PUBLIC ACCOUNTABILITY AND TRANSPARENCY

# Public Accountability and Transparency
## The Imperatives of Good Governance

MADHAV GODBOLE

Orient Longman

ORIENT LONGMAN PRIVATE LIMITED

*Registered Office*
3-6-752 Himayatnagar, Hyderabad 500 029 (A.P.), India

*Other Offices*
Bangalore, Bhopal, Bhubaneshwar, Chandigarh, Chennai, Ernakulam, Guwahati, Hyderabad, Jaipur, Kolkata, Lucknow, Mumbai, New Delhi, Patna

© Orient Longman Limited 2003
First Published 2003

ISBN 81 250 2515 4

*Typeset by*
Scribe Consultants
New Delhi

*Printed in India at*
Baba Barkha Nath Printers
New Delhi

*Published by*
Orient Longman Private Limited
1/24 Asaf Ali Road
New Delhi 110 002

*To my very special grand-daughter
Gaayatri*

# Contents

*Preface* / ix
1  We, the People / 1
2  Indian Democracy: The Unfinished Agenda / 73
3  Reinventing the Government / 137
4  Governance—Some Major Concerns / 196
5  Corporate and Co-operative Governance / 267
6  The Judiciary, the Media and Civil Society / 323
   *Abbreviations* / 384
   *Index* / 391

# Preface

Rabindranath Tagore, in his *Geetanjali*, had a beautiful and uplifting dream for his country which a large number of his fellow-countrymen fervently shared:

> 'Where the mind is without fear and the head is held high;
> Where knowledge is free;
> Where words come out from the depth of truth;
> Where tireless striving stretches its arms towards perfection;
> Where the clear stream of reason has not lost its way into the dreary desert sand of dead habit;
> Where the mind is led forward by thee into ever-widening thought and action;
> Into that heaven of freedom, my Father, let my country awake'.

More than half a century after Independence, it is clear that Tagore's dream has failed to inspire action. What is most disturbing is the fact that there is no national will to address the core issues facing the country. John K. Galbraith described India as a 'functioning anarchy'. Even a die-hard Communist like Krushchev is reported to have said, 'If any proof is required of the existence of God, one has only to look at India'. A highly respected former union finance minister of India commented that the Indian passport had become a liability for Indians!

Foreigners look at us no differently. Prince Philip, Duke of Edinburgh, during a visit to an electronics company in London, was conducted through rooms filled with state of the art technology. On seeing a crudely designed fuse box, he remarked that it looked as if it had been 'put in by an Indian'. (*Times of India*, 12 Aug 1999). India has been ranked at the bottom of a table on transparency rankings of international property markets. The study, conducted by major property services agency Jones Lang LaSalle, has put India in the 'opaque' tier-5 category, along with Eastern Europe, Greece, Portugal and Vietnam. The transparency rankings of the property markets have been worked out on the basis of five attributes: presence of public and private performance indices; quality of market fundamentals research; availability of reliable financial statements; alignment of interests among directors, managers and investors/shareholders; and taxes and restriction on cross-border transactions.

In January 2001, Pricewaterhouse Coopers unveiled at the annual meeting of the World Economic Forum in Davos, Switzerland, an index that measures the impact of business, legal and ethical transparency on the cost of capital in 35 countries—the Opacity Index or O-Factor. In this study, primarily intended to assist policy makers and investors, opacity is defined as the lack of 'clear, accurate, formal and widely accepted practices'. The O-Factor for India is 64 as compared to 29 for Singapore, and 36 for USA and China. The corresponding tax equivalent, which shows the effect of opacity when viewed as if it imposes a hidden tax burden, in percentage terms, was 0 for Singapore, 5 for USA and China, and 28 for India. The opacity risk premium, which indicates the increased cost of borrowing faced by countries due to opacity, expressed on the basis of points (100 basis points = one percentage point), was 0 for Singapore and USA, 3 for China and 719 for India.

There is an urgent need to revise decision-making processes to make India an attractive destination for foreign investors. The Prime Minister of Singapore, Goh Chok Tong, during a visit to India, was frank enough to admit that many potential investors in India were reluctant to invest in the country because, among other factors, many rules were not transparent. (*Indian Express*, 7 Jan 1995). Michael Heseltine, the then president of the Board of Trade and Secretary of Trade and Industry of the United Kingdom, during his visit to Delhi, commented that 'transparency of procedures was in everybody's interest because it would remove the opportunities for corruption'. (*Financial Express*, 16 Feb 1995). Frank Wisner, the then United States ambassador to India, emphasised that a regulatory framework comprising independent and transparent regulatory bodies is imperative for protecting an efficient market economy and India needs to ensure that market participants are comfortable with the integrity of the market. Hundreds of billions of dollars will flow to India once investors are assured that this country offers an environment that is attractive to investors, a playing field that is level, and rules that are equally applied and transparent. (*Times of India*, 16 Feb 1995). The Chairman of Grindlays Bank, Sir Brian Shaw, said that transparency in policy-making which would accompany privatisation would help achieve clarity and speed in the flow of investment capital. (*Economic Times*, 13 Feb 1995). John Major, former British prime minister, leading a 120-member delegation to India, highlighted the growth in British investment in India but cautioned that, 'bureaucratic inertia and a lack of transparency in the award of contracts continue to discourage foreign investors.' (*Frontline*, 7 Feb 1997). The perception that transparency will greatly aid the inflow of investment is indeed widespread.

The Lok Sabha created history with its longest-ever sitting of about 22 hours in the special five-day golden jubilee session debating issues of national importance. A total of 225 members participated in the marathon debate as if they were being paid by the word! But 'a speech to be immortal does not have to be eternal'. P.A. Sangma, the then speaker of the Lok Sabha, gave a rousing call for a 'second freedom struggle'. Such is the empty rhetoric and futile debating that takes place in the most exalted of our public arenas.

Transparency International (TI), a non-government organisation (NGO) dedicated to the reduction of corruption as a means to hastening economic development, classified India as one of the ten most corrupt countries in the world, on the basis of annual surveys. Even according to the latest corruption perception indices published by TI, India remains where it has always been—down among the more bribable nations—scoring 2.9 (on a scale of 1 to 10, 1 being most corrupt) and ranking 72 among 99 countries, alongside Columbia.

Time and again, decisions taken in individual cases have shown the clout of mighty lobbies in the corridors of power in Delhi. This has created public misgivings and raised uneasy questions about the continuance of crony capitalism even in the regime of economic liberalisation. Equally important is the growing public perception that the so called case-by-case decision-making approach adopted in most cases is in reality a suitcase-by-suitcase approach (à la Harshad Mehta).

The close nexus between powerful businessmen and ministers, including prime ministers, has shaken the faith of the common man and demoralised and subverted the system. The links of the Ambanis, Hindujas and others with the high and mighty in the government is no longer a secret. The Ambanis have been a force to reckon with in every government at the centre since the days of Indira Gandhi and have subjugated even those at the highest levels of bureaucracy and the political elite. Senior bureaucrats in Delhi are openly classified into two categories: RH—Reliance and Hindujas—(positive) and RH (negative)! A few who refused to fall in line have had to pay a heavy price which taught a lesson to several others who quickly learned to crawl when asked to bend. It was as if the whole system had been mortgaged to them.

Kamal Nath, former central minister for forests and environment, went to the extent of diverting the flow of a river in Himachal Pradesh for the sake of his holiday resort. This must be a unique case of its kind deserving a mention in the Guinness Book of Records!

Respect is no longer accorded on the basis of a person's character, ethical standards and moral principles. People with money and power are respected and become role models, irrespective of their background and past record. This is as true of business tycoons like the Ambanis as it is of politicians and professionals in several walks of life. It is not, therefore, surprising that Dhirubhai Ambani had been declared the most notable Indian Businessman of the Century in the *Business Baron*'s multi-media poll. (*Loksatta*, 7 Dec 1999). He has also been voted as one of the top four Indians of the century along with Mahatma Gandhi, Swami Vivekananda and Lata Mangeshkar in the *Times of India-Online*'s 'Indians of the Century' poll! (*Economic Times*, 7 Jan 2000). It should not be surprising if the *Bharat Ratna* is conferred on him posthumously. Mukesh Ambani is among the 17 outstanding Asians identified by *Time International* in a new 'Global 100' directory of young world leaders. (*Business Standard*, 29 Nov 1994). Harshad Mehta, the prime accused in the bank and securities scam, who also headed the list of large income tax defaulters, was elevated to the position of an investment columnist in some of our leading dailies. (*Sunday*, 22/28 Nov 1998). Lala Lajpatrai College in Mumbai even appointed him a visiting professor! (*Maharashtra Times*, 30 Oct 1997).

A 'time-capsule' of the post-Independence period can bring into sharp focus the rapid decline in the institutions, moral fibre and standards of public life in the country. What is striking is that every field of public life has become tainted and there is a growing cynicism. This situation will not change by merely criticising what is wrong. Ways will have to be found to address problems and mend matters, howsoever slow the process may be. It will call for infinite patience, tact and perseverance to mould public opinion in favour of a change. As I was working on this book, a colleague asked me what the subject of my book was. When I told him that it was on public accountability and transparency, his immediate response was, 'I did not know that you had taken to writing fiction!'

I stayed in Delhi for six weeks in December 1996–January 1997 to work in the library of Parliament for this book and found the librarian and staff most helpful. I am grateful to them. I owe a debt of gratitude to my colleague Shri R.C. Jain for hospitality extended to me during my stay at his residence in Delhi. I am also grateful to Smt Meena Kasbekar and Shri Pandya of the library of the State Bank of India in Mumbai for their help and assistance in getting me the relevant reading material. The National Centre for Advocacy Studies, Pune, kept me supplied with the reading material I needed.

I am grateful to Prof. S.V. Kogekar, Shri B.S. Raghavan, Shri K.V. Ramanathan and Shri B. Vijayaraghavan for going through the draft and making several perceptive and useful comments. However, I alone am responsible for any deficiencies and weaknesses which may have remained in the book. Finally, I must place on record my deep sense of gratitude to my wife Sujata for all her help and assistance.

MADHAV GODBOLE

# 1

# We, the People

**Democracy: In Action**

The Lok Sabha completed fifty years of its existence in May 2002. The hallmark of democratic governance is parliament's supervision and control over the executive. In India, this task remains undone. A common person can see the unseemly sight of democracy in action when the proceedings of parliament and state legislatures are telecast. The pros and cons of televising parliamentary proceedings have been debated extensively in India and abroad.[1] Subhash C. Kashyap has brought out the disadvantages of televising such proceedings.[2] While one may not agree with the view that the decision to televise the proceedings of parliament and state legislatures was wrong, it will have to be admitted that it has proved our worst fears and brought these institutions to public ridicule. This is aptly brought out in the cartoon by R.K. Laxman in 'You Said it', in the *Times of India*, (26 Nov 1997) in which an angry father

---

[1] R.C. Bhardwaj, Televising of Parliamentary Proceedings, *The Journal of Parliamentary Information*, Lok Sabha Secretariat, Vol. XL, No. 2, June 1994, pp. 188–197.

[2] Subhash C. Kashyap, Should Parliamentary Proceedings be Televised?, Black and White, *Sunday Times*, 20 April 1997.

shouts at his rowdy children and says, 'Not here. Go and play Lok Sabha or Rajya Sabha on the street. Do you think you are grown up enough to play it in the house?'

The televised proceedings of the Uttar Pradesh (UP) legislative assembly during the vote of no confidence in the Kalyan Singh government, which showed the disgraceful behaviour of legislators, shamed the nation. A number of legislators and ministers were seriously injured. These proceedings were shown on television all over the world again and again and brought the entire country and its democratic governance into disrepute. P.A. Sangma, the then speaker of the Lok Sabha, candidly remarked that Article 105 of the Constitution only conferred immunity for speeches made and voting in the House. For all other actions, the members are liable for prosecution. On the issue of non-members reportedly being present in the assembly when voting was taking place, he said, 'I am shocked that something like this was allowed to happen. It really is unbelievable. It is clearly a contempt of the House.' A formal inquiry into the episode was ordered. The inquiry report was received by the speaker of the assembly but nothing further has been heard in the matter, nor has the report been published.

Realising how devastating the impact of televising the unseemly and rowdy proceedings has been, the presiding officers of parliament and state legislatures have started ordering that television cameras be switched off whenever proceedings take an ugly turn or are not likely to further the interest of the ruling party. Thus, the entire debate in parliament on the Gujarat communal conflagration and the failure of the state and central government in containing it was not permitted to be telecast in April–May 2002.

Unfortunately, this is not the only case of its kind. As Margaret Thatcher, former prime minister of United Kingdom, had said, 'When you are in the government, five years is a very short time. When you are in opposition, it is hell of a long time.' This impatience of opposition parties is evident all the time. A DMK minister was physically assaulted in the Tamil Nadu assembly by a member of the opposition. The proceedings of legislative assemblies in several other states have been held to ransom for days at a time. The Maharashtra legislative assembly witnessed the mock funeral procession of a member in July 1997. Even such a solemn occasion as the Governor's address to the joint session of the legislature has been marred by rowdy behaviour in some states. The Governor of Rajasthan was hurt while delivering a speech in the Rajasthan assembly in January 1997. The Governor of UP was heckled and pelted with paper balls when he addressed the joint session of the legislature in May 2002 and, as a result, he read only the first and the last sentence of his address to the legislature.

Proceedings in parliament have been no better. 'Shouting brigades' encouraged and given respectability by Rajiv Gandhi during his tenure as the PM and leader of opposition have now become a part of the accepted system. Walking into and shouting from the well of the House has become the accepted pattern and some members take pride in being known as those elected to the well of the House rather than to the House. The members seem to believe that stalling the business of the House for days at a time or boycotting it is the best way to serve the public interest. The opposition parties boycotted parliament for 16 days in July–August 1994 after the ATR on the bank scam was presented in the House. The telecom scandal involving Sukh Ram, former minister for communications, rocked parliament in December 1995. Both Houses of parliament adjourned *sine die* on 22 December after having failed to resolve the 13-day deadlock between the government and the opposition. Over ten per cent of the time of the tenth Lok Sabha was wasted in such hold-ups of business. Except for the presentation of the railway and general budget and a discussion of the issue of the Gujarat government orders permitting its employees to become members of the Rashtriya Swayamsevak Sangh, not much else happened in the budget session of February–March 2002. No business was transacted for at least eight days during this session. From 1992 onwards, the Lok Sabha has been adjourned for 111 hours over the Ayodhya controversy (excluding the number of hours lost in December 2001), while only 40 hours have been devoted to a substantive discussion of the issue. Premature winding up of the session has now become the order of the day.

The 'zero hour' which follows the question hour is a misnomer—it is meant to invite the attention of the government to matters of urgent public interest which cannot wait to be raised through other normal channels such as a starred, unstarred or short-notice question, a notice for calling attention, or a half hour discussion. In theory, such brief mention of items should not take more than a few minutes. In practice, however, it is seen that the 'zero hour' not only runs for an hour but even stretches much beyond, cutting into the time for other business. If there is one institution in the country which calls for a 'time and motion study', it is parliament!

A decade ago, there was 'a growing realisation that the various mechanisms of parliamentary scrutiny needed to be strengthened to give greater meaning to the concept of administrative accountability to the legislature and through it to the people. What is important is how parliamentarians make the best use of every minute and every second or in other words, how the time at the disposal of the House could be used most purposefully.'[3] During the golden jubilee celebrations of India's independence in 1997, MPs had vowed to improve their behaviour in parliament. But, this made no difference. During the winter session of parliament in 1998, the Lok Sabha had to be adjourned twenty times leading to a wastage of 32 hours. The Rajya Sabha was adjourned four times leading to a wastage of eight hours. (*Maharashtra Times*, 26 Dec 1998). A Code of Conduct was adopted on 25 November 2001 on discipline and decorum in parliament and state legislatures but this too has not made any difference to the functioning of parliament. The situation seems to go from bad to worse in each successive session as was seen in the winter session of 2001 and the budget session in March–May 2002.

The Budgetary allocation for parliament has gone up steeply

---

[3]C.K. Jain, *All India Conference of Presiding Officers, Leaders of Parties and Whips on Discipline and Decorum in the Parliament and State Legislatures*, Lok Sabha Secretariat, September 23–24, 1992, pp. 180–181.

over the years from Rs 12.49 crore in 1983–84 to Rs 173.09 crore in 2000–01. Even with a number of items of expenditure not quantified fully, it is estimated that the government spends Rs 17,000 per minute of parliament's time. The new library building of parliament, constructed at the cost of Rs 191 crores, was inaugurated in May 2002. Reportedly, the expenditure on air-conditioning, interior decoration and furniture totalled Rs 35 crore. The library already has 11 lakh books and a provision has been made for keeping 30 lakh books. It should be a subject of research as to how many of our lawmakers make use of the library. The evaluation of the efficacy of such extravagant expenditure is important because, unlike the library of Congress in the US, in India, due to security and other reasons, parliament precincts are mostly inaccessible to ordinary researchers, visitors and students. In practically every session, the opening day is declared a holiday on the ground that some sitting MP has died. It is high time to discontinue such paid holidays at the cost of the taxpayer.

In this context, two issues merit attention. Over the years, the time parliament spends in sessions has progressively decreased. In the initial 15–20 years after parliament came into being, the three parliament sessions in a year consisted of 120 sittings spread over 23–24 weeks. The number of sittings of the Lok Sabha came down to 78 in 1995 and 65 in 1997. The same trend has continued. This is also true of the state legislatures. During the last five years, the Maharashtra legislature has met, on an average, only for 44 days in a year. The National Commission to Review the Working of the Constitution (NCRWC) has, therefore, rightly recommended that the state legislatures/parliament should transact business for at least 50 days in a year in the case of state legislatures with less than 70 members, 90 days in the case of other legislatures, 120 days in the case of the Lok Sabha and 100 days in the case of the Rajya Sabha.[4]

Also, in the time spent in sessions, less and less time is accorded to legislative business. The first Lok Sabha spent 49

---

[4]Government of India, Ministry of Law, *Report of the National Commission to Review the Working of the Constitution*, 31 March 2002.

per cent of the total time on issues of legislation. This came down progressively to 16 per cent in the ninth Lok Sabha. The record has been equally disturbing thereafter. Each session ends with a number of Bills pending in both Houses. Thus, for example, the Banking Bill introduced in 2000 and the Electricity Bill of 2001 are still pending. The Confederation of Indian Industry (CII) advocated in all seriousness that the government should adopt the ordinance route for pending economic legislation. The advocacy of *ordinance raj* by a responsible body like the CII is a reflection of the helplessness and despondency at the working of parliament. This was also borne out by the repeated issue of ordinances for setting up the central vigilance commission and the prevention of terrorism.

Discussion of budgets (general, railways, and of states under President's rule), took 23.2 per cent of the total time of the House in the sixth Lok Sabha. This came down steeply to just 14.6 per cent in the twelfth Lok Sabha, in spite of the fact that, during this period, there was a sharp deterioration in the financial health of the country. For several years in the recent past, the House has not been in a position to scrutinise the functioning of even important ministries. The standard practice now is to pass the budget without a thorough discussion. The percentage of demands for grants that have been guillotined has gone up steadily from 63 per cent of the total in 1990–91 to 93 per cent in 1996–97 and 97 per cent in 1998–99. In the budget for 2002–03, demands of all ministries, other than agriculture, were guillotined. When the budget discussion was in progress in April 2002, against the total strength of 545 members in the Lok Sabha, only 37 members were present. Since this was less than the quorum required (55 members), the House had to be adjourned. It was for the first time in the history of parliament that a budget discussion had to be adjourned and thereafter postponed in this manner for want of quorum. (*Maharashtra Times*, 29 Apr 2002). What an example to set during the golden jubilee year of parliament! There is never any discussion on the budgets of the states under President's rule. Supplementary demands are mostly passed without any discussion.

On an average, the government answers 75,000 questions in parliament each year. A long time is spent by the ministries in preparing replies to starred questions and briefing ministers on supplementaries likely to be raised in the House. The question hour is the real test of the government's accountability. It is considered a sparring ground for testing the worth of a minister or a member. Here also, the time spent on questions has been reduced from 15 per cent of the total each in the first, second and third Lok Sabha to 13 per cent in the eighth Lok Sabha and 10 per cent in the ninth Lok Sabha. The number of questions answered each day ranges between one to four.[5] The former speaker of the Lok Sabha, G.M.C. Balayogi, had bemoaned the fact that the number of members present in the House during question hour had declined perceptibly and a number of members whose questions were listed for oral answers were absent. (*Loksatta*, 4 Dec 1999). In the eighth session of the thirteenth Lok Sabha in 2001, out of the 420 starred questions which were listed, only 38 could be answered orally. On this background, Rajya Sabha created history on 2 December 2002 by taking up all the starred questions listed for that day.

A brief reference must be made to the judgement of the Supreme Court in the Jharkhand Mukti Morcha (JMM) case. It shocked the conscience of the country that the then prime minister, P.V. Narasimha Rao, and his colleagues in the Congress party had paid hefty bribes to some opposition MPs to ensure that the government would survive a vote of confidence in the House in July 1996. Though the judges could not come to a unanimous conclusion on other major issues pertaining to the ambit of the privilege of a MP, brought out later, the judgement took the fight for a clean public life forward, at least to some extent, in that all the five judges unanimously held that an MP is a public servant and he holds an office and performs a public duty. This set at rest the doubts raised on this

---

[5]Lok Sabha Secretariat, *Time Spent on Various Kinds of Business in Lok Sabha—An Appraisal*, New Delhi, November 1996.

question by the earlier contradictory judgements of the Bombay and Orissa high courts.

It may be recalled that, soon after the receipt of the Orissa high court judgement that MPs are public servants and are, therefore, covered by the provisions of the Prevention of Corruption Act (PCA), 1988, there were pressures by a large number of MPs, cutting across party lines, to amend the PCA so as to exclude the legislators from its purview. This move was co-ordinated by none other than the then prime minister H.D. Deve Gowda and two of his predecessors, Atal Behari Vajpayee (who is now the current PM) and Chandrashekhar.[6] An all party meeting was even convened to discuss the matter. Fortunately, wiser counsels prevailed. But, the political culture in the country has reached such a state of moral degradation that, without such an unambiguous pronouncement by the Supreme Court on this vital issue, it is quite likely that the PCA would have been amended at some future date.

Though the Supreme Court was unanimous that an MP is a public servant, there was a difference of opinion among the judges on another important issue. The majority judgement underlined that merely because there is no authority to remove an MP from his office, he does not cease to be a public servant for the purpose of PCA. The court held that till a provision is made by parliament in that regard by suitable amendment in the law (as to the authority competent to grant sanction for prosecution), the prosecuting agency, before filing a charge-sheet in a criminal court, shall obtain the permission of the chairman of the Rajya Sabha/speaker of the Lok Sabha, as the case may be. But, the minority judgement held that section 19 is applicable only to a public servant who is removable from his office by a competent authority. If the court fails to identify the authority competent to remove the public servant, he would not be liable to be prosecuted under section 7, 10, 11, 13 and 15 though he would be liable to be prosecuted for any other offences under the Act.[7]

[6]Editorial, 'Action, Not Words', *Times of India*, 27 December 1996.
[7]*P.V. Narasimha Rao* v. *State* (CBI/SPE), (1998) 4 Supreme Court cases 626, 17 April 1998.

## Parliamentary Committees

John P. Mackintosh observed, 'All over the world, where democratic systems of government survive, it is being said that legislatures are losing ground to the executive. The reason is partly the increased complexity of government and partly that the public tend to be more interested in the executive.'[8] Considerable thought has, therefore, been given in several countries towards increasing the supervisory role of legislatures. In Britain, for example, the most significant structural reform for more than half a century was witnessed with the creation of new select committees which have led to other noteworthy structural, procedural and also behavioural changes.[9] In many other countries such as USA, Canada and South Africa, the committees almost serve as 'mini legislatures'. Indira Gandhi had accepted the concept of a committee system for a while in 1976. The idea was to shorten plenary sessions so that parliament could devote half of its time to purposeful committee work. But she changed her mind and nothing came of it.

Twenty-two committees are now in operation in parliament. Apart from the traditional committees such as the estimates committee, the public accounts committee (PAC), the public undertakings committee (PUC), the committee on privileges and the subordinate legislation committee, there are 17 department-related standing committees which were inaugurated on 31 March 1993. In addition there are consultative committees for the ministries which are presided over by the minister in charge of the ministry.

The importance of committees depends, to a considerable extent, on the government, and particularly on the prime minister. Rajiv Gandhi, for example, had scant respect for established parliamentary conventions. As a convention, it is always a prominent opposition leader who is appointed

---

[8]John P. Mackintosh, (ed.), *People and Parliament*, Saxon House, The Hansard Society of Parliamentary Government, 1978, p. 209.
[9]Philip Norton (ed.), *Parliament In The 1980s*, Basil Blackwell Ltd., UK, 1985. p. 138.

Chairman of the PAC. But under Rajiv Gandhi, an MP from a non-Congress party, which had supported the Congress, was appointed as the chairman. As a mark of protest, all the opposition MPs withdrew from all three financial committees of the House.[10]

At the time of the creation of the standing committees, the former speaker of the Lok Sabha, Shivraj V. Patil, had expressed the hope that 'these committees shall help the people, the parliament and the executive to use the system in a most cost-effective, democratic and purposeful manner'. It is too early to assess the impact or the effectiveness of these committees but the brief details in the following paragraphs show that there is considerable room for improving and strengthening the system.

The reports of a number of standing committees show that they are replete with sentences such as: 'the committee deplores the approach and attitude of the government'; 'the committee is dismayed at the explanation given by the department'; 'the committee notes with regret'; 'the committee is not at all convinced with the reasons given by ministry and finds its approach casual and perfunctory'; and so on. Such an attitude needs to be replaced by much more exhaustive analysis with a focus on the short and medium term issues in each sector. If the committees were to do such work, they would automatically command the respect of the ministries.

This is brought out by a look at the reports of the standing committees pertaining to a few ministries. The atomic power stations (APS) have had very large time and cost over-runs. Obviously, the explanation that the cost over-run was mainly due to the inclusion of the element of interest during construction is not adequate and begs the question. The parliamentary standing committee has failed to go into these issues at any length. The safety issues in nuclear installations have been causing concern. The study carried out by the atomic energy regulatory board (AERB) had documented a number of safety issues in the nuclear installations under the department of

S. Gill, *The Dynasty*, 1996, p. 506.

atomic energy (DAE) which warrant urgent corrective action. There was, for example, a controversy regarding re-engineering of the dome of the Kaiga APS. This had led to the work on the Rajasthan APS Units III and IV, which were identical to Kaiga Unit I, being suspended. Excessive reliance on domestic technology and indigenisation of equipment, which has led to long delays in the completion of power projects, apart from adding to the cost of power, are the other issues which need to be carefully considered. Whether India should plan for an ambitious atomic power generation capacity of 20,000 MW by 2010 is also an issue which requires consideration. The unsatisfactory state of performance budget of DAE has been referred to by the committee but without going into details of the manner in which it needs to be recast. None of these issues find any worthwhile, indepth or comprehensive treatment in the reports of the standing committee.

The ministry of defence (MOD) is also treated as sacrosanct, and outside the pale of criticism. In the name of secrecy, issues such as the necessity, efficiency and productivity of expenditures are hardly ever addressed. The bogey of national security would deter the bravest from forcing the issues. As can be seen, even the standing committee on defence had to face such stonewalling by the ministry. The committee, while examining the demands for the grants of the MOD for the year 1993–94, had recommended in their first report that the report of the committee on defence expenditure [Arun Singh committee] be made public as early as possible. The committee lamented that the report was still under examination by the committee of secretaries... 'The committee is of the view that a little more openness even in matters relating to defence will not militate against the national interest, and therefore, reiterate their earlier recommendation to make the report public as early as possible.'[11] As was to be expected, the report of the committee on defence

---

[11] Lok Sabha Secretariat, *Standing Committee on Defence (1994–95), Tenth Lok Sabha, Ministry of Defence, Demands for Grants (1994–95)*, Second Report, New Delhi, April 1994, p. 13.

expenditure is still under examination by the committee of secretaries. Though over a decade has elapsed since the report was submitted, it has not been permitted to see the light of day! Another example is the refusal of MOD, in January 2002, to make available to the Public Accounts Committee (PAC) a copy of the report prepared by the CVC on major defence procurement transactions since 1989, on grounds of secrecy. The report was prepared at the instance of the government with the ostensible purpose of furthering greater transparency. What is most surprising is that the CVC is supposed to have recommended not publicising this report. This raises the important issue of the accountability of a statutory body, such as the CVC, to parliament. If the findings of such bodies are to be kept from parliament, what is the use of setting up such bodies?

The exasperating and scandalous delays in the MBT (Arjun) tank project is another example of delays and wastages: There had been a *seventeen-fold escalation* in the project cost which was originally sanctioned for Rs 15.50 crore in March 1974 with the probable year of completion being 1984. It increased to Rs 56.55 crore after first revision in October 1980 and to Rs 280 crore in May 1987. The standing committee was understandably not satisfied by the justification given by the MOD that the specifications of the tank were revised twice in less than five years, after being specified originally in 1972, on the ground of change in the threat perceptions beyond the year 2000. Finally, the first phase of user trials were carried out by the Army in 1995 and a symbolic replica of the tank was handed over to the prime minister on 9 January 1996—22 years after the project was sanctioned! According to the information given by the defence minister in the Rajya Sabha, after all these years of research, the tank will have an imported engine. Tests with the armour-plating are yet to be done. (*Times of India*, 25 Dec 1999). It is only in India that such a leisurely pace is accepted, even in the strategic field of defence. Here again, the successive reports of the standing committee leave the reader with a feeling of justice not being done to an extremely important subject. The reports of the committees on the ministries of agriculture, welfare, rural development, urban development and others also show that the committees had not gone into the question of proper utilisation of funds, leakages, accounting procedures, advisability of releasing funds directly to village panchayats, supervision and monitoring arrangements, efficacy of local fund audit and so on. The examination by the committees was largely target-oriented, whether physical or financial, and the emphasis was mainly on providing larger budgetary outlays. The emphasis was on why there was under-utilisation of funds, not on how the funds were used. It is also significant to note that the reports were wholly based on discussions with the officers of concerned ministries.[12] There were no outside inputs from NGOs, academics, specialists, public policy analysts, and others. The discussions of the committees were focused on ensuring a greater number of beneficiaries and higher targets, not on reliability of data and independent scrutiny of beneficiaries.

The standing committees on urban and rural development failed to examine in depth why the 73rd and 74th amendments of the Constitution, relating to democratic decentralisation, had not been acted upon purposefully by the states so far though years have elapsed since these amendments were adopted by parliament. (See chapter 2, section II below). This is a glaring omission.

The reports of the standing committees of some of the other departments show that except for honourable exceptions, the committees have not done any in-depth sector work which could have provided useful insights. Often, each committee seems to take a compartmentalised view of the budget and as a result makes recommendations for a larger and larger budget allocation. Hardly any committee has looked at the forward and backward linkages of the sector and whether there were adequate budget provisions for all such activities. The imperatives of economic liberalisation, globalisation or World Trade Agreement

---

[12] I.K. Gujral as the Prime Minister, broke this convention in October 1997 and spoke at the meeting of the Standing Committee of the Ministry of External Affairs to brief the members on his visit to the US. (*Indian Express*, 19 October 1997).

do not find any significant reflection in the reports. Non-plan expenditure, including maintenance expenditure, was hardly ever discussed. One would have expected the committees to comment on issues such as proliferation of ministries at the centre, large staff in ministries, relevance of continuing an institution such as the planning commission after the introduction of economic reforms, and the down-sizing of the government.

A brief reference may be made to yet another aspect of the relevance, or rather irrelevance, of the standing committees to policy-making in the government. The importance and public standing of these committees will increase only if the government is seen to be giving due respect to their recommendations. When the government decides not to accept a recommendation, the least that can be expected is that it would give cogent and well-reasoned arguments for its decision. These rudimentary requirements were not fulfilled in the case of the standing committees on petroleum and chemicals and finance. The former committee in its successive reports had recommended that the cess collected under the Oil Industry Development Board (OIDB) Act, since 1974, amounting to over Rs 31,000 crore, by the central government should be made available to the oil companies for projects in the field of exploration, production, refining and marketing of oil and gas. The committee had noted that against this large collection, an amount of only Rs 902 crore had been paid to the oil companies.[13] The attorney general, in his opinion given in January 1995, had clearly held that the cess was meant for the development of the oil industry. He had also opined that 'in cases where Act gives authority of direction, it should be exercised in a reasonable manner.' The Comptroller and Auditor-General too has supported this view. He had observed that 'as the funds generated from the cess are largely not being applied for the purpose for which it is levied, the imposition of cess itself loses

---

[13]Lok Sabha Secretariat, *Standing Committee on Petroleum and Chemicals (1998–99), Twelfth Lok Sabha, Ministry of Petroleum and Natural Gas, Demands for Grants (1998–99)*, Seventh Report, March 1999, pp. 3–6.

much of its justification.' The standing committee on finance had also supported the stand of the committee on petroleum and chemicals and had observed that the 'cess receipts should be used for the purpose for which these are collected... A good part of collection of cess is in the nature of excise duty. Had it been regularised as such, it would have come under the divisible pool and the resources of the states would have increased to that extent.' The committee had suggested that 'the union government should review the matter in this light.'[14] In spite of these weighty arguments, the ministry of finance has refused to concede the point and has continued to dodge the issue—hardly the response one would expect from a government in a democracy!

Having said the above, it must be underlined that since parliamentary committees work as 'mini legislatures', it is of utmost importance that the committees' recommendations on new legislation subserve the larger interests of the country. This will be possible only when the evidence before the committees is balanced and not overwhelmingly in favour of any sectarian interest. Viewed in this light, the report of the standing committee of finance on the Foreign Exchange Management Bill, 1998, raised some uneasy questions as it recommended the substantial watering down of the provision of the Bill.[15] There are as many as six notes of dissent in the report which bring out why it will not be in the national interest to go by the majority recommendations of the committee.

Attention was first invited to the question of capital flight in a major way when US Treasury Secretary, James Baker, noted in the World Bank-IMF meeting in 1985, that 'as a practical matter, it is unrealistic to call upon the support of voluntary lending from abroad, when domestic funds are moving in the

[14]Lok Sabha Secretariat, *Standing Committee of Finance (1996–97), Eleventh Lok Sabha, Ministry of Finance, Demands for Grants (1996–97), Second Report,* August 1996, pp. 39–40.
[15]*Lok Sabha Secretariat, Standing Committee of Finance (1998–99), Twelfth Lok Sabha, Ministry of Finance, (Department of Economic Affairs and Revenue), The Foreign Exchange Management Bill, 1998,* Eleventh Report, December 1998.

other direction. If a country's own citizens have no confidence in its economic system, how can others?'

In a study published in 1996, it has been highlighted that, 'the economic benefit of detecting and deterring capital outflows related to abnormal transaction prices is substantial. The application of the global price matrix as a means of determining optimal audits and inspections will facilitate the detection process based on economic benefit-cost criteria'.[16]

As Kannan Srinivasan has commented, India's exports have reacted to the value of the rupee by growing when it appreciates and falling when it depreciates! India doesn't export goods, it exports money—by under-invoicing exports and over-invoicing imports... Now, an excellent study by three academics, has analysed every single India-United States import and export transaction for the years 1993, 1994 and 1995, to determine over-invoicing, under-invoicing and consequent capital flight. In the most recent year studied, 1995, capital flight to the United States is estimated to be about $5.6 billion. We can infer by extrapolation that India witnessed a flight of capital of $46.1 billion on its total exports and imports to and from all countries of $75.1 billion in 1998–99—or over half the value of India's international trade.[17]

The statement of S.P. Hinduja, quoted in the section on overdue electoral reforms (chapter II, section I) shows the quantum of funds siphoned off by Indian politicians, another highly influential class in society, in foreign banks abroad. The fact that none of these transactions could be hauled up under the Foreign Exchange Regulation Act (FERA) should have brought home to the standing committee the imperative need to strengthen the existing provisions of the law, rather than to dilute them further.

It can thus be seen that while the view of industry and trade

---

[16] John S. Zdanowicz, William W. Welch and Simon J. Pak, Capital Flight from India to the US through Abnormal Pricing in International Trade, *Finance India*, Vol. X, No. 4, December 1996, p. 885.

[17] Kannan Srinivasan, Control Mechanisms—Reversing the Flight of Capital, *Times of India*, 5 November 1999.

was strongly represented before the committee, the same cannot be said of those who would have liked the government to take strong action against those who contravene the law. This is also true of the report of the committee on the Prevention of Money Laundering Bill, 1998.[18] Here too, the committee has watered down the provisions of the Bill considerably. There are two well-articulated notes of dissent which bring out the hazards of accepting the majority recommendations of the report. Considering the importance and complexity of the subject, it has to be said that the committee's report is far from satisfactory. The Lok Sabha passed the revised industry-friendly Prevention of Money Laundering Bill, 1999, and the Foreign Exchange Management Bill, 1999, incorporating the recommendations of the standing committee on the earlier Bills, on 2 December 1999, with barely 30 members present in the House! A number of amendments in the names of Congress and other opposition members opposing certain provisions of the two Bills could not be taken up in their absence. (*Deccan Chronicle*, 3 Dec 1999). The lack of interest of parliament in such important legislative business is indeed shocking. The Foreign Exchange Management Bill has been passed by the Rajya Sabha. But, amazingly, even the much diluted version of the Money Laundering Bill was found to be draconian by the Rajya Sabha and referred, at the instance of the Congress party, to a select committee of the House for further review of the provisions. It was over four years after the introduction of the Bill in parliament, that it was passed in a highly diluted form in December 2002. It was disconcerting to see the inordinate delays in the passing of the competition law in December 2002. If this is what economic liberalisation and globalisation mean, no wonder the common man has serious reservations about where the country is being taken by vested interests and powerful lobbies.

The experience of three other major Bills scrutinised by the

---

[18]Lok Sabha Secretariat, *Standing Committee on Finance*, (*1998–99*), *Twelfth Lok Sabha, Ministry of Finance* (*Department of Economic Affairs and Revenue*), *The Prevention of Money Laundering Bill, 1998*, Twelfth Report, January 1999.

standing committees of the concerned ministries is equally disconcerting. The standing committee for the department of personnel has watered down the provisions of the Central Vigilance Commission Bill to such an extent as to make the new office meaningless. In spite of the strong pleas made to the standing committee to review and modify the provisions of the Freedom of Information Bill, the committee had largely gone along with the restrictive provisions of the Bill moved by the government and had merely referred back to the government the various suggestions made to the committee to modify the Bill, thereby effectively weakening the cause of right to information. Yet another case is that of the Budget Management and Fiscal Responsibility Bill. The committee has recommended dilution of the proposed provisions of the Bill to such an extent as to frustrate the basic purpose underlying the Bill.

It can thus be seen that while the setting up of standing committees is a step in the right direction, a great deal still remains to be done before they acquire stature and public recognition as the sentinels of democracy.

It is interesting to see how little time is spent by parliament in debating the provisions of legislative measures. In the seventh session of the thirteenth Lok Sabha in 2001, of the 9 Bills passed, the Salaries and Allowances of Ministers (Amendment) Bill, 2001, was passed in four minutes! Two other Bills were passed in 26 and 37 minutes respectively. Of the remaining Bills, the longest time taken was of three hours and 28 minutes. It is important to note in this context that though legislative proposals receive such scant attention, as opposed to what happens in some other countries, there is no 'sunset' provision in almost any legislation in India. As a result, the laws continue to be in force for years without any periodical review of their relevance or adequacy.

A brief reference may be made to the committee on subordinate legislation. Though an important committee, first set up in December 1953, it is not one of the sought after committees. The need for subordinate legislation arises because all details cannot be incorporated in a legislation. There are also unforeseen contingencies which arise during the implementation

of a legislation. Th[...] tter also entails
dealing with the iss[...] lation. Pressures
of time make it [...] ent for frequent
amendments of a[...] merely lay down
broad policy and [...] ving the details to
be worked out by [...] of rules, regulations
and by-laws.

The committe[...] ordinate legislation
at two stages: Fi[...] e powers to frame
subordinate legi[...] ond, at the 'order'
stage when the [...] d by the executive
in pursuance o[...]

Slippages m[...] of a law and its
execution. Pa[...] d to be skeletal,
containing on[...] s, omitting matters
of substance [...] ing on the life of a
citizen. Powe[...] ide as to subject the
citizen to har[...] y the administration.
Some powers [...] at the areas intended
to be covered [...] It is also possible that
the executive [...] rule-making powers,
transgress the [...] liament.[19] Thus, while
some delegation of legislative powers is inevitable and
indispensable, it has to be ensured that these powers are exercised
prudently and with due diligence.

Excessive delegation of powers and unguided discretion to the
executive under various legislations has become a cause for
serious concern. One of the foremost examples is the Urban
Land (Ceiling on Holding) Act, 1976. Delegated powers under
several sections of the Act have been a virtual goldmine for
implementing authorities. A number of other examples can also
be cited. In future, the scope for subordinate legislation, and
particularly the areas of discretion, will have to be curtailed with
a firm hand. The committees on subordinate legislation will have

[19]Lok Sabha Secretariat, *Parliament in India—The Ninth Lok Sabha, 1989–91,
A Study*, Northern Book Centre, New Delhi.

to insist on the framing of clear and unambiguous guidelines which are made public in all cases wherever discretionary powers are to be used by the executive. It will have to be admitted that the subordinate legislation committees have not been successful so far in addressing this task adequately. In this light, it is surprising that the NCRWC, instead of suggesting the strengthening the committee, has recommended its abolition and substitution by a committee on legislation which would advise the government on legislative programmes from time to time.

Weak expenditure control by parliament has emerged as yet another area of serious concern in a number of countries, including India. Based on her analysis of the experience in UK, Ann Robinson has emphasised that there are too many institutional and attitudinal barriers to an extension of parliamentary influence. 'What Parliament needs is not a hollow power of life or death, but a little larger share in the process of deciding who gets what of public spending in Britain. The House of Commons will only get a larger share of power and influence when political attitudes towards the respective roles of executive and legislature change.'[20] The estimates committee in UK has since 1970–71 been restyled as the expenditure committee with amended terms of reference. This is intended to enable the committee to focus its attention on public expenditure rather than on supply estimates and to examine a wider selection of issues arising in this field. Further, it was suggested by the select committee on procedure appointed by the House of Commons that the two committees, namely, the PAC and the estimates committee could with advantage be combined into a single committee to be called the public expenditure committee...(as) the sums which appear this year as estimates of expenditure will eventually become items in the corresponding appropriation accounts. The difference is one of time rather than of subject matter or method.[21]

[20]Ann Robinson, *Parliament and Public Spending, The Expenditure Committee of the House of Commons, 1970–76*, Heinemann, London, 1978, p. 161.

[21]M.N. Kaul, *Parliamentary Institutions and Procedures*, National Publishing House, New Delhi, 1978.

Legislators in most countries are at sea regarding budget matters. Speaking about the $520 billion, 4,000-page omnibus spending bill passed by the US House of Representatives, West Virginia Senator Robert Byrd said, 'Do I know what's in this bill? Are you kidding? Only god knows what's in this conference report.' (*Newsweek*, 2 Nov 1998).

In India the scrutiny of public expenditure by parliament leaves a great deal to be desired. The efficacy and productivity of government spending have remained largely unexplored by legislatures. The Comptroller and Auditor-General's report on Bihar released in 1997 showed that the government spent three rupees to earn one rupee. The report on the accounts of the union government for 1995–96 found that parliament does not exercise any effective control over as much as 80 per cent of the expenditure. In the five years from 1991–92 to 1995–96, the 'charged expenditure' of the union government has increased from 66 per cent to 72 per cent of its total expenditure.[22] In addition, the expenditure on salaries and allowances, which is inflexible in the short run, accounts for another 8 per cent. Over Rs 85,000 crore of expenditure incurred by state governments over the last twenty years is yet to be regularised by obtaining approval of their legislatures. (*Economic Times*, 28 Sep 1999). Hidden tax subsidies given by the centre and the states have escaped close scrutiny. In a penetrating article, D.R. Pendse had brought out the erosion of the budget process and how the union budget for 1999–2000 was full of fudged facts and figures.[23] As S. Venkitaramanan has brought out, 'the gimmick of extra budgetary resources under which PSUs [public sector undertakings] raise resources, not according to what each needs but according to what each entity can, is also a contributory

---

[22]This expenditure is debited to the Consolidated Fund of India but is not voted by Parliament, and includes interest payments, grants-in-aid to state governments under Article 275 of the Constitution, payment of states' share of Union excise duties, repayments of internal and external debt of the Centre and loans of state governments, and salary and allowances of a few statutory functionaries.

[23]D.R. Pendse, Erosion of the Budget Process, *Economic Times*, 26 March 1999.

factor to masking financial responsibility.'[24] Earlier, a reference was made to the perfunctory nature of the discussion on the budget in parliament. During the three years from 1986–1989 when Maharashtra adopted zero based budgeting (ZBB), annual reports on subsidies contained in the budget, performance of PSUs and progress of implementation of ZBB were placed before the state legislature at its budget session but there was no discussion on any of these reports.

The demand for introducing Performance Budgets (PBs) was made in the Lok Sabha as far back as 1954. The estimates committee, in its twentieth report on budgetary reforms in 1959, made a recommendation on preparation of PBs and repeated it in 1959 and 1960. The Administrative Reforms Commission made a similar recommendation in 1968. The PBs were, *inter alia*, expected to enhance the accountability of the management and at the same time provide an additional tool for management control of financial operations. They were also expected to render performance audit more purposeful and effective.[25] Experience shows that the PBs have become a routine and mindless form-filling exercise. (see chapter 4, section III).

## Parliamentary Privileges

Article 105 of the Constitution provides for the powers, privileges and immunities of the Houses of parliament and of the members and the committees thereof.[26] The corresponding

[24]S. Venkitaramanan, Time to Restore Fiscal Sanity, *Economic Times*, 6 February 1995.

[25]A. Premchand (ed.), *Government Financial Management—Issues and Country Studies*, International Monetary Fund, Washington D.C., 1990.

[26]Section 15 of the Constitution (Forty-fourth Amendment) Act, 1978, came into force with effect from 20 June 1979. Prior to that, Clause (3) of Article 105 provided that, 'in other respects, the powers, privileges and immunities of each House of Parliament and of the members and the committees of each House shall be such as from time to time be defined by Parliament by law, and until so defined, shall be those of the House of Commons of the Parliament of the United Kingdom, and of its members and committees at the commencement of the Constitution i.e., on 26 January 1950.'

provisions relating to the powers, privileges and immunities of the Houses of state legislatures and of the members and committees thereof are contained in Article 194 of the Constitution which are the same as those in Article 105 relating to parliament.

Justice A.N. Grover, former chairman of the Press Council of India (PCI), had opined that the language of Article 105 seemed to suggest that it was intended that there should be legislation on the subject. It appears that the framers of the Constitution wanted to leave it to parliament to define these privileges by enacting laws in due course, and during the interim period, the powers, privileges and immunities of the House of Commons were to be followed. However, no law has been enacted by parliament and state legislatures in pursuance of clause (3) of Article 105/194 of the Constitution to define their powers, privileges and immunities.

The main issue which requires consideration is whether the privileges of parliament and state legislatures should remain uncodified. Frequent invocation of privilege by members of these bodies has become a point of serious concern. Though in a large number of these cases, the persons and organisations charged with breach of privilege have not been held guilty by the committees on privileges, it must be said that such inquiries lead to a great deal of mental anguish and harassment, and also waste the time and resources of those charged.

Subhash C. Kashyap, former secretary general of Lok Sabha, has rightly emphasised that the people and the Press are entitled to ask and know what the 'blessed' privileges are before they can exercise all the care not to breach them. The MPs should not forget that they are not above the people...To prevent ugly situations appearing again and again in the name of protecting parliamentary privileges, the only honest and straightforward course would be for parliament and state legislatures to abide by the constitutional provision and codify their privileges by law.[27]

[27]Subhash C. Kashyap, Parliamentary Privileges: Use and Misuse, *Indian Express*, 20 January 1995.

This issue has assumed special significance in the context of the JMM case referred to earlier. The Supreme Court decision in this case has raised issues of far-reaching significance. The court has, *inter alia*, held that the alleged bribe-takers who voted upon the no-confidence motion are entitled to the immunity conferred by Article 105(2). However the MP who, despite having received the bribe pursuant to the conspiracy, had abstained from voting would not be entitled to such immunity since protection under Article 105(2) must relate to the vote actually given or speech actually made in parliament by an MP. Therefore, prosecution against such an MP must proceed. The court also observed that parliament may, however, proceed against both bribe-takers and bribe-givers for breach of privilege and contempt. However, as per the minority judgement, immunity under Article 105(2) is available only to give protection against liability for an act that follows or succeeds as a consequence of the making of the speech or giving of a vote by an MP and not for an act that precedes the speech or vote and that gives rise to the liability which arises independently of the speech or vote. The minority view therefore was that the offence of criminal conspiracy under section 120-A of IPC made out on conclusion of the act pursuant to the agreement is immaterial. The act of acceptance of bribe for speaking or giving a vote against the motion arose independently of making the speech or giving of vote by the MP. Hence liability for the offence cannot be treated in respect of anything done or any vote given in parliament and neither the bribe-takers nor the bribe-givers are entitled to any immunity under Article 105(2). These issues came into prominence once again due to the withdrawal of support by some MLAs of the political parties in the ruling democratic front government in Maharashtra in June 2002. News reports indicated that huge sums of two to five crore rupees had been paid to each of the defecting MLAs to topple the government. Against this background, it is important to note that the NCRWC has recommended that Article 105(2) of the Constitution may be amended to clarify that the immunity enjoyed by MPs does not cover corrupt acts committed by them in connection with the duties in the House or otherwise. The commission has recommended that Article 194(2) may also be similarly amended in relation to the members of state legislatures.

It is unfortunate that the government has not initiated any steps to comprehensively examine the issues arising from the above judgement of the Supreme Court. The delay, on the part of the government, in filing the review petition in the court for referring the case to a larger bench was simply inexcusable and raises doubts whether the government was really serious in the matter or was merely making a token gesture and going through the motions for public consumption.

It is interesting to note that four different notices of privilege were received by the speaker against the then prime minister, P.V. Narasimha Rao, in February 1996. In replies to these notices, Rao had denied the allegations levelled against him. The speaker, Shivraj V. Patil, disallowed, on 11 March 1996, the notice given by Arjun Singh and observed that, 'The matter is before the court which may take a proper decision on the basis of evidence that may be produced before it. Three years back some allegations were voiced about the illegal payments. At that time itself, the House could have been asked to look into it. On the basis of other kinds of inducements, the matter could have been asked to be looked into by the House. In view of these facts and the available evidence, I find it very difficult to give the consent.'[28] Later, on the same grounds, the other three notices were also disallowed. It can be seen how shallow and unconvincing were the arguments put forth by the speaker for rejection of the notices. Surprisingly, none of the members pressed for the admission of the notices and their reference to the committee on privileges. Since then, even though the Supreme Court, in its judgement, had stated that 'Parliament may, however, proceed against both bribe-takers and bribe-givers for breach of privilege and contempt', no action was initiated in

[28]Lok Sabha Secretariat, *The Journal of Parliamentary Information*, Vol. XLII, No. 2, June 1996, p. 187.

the matter. This is an eloquent commentary on the scant importance attached by parliament to improving its public image and dealing with corruption among its members firmly and in a transparent manner.

A former speaker of the Lok Sabha, P.A. Sangma, had, in the wake of a letter purportedly written by some MPs to the speaker and the prime minister regarding parliamentary privileges in the context of the JMM case, called for a consensus among political parties on the issue of special privileges enjoyed by elected representatives. He had observed that suggestions had been made that these privileges be codified, but put in Schedule IX of the Constitution which grants immunity from review by courts. 'Now, it is for political parties to hammer out a solution', he added. (*Times of India*, 16 Mar 1997). On the other side, Shivraj Patil, the former speaker of the Lok Sabha, had argued that complete codification of parliamentary privileges is not possible because the parliamentarians feel that such a move would curtail their privileges and lead to problems in protecting them. (*Hindustan Times*, 18 Dec 1996). According to M.N. Kaul, the 'problem here is not one of defining privileges but of developing suitable conventions...The idea underlying privileges of the House was that there should always be the reserve power in parliament emphasising sovereignty, in the same manner in which courts have power to punish contempt, and its authority, as the highest tribunal in the land in the sphere of legislation, should not be held to ridicule. But it does not mean that it amounted in any way to restriction of the liberty of the Press or the citizen's liberty of criticism... Privilege is impossible to define, nor is it desirable to define it precisely for very good reasons.'[29]

The ludicrousness, in today's world, of one of the privileges enjoyed by the legislators of a bygone era was brought out by P. Shiv Shanker, former union law minister, in the training session for the new MPs. This pertains to the immunity from arrest by the police during a period of forty days preceding and

[29]M.N. Kaul, *Parliamentary Institutions and Procedures*, National Publishing House, New Delhi, 1978, pp. 200–201.

succeeding the session of parliament. This was given in the days in which MPs in the United Kingdom travelled on horse-back to and from their constituencies for each session. (*Maharashtra Times*, 1 Sep 1998). But, the same privilege still continues. As a result, according to news reports, Mohan Rawle, Shiv Sena MP, could not be arrested by the police though he sat fasting in Mumbai, in a police station, to protest against the arrest of Arun Gavali, the notorious crimelord, in February 1997. The police in Mumbai admitted delaying the arrest of ex-Shiv Sena MLA Gurunath Desai for over a month as the Shiv Sena-BJP was in power. A senior IPS officer said, 'You will come across very few policemen taking a risk of arresting a politician, especially someone from the ruling party. Nobody wants to be in the limelight for a single day and get transferred to a side posting the very next day.' (*Times of India*, 28 Oct 1999). According to a convenient excuse trooped out by police, the late Phoolan Devi, MP, could not be arrested, in spite of a court warrant, as parliament's budget session was on and the speaker's permission was required for her arrest. It was shocking to see that an MP whose electricity supply was disconnected by the New Delhi Municipal Committee (NDMC) for the non-payment of bills had the temerity to give a notice of privilege motion against the concerned officers of the NDMC. It is another matter that the motion was not admitted by the chairman. (*Economic Times*, 14 Nov 1999). But this shows the mindset of the representatives of the people! In yet another shocking instance, the chairman of the Maharashtra legislative council had referred to the privileges panel the complaint of a member regarding the refusal of the railway authorities to provide him with a reservation on a train. (*Times of India*, 23 Dec 1999).

The Bihar IAS officers' association in its resolution in October 1991 had, *inter alia*, expressed concern over 'the growing practice of hauling up civil servants in the name of breach of privilege which has been extended to cover matters having no conceivable concern with the legislators' law-making powers. The deliberate harassment caused to the civil servants in such cases, together with the unseemly publicity that such cases are guaranteed to attract, can by no stretch of imagination be said to further the requirements of public interest or fulfil the electorate's mandate. The association is of the view that immediate definition and listing of privileges of legislators is imperative in order to cry a halt to irresponsibility in public life.' (*Hindustan Times*, 5 Oct 1991).

It was in the early 1970s that an IPS officer of the Maharashtra cadre was called before the bar of the Lok Sabha for having misbehaved with an MP and reprimanded. This led to widespread demoralisation among police officers all over the country. In another case, a woman district magistrate in Katihar district in Bihar was held guilty of breach of privilege and was summoned to the bar of the assembly and reprimanded. This made legislative history in Bihar. (*Hindustan Times*, 15 Nov 1991). Against this background of misuse of parliamentary privileges, it was not surprising that the former speaker of Lok Sabha, P.A. Sangma, threatened district officers all over the country that any delay in implementation of the Members of Parliament Local Area Development Scheme (MPLADS) would be treated as contempt of the House.

The *Privileges Digest* brought out by the Lok Sabha secretariat gives a series of cases of breach of privilege coming up before the speakers of the Lok Sabha and state assemblies and presiding officers of upper Houses as also their committees on privileges. Even a cursory look at these cases leads one to the conclusion that parliamentary privileges have become a holy cow. The present position is clearly untenable and needs to be reviewed urgently.

In order to alleviate some of the uncertainty traditionally inherent in the exercise of their privileges, many parliaments based on the Westminster model have opted to codify their privileges. Australia is one of the latest to do so. In 1987, the Australian parliament passed legislation declaring, clarifying and substantially changing the law of parliamentary privileges. Partly in consequence of the legislation, the Australian Senate passed a series of resolutions substantially codifying its practices in matters relating to privilege... This was done not with great enthusiasm and reforming zeal, but as a matter of necessity. The legislation was occasioned by two judgements of the Supreme Court of New South Wales which severely restricted parliament's privilege of freedom of speech.[30] Harry Evans has suggested that 'the changes to the law will not satisfy the most zealous reformers, in that the Houses retain their power to deal with contempt. Only the conversion of contempt of parliament into statutory criminal offences prosecuted in the courts, and perhaps, some weakening of the privilege of freedom of speech, would quieten the determined critics. It is unlikely that any further changes, much less such drastic changes, will be made, partly because members of parliament will resist them, partly because the law is now much more acceptable.'[31]

The United Kingdom has not opted for codification of privileges but it has altered its way of dealing with them. The UK select committee on parliamentary privileges which submitted its report in 1967 made a significant recommendation to forsake the term 'privilege' for 'rights and immunities'. The committee underlined that, 'if the basic concept of "privileges" or "privilege" is abolished, it will be easier to understand and to concentrate upon the provision of the essential protection which is required by the House, its members and officers.'

As a part of the on-going reforms based on the 1967–68 select committee report, the House of Commons adopted the self-denying principle that, while not relinquishing its privileges, it would not always seek to enforce them. It decided that it should exercise its penal jurisdiction as sparingly as possible and only when it is satisfied that to do so was essential in order to provide reasonable protection for the House, its members or its officers... The House no longer entertains complaints about

---

[30]'Privilege in the Modern Context', Paper Prepared by Table Research Branch, House of Commons, Canada, published in Lok Sabha Secretariat, *Privileges Digest*, Vol. XXXIX, No. 2, October 1994, p. 18.

[31]Harry Evans, Parliamentary Privilege: Changes to the Law at Federal Level, published in Lok Sabha Secretariat, *Privileges Digest*, Vol. XXXVIII, No. 2, October 1993, p. 28.

actions which do not cause actual or threatened damage to the working of the House in a substantial way. This has almost eliminated the pursuit of trivial complaints. It was noted that the more often the House exercises its penal powers, the more frequently it will find itself in conflict with the courts in matters of interpretation.[32]

The new procedure has had a dramatic effect on the number of claims to privilege raised in the British House of Commons. The use of the word privilege to gain the speaker's ear and to secure the chance to raise a political issue unrelated to real privilege...is now almost unknown. Secondly, *there are now far fewer trivial cases referred to the committee of privileges. In particular, since 1978, there have been no cases of privilege involving what is often referred to as 'constructive attempts', that is rude or derogatory reflections on Members. In this sense, the new privilege practice has helped to cure a problem first suggested in the 1967 report that the Members of the British House of Commons were too sensitive in their reactions to Press criticism. Finally, the total number of privilege matters of all kinds referred to the committee has been significantly reduced.*[33] (Emphasis added; this is in sharp contrast to the situation in the Indian parliament and state legislatures.)

The special committee on the rights and immunities of members in Canada also echoed the recommendation of the 1967 British select committee and found that the term privilege was likely to give rise to misconceptions on the part of the public and so preferred the use of the term 'rights and immunities'. Further, the committee found that the rights and immunities of members had not been frequently violated and that it had rarely been necessary to invoke the penal powers of the House... The House has quite rightly held a very limiting view of its privileges and has always been reluctant to use its powers harshly.[34]

[32]*Ibid.*, p. 19.

[33]'Privilege in the Historical Context', Paper Prepared by Table Research Branch, House of Commons, Canada, published in Lok Sabha Secretariat, *Privileges Digest*, Vol. XXXIX, No. 1, April, 1994, pp. 24–25.

[34]*Op. cit.*, pp. 26–27.

In spite of these winds of change in other Commonwealth countries, in India, parliament and state legislatures seem to be not only reluctant to codify their privileges but are even reluctant to do any rethinking on the subject. The fourth report of the committee of privileges submitted in December 1994 contains a solitary recommendation, namely, 'that it is not advisable to codify parliamentary privileges.'[35] The report stated, 'The committee are of the view that the legislatures' powers to punish is more or less akin to and analogous to the power given to the courts to punish for their contempt. Even the Contempt of Court Act, 1971 does not specify the matters which constitute contempt. Contempt of court in a given case has to be judged according to the facts and circumstances of each case. Likewise, the committee feel that a breach of privilege or contempt of the House can best be decided according to the facts and circumstances of each case rather than by specifying them in so many words.'

Even if the conclusion of the committee were to be accepted as logical and reasonable, one would have expected the committee to make a critical appraisal of the actions taken in the past in breach of privilege complaints. It would also be expected that the committee would at least suggest measures to tighten the present procedures so as to reduce the grievances of harassment and mental torture of those against whom complaints are filed and to change the mindset of MPs which leads to innumerable complaints concerning their hurt egos and offended feelings of self-importance.

It is unfortunate that legislators in India are not prepared to learn from their counterparts in other Commonwealth countries. It is only under pressure of public opinion and intervention by the higher judiciary, as is the case in some other countries, that our legislators can be made to see reason. A step in this direction is the recommendation of the NCRWC that the privileges of legislators should be defined and delimited.

[35] Extracts from the Fourth Report of the Committee of Privileges, Lok Sabha, regarding Codification of Parliamentary Privileges, published in Lok Sabha Secretariat, *Privileges Digest*, Vol. XL, December 1995, p. 35.

## Some Outstanding Failures

A reference must be made, briefly, to some outstanding failures of parliament which have contributed to the erosion of the confidence of the people in its capacity to deliver. These failures also cast serious doubts on the capacity of parliament to deal with important national issues decisively. It further highlights the weaknesses of the mechanisms provided by the Constitution for effective surveillance by parliament. The first of these failures is in respect of the inquiries through the joint committees of parliament. The two high profile joint parliamentary committee (JPC) enquiries pertaining to the Bofors contract and the irregularities in securities and banking transactions brought out the utter futility of entrusting any such enquiries in future to such committees.

### JPC on the Bofors Contract

The motion for setting up the joint committee on the Bofors contract was adopted by the Lok Sabha and the Rajya Sabha on 6 August and 12 August 1987, respectively, after a marathon debate lasting for 22 hours in each House spread over a period of 19 days. The committee consisted of B. Shankaranand as chairman and 19 other members from the Lok Sabha and 10 members from the Rajya Sabha. The committee held 50 sittings. Of these, 30 were for recording evidence, 7 for the study of classified documents and the remaining 13 for in-house deliberations.

The boycott of the committee by most of the opposition parties helped it to white-wash the enquiry completely. The committee's conclusions bring this out fully. The committee, *inter alia*, concluded:

- The committee is firmly convinced that the procedure followed for the selection of the Bofors gun system was sound and objective, and the technical evaluation of the various gun systems considered was thorough, flawless and meticulous.
- *No middleman was involved* in the commercial negotiations

leading to the finalisation of the price and the other terms of the contract with Bofors.
- The committee has noted with satisfaction that the price of the Bofors gun system in the Indian contract was the lowest compared with prices in contracts with other customers.
- No extraneous influence or consideration such as kickbacks or bribes as alleged in the media affected at any stage the selection and the evaluation of the gun systems or the commercial negotiations with the competing suppliers.
- The evidence before the committee conclusively establishes that the decision to award the contract to Bofors was purely on merit.
- There is also no evidence to substantiate the allegation of commissions or bribes having been paid to anyone.
- There is no evidence of any other payment having been made by Bofors for winning the contract.[36]

The committee's findings, in effect, belittled parliament itself in the eyes of the public. What is most shocking is not the utter failure of the joint committee to unearth the truth but its misuse by the government to bury the truth. Even though more than a decade has elapsed since the submission of the report of the joint committee, the Bofors controversy remains a shameful episode in the national conscience. Up to the beginning of 1997, over 202 hours had been spent on discussion of Bofors in parliament and its committee and over Rs 80 lakh spent on its investigation. The FIR in this case was filed in 1990. Ultimately, nine years after the filing of the FIR, a new chapter was opened in October 1999, by the CBI filing a formal chargesheet in a criminal court in New Delhi against some persons, including the late Rajiv Gandhi, under several sections of the IPC and the PCA. It was only in October 2000 that the chargesheet was filed by the CBI against the Hinduja brothers. By its judgment dated 10 June 2002, the Delhi high court had quashed the chargesheet

[36]Lok Sabha Secretariat, *Report of the Joint Committee to Enquire into Bofors Contract*, Eighth Lok Sabha, April 1988, pp. 189–192.

against the Hinduja brothers on the ground that the CBI had bypassed the CVC while filing the chargesheet. The CBI had to go in appeal against this decision. Clearly, the case is not likely to conclude for several more years, in spite of the orders of the Supreme Court that the case should be heard on a day to day basis by a special court as at each stage, appeals are being filed in the High Court and the Supreme Court. In the meantime, two of the accused, S.K. Bhatnagar, former defence secretary and Win Chaddha, have died. The third accused, Rajiv Gandhi, was assassinated even before the chargesheet against him was filed. [The extradition case against Octavio Quattrocchi in a Malaysian court is dragging on interminably.]

### JPC on the Bank Scam

Looked at purely in terms of numbers, though it would perhaps be wrong to do so, the Rs 64 crore Bofors scam pales into insignificance when compared to the bank scam involving over Rs 10,000 crore. It is shocking that the parliamentary joint committee's report on the subject acknowledges it as a scam in chapter II but, in the title of the report, refers to it as mere irregularities in securities and banking transactions![37] The report bemoans that, 'The most unfortunate aspect has been the emergence of a culture of non-accountability which permeated all sections of the government and banking system over the years. The state of the country's system of governance, the persistence of non-adherence to rules, regulations and guidelines, the alarming decay over time in the banking systems has been exposed. These grave and numerous irregularities persisted for so long that eventually it was not the observance of regulations but their breach that came to be regarded and defended as "market practice".'[38]

The finance minister (FM) while replying to a call attention motion on the strike by sharebrokers, had stated in the Lok Sabha on 30 April 1992, in a lighter vein, '...but that does not

[37] Lok Sabha Secretariat, *Report: Joint Committee to Enquire into Irregularities in Securities and Banking Transactions*, Vol. I, December 1993.
[38] *Ibid.*, p. 7.

mean that I should lose my sleep simply because stock market goes up one day and falls the next day.' Referring to this statement of the FM, the committee observed that 'it is good to have a FM who does not lose his sleep easily but one would wish that when such cataclysmic changes take place all around some alarm would ring to disturb his slumber'. But these sentiments, observations and barbs are no substitute for the solid homework that goes to the root of the problems, and exposes the persons who perpetrated the scam.

'Where has all the money gone?' remained an unanswered question at the end of the day. All that the committee came up with was the observation that 'The tracing of end-use monies to their final destination, particularly when large sums are involved and when intricate mechanisms have been employed to cloak transactions, is the task of a team comprising of (*sic*) specialists in the field of accountancy, taxation and criminal investigation. The committee, therefore, recommend that such a team be constituted under the overall co-ordinating responsibility of the MOF and with due and proper representation of such other agencies as it may deem fit; the task of identifying the end-use monies be entrusted to this committee; it may be directed to report within six months of appointment and the report also be presented to parliament.'[39] The committee dumped the problem of reconciling the contradictory statements of witnesses who appeared before it into the lap of another group by observing that, 'during the course of the enquiry the committee found various discrepancies/contradictions in the statements made by various witnesses. Considering the nature of this case and the complexities of the transactions, the committee recommend that the matter should be enquired thoroughly by a joint team consisting of CBI [Central Board of Investigation], CBDT [Central Board of Direct Taxes], SEBI [Security and Exchange Board of India], Department of Company Affairs and RBI [Reserve Bank of India].'[40]

[39] *Ibid.*, p. 319.
[40] *Ibid.*, p. 321.

The committee admitted that it had 'come across various instances of close nexus between prominent industrial houses, banks and brokers'. Such a bland statement amounts to stating the obvious. The committee failed to go deeper into the matter and expose the nexus with authentic facts and figures. It also failed to make any concrete recommendations regarding action which should be taken against those responsible.

Debashis Basu and Sucheta Dalal have cogently demonstrated how most of the members of the JPC were neither interested in understanding the market and the system, nor did they ask any questions regarding the ramifications of their investigation. Though the report was voluminous, no breakthrough was achieved. This happened because there was simply no strategy either at the collective or at the individual level to deal with such a large and complex issue. The JPC started off by calling for truckloads of information which nobody read... If only the JPC members had first done their homework by talking to the right brokers and bank treasury officers, they would have narrowed down their focus. In fact, the JPC got very close to the real can of worms, prised it slightly open and left it at that.[41]

Some political parties were trying to mount a campaign for a JPC on yet another scam (CRB scam) which unfolded in 1997. However, in the light of the very disappointing experience of the earlier two JPCs, there was hardly any enthusiasm in the country for another JPC. Thus, potentially one of the most effective instruments for parliamentary scrutiny has fallen into disuse. This is once again convincingly brought out by the report of the joint parliamentary committee on the stock market scam in December 2002. After interminable discussions and four extensions, the committee has not come out with anything which was not already known and has merely harped on systemic deficiencies, without holding hardly anybody accountable.

### Proceedings for the Removal of a Supreme Court Judge

Article 124(4) of the Constitution of India states that a judge of

---

[41]Debashis Basu and Sucheta Dalal, *The Scam: Who Won, Who Lost, Who Got Away*, UBS Publishers' Distributors Ltd., New Delhi, 1993, pp. 270–271.

the Supreme Court shall not be removed from office except by an order of the President passed after an address by each House of parliament supported by a majority of the total membership of that House and by a majority of not less than two thirds of the members of that House present and voting has been presented to the President in the same session for such removal on the ground of proved misbehaviour or incapacity.

In keeping with this provision, a motion for presenting an address to the President for removal from office of Justice V. Ramaswamy of the Supreme Court of India for his acts of misbehaviour and a motion for considering the report of the inquiry committee to investigate into the grounds on which the removal of Shri V. Ramaswamy, Judge, Supreme Court of India, was sought were moved by Somnath Chatterjee, MP, on 10 May 1993.

Earlier, a committee comprising P.B. Sawant, a Supreme Court judge, P.D. Desai, Chief Justice of the Bombay high court, and D. Chinnappa Reddy, a distinguished jurist had inquired into the charges against Justice V. Ramaswamy and come to the conclusion that the charges against him were established. In such a situation, it was shocking to see the Congress party, then in power, deciding to abstain from voting on the flimsy and ridiculous ground that the matter reeked of discrimination against south Indians. The final voting was: Ayes 198, Noes Nil, and Abstentions 207. Accordingly, the motion and Address (to the President) were declared as not carried by the required majority in accordance with Clause (4) of Article 124 of the Constitution of India.

Proceedings for the removal of a judge of the Supreme Court are highly sensitive and far too important to be treated in this cavalier manner. In every sense of the term, parliament was on test and it failed miserably, shaking the confidence of the people in the highest institution of democracy. Time and time again, parliament has tried to assert its supremacy *vis-a-vis* the judiciary. But, on the one occasion when it had to prove its mettle, it failed and came down heavily in the estimation of the people. This will be written down as one of the most ignominious chapters in the history of parliament.

It is also interesting to note that, after failing to act against the indicted judge, parliament did not even bother to ask the government to get the various legal and procedural issues raised by Kapil Sibal, who appeared as the lawyer for the indicted judge, examined in depth so that there would not be any scope for ambiguities and infirmities in similar cases in the future. The government could even have been asked to seek the advisory opinion of the Supreme Court under Article 143 of the Constitution. But, parliament decided to turn a blind eye to all these matters. This is a sad commentary on the working of the highest legislative body in the country.

**The Lok Pal Bill**

The Lok Pal Bill must have set some kind of record. It has been under consideration for a period of over 34 years. The first Bill on the creation of the institution of Lok Pal or ombudsman was introduced in parliament way back in 1968. Thereafter, revised versions of the Bill were tabled in 1971, 1977, 1985, 1989, 1996 and 1998 and the last word on the subject is still to be written.

One can understand and live with differences of perception and views on any subject. It is only fair that all such views are considered carefully. One can also understand the spirit of accommodation which is necessary to reconcile the views of various parties. But the travails of the Lok Pal Bill show interminable analysis leading to paralysis of action. This is a case of the best being an enemy of the good.

This is not the place to go into the details of the provisions of the various Bills or the *pros* and *cons* thereof. A treatise can be written on the subject. What is relevant here is the efficacy of the institution of parliament in addressing issues, such as corruption in high places, which are crucial for cleaning up public life. The NCRWC has, therefore, rightly recommended that the Constitution should provide for the appointment of a

Lok Pal. It has further recommended that the prime minister should be kept out of the purview of the Lok Pal.

It is interesting to note that although governments of almost all political parties, except the Communist parties and the Bahujan Samaj Party, have been in power or have supported the government at the Centre during all these years, none of them were really committed to getting the Bill passed in parliament. The Lok Pal Bill is once again on the agenda of the National Democratic Alliance government at the centre. But, there are serious differences among political parties regarding the powers and functions to be entrusted to the proposed institution of Lok Pal. A PIL has been filed by an NGO in the Supreme Court with a request that the government be directed to come up with a time-bound action plan for converting the Bill into a Law. But, it is time the limitations of the higher judiciary are recognised. The apex court cannot force parliament to legislate on any subject, particularly when parliament is reluctant to do so.

### The Nexus between Criminals, Politicians and Bureaucrats

A committee was appointed by the central government on 9 July 1993 to look into the links of crime syndicates/Mafia with government functionaries and 'political personalities'. The committee, headed by the then union home secretary, N.N. Vohra, submitted its report on 5 October 1993.[42] Over nine years have elapsed since the submission of the report. In the meantime the matter was also brought before the Supreme Court through a PIL. Unfortunately, there is nothing worthwhile to show in the way of concrete action except for the setting up of a nodal group under the chairmanship of the union home secretary. No details of any other action taken in pursuance of the report have been made public. Significantly, parliament has not insisted on any time-bound action by the government. Attention must be invited in this context to a pertinent observation in the Vohra report: 'I perceived that some of the

[42]Government of India, Ministry of Home Affairs, *Vohra Committee Report.*

members [of the committee] appeared to have some hesitation in openly expressing their views and also seemed unconvinced that government actually intended to pursue such matters'. Quite a prophetic observation!

The heads of various central organisations had made some very candid and devastating observations—all over India, crime syndicates have become a law unto themselves; the network of Mafia is virtually running a parallel government pushing the state apparatus into irrelevance; and the existing criminal justice system, which was essentially designed to deal with individual offences/crimes, is unable to deal with the activities of the Mafia; the provisions of law in regard to economic offences are weak; there are insurmountable legal difficulties in the confiscation of the property acquired through Mafia activities that the committee has taken cognisance of.

This report was placed on the table of parliament and received nation-wide publicity. But our lawmakers have failed to grasp the enormity and urgency of the problem. The Supreme Court, in its decision on the PIL, had suggested to the government that a high level commission should be appointed to pursue these matters. The court had also underlined the importance of ensuring the independence of such a commission. It is a pity that the government has had no time to look into these vital issues. Parliament too has failed in its responsibility to force the government to take follow-up action.

## A Framework of Parliamentary Reforms

It may be useful to begin the discussion in this section with a brief reference to how far we have strayed from parliamentary norms and standards of the period soon after Independence. Jawaharlal Nehru regarded parliament as the high temple of democracy and a 'grand inquest of the nation'. An illustrative reference may be made to just two instances to bring home the point. The opposition wanted some information but the minister stalled it on the plea that it could not be given in the public interest. A visibly agitated Nehru was soon up on his feet to intervene and assert, 'Mr speaker, sir, I see no public interest involved. The minister should give the required information.' The other instance is equally striking. In June 1951, independent India witnessed its first parliamentary probe against H.G. Mudgal, a then member of parliament, involving a sum of only Rs 5,000. Nehru himself went into the facts of the case and recommended the appointment of a five-member committee. Once the facts were clear and precise, he insisted that parliament's decision 'should also be clear, precise and unambiguous.'[43]

It may be useful to take a look at the changes which are contemplated or are being attempted in other leading democracies such as the UK and the US. Speaking in the House of Lords in 1977, Lord O'Hagan declared, 'Parliament dies if it does not update its procedures. Procedures are the muscle and sinew of parliament. If we do not exercise that muscle and keep it in good trim for contemporary challenges, then we shall have no real job left to do.'[44]

Inder Jit has brought out some of the reforms which have been implemented in the UK.[45] The select committee on procedures set up by British House of Commons in 1976 produced 76 recommendations 'to enable the House as a whole to exercise effective control and stewardship over ministers and the expanding bureaucracy of the state for which they are answerable.' It rejected proposals for streamlining the procedures to give ministers greater power to make delegated legislation. The committee's major recommendation was on the select committee system. It drew attention to the piecemeal growth of select committees since the War and urged the replacement of

[43]Inder Jit, Parliament Requires Reform, in Lok Sabha Secretariat, *Parliament of India, Ninth Lok Sabha—1989–1991—A Study*, Northern Book Centre, New Delhi, 1992, p. 19.
[44]Recent Structural and Procedural Changes in the House of Commons (Appendix I) in Philip Norton (ed.), *Parliament in the 1980s*, Basil Blackwell, UK, 1985, p. 163.
[45]Inder Jit, *op. cit.*, pp. 20–22.

these with a comprehensive range of committees to monitor all aspects of expenditure, administration and policy within the responsibilities of the various government departments and agencies.

The incoming government in Britain in 1979, headed by Margaret Thatcher, accepted both the procedure committee's order of priorities as well as the essentials of its recommendations, especially in regard to the appointment of permanent select committees. As Michael Rye, principal clerk (overseas office) observed in the *Commons Today*, 'in the end, the development (setting up of select committees) must flow from a recognition, by all those concerned with ascertaining that parliament keeps a proper critical eye on ministers and civil servants alike, that the growing volume and complexity of government can no longer be scrutinised effectively by the old process of debate on the floor or in standing committees; committees able to call for papers and examine witnesses closely provide a much more searching technique.'

The committees are empowered to appoint any number of part-time specialist advisors to assist them in their enquiry. Many men of distinction in their particular fields of expertise had spared time to give committees their invaluable guidance. The new committees were making full use of part-time advisors numbering over 70 at one stage. Parliamentary activities in Britain have become progressively more 'open' through grass-root enquiries. Until 1965, no select committee had heard evidence in public for many years. Now, the great majority of hearings are open to the public (except where strictly confidential evidence is being given). Advance notices are published in the press.

John Biffen has observed that the 'select committees have entered into the "bloodstream" of British politics. They have not changed the working relationship of parliament and the executive, but they have at least improved it'.[46]

[46]Stephen J. Downs, Structural Changes—Select Committees: Experiment and Establishment, in Philip Norton (ed.), *op. cit.*, p. 67.

In January 1980, a liaison select committee, comprising the chairmen of the select committees and some additional members, was appointed. In the Commons' reforms group survey of MPs in 1984, almost 60 per cent of respondents rated the select committees as being successful or very successful. Beginning in the first session of 1980, the House of Commons witnessed an experiment with the appointment of a number of special standing committees.

In 1982, 29 'supply days' (on which certain topics such as Scottish affairs were debated and the remaining topics for discussion were chosen by the opposition) were abolished. They had little to do with supply. In order to rationalise the procedure, they were replaced by 19 Opposition Days, days on which opposition was recognised formally as having the right to choose the topics of the debate.[47]

A reference must also be made to another important area of interest pertaining to the representatives of the people. As Sandra Williams has brought out, 'Initially, concern focused on the executive branch of government, but increasingly embarrassing relevations have forced legislatures to consider putting their own house in order. The fact that definition and regulation have largely eluded them has major implications for contemporary politics.'[48]

The 1969 select committee on members' interests had reached its conclusion not to recommend a register of members' interests on the assumption that MPs should be treated no differently from other citizens. But, finally, a compulsory register was considered necessary to restore public confidence in parliament. A number of questions were relevant in this context. For example, should such a register be set up by a statute rather than by a resolution of the House? Whether the issue of members' interests is a House issue or a party issue? Is the topic of disclosure of members' interests a part of the wider debate about

[47] *Ibid.*
[48] Sandra Williams, *Conflict of Interest—The Ethical Dilemma in Politics*, Gower Publishing Company Ltd., England, 1985, p. 1.

open government? The Liberal Party believed that a register could be established without an Act of parliament. Consequently, in June 1967, they established a voluntary open register of MPs' interests, subject to revision every six months. Finally, the House of Commons adopted the register of members' interests in 1974. The first edition of the register, posted in accordance with replies received by the registrar of members' interests was published in 1975. the register takes note of nine specific classes of pecuniary interests or benefits. Members who failed to comply with the requirement of the register now total five... To date no action has been taken against members who refused to comply with the register.[49]

In the mid-1990s, the issue of MPs accepting cash for asking questions in parliament led to a storm in Britain. The issue received a high priority for the political agenda of all parties and agitated the public and the media. Since parliament acts as judge and jury on MPs' behaviour, its only sanction in such cases can extend to expelling the members from the House. This was considered to be grossly inadequate. There was a persistent demand that a special law may be enacted to punish such MPs for a criminal offence.

In the US, the Ethics in Government Act, 1978 codified the public financial disclosure provisions of both chambers and enabled civil penalties, fines in particular, to be imposed for wilful violations. This Act was passed in the wake of the Watergate scandal, at a time when President Carter had made ethics an important issue. There had also been considerable government activity at state level with respect to financial disclosure legislation. As of August 1977 about 36 states required some form of annual financial disclosure by public officials. The Act provided that the designated ethics committees in the House and Senate should review all reports to see if they were properly and completely filed and required the committees to notify any reporting individual who did not file an accurate report and give the individual an opportunity to correct it.[50]

[49] *Ibid.*, pp. 91–92.
[50] *Ibid.*, p. 122.

Unfortunately, despite continuing cases of financial misconduct of members, there has been a gradual watering down of the codes of ethics in both chambers since their initial passage. The main effect of these changes has been to make it more difficult for the electorate to assess the financial status and interests of their representatives.

Sandra Williams comes to the conclusion that, 'In the final analysis, as the American experience illustrates, even the most stringent of financial ethics code is difficult to enforce and cannot ensure ethical behaviour...inevitably individual responsibility and integrity, whether nurtured or tested by the prevailing morality of society, have to be the mainspring of a public service ethics. Nevertheless, external controls in the form of ethics codes, financial disclosure provisions and income limitations have become a necessary and secondary support system, if only to sharpen the moral judgements of those who know that against such controls their actions can be challenged.'[51]

The US Supreme Court Judge, Justice John Paul, used a remarkable phrase as he announced the court's dramatic decision that President Clinton must face sexual harassment charges by Paula Jones. President Clinton, Stevens said from the bench in an almost off-handed way, is 'an individual who happens to be the President'. (*Times of India*, 4 Jun 1997). Instances like this bring out the vitality and the strength of democratic institutions and accountability of the holder of even the most powerful office in the world.

There are a number of other countries which have laid down requirements concerning public disclosure of the assets of the members of their legislatures. These include Argentina, Australia, Germany, Great Britain, Japan, Singapore, and so on.[52]

This discussion would not be complete without a reference to

[51] *Ibid.*, p. 138.
[52] Congressional Research Service, The Library of Congress, *Legislative Ethics in Democratic Countries: Comparative Analysis of Financial Standards*, CRS Report for Congress, April 1994.

the Nolan Committee Report on Standards in Public Life. The committee was appointed by the British government on 25 October 1994 with wide terms of reference. It was constituted as a standing body with its members appointed for three years. The committee made far-reaching recommendations in respect of holders of various public offices. As far as MPs are concerned, the recommendations included, among others, the introduction of a code of conduct for MPs, avoidance of conflict of interest, disclosure of interests and maintenance of a register for the purpose, steps to clarify the position in respect of the bribery of an MP, appointment of a parliamentary commissioner of standards, and so on. Equally important are the seven principles of public life, enunciated by the Nolan Committee, which should apply to all aspects of public life. These are

*Selflessness*—Holders of public office should take decisions solely in terms of the public interest. They should not do so in order to gain financial or other material benefits for themselves, their family, or their friends.

*Integrity*—Holders of public office should not place themselves under any financial or other obligation to outside individuals or organisations that might influence them in the performance of their official duties.

*Objectivity*—In carrying out public business, including making public appointments, awarding contracts, or recommending individuals for rewards and benefits, holders of public office should make choices on merit.

*Accountability*—Holders of public office are accountable for their decisions and actions to the public and must submit themselves to whatever scrutiny is appropriate to their office.

*Openness*—Holders of public office should be as open as possible about all the decisions and actions that they take. They should give reasons for their decisions and restrict information only when the wider public interest clearly demands such restriction.

*Honesty*—Holders of public office have a duty to declare any private interests relating to their public duties and to take steps to resolve any conflicts arising in a way that protects the public interest.

*Leadership*—Holders of public office should promote and support these principles by leadership and example.

The British government is reported to be planning to introduce an 'anti-sleaze' legislation to clean up political life. Under the proposed law, MPs will no longer be protected by the right of parliamentary privilege. (*Times of India*, 16 Dec 2002)

Reference must also be made to yet another milestone in the quest for better democratic governance. The Republican National Committee in the US put forth, in 1994, what it called, *Contract with America* 'to change the nation'.[53] Though presented before the election manifesto, it was claimed to be a meaningful mandate for change. It was also considered to be a document for holding Congress accountable. The Republican party, if returned to power, undertook to pass some major reforms. Of these, the more significant, which are relevant to the discussion in this book, may be briefly stated as under:

- Require that all laws that apply to the rest of the country also apply equally to Congress.
- Select a major independent auditing firm to conduct a comprehensive audit of Congress for waste, fraud or abuse.
- Cut the number of House committees, and cut committee staff by one-third.
- Require committee meetings to be open to the public, and
- Guarantee an honest accounting of the federal budget by implementing zero base-line budgeting.

Significantly, among the Bills which the Republican candidates promised to sponsor were the following:

- The Fiscal Responsibility Bill for a balanced budget with tax limitation amendment, and
- The Citizen Legislature Bill. 'This is to be a first-ever vote on term limits to replace career politicians with citizen legislators.' This will involve limiting the term of representives [Members of Congress] to six years and Senators to 12 years.

[53]Republican National Committee, *Contract with America*, 1994.

It will also contain a limit of a total tenure of 12 years in both Congress and the Senate, put together, for any member.

It is often argued by the Indian political elite that politics is a dirty game all over the world and India can be no exception. This may be true. But, as Oscar Wilde said, 'We are all in the gutter, but a few of us are looking at the stars.' It is therefore refreshing to see the preoccupation, in a number of countries, with addressing issues of ethics in political life and emphasising their relevance to democratic institutions. In this light, the situation in India is indeed alarming. Even more frightening is the mindset of the political elite in India that ethics has nothing to do with the profession (or rather business) of politics and the governance of the country. In this sense, India is one of its kind, a case *sui generis*. It is not surprising that there is a widespread disenchantment with democracy and its institutions, of which 'election fatigue' is only a symptom. The real disease is the basic distrust of the politician and the disgust with political life in the country. Equally important is the weakening of the moral fibre of the country. These are formidable challenges which must be addressed and parliament must take a lead in the matter. A suggested programme of action for this purpose is given below:

### Code of Conduct for MPs and MLAs

At present, there is no code of conduct for legislators. There is however, an increasing demand that all responsible sections of society must lay down for themselves a code of conduct by which they can be judged. MLAs and MPs themselves are up front in pressing this point when it concerns others but not when it comes to laying down a code for themselves. The then speaker of the Lok Sabha, Shivraj Patil, had prepared a draft of such a code of conduct way back in 1992 and forwarded it to the vice chairman of the Rajya Sabha and the minister for parliamentary affairs. (*Sakal*, 26 Aug 1997). There has been no follow-up action on this. The need for such a code was accepted at the special session of parliament held to commemorate the golden jubilee of India's Independence in August 1997. The conference of chief whips of all political parties held in Srinagar in August 1997 had passed a unanimous resolution in favour of adopting such a code. Parliament was to take a very early initiative to adopt a code of conduct and ethics for its members and appoint an Ombudsman for the purpose. The committee of ethics of the thirteenth Lok Sabha presented its first report on Ethical Norms and Code of Conduct to the speaker on 31 August 2001. Though disappointing and out-of-step with the world view on these matters, it was laid on the table of the House on 22 November 2001. It is imperative that early decisions are taken thereon. This will goad the state legislatures to follow suit. Hopefully, this will also be emulated by other elected bodies such as municipal corporations, municipal councils, and zilla parishads.

## Code of Conduct for Ministers

The central government had formulated a code of conduct for ministers of both union and state governments and placed it on the table of parliament in 1967. The modified document has not so far been placed before parliament. It is imperative that the code of conduct is revised and brought up to date in the light of widespread concerns regarding the urgent need for cleaning up public life. Ministers must set an example of highest integrity, honesty and rectitude. It is essential that the code be published so that people can assess the conduct of ministers on this basis.

## Declaration of Assets by MLAs/MPs

This is another reform which is long overdue. It must be made incumbent by law on each MLA and MP to declare the assets possessed by himself and his dependents, on taking the oath of office and thereafter each year, for as long as he continues to hold office. This information must be published at regular intervals, at least once every year, and at the end of the tenure of the member. Any member of the public should have free access to this information.

## Declaration of Assets by Ministers

The Atal Behari Vajpayee-led government has issued orders for the declaration of assets by central ministers. (*Loksatta*, 21 Jan 1999). Similar action has been taken by a few state governments such as Andhra Pradesh, Goa and Gujarat, apart from the government of Delhi. It is necessary for all central and state government ministers to declare their assets regularly each year. The NCRWC has, in fact, recommended that every holder of a political position must declare his assets and liabilities along with those of his close relations. It is not enough that this information is merely placed in the parliament/legislature library. People must have free access to this information from a designated office. Copies of the statement of assets must also be made available to the media.

## Pay and Allowances of MPs

Democracy does not come cheap, and society must accept this and be prepared to pay its law-givers well. Legislators have been frequently sanctioning hefty increases in their salaries and allowances, without any public discussion of the issues. Most of these emoluments are in the nature of allowances which are free from income tax. Thus, for example, legislators get a *per diem* allowance even for the session period, though all of them stay in regular government accommodation allotted to them. It is not uncommon to see news reports of legislators claiming travelling and daily allowance for more than one meeting attended during the same visit to a place. As a result, the true cost of each legislator to the taxpayer is not evident. L.K. Advani, deputy prime minister, is reported to have asked the CII to suggest a new remuneration pattern for MPs. (*Economic Times*, 15 Oct 2002). This raises several important questions including whether emoluments of MPs should have any relationship with corporate sector emoluments.

## Local Area Development Scheme

A highly controversial decision taken by the P.V. Narasimha Rao government was to sanction the Member of Parliament Local Area Development Scheme (MPLADS) under which an amount of Rs 1 crore is placed at the disposal of each MP, every year, for undertaking development works in his constituency. Amazingly, this scheme has also been made applicable to Rajya Sabha MPs though their elections are indirect. The amount available under the scheme was increased to Rs 2 crores per MP per year in 1998, requiring an annual outlay of Rs 1,600 crores! There is now a demand that this should be increased to Rs 3 crores per annum.

The MPLADS can be faulted on a number of counts. To mention only a few, it is a travesty to argue that, in a democracy, the elected government does not understand the felt needs of the people and that these have to be fulfilled by an MLA/MP of the area. It is not in the domain of the elected representatives to undertake such functions. It also queers the pitch in favour of the sitting MLA/MP, and a new candidate in the election finds it that much more difficult to dislodge him. This is contrary to the stated ideal of ensuring a 'level playing field'. It is not binding on the newly elected MLA/MP to allow additional expenditure towards the completion of works undertaken by his predecessor. This can lead to infructuous expenditure as also time and cost over-run on incomplete works. More importantly, MPLADS is against the scheme of separation of the roles of parliament and executive, as envisaged in the Constitution. When governments, both at the centre and in the states, are faced with a serious constraint of resources, this drain of a huge sum of money each year on this scheme is difficult to justify except on the grounds of political expediency of each successive government, coupled with the incapacity to take the hard and unpopular decision to scrap the scheme. The NCRWC has also recommended that the scheme, being inconsistent with the spirit of the Constitution in many ways, should be discontinued immediately. But, this is bound to prove to be a cry in the wilderness. Inevitably, as in several other similar cases, the problem has been put in the lap of the judiciary by filing a PIL in the Supreme Court. This PIL is still pending.

## Complimentary Railway Passes for Former MPs

Along with a pension, former MPs are given complimentary railway passes. It is difficult to justify such expenditure. This became the subject of a PIL in which a division bench of the Allahabad high court ordered, in December 1998, that all such passes should be cancelled forthwith. This led to a heated discussion in the Lok Sabha. There was near unanimity that the high court's order should not be followed and only the speaker's decision should prevail. The reply given by M.L. Khurana, the then minister for parliamentary affairs, to the discussion on the subject shows how successive governments have been pandering to the demands of MPs without showing any concern for the taxpayer. The minister disclosed that the government was going to bring an amendment in the law passed in the previous session which would enable the wives of sitting MPs to enjoy free rail travel along with their husbands. (*Times of India*, 21 Dec 1998).

## Discretionary Quotas

The subject of discretionary quotas for MPs has raised a hornet's nest. Following a decision in a PIL, the then speaker of the Lok Sabha, P.A. Sangma, had, in February 1997, suggested to the government that the discretionary quotas placed at the disposal of each MP for sanctioning LPG gas and telephone connections should be cancelled. This led to such an uproar that the next Lok Sabha speaker, G.M.C. Balayogi, not only reinstated the quotas but increased them. (*Maharashtra Times*, 2 Jun 1998). The matter led to an uproar once again in December 1998 when the Kerala high court decided against such quotas. MPs, cutting across party lines, questioned the authority and jurisdiction of the courts in the matter. V.K. Ramamurthy, the then minister for petroleum, accused the courts of 'blackmailing' the legislature. Former defence minister, Mulayam Singh Yadav, complaining about the court's intervention, went so far as to say that the legislature was the primary authority in this country, the judiciary's powers being derivative! (*Economic Times*, 8 Dec 1998).

Whatever the noises in its favour, this system which is detrimental to a modern and democratic system of governance, needs to be eradicated with a firm hand. Despite widespread public resentment against these quotas and their misuse, it is most unlikely that they will ever be abolished by the government. The judiciary is the only institution which provides reason for hope.

**The Rule of Law**

In the eyes of the law, everyone is supposed to be equal. But, in reality, some are more equal than others. There is growing public perception that the law-makers in India are often the law-breakers. This is borne out by many instances of legislators taking the law into their own hands. Two recent instances can be cited to bring home this point. After the general elections in September 1999, some newly elected Maharashtra MLAs broke open the locks on the rooms of the old MLAs' hostel in Mumbai and forcibly occupied them even though they had been allotted accommodation in the new MLAs' hostel. No action has been taken against any of them. Some MLAs belonging to the Nationalist Congress party, Shiv Sena and BJP forcibly occupied accommodation in the reserved compartment of the Mumbai-Nanded Devgiri Express on 23 October 1999. As a result of the protest by those passengers who had reserved their seats in advance, the train was held up at Chatrapati Shivaji Terminus and Dadar station for one and two hours respectively. Finally, the train left Dadar with all the encroacher lawmakers and their companions on board while fourteen passengers with reserved seats were forced to cancel their journey! According to newsreports, all that the railway authorities did was to send a report to the chief secretary. (*Times of India*, 25 Oct 1999). This shows the impotence and helplessness of the whole system, which is corrupted by the law-makers themselves. Countless instances of unlawful and unruly behaviour by MLAs and MPs are reported, from time to time, in the media all over the country. It is not, therefore, surprising that the public image of MLAs and MPs is so poor.

It is necessary that this situation be remedied at the earliest by parliament and state legislatures by passing an unambiguous resolution on the subject for the guidance of all law enforcement agencies to treat a law-breaking lawmaker no differently from any other citizen in a similar situation. It is also necessary that parliament and state legislatures set up special committees to take suitable punitive action against their members in such cases.

### Parliamentary Privileges

Parliament should amend Article 105(2) of the Constitution to deal with the issues raised by the Supreme Court judgement in the JMM case. Let Indian MPs assert, as Lord Salmon did, that 'a privilege of a member of parliament is a charter for freedom and not corruption.'[54] Additionally, parliament and state legislatures must take very early steps to codify their privileges.

The committee on privileges in a report submitted to the speaker in December 1997 had, *inter alia*, recommended that the committee on privileges should be renamed the committee on privileges and ethics, with a clear mandate to monitor complaints against members. (*Times of India*, 6 Dec 1997). It is high time for a decision to be taken in this regard. As an alternative, each House should appoint an ethics committee to go into the conduct of its members and to make suitable recommendations regarding the punishment, including suspension, removal, and in extreme cases even disqualification for re-election, to be imposed on a member. Parliament must also frame rules for dealing with sanction of prosecution against MPs under the PCA.

### Sanction of Prosecution of PM/CM/Ministers

Under the present system, such sanction in the case of the PM and central ministers has to be given by the President of India. In the case of a CM and ministers in a state government, it is the prerogative of the Governor to sanction the prosecution. In

---

[54]Murlidhar C. Bhandare, MPs' Immunity: Amend the Statute, *The Times of India*, 30 April 1998.

the case of certain requests, such proposals were pending in Rashtrapati Bhavan for an unduly long time. These delays were even more scandalous in the case of Governors. The worst case of its kind was the delay of several years in the sanction of prosecution of J. Jayalalitha by the then Governor of Tamil Nadu, Chenna Reddy. The Governor of Assam took considerable time to decide on the request of the CBI for sanction to prosecute the then chief minister Prafulla Kumar Mahanta. Finally, the Governor rejected the request and this led to considerable controversy. Similar delays have taken place in the sanction of prosecution of the two former chief ministers of Bihar, namely, Laloo Prasad Yadav and Jagannath Mishra in the fodder scam cases. The only recent case in which a governor took prompt decision is that of sanction of prosecution, in November 1999, of K. Karunakaran, former chief minister of Kerala, on corruption charges pertaining to import of palm oil from Malaysia in 1991. It took nine years for the case to come up to the stage of sanction of prosecution! As it is, the judicial delays in such cases are phenomenal. Besides, if the very process of sanction of prosecution is delayed inordinately, particularly where the accused are or have been holders of high office, the confidence of the common man is shaken.

Against this background, it is necessary to lay down some golden rules:

- Each request by an investigating agency for sanction of prosecution must be decided by the competent authority within a period of three months at the latest from the date of receipt of the request.
- If the case is not decided by the competent authority within the stipulated period, it will be presumed that the prosecution has been sanctioned, and
- In a case where the request is rejected by the competent authority, a speaking order, giving detailed reasons for the rejection of the request, will be passed and released for wide publicity.

## Opposition Day

Ways and means have to be found which would enable the opposition to raise issues and initiate discussion in the House. 'Interestingly, a formula for dividing time went through in 1974 when the opposition was blocking business and the government was anxious to get on with the job. But the idea fell through when the opposition insisted on getting one more hour!'[55]

One way to reduce the interruptions, walkouts and similar other distractions which lead to unseemly wrangling, shouting from the well of the House and so on, is to set apart a day, once in two weeks, entirely for matters which are important to the opposition parties. Except for the initial standard daily business, (question hour, zero hour, calling attention motion and short-notice question) the remaining agenda for the opposition day should be finalised by the Business Advisory Committee presided over by the speaker/chairman. Private Members Bills should also be shifted to this day. This will provide an adequate opportunity for opposition parties to bring up for discussion issues which they consider urgent and important. The remaining time of the House can then be devoted to government business in a business-like manner.

## Functioning of Committees

Parliament must increasingly work through its committees to exercise more effective supervision and control over the executive. This will also make its functioning more apolitical. This will call for the following changes in the existing system, among others:

- The committees need to be reviewed so as to reduce their number and to avoid an overlap in their jurisdiction. Thus, for example, after the setting up of department-related standing committees, there is no justification for the continuance of the consultative committees attached to each ministry.
- The present term of each member on a committee is just one

[55] Inder Jit, *op cit.*, p. 22.

year. This is too short a time for a member to understand the issues, to develop insights and contribute anything significant. It is necessary that the term be extended to at least two years, if not three.
- Presently, the reports of the committees lack adequate depth. A large number of recommendations are of a routine nature. In most cases, the recommendations of committees have not led to any significant improvement in the working of ministries. The committees must make greater use of expertise available from outside the government to scrutinise the government's actions, policies and programmes. The present system of calling for suggestions from members of the public by giving a notice in the media is far from satisfactory. The secretariats of the committees must maintain standing lists of organisations, academics, experts, public policy commentators, NGOs and other knowledgeable persons in the given subjects. These must be updated regularly, and these institutions and individuals must be kept informed, on a continuous basis, of issues coming up before the committees for deliberation so as to enable them to send in their suggestions and comments. Greater interaction between such bodies and the representatives of the government through the committees is needed.
- The secretariats of the committees should have some part-time experts in various fields. The secretariats also need to be more broad-based. Excessive reliance on the parliament secretariat for filling the posts in these secretariats militates against the objective of making the committees more effective and insightful.
- The committees' deliberations must be open to the media and members of the public, as is the case in UK, Canada and Australia, except when the evidence to be taken is confidential or secret.
- The formats of performance budgets need to be completely revised, to make them more focused and purposeful to ensure transparency in and accountability of administration.
- A separate channel of Doordarshan needs to be started, as a public service, along the lines of the Public Broadcasting

System (PBS) in the US, till such time as private channels come forward to play this role. This channel should be used to telecast the deliberations of the committees of parliament and state legislatures, particularly when important issues of public concern are under discussion. This will also help in counter-balancing the adverse impact of the televised broadcasts depicting the unruly and indisciplined behaviour of the law-makers referred to earlier.

Since the reach of the radio is currently wider than that of television, it is necessary to make more use of radio broadcasts to carry the proceedings of parliament and its committees to the people, to especially those living in remote areas.

- The details of the meetings of the standing committees show that, on an average, these committees meet for a very short time.[56] In many cases, the duration of meetings ranges between just half an hour to two hours. Very few sessions exceed three hours. Considering the fact that members have to come for the meetings from all over the country, and keeping in mind the heavy expenditure on travelling allowances and daily allowances of members, it is necessary that the meetings are held at least for a whole day, if not for two consecutive days at a time, to get the maximum work done.
- The cost-effectiveness of field visits too requires careful consideration. Often very few members join in these visits which themselves are for a very short time. MPs are very vociferous in criticising the government for wasting money. Taxpayers have a right to be reassured that their representatives are more careful in this regard.
- The reports of the committees of parliament and state legislatures should be made available to media, academic and research institutions, public libraries, NGOs and other interested organisations and persons, on nominal payment, on an institutionalised basis, soon after they are submitted to parliament. They also need to be put on the internet regularly.

[56]Lok Sabha Secretariat, *Departmentally Related Standing Committees 1993–94, A Review*, New Delhi, August 1994.

## Calling Ministers before Parliamentary Committees

The present practice of calling only government officers to give evidence before the committees needs to be changed. Ministers also need to be called before the committees when larger policy questions come up or where certain decisions have been taken on the explicit orders of a minister.

During the debate for setting up the joint committee on the Bofors contract, a suggestion was made that the proposed committee should be empowered to summon ministers to give evidence before it. In reply, the defence minister had observed that 'as per practice obtaining in Westminster (UK), the ministers being answerable to parliament, are not summoned before parliamentary committees. In the Lok Sabha, under Direction 99(1) of the directions of the speaker, ministers are not to be called before the financial committees for formal evidence. However, if a minister wanted to place some facts before the committee of his own, he could do so.'[57]

It does not make sense to say that since ministers are responsible to parliament, they should not appear before the committees. This is all the more ludicrous since the committees of parliament enjoy the same status, rights and privileges as parliament and function as mini-legislatures. The present directions of the speaker on this subject, therefore, need to be changed and a suitable rule needs to be formulated to enable ministers to be called to give evidence before parliamentary committees. This is imperative if parliament is to work increasingly through its committees.

## Joint Committees of Parliament

The highly disappointing experience of the three previous joint committees, namely, on Bofors, bank scam and the stock market scam must not be permitted to be repeated in respect of similar committees in the future. This important mechanism should also

---

[57]Lok Sabha Secretariat, *Report of the Joint Committee to Enquire into Bofors Contract*, Eighth Lok Sabha, April 1988, p. 21.

not be permitted to fall into disuse because the earlier committees had failed to deliver. This is imperative if the role of parliament in overseeing the executive is to be strengthened. This would mean learning from the past and laying down some salient guideposts for the future:

- The government should not resist the demands for appointment of such committees, if it has nothing to hide. Opposition parties themselves will be reluctant to voice such demands if in some cases the government's actions are upheld by the joint committee after making in-depth inquiries in a transparent manner.
- The committee should invariably be headed by a respected and reasonable leader of one of the opposition parties. The selection of such a person should be left to the Business Advisory Committee presided over by the speaker.
- The committee should be empowered to call any minister, including the PM, to give evidence.
- The committees should have access to all relevant papers, including those which are secret. It should be left to the discretion of the committee as to the manner in which such papers may be used in finalising its report.

### Parliament—A Goldmine of Information

Information furnished by government to parliament, in reply to the starred and unstarred questions and during the course of the transaction of other business, can be a goldmine for researchers, NGOs, media and members of the public. For example, information on thousands of questions tabled by members is compiled and presented by the government at tremendous cost to the exchequer during every session of parliament. Unfortunately hardly any use is made of this information. There is also no institutionalised arrangement for the widest possible dissemination of all such information to the people at large. Ways must be found to address this question urgently. We must translate into practice the adage, 'information is power'. There can be no better and more cost-effective way of empowering people.

### White Papers

The government must bring out white papers from time to time on major national and state level issues for educating public opinion, and for constructive debate and discussion. Recent efforts in this direction include white papers released by the central government on subsidies, India's external debt and the railways. However, such initiatives are still very few. They are particularly rare in the state governments. The presentation of white papers can go a long way in taking public policy formulation away from a populist mode. If the people are taken into confidence, even unpopular and unpalatable decisions will meet with much less resistance.

### Subordinate Legislation

In future, the scope for subordinate legislation, and particularly the areas of discretion for the government, will have to be curtailed with a firm hand. The committee on subordinate legislation will have to insist on clear and unambiguous guidelines being framed and made public in all cases wherever discretionary powers are to be used by the executive.

### Financial Control

The present mechanisms for the financial control of the legislature over the executive are far from satisfactory. With the introduction of the system of department-related standing committees, there is not enough justification for the continuance of the estimates committee. This committee can, with advantage, be renamed the public expenditure committee with much wider terms of reference which would enable it to look at all government expenditures much more holistically. This committee may also be authorised to look at policy issues and to advise the government suitably. This is all the more important in the Indian context where competitive populism among political parties has perpetrated fiscal crises both at the centre and in the states. Only by arriving at a consensus among political parties will it be possible to take some unpopular and harsh steps to deal with the situation.

**Upper Limit on Size of Ministry**

With the emergence of regional parties, smaller parties, splinter groups and so on, coalition governments have become the order of the day. In the name of political compulsions, larger and larger councils of ministers are being formed at the centre and in the states. The BJP-led coalition ministry formed at the centre after the general elections in 1999 which had 70 members was further expanded and now has 74 members—this is the largest-ever ministry at the centre. One-third of BJP MPs are now ministers. This unhealthy trend has now spread to the states. Even a state like Karnataka, where, in the elections in 1999, the Congress party got a clear majority, has not escaped. The earlier description of 'jumbo cabinet' first used to describe the ministry in AP of about 60 persons has now become out-of-date. The ninety-member Kalyan Singh Ministry formed in UP in 1998 made a world-record, at the time it was formed. It constituted over 40 per cent of the total strength (222) of the parties who had come together to form the government. All defectors were accommodated in the ministry. The Ramprakash Gupta Ministry in UP was even bigger and consisted of 91 members. Rabri Devi's ministry in Bihar has 74 ministers when the strength of the ruling party is just 136 members. In Maharashtra, for the first time since Independence, a ministry of 61 persons was sworn in after the elections in 1999, when the total strength of the parties in the coalition government was just 150. This led to such adverse reactions from all over the state that, in a most unusual and unprecedented move, six ministers were dropped even before the portfolios were distributed and the number was brought down to 55. This number has now gone up to 58. This is too large as compared to the successive councils of ministers of less than 48 in the past. Several other states too have similarly large ministries. India is no longer merely the world's largest democracy, it also has the world's largest ministries.

The formula suggested by the Sarkaria Commission on

Centre-State Relations for the maximum size of the ministry has also been ignored. 'Narasimha Rao blew the concept sky high by decreeing that, under the formula, he was entitled to appoint not only 10 per cent of the strength of the Lok Sabha but 10 per cent of the combined strength of both the Lok Sabha and the Rajya Sabha, namely a total of 79 ministers.'[58] The same stand was taken by the union finance minister Yashwant Sinha in an interview given to the *Economic Times*. When asked about the upsizing of the council of ministers by Atal Behari Vajpayee, Sinha answered, 'I will not call it upsizing... We have 800 MPs [in parliament]... and a government can have 80 ministers. So 70 is not an abnormal number.' (*Economic Times*, 15 Oct 1999).

Note must also be taken of yet another development in recent years. This pertains to a much larger single party or a group of parties giving outside support to a ministry headed by a small party. Such an arrangement needs to be firmly rejected by the President/Governor while inviting a party to form the government, in the interest of ensuring the stability of the government. Further, in such a situation, to consider the total membership of both the Houses as the ceiling on the size of the ministry becomes meaningless. It will be recalled that the Janata Dal faction led by Chandrashekhar had a huge ministry at the centre in 1990–91, as compared with its total strength in parliament.

The recommendation of the NCRWC in this regard is to confine the size of the council of ministers to 10 per cent and appointments to other offices to 2 per cent of the total strength of the lower House. But, perhaps, a time has come to relate the maximum size of the ministry to the total strength of the party/parties forming the government. It must be laid down that the size of the ministry (including appointments in other positions outside the ministry) should not be larger than 15 per cent of the total strength of the political party/parties forming the government. It is also necessary to lay down this limit

---

[58]Inder Jit, A Fraud on Democracy, *The Hindustan Times*, New Delhi, 20 November 1997

statutorily to strengthen the hands of the leader of the party who is called upon to form the government. This will be in line with the objective of down-sizing the government from which there is clearly no escape.

### The Face of the Ministry

Apart from its size, the face or the image of the ministry is equally important if the credibility of democratic governance is to be restored. It has to be accepted that the image of a typical minister has taken a serious drubbing. This is not just because of the caricature of politicians in literature, Bollywood movies and movies in regional languages which represent politicians as persons bereft of any moral principles, prepared to adopt any means to achieve nefarious objectives. In fact, it is difficult to tell whether art imitates life or the other way round.

In a democracy, it is taken for granted that a person heading a ministry as PM/CM would belong to the lower House and would have been directly elected by the people. In the last five decades of democratic governance in this country, we have, however, demolished all conventions, guidelines and basic principles governing the parliamentary form of government. H.D. Deve Gowda was nominated as a candidate for prime ministership by the United Front though he did not belong to either House of parliament. Amazingly, he preferred to make a backdoor entry as a Rajya Sabha MP rather than contest an election to the Lok Sabha. Earlier, P.V. Narasimha Rao was similarly elected as the leader of the Congress parliamentary party though he was not an MP. It must be said to his credit that he contested the election to the Lok Sabha soon thereafter. But, it is time this practice is reviewed. It must be laid down that only a person belonging to the legislature party and who is a member of the lower House would be eligible to be elected as the leader of a party. Further, it is necessary to lay down that, if this is not feasible, such a person will have to contest election to the lower House within a period of six months.

It is not unusual to see persons with a criminal background

being sworn in as ministers. *Sunday* magazine observed that the Rabri Devi cabinet in Bihar 'reads like a roll-call in the state's crime branch—no less than 29 of her 74-member team are history-sheeters'. (*Sunday*, 17–23 August 1997). During the 12-year regime of Laloo Prasad Yadav and his wife, as many as eleven ministers had to undergo imprisonment. This was also true about the Kalyan Singh's ministry in UP where at least a dozen persons had dubious records. It is a travesty when a criminal takes the solemn oath of office as minister, in the splendour of Rashtrapati Bhavan or a Raj Bhavan, 'that I will bear true faith and allegiance to the Constitution of India as by law established, that I will uphold the sovereignty and integrity of India, that I will faithfully and consciously discharge my duties...'.[59]

It is no longer unusual to see persons indicted by courts or whose actions have been commented upon adversely occupying ministerial berths. One of the latest such cases was the induction of Manohar Joshi, as union minister for heavy industry in 1999. He had been indicted by the Bombay high court in a PIL pertaining to the permission given to his son-in-law to construct a multi-storied residential complex on a plot of land in Pune reserved for a school building. The appeal filed by him against this decision is still pending in the Supreme Court. He has now been elevated to the post of speaker of the Lok Sabha. It may be recalled that the Rajasthan Lok Ayukta had recommended that persons who are indicted by the Lok Ayukta should not be appointed as ministers. It may be worthwhile to lay down that any person who has been indicted by a statutory/constitutional authority will not be eligible to be appointed to any public office for a period of five years or till the appeal filed by him is decided in his favour, whichever is earlier.

It is common to see ministers continuing in office even after charges have been framed against them by courts in criminal cases. The most prominent cases in this regard are those of persons who are charged in the Babri Masjid demolition case. Their continuance in the ministry, in spite of being charge-

[59]Third Schedule of the *Constitution of India*.

sheeted in the case, is justified by prime minister Atal Behari Vajpayee on the specious plea that they are not involved in any corruption case nor have they been charged with misuse of their office! In an interview given to *Frontline*, L.K. Advani has argued that the Babri Masjid demolition case is a political case. 'There is a clear distinction between a political case and being chargesheeted in any other case, however motivated it may have been', avers Advani. (*Frontline*, 20 Dec 1999). These arguments are preposterous, to say the least. The law minister of Gujarat is reported to be an accused in a murder case, along with a central minister. It must be prescribed that any person against whom charges have been framed by a criminal court will not be eligible to hold any public office till the case is decided by the court and he is acquitted, without any blemish, and not just on technical grounds.

Yet another disturbing development is to appoint as ministers those who have been defeated in elections. The ploy adopted in the past was to wait for some time till a person is brought in as a Rajya Sabha MP. This is also not observed any longer. The most recent prominent cases in this respect were those of Jaswant Singh and Pramod Mahajan who were appointed as central ministers in the Atal Behari Vajpayee government in 1997. Other recent cases of this type were of two ministers, belonging to the Congress and the Nationalist Congress party, who were inducted into the Maharashtra council of ministers in October 1999 though they had been defeated in the elections. There are any number of other such instances all over the country. This is tantamount to an outright trampling of democratic norms.

All these kinds of cases have shaken the confidence of the common man in democracy. It is obvious that political parties, with pulls and pressures from influential interest groups, will not be able to deal with these issues firmly and in a principled manner. It is time the norms and criteria for heading a ministry and induction of persons into the ministry are spelt out unambiguously in a statute titled 'Ethics In Democracy Act'. This is all the more necessary in the present era of coalition governments as the prime minister no longer has the absolute and unquestioned freedom to appoint or drop ministers representing the coalition partners in the ministry. It is the satraps of these political parties who nominate the persons for induction into the ministry. It may not be easy to build a consensus on this subject among political parties to enact such a law but efforts in this direction ought to begin in earnest. It is only by building up the pressure of public opinion that political parties can be made to see reason.

**Anti-Defection Act**

The *Aaya Ram, Gaya Ram* phenomenon (members shifting their loyalty from one party to the other) as also horse-trading have afflicted Indian polity for several years now. As K.N. Singh has written: 'In the second half of the sixties, the politics of defection came to acquire threatening dimensions. According to one survey for the years 1967–71, out of 3,500 legislators, more than 500 were found to have staged defections at one time or the other. Subsequent to the mid-term poll in 1971, the practice of to and fro defections touched perilous dimensions... Between 1967 and 1983, about 2,700 defections were recorded and of these, some 15 members eventually became chief ministers, 212 occupied ministerial offices and a sizeable number of them came to head various statutory corporations or other like bodies.'[60] The latest instance of this type is the defections from the Nationalist Congress party leading to efforts to destabilise the Democratic Front government in Maharashtra in June 2002.

The Constitution (Fifty-Second Amendment) Act, 1985, popularly known as the anti-defection legislation, was enacted with much fanfare to give a body-blow to the rampant practice of defections. Unfortunately, the law has not quite achieved its objective. It has put an end to defections by individuals, but has been misused to stage mass defections. The law has conferred unlimited powers on the speaker to decide the question of

---

[60]K.N. Singh, Anti-Defection Law and Judicial Review, in C.K. Jain (ed.), *Constitution of India—In Precept and Practice*, CBS Publishers and Distributors, New Delhi, 1992, p. 148.

disqualification of members. There is no provision making the speaker accountable for his decision. Furthermore, the speaker's decision is final, since no appellate authority has been provided under the Act. The law also does not stipulate any process to be followed by the speaker before deciding on a defection case.

Over the years, the Act has been blatantly misused to shield defectors. The presiding officers of legislative assemblies and parliament have, by their judgements in defection cases, subverted the law and brought it into public ridicule.[61] 'There have been cases where the speaker has repeatedly adjourned the hearing of the disqualification petition and thus enabled the member who had clearly incurred disqualification to enjoy the fruits of his disqualification.'[62] The 'UP assembly speaker K.N. Tripathi, has an all-new interpretation of the Act. According to him, a third of a political party does not necessarily have to break away for the move to be formally recognised as a split... [Tripathi] seemed to think the split could take its own time for completion. The 10 MLAs needed to make up the shortfall could well be making up their mind, he argued. This gives a fresh twist to a piece of legislation that has already been all but rendered ineffective by many earlier interpretations.'[63] Rabi Ray, the then speaker, who had to decide on the validity of defections from the V.P. Singh-led Janata Dal gave the 'benefit of the doubt' to the group which subsequently joined former prime minister Chandrashekhar's faction on the grounds of legal lacunae. 'Shivraj Patil, speaker of the tenth Lok Sabha, did worse even as he lamented about "some weak points" and "defects" in the Act. He ruled that it was not the job of the speaker under the Tenth Schedule to see whether a split had taken place in the original party or not. The speaker was only required to ascertain whether the group consisted of not less than one-third of the

---

[61] Jashwant B. Mehta, *Quest for a Better Democratic Alternative*, N.M. Tripathi Private Limited, Mumbai, 1995, pp. 168–207.

[62] Soli J. Sorabjee, Defectors, Codes of Conduct and Poetry, in the column 'Out of Court', *Times of India*, 6 November 1997.

[63] Editorial, 'Defective Act', *Times of India*, 28 October 1997.

members of the legislature party. That was not all. He did something incredible. He recognised a split within a split... Equally incredibly, the speaker took almost ten months to give his decision in the crucial matter.'[64]

The speakers' decisions have been challenged in a number of cases in the high courts and the Supreme Court. The Supreme Court decision in the UP Bahujan Samaj Party split raised a number of issues such as: At what point of time does a 'split' in a legislature party start, and what is the court's power to adjudicate on an appeal against the speaker's order if it suffers from perversity.

The basic question in all defection cases is that of ethics in a democracy. Should a legislator be permitted to go against the mandate which he had sought from the electorate? Should he be free to change his party irrespective of the mandate on which he had fought the election and won the support of the electorate?

The other equally important question is whether the speaker should be given such judicial powers to be exercised in a totally unguided manner? This is particularly relevant in the context of the scandalous decisions given by a number of speakers during the last decade. In India, a speaker is not above the dictates of his party. As M.S. Gill, former chief election commissioner, has underlined, 'We have not been able, unlike the British parliament, to give the speaker's office total security and neutrality by ensuring automatic unopposed election, once chosen by all parties by consensus. In England, the speaker's chair is filled every 20–30 years when he chooses to retire and no party challenges him in the field during elections. That's a unique status, a moving away from active politics.'[65]

Against this background, it needs to be seriously considered whether the power to decide such cases should be given to the EC. The Representation of People Act (RPA), 1951, has already

---

[64]Inder Jit, A Fraud on Democracy, *Hindustan Times*, New Delhi, 20 November 1997.

[65]Interview with M.S. Gill, 'We Can Rule on Defectors instead of the Speaker', *Outlook*, 30 March 1998, p. 10.

imposed a duty on the Election Commission under section 8-A, which deals with disqualification on grounds of corrupt practices as determined by a court. Such cases go to the EC in automatic reference by the Governor/President of India. The EC sits as a judicial body, hears all parties and sends its recommendations to the Governor/ President. The same procedure could be laid down in deciding defection cases. P.A. Sangma, the then speaker of the Lok Sabha, had mentioned that a unanimous resolution was passed in the speakers' conference held in Shimla in 1997 that the 'anti defection law needs to be reviewed' and that 'defection in any form should be legally banned.' (*Times of India*, 4 Nov 1997).

It is thus abundantly clear that the Act needs to be repealed and substituted by a new enactment, Ethics In Democracy Act, mentioned earlier, containing the following broad principles:

- Any member who defects from the party on whose symbol he had contested the election will forthwith cease to be an MP/MLA and will have to resign. Till he tenders his resignation, he will stand suspended from the House. Such action will be irrespective of the number of persons who leave the party.
- A defector will not be eligible to hold any public office for a period of three years from the date of his defection from the party or till the time he has been re-elected, whichever is earlier.
- All disputes pertaining to the subject will be decided by the EC. Appeal over the commission's decision will be heard only by a division bench of the Supreme Court.

### Age Limit for Holding a Public Office

In India politics is not just a full time profession, but a business. Sometimes it is a family business. As in the princely states of a bygone era, public office is also treated as a hereditary office by the political rulers. Dynastic rule is not just confined to the Gandhi-Nehru family. Now, even a small-time politician dreams of establishing a dynasty in his fiefdom.

If the political life of the country is to be enriched, people from all walks of life—professionals, technocrats, academics, writers, and makers of public opinion—must be encouraged to take an active part in the political life of the country for a period of five to ten years. But, this is easier said than done.

Since politics is considered a profession in India, it may be difficult to lay down the maximum age for contesting election since there are no such restrictions on other professions. But, it would be in order to lay down the maximum age for eligibility for holding any public office. In the past twenty years, some prime ministers and Presidents of India have been well over the age of 70. India's longest serving Chief Minister Jyoti Basu of West Bengal, was more than 86 years old when he stepped down from office. It was amazing to see that the CPI(M) could not find a replacement for him and he had to be asked by the party to continue in office in spite of his failing health and desire to step down! Considering the fact that the retirement age in both the public and the private sector is generally 60 years, it should be reasonable to lay down an upper age limit of 65 years for this purpose. This age-limit should apply uniformly to Constitutional or statutory office.

## Only One Term for Certain Constitutional Offices

It is seen that holders of certain offices such as the President of India and Governor need to be much more independent than has been possible so far. This is primarily because the holders of these offices wish to get a second term so they are reluctant to displease the ruling political party. They often fail to exercise judicious discretion and independent judgement, sometimes at the cost of national interest.

It is well known that several Presidents have been averse to displeasing the government at the end of their first term in the hope of getting a second term. Khurshed Alam Khan went to Karnataka as Governor after spending some time as Governor of Goa. His tenure in Karnataka extended for a further period of nearly ten years. The former Governor of Maharashtra,

P.C. Alexander, served two terms as Governor there. Earlier, he was Governor of Tamil Nadu.

It is necessary to restrict the term of office of the President of India, Vice President of India and Governors to one term only. This principle should also apply to holders of other offices such as Lok Pal, if and when such an institution comes into being, Lok Ayukta, and chairmen and members of other statutory bodies.

# 2

# Indian Democracy: The Unfinished Agenda

**Long Overdue Electoral Reforms**

At the outset, it may be useful to note some significant details about the election exercise in India. The number of voters has risen from 17.32 crore in 1952 to 60.23 crore in 1998. During the same period, the number of polling stations has gone up from 1.96 lakh to 7.65 lakh. As many as 850,000 to 900,000 polling booths had to be erected for the general elections in 1999. To manage the booths, 45 to 50 lakh personnel had to be deployed. This is in addition to the police, home guards, NCC cadets and paramilitary personnel deployed on security duty.

Government expenditure on conducting elections has gone up steeply from just Rs 11 crore in 1952 to Rs 626 crore in 1998 and a staggering Rs 900 crore in 1999. Because of the increasing problems of lawlessness and violence, paramilitary forces have to be moved across the country. Their presence is also insisted upon by the candidates themselves in some states due to the politicisation of the local police and home guards. This has meant holding Lok Sabha and legislative assembly elections in some states in a staggered manner—in five phases spread over a period of five weeks. Due to the weakening of national political parties on the one hand and the emergence of regional parties and splinter groups on the other, political stability has been seriously compromised in both the centre and the states. The 1999 Lok Sabha election was the fourth in less than five years. The last UP legislative assembly election was the fifth in seven years. The increasing frequency of elections has serious long-term implications which cannot be ignored.

The composition of candidates contesting elections is also undergoing a perceptible change. The typical khadi clad Congress politicians donning white khadi caps, largely representing the well-to-do large land owners, are giving way to more diversified political representation particularly from the lower social and economic strata of society. Now, the khadi cap is a rare sight among MPs. Criminals and persons from the business world have also entered politics, though the strides by the former group are much more than the latter.

Politics is still largely the preserve of professional politicians. Hardly any professionals, technocrats, grass-roots social workers dare enter this field. *Outlook* magazine (13 Sep 1999) published a cover-story titled 'Voting to Abstain—They have the real campaign and are close to the masses, yet they keep away from elections' in which it gave the reactions of some of the stalwarts of society such as Verghese Kurien, a pioneer of the co-operative milk movement, Baba Amte, a well-known Gandhian and an eminent social worker in the field of leprosy eradication, Chandi Prasad Bhatt, pioneer of the *Chipko* movement, and others, on electoral politics in the country. Their observations, which made depressing reading, will be shared by a large cross-section of people in the country.

It is interesting to note that in the UK, the 'temple of democracy', although there is a great deal of electoral law, there is very little electoral litigation. At the parliamentary level, no victorious candidate has been unseated for illegal practices since 1924, and no serious petition on the grounds of corrupt or illegal practices has been brought since 1929 (though two candidates have been disqualified on petition).[1] This shows the intrinsic strength and vigour of democracy in that country. By comparison, the Indian electoral system is a minefield. Practically every section of the Representation of the People Act (RPA) and the Rules, as well as the Code of Conduct laid down by the election commission (EC) have been contravened again and again. The litigation in election petitions has gone not only to the high courts but to the Supreme Court. Looking at this experience, it is evident that the provisions of the Constitution pertaining to the EC and its powers are too weak and do not show the kind of farsightedness and acumen which is seen in some other parts of the Constitution, including in its basic structure.

*Neglect of Electoral Reforms*: Though we take pride in declaring that we are the world's largest democracy, the subject of electoral reforms has been consistently neglected by all political parties for over five decades since Independence. It is interesting to see that a joint committee on amendments to election law submitted its 121-page report to parliament as far back as 1972. Among its members were Somnath Chatterjee, Atal Behari Vajpayee and L.K. Advani who continue to be leaders in parliament even today. Three decades have elapsed since then and these venerable members have gone places in their political careers but the electoral reforms have remained where they were! The Goswami Committee on Electoral Reforms had rightly emphasised that, 'electoral reforms are correctly understood to be a continuous process. But the attempts so far made in this area did not touch even the fringe of the problem.'

Time and time again, political parties have talked about the imperative need for electoral reforms in their election manifestos but these have remained paper promises. In the last decade, each in-coming government had begun with the assurance that it would introduce a comprehensive Bill for electoral reforms but it has never been translated into practice. The only serious effort in this direction was during the V.P. Singh government in

---

[1]David Butler, 'Electoral Reforms', in Jeffrey Jowel and Dawn Oliver (eds.), *The Changing Constitution*, Third Edition, Clarendon Press, Oxford, 1994.

1989–90 but since the government lost majority, this initiative too was a non-starter.[2] Even the special session of parliament called during the term of the P.V. Narasimha Rao government failed to arrive at any consensus on the outstanding issues relating to electoral reforms. Now, once again, the BJP-led coalition government headed by Atal Behari Vajpayee has announced that a comprehensive electoral reforms Bill, to cleanse the polling process and introduce proxy voting for defence and security forces, will be brought up in parliament. It remains to be seen how far and when this gets translated into reality.

Though the EC came into prominence and caught the imagination of the people during and after the tenure of T.N. Seshan as CEC, the previous CECs too had worked silently and diligently on the subject of electoral reforms and had submitted to the central government, from time to time, detailed and highly sensible proposals for electoral reforms. Unfortunately, they did not receive any attention. As the late S.L. Shakdhar, the then CEC had lamented, 'Despite a wide measure of agreement on the subject, the question of electoral reforms generally seems to come up only on the eve of a general election when the stock answer is that it is too late and that such ideas had better be postponed until "next time". That "next time" has not arrived.'

It is not possible to deal with all issues relating to electoral reforms within this book. In the rest of the chapter, an effort is made to list some of the more important and critical issues which can make a significant difference towards cleansing the electoral system of the country and ensuring its public accountability and transparency.

### The Election Commission of India

The question of the inherent powers of the EC needs to be reviewed afresh in the light of the problems being encountered in holding peaceful, orderly and fair elections in the country.

---

[2]Ministry of Law and Justice, Legislative Department, Government of India, *Report of the Committee on Electoral Reforms*, (*Goswami Committee on Electoral Reforms*), May 1990.

# Indian Democracy: The Unfinished Agenda

The history of electoral reforms has shown that political parties are unlikely to agree on any significant and fundamental changes that would rid the system of several ills and malpratices. It is a distressing fact that violence continues to mar the election process in a number of states. Booth-capturing, intimidation and impersonation of voters, and similar other serious electoral malpractices are rampant. It was not, therefore, surprising that in the 1999 elections, two ministers of the Bihar government had to be arrested for electoral malpractices. The EC had to order the chief minister of Haryana, Om Prakash Chautala, to leave Bhiwani district from where his son was contesting the election. (*Indian Express*, 25 Sep 1999). On an all-India basis, the election process has had to be extended to an exasperating and frustrating long period of nearly six weeks to ensure the holding of orderly elections. A number of these problems were not foreseen by the founding fathers of the Constitution. If India is to survive as a democracy, the question of inherent powers is as important in the case of the EC as it is in that of the higher judiciary.

Against this background, it is imperative to amend the Constitution, and give wide powers to the EC to conduct elections in the best manner possible so as to enhance the credibility, integrity, fairness and purity of the process. Now that the commission has been made into a multi-member body, there need be no hesitation in giving such wide and, in a sense, undefined powers to the EC. It is also necessary to remember that the EC's actions will always be subject to review by the higher judiciary. While undertaking such a constitutional amendment, the following points may also be incorporated therein:

- The maximum number of members in the commission should be specified as three, so as to ensure that, in future, the government does not try to pack the commission with its own nominees, as the Rajiv Gandhi government tried to do in 1989. Till then, the EC consisted of only a CEC. When the government found CEC Peri Sastry inconvenient and far too independent, it added two members to the commission. It was only when the V.P. Singh government came to power in

December 1989 that the two additional members were removed. There were news reports that the Atal Behari Vajpayee government was planning to expand the EC to 5 members. (*Times of India*, 25 Nov 1999). It is time to stop such pressure tactics, once and for all, by making a requisite change in the Constitution to fix the strength of the EC at 3 members.

- The selection of the CEC and the other members may be done by a committee comprising the prime minister, vice president of India, speaker of the Lok Sabha, chief justice of India and the leader of opposition and, in his absence, the leader of the largest opposition party in the Lok Sabha. In the case of members of the EC, the CEC should also be consulted.
- All members of the commission should enjoy the same terms and conditions of service, and privileges and immunity as the CEC.
- The CEC and the members of EC should be made ineligible not only for any appointment under the government but also to hold any office, including the office of Governor, appointment to which is made by the president.[3]
- The protection of salary and other allied matters relating to the CEC and the election commissioners should be provided in the Constitution on the analogy of the provisions in respect of the chief justice and judges of the Supreme Court.[4]
- The provision regarding the appointment of regional commissioners should be scrapped since each state now has an election commissioner who works under the control and supervision of the EC.
- At present, the model code of conduct (MCC) issued by the EC does not have any legal sanction. It is imperative that the MCC should be recognised as having been issued in pursuance of the inherent powers of the EC and should have Constitutional sanction. If for any reason this is not considered feasible, a separate legislation may be passed for the purpose. In addition, to give some teeth to the legislation,

[3] *Ibid.*
[4] *Ibid.*

as suggested by the Goswami Committee, the violations of these provisions should be made an electoral offence and not be treated just as a corrupt practice.
- Section 77(3) of the RPA should be amended so as to empower the EC to revise the ceilings for election expenses, from time to time, and powers in this regard need not vest in the government.
- Any ambiguity in respect of the powers of the EC to suspend or withdraw recognition of a national or a state party which fails to hold organisational elections at regular intervals; keep regular accounts; have them audited; file income tax returns; file an annual return to the EC confirming compliance of all these and such other requirements which may be laid down from time to time; and comply with the MCC, should be removed.
- The EC should have all powers to give such directions as may be necessary from time to time to hold free and fair elections and to safeguard their integrity and credibility in every way.

Political Parties

As is the case in some other countries, there must be a parliamentary law pertaining to the registration, structure and functioning of political parties in India, both at the state and the national level. Unless a party is registered under such a law, it should not qualify for recognition by the EC, allotment of a symbol and state funding in the elections. Such a law must ensure internal democracy in each party. The elections of all political parties must be held under the supervision of persons to be nominated by the EC in a transparent manner. This might be considered odd by some but looking at the state of affairs of most political parties, such an extreme step is justifiable. One can understand a Fascist party like the Shiv Sena resisting the demand for holding organisational elections but the Congress party has also tried to put off its organisational elections time and again. It is meaningless to talk of democracy if the political parties which are its bulwark are to be permitted to be run as personal fiefdoms or dynastic outfits.

Madhu Limaye described the opposition as being capable of 'infinite fissionability'. This is a feature of all political parties in India. It is interesting to note that as many as 537 political parties are registered with the EC. During the 1998 elections, 176 political parties participated. The question, therefore, arises whether any special efforts need to be made to bring about the polarisation of the political process in the country. The Law Commission of India has made certain recommendations in this regard with a view to arresting and reversing the process of proliferation and splintering of political parties. The aim of the commission is to reduce the number of political parties or pre-election political fronts to three or four parties/fronts. The commission has, *inter alia*, recommended that any political party, whether recognised or not, which obtains less than 5 per cent of the total valid votes cast in an election to the House of the People shall not be entitled to any seat in that House. Any constituency which has elected the candidate of a political party which is deprived of a seat in the House of the People or in the legislative assembly... shall be represented by the candidate of a political party which has obtained the next highest votes provided that his political party obtains 5 per cent of the total valid votes cast in that election and that he has not lost the security deposit.[5]

The recommendations of the commission are clearly short-sighted. Political polarisation cannot be brought about by *fiat* or mere Constitutional amendment. And, this is especially true in a country as diverse linguistically, culturally, socially and religionwise as India. It is bound to take a long time to achieve political polarisation, so enough time will have to be given patiently for this purpose. It will have to be noted that splintering of political parties and emergence of regional parties has come about, in no small measure, due to the weakening of national parties, lack of any ideology or principles in political parties and parties becoming fiefdoms of certain families and

[5] Law Commission of India, One Hundred Seventieth Report, *Reform of the Electoral Laws*, May 1999, pp. 184–185.

individuals. It is only by learning from experience, passage of time and the lure of gaining power that political parties will shed their individual identities and merge themselves into a large entity, or at least form viable coalitions before the elections. This is amply borne out by the experience at the centre as also in some major states. It must also be remembered that a number of small parties represent the minorities or special interest groups. Their separate identity as political parties is important to them, not only for safeguarding the interests of their members but also for giving them a sense of security against majoritarianism and elements hostile to them. Forcibly erasing their identity will lead to social and political tensions as in Punjab or Jammu and Kashmir. The Law Commission's recommendation in this regard is therefore not only ill-conceived but against the national interest of fostering a united and strong India. The focus of attention must, therefore be on the enactment of a law for registration and regulation of political parties and not on the curtailment of the freedom of the people to form political parties.

**Electoral Funding**

Money and muscle power have dominated the elections in India over the last five decades. Muscle power itself is largely dependent on the monetary clout of a candidate. Thus, the root cause of a large number of ills can be traced to money power or 'moneyfestos' as picturesquely described by V.P. Singh. S.L. Shakdhar, former CEC, had also highlighted the danger of 'captive politics' on the analogy of the saying 'he who pays the piper, calls the tune.'[6]

The nexus between black money and election spending has been established since the early 1970s at least, if not even earlier. One of the recommendations of the Direct Taxes Enquiry Committee (Wanchoo Committee) Report, received in 1971, was the demonetisation of high value currency notes. When the

---

[6]The Voters' Council and Citizens for Democracy, Delhi, *Electoral Reforms in India*, address by S.L. Shakdhar, Chief Election Commissioner, 26 September 1980, pp. 1, 7.

then union finance minister, Y.B. Chavan, went to prime minister Indira Gandhi to seek her approval for implementing the recommendation, she asked Chavan only one question: 'Chavanji, are no more elections to be fought by the Congress party?' Chavan got the message and the recommendation was shelved.[7]

V.V. Giri, then president of India, in his message to the nation on the eve of Independence Day in 1974 had warned: 'It has been a most regrettable development in recent years that money power has come to play such a dominant role in the elections to legislatures. This, to my mind, is at the root of corruption and corrupt influences in our public life.'

Some years later, M.C. Chagla said that elected members do not represent the people; they represent money power. Raj Krishna, eminent economist, was right when he said Indian politics was becoming increasingly capital-intensive.

The National Institute of Public Finance and Policy, in its report, *Aspects of Black Money in India*, has rightly emphasised:

> Even if economic policies such as tax and industrial import policies are changed to scale down the generation of black money, so long as there is persistent demand for black money or the clandestine receipt of unaccounted money on the part of politicians, some of whom may be already in authority and others who are likely to assume leadership, business would have the need and temptation to spawn black money.

The ridiculously low ceilings on maximum permissible expenditure by a candidate, laid down from time to time (currently Rs 15 lakhs for parliament and Rs 6 lakhs for assembly election), are observed more in the breach. A newly elected legislator begins his tenure by knowingly and wilfully filing a false affidavit that the expenditure incurred by him does not exceed the ceiling laid down by law. In its judgement in *Gadak Y.K.* vs *Balasaheb Vikhe Patil* in November 1993, the

[7] Madhav Godbole, *Unfinished Innings—Recollections and Reflections of a Civil Servant*, Orient Longman, 1996, pp. 87–88.

Supreme Court observed that the 'prescription of ceiling on expenditure by a candidate is a mere eyewash and there is no practical check on election expenses for which it was enacted to attain a meaningful democracy... This provision has ceased to be even a fig leaf to hide the reality'. There is no ceiling on the expenditure which a party may incur on its candidates.

Huge unaccounted expenditure by candidates is perhaps the most serious issue in any programme of electoral reforms. The estimates of such expenditure vary from constituency to constituency. A great deal depends on the candidates contesting the election and the prestige attached to winning the seat. But, leaving aside these exceptional cases, the average expenditure of a serious candidate for parliament election in 1999 was estimated at Rs 2–3 crore. According to another estimate, it was Rs 1.3 crore in the 1998 election. According to the national election audit report prepared by the EC of elections held in 1999 and 2000, the average visible compaign expenditure of rich, very rich and super rich candidates was over Rs 83 lakh against the legal ceiling of only Rs 15 lakh. Where does this money come from? It comes partly from the candidate, his friends, supporters and well-wishers. But, a big chunk comes from the political party which sponsors him. Therefore, it is necessary to go into the question of financing not only by the candidates but more importantly, by the political parties.

Let us first take up the question of foreign money in elections. The issue was first raised in parliament as far back as 1968. Chitta Basu, in a discussion during the question hour in the Rajya Sabha, had referred to a news item from the *New York Times* published in the *Economic Times* of 14 June 1967 that the US Central Intelligence Agency had given substantial sums of money to right wing parties and candidates. The government had admitted that the Intelligence Bureau (IB) had been asked to prepare a report on the use of foreign money in the general elections held in 1967. But, the government declined to share the report with the Lok Sabha. The reply of the then union home minister (HM), Y.B. Chavan, was evasive and full of platitudes. He said, 'A very effective public opinion and political thinking has to be created in this country and that cannot be done overnight.'[8] Later, under persistent demands, the HM laid a statement in regard to the IB report on the table of the House on 14 May 1969.[9] The statement admitted that, 'Any precise quantitative assessment of the financial assistance received is not possible, but the indications are that it is selective and is not so small as to be ignored. There is also reason to think that funds obtained from foreign sources were used in the last general elections. Keeping these aspects in view, government proposes to bring forward a comprehensive legislation to impose suitable restrictions on receipt of funds from foreign organisations, agencies or individuals.' The HM underlined that, 'The single most important issue before the House is: what should be done to ensure that our parliamentary institutions, political organisations, academic and other voluntary organisations working in important areas of national life, are able to function in a manner consistent with the values of a sovereign democratic republic.'

The question of foreign money came up again on 12 April 1979 when Kanwar Lal Gupta raised the matter 'regarding reported disclosure made by a former US ambassador about Indira Gandhi having received US money'. The subject came up for detailed discussion in the House in May 1979.[10] The reference was to certain disclosures by Daniel Patrick Moynihan in his book *A Dangerous Place*. In reply to the debate, H.M. Patel, HM, in effect said that there was no point in making any inquiries as nothing is likely to come out of it. But, during the course of his speech, he also observed, 'It is not a matter of whether Mr Moynihan is telling the complete truth or partial truth. But, certainly, if a person like him has gone on record, then there must [be] something in it. It may not be the whole truth.'

In reply to a question by K. Pradhani in the Lok Sabha on 8 August 1980, regarding foreign money received for use in tribal

[8] Starred Question No. 62 on Use of Foreign Money in Elections, *Rajya Sabha Debates*, 20 November 1968.
[9] *Lok Sabha Debates*, 14 May 1969.
[10] Alleged Payment of Foreign Money for Elections in India by American Government, *Lok Sabha Debates*, 7 May 1979.

areas, the then finance minister (FM), R. Venkataraman, had replied that the provisions of the Foreign Contribution (Regulation) Act (FCRA), 1976, were adequate for the purpose.

A reference must be made to unstarred question No. 1523 tabled by Jyotirmoy Bosu in the Lok Sabha regarding the statement of the former prime minister, Charan Singh, on the withdrawal of huge sums by prime minister Indira Gandhi from a Swiss bank for election in 1980. As was to be expected, the then FM, R. Venkataraman, denied the allegation. However, the remaining part of his written reply was more significant. He said, 'The policy of the present government is not to collect any information about expenses incurred by any of the political parties for contesting elections or sources from which they have financed such expenditure.' It can be seen how far the Indira Gandhi government had travelled between 1968 and 1980 on the funding of elections in the country. The government had decided to close its eyes to the problem and had become totally oblivious to the hazardous legacy it was leaving behind for the country.

It was shocking to see that the same nonchalant attitude to this grave problem continued in the I.K. Gujral government in the case pertaining to the donation of Rs 3.75 crore received by the Congress party from abroad, during the term of Sitaram Kesari as the party treasurer, between 1993 and 1995. The additional solicitor general of India, Abhishek Manu Singhvi told the Delhi high court, in a PIL, that the central government had not taken any final decision on the applicability of FCRA in this case. (*Indian Express*, 30 Jul 1997). This was in spite of the explicit provision in section 4(i) of FCRA. In fact, later, in the affidavit filed by the government it asserted that donations received by the Congress party from abroad were legal. What is surprising is the 'opinion' of three former chief justices of India. All three say these donations do not fall under the FCRA.[11] The much touted FCRA has been a dead letter in so far as funding of political parties from abroad is concerned. It has been used

---

[11] T.V.R. Shenoy, While We Looked Away—Congress Foreign Receipts, in *Indian Express*, 2 August 1997.

almost exclusively by the centre against academic institutions and NGOs in the name of their compromising the independence and integrity of the country!

It may be relevant in this context to refer to what S.P. Hinduja, one of the richest businessman of Indian origin, had to say on this subject. He has 'disclosed that Indian politicians collecting money abroad, ostensibly for party funds, were stashing away large portions of it in foreign banks for their personal use...Even way back in the early 1970s, the economy had to be drained of as much as Rs 250 crore to provide just one-tenth of that amount for the elections. Almost 25 years later, perhaps, even our richest businessmen are finding it difficult to generate enough black money to feed the insatiable hunger of our politicians.'[12] It is not surprising that successive governments at the centre, belonging to almost all major political parties, are reluctant to go deeper into the funding of elections. Even in 1972, the joint committee on amendments to electoral law had come to the conclusion, 'The committee have also considered the recommendations made by the EC in their reports to the effect that the political parties might also be called upon to account for the expenses incurred by them for the election campaign of their candidates. After careful scrutiny, the committee have come to the conclusion that due to various practical difficulties, it is not possible to pursue such a course.'[13]

At the heart of the matter is the maintenance and audit of the accounts of political parties. The present situation in almost all parties is best described by a popular saying about the Congress party during the long tenure of Sitaram Kesari as its treasurer: '*Na khata na bahi, jo Kesri kahe wahi sahi*' (there is no ledger, no notebook, what Kesari says alone is true).

Section 13A and 139(4B) of the Income Tax Act prescribes that (i) every political party has to maintain detailed accounts of

[12]Bet On This, *Economic Times*, 8 February 1996.
[13]The only minute of dissent was by Mahavir Tyagi. See Lok Sabha Secretariat, Joint Committee on Amendments to Electoral Law, Report, Part I, January 1972, p. 65.

income and expenditure, (ii) in the accounts there has to be a specific mention of receipt of any donation of above Rs 10,000 along with the name and address of the person or company making the donation, and (iii) the accounts of a political party must be audited every year by a chartered accountant. The law also imposes an obligation on the designated functionary of a political party to ensure that the income tax return is submitted every year in the prescribed form setting forth the requisite particulars.

Section293(A) of the Companies Act, 1956, lays down that no company can make a contribution to a political party unless the proposal is first passed by its board of directors, a proper resolution is passed and recorded and the contribution appears in the accounts of the company for purposes of audit. In the case of default, the imposition of a heavy penalty on the company and imprisonment of its functionaries have been prescribed. As T.N. Pandey has brought out, by and large, the view taken by the courts was that political donations cannot be a charge against the profits of a business. However, if the nexus between the payment made and the advantage to the business can be established, the claim would be admissible under section 37(1) of the Income Tax Act on the ground of it being incurred wholly and exclusively for business purposes.[14]

It is interesting to see that in spite of these explicit provisions in the relevant Acts, the income tax department did not take any action against political parties for infringement of the provisions. Finally, Common Cause, an NGO in Delhi, filed a PIL in the Supreme Court. It came to light in the context of this writ petition, that the income tax department had noted on the relevant file on 31 March 1993; 'it is hereby assumed that they [the political parties] do not have any income to declare; accordingly the proceedings are hereby dropped'!

Fortunately, the Supreme Court decision in the above PIL

[14]T.N. Pandey, Tax Deductibility of Political Donations, *Financial Express*, 6 July 1999.

was a major step forward in the crusade for a clean public life. The Court, *inter alia*, decided that:

1. Political parties are under a statutory obligation to file return of income in respect of each assessment year in accordance with the provisions of the Income Tax Act. The political parties...who have not been filing returns of income for several years have *prima facie* violated the statutory provisions of the Income Tax Act.
2. The income tax authorities have been wholly remiss in the performance of their statutory duties under law. The said authorities have for a long period failed to take appropriate action against the defaulter political parties.
3. A political party which is not maintaining audited and authenticated accounts and has not filed the return of income for the relevant period, cannot, ordinarily, be permitted to say that it has incurred or authorised expenditure in connection with the election of its candidates in terms of Explanation 1 to section 77 of the RP Act.

Such is the state of governance, so insensitive are the political parties to public opinion and such is the utter disregard for the explicit orders of the highest court that Common Cause had to file yet another petition in the Supreme Court to get the previous orders of the court on maintenance of accounts by political parties implemented expeditiously. During the hearing of this petition it came to light that, 'except one party, all others had declared 'nil' return. They were seeking to convince the court that without any income they were able to manage the party affairs. No small achievement!'[15]

At long last, the Central Board of Direct Taxes (CBDT), issued orders for the compulsory scrutiny of all pending and forthcoming returns filed by political parties. It has also decided that assessment should be made only after an indepth study of

[15]Rakesh Bhatnagar, Law Commission Report on Key Electoral Reforms Gathers Dust, *Times of India*, 12 January 1999.

returns under section 143(3). (*Economic Times*, 27 Aug 1999). The effectiveness of these orders can only be assessed after they have been in force for a few years.

The funding of political parties by business and industry has always been a dubious affair. Almost all such transactions are in black money and cash. In a controversy surrounding certain favours allegedly shown to Mesco airlines by the National Airports Authority, the chairman of this group of companies admitted having paid Rs 3 crore to the Congress party by cheque when P.V. Narasimha Rao was the PM. In a candid admission, he said, 'I will never make any payment in cheques in future'. (*Times of India*, 3 Jul 1997).

Against this background, it is interesting to note the proposal of Tata Sons to set up an electoral fund for donations to political parties. The objective is to make political contributions in a manner that is transparent, non-discriminatory and non-discretionary in order to create a climate where business and industry can be carried on more economically and efficiently. The money would be distributed in two phases. In the first phase it will be given to parties (and not individuals) which hold more than five per cent of seats at the start of elections, and, in the second phase, to parties which secure more than five per cent of seats in the election. Up to five per cent of each company's average net profits during the preceding three years will be disbursed in this manner.

Understandably, while larger parties broadly supported the proposal, the small parties and the communist parties scoffed at the idea. The Communist Party of India (Marxist) (CPM), in fact, returned the donation sent by the Tata Electoral Trust. Most other industries and business houses were unresponsive. The proposal was faulted by Swaminathan S. Anklesaria Aiyar who asserted, 'Democracy means representation of the people and not companies, so the latter should be kept as far away from the electoral process as possible'. (*Economic Times*, 26 Aug 1997). While this is unexceptionable as a principle, the basic question is how to put an end to the murky dealings between industrial and business houses and political parties.

The main question is whether the present system of funding elections should continue or be replaced by state funding of elections. The joint committee on amendment to electoral laws had recommended in 1972 that, 'a process should be initiated whereby the burden of legitimate election expenses should be progressively shifted to the state'.[16] Very limited state funding of elections was recommended by the Goswami Committee on Electoral Reforms in 1990. The Committee on State Funding of Elections (Indrajit Gupta Committee), which submitted its report in December 1998, recommended *inter alia*, that:

(i) State funding of elections is fully justified—Constitutionally, legally and also in the larger public interest.
(ii) State funding should be confined only to the parties recognised as national or state parties by the EC, and to the candidates set up by such parties.
(iii) Given the budgetary constraints and the present financial stringency, only part of the financial burden of funding political parties may be shifted to the state, for the time being, and
(iv) Any state funding should be in kind, and not in cash.[17]

The recommendation appears half-hearted and makes only a token gesture to state funding. In that sense, it is no better than the view propounded by the joint committee of parliament, referred to earlier, in 1972. The Indrajit Gupta committee has also not made any recommendation regarding the manner in which financial resources should be raised by the government for this purpose.

The Law Commission Report on Reform of the Electoral Laws, submitted in May 1999, recommends that, 'in the present circumstances only partial state funding could be contemplated more as a first step towards total state funding but it is absolutely

[16]Lok Sabha Secretariat, *op cit.*, p. 64.
[17]Government of India, Ministry of Law, Justice and Company Affairs, Legislative Department, *Committee on State Funding of Elections, Report*, December 1998, pp. 57–58.

essential that before the idea of state funding (whether partial or total) is resorted to, the provisions suggested...relating to political parties (including the provisions ensuring internal democracy, internal structures) and maintenance of accounts, their auditing and submission to EC are implemented...state funding, even if partial, should never be resorted to unless the other provisions mentioned aforesaid are implemented lest the very idea may prove counter-productive and may defeat the very object underlying the idea of state funding of elections.'[18] It is disappointing to see that even the Law Commission has failed to do justice to the subject and has made only a token gesture. It is a pity that the above recommendations of the Law Commission have been endorsed by the NCRWC which has suggested that the proposal for state funding be deferred till the regulatory mechanisms pertaining to political parties and the financial limits are firmly in place.

The successive reports on this critical issue during the last three decades have failed to grasp that what is at stake is not just the purity and integrity of elections, but, more importantly, combating the evil of black money, improving the credibility of democracy and cleansing public life of the cancer of corruption. To achieve these objectives, no price should be considered too high. In fact, state funding is the 'least cost solution' to these formidable and intractable problems. It is necessary to appreciate that all political parties are bound to oppose any legislation to regulate their working. If state funding of elections is to depend on the passage of such a law and its enforcement over a period of some years, then state funding will remain a topic of mere academic interest, and there will be no change in the present situation. As regards resources for undertaking such a scheme, it should be possible to find over Rs 2,000 crore each year quite easily by discontinuing the MPLADS and similar other ongoing schemes for MLAs, municipal corporators/councillors, zilla parishad members and others. This could result in the collection

---

[18] Law Commission of India, *One Hundred Seventieth Report on Reform of the Electoral Law*, May 1999, pp. 118–119.

of Rs 10,000 crore over a five-year period. If necessary, this sum could be supplemented by the levy of a small election cess on some state and central taxes. This will be much cheaper than the rampant corruption which currently feeds all election expenditure. Even if some additional money has to be found, it will be well worth finding it by curtailing other low priority expenditure. In this connection, please see the discussion in the next chapter on downsizing the government.

From the foregoing discussion, some major points emerge for consideration. First, there is an urgent need to enact a comprehensive law to regulate the functioning of political parties but the introduction of the scheme for state funding of elections should not be held up on this account. Both these actions can proceed on a parallel track. Second, as a precondition of state funding, section 77 of the RP Act which allows a political party to spend any amount of money on its candidates should be amended so as to include such expenditure in the ceiling on total expenditure prescribed for a candidate. Third, it is time the Income Tax Act is amended to make it obligatory on the income tax authorities to give wide publicity to the returns filed by political parties and the assessment orders passed thereon. This will be the best way to ensure that the provisions of the Act are implemented faithfully. Fourth, the expenditure statements filed by each candidate before the EC should also be made public for scrutiny by the people and their watch-dog organisations. Fifth, a law must be passed which provides the entire funding of election expenditure of candidates from the public exchequer. It should provide for a total ban on funding of candidates by political parties. The proposed amendment of the RPA as suggested above will ensure that if the ban is violated, the expenditure incurred by a political party on its candidate will form part of his total expenditure. The expenditure on state funding should be shared by the centre and the states in the proportion of 75:25. The scheme of state funding will apply only to the candidates sponsored by recognised political parties in proportion to the total number of votes polled by each party. The candidates themselves will not be permitted to spend anything over and above what is provided by the state. State funding will not be available to candidates who contest as independents.

### Decriminalisation of Politics

The criminalisation of politics and the politicisation of criminals has become a shocking reality in India. Criminals are no longer satisfied by supporting certain candidates in elections. They now aspire to the seats of power themselves. Some have even floated their own political parties. Thus, for example, Arun Gawli, a dreaded crime-lord, has floated his own political party called *Akhil Bharatiya Sena*. Amazingly, Anna Hazare, the well known social activist, has blessed these efforts of Arun Gawli! (*Loksatta*, 11 Jul 1997).

Criminals have made inroads into all political parties, both at the national and regional levels. In the 1996 Lok Sabha elections, more than 1,500 candidates had a criminal background. It is interesting to see that these candidates found representation almost all over the country. This author joined former Supreme Court judge Kuldeep Singh, and social activist Swami Agnivesh in a citizen's panel set up by the weekly magazine *Outlook* in connection with the Lok Sabha elections in 1998. The panel compiled a list of 72 candidates contesting elections against whom criminal proceedings were pending, though within the short time which was available between the filing of the nominations and the holding of elections, the panel could compile and scrutinise the data in respect of only 500 of the 4,693 candidates in the fray. It was disconcerting to see that in the Bihar legislative assembly elections in February 2000 more than twelve notorious criminals were elected as MLAs.

'Winnability' has become the sole criterion for selection of candidates by political parties.[19] Such is the level of cynicism on this subject that Bal Thackeray, Shiv Sena supremo, when asked by news reporters about a large number of criminals getting Shiv

---

[19]Madhav Godbole, Crime and Blandishment—My Thug Is Better Than Yours, *Times of India*, 18 April 1997, *The Changing Times—A Commentary on Current Affairs*, Orient Longman, 2000, p. 50.

Sena tickets in the elections, had the temerity to say that these persons were political activists and if they were to be called criminals then Gandhi and Nehru would also have to be called criminals. (*Sakal*, 20 Feb 1997). The Shiv Sena organised a function to felicitate a municipal councillor in Mumbai who was arrested and charged by the police under section 5 of TADA for possession of five revolvers, including four imported ones, during the communal riots in Mumbai in 1993. Speaking at the felicitation function, Bal Thackeray warned that he would not hesitate to ask *shiv sainiks* to store weapons illegally if it was found that the government was harassing political activists. (*Indian Express*, 21 Jun 1995).

In 1997, one out of every fourteen MPs and as may as 700 MLAs had a criminal background. (Editorial, *Loksatta*, 23 Aug 1997). Though consolidated data in respect of the 1999 Lok Sabha and Assembly polls is yet to become available, from UP alone, at least seven MPs with a criminal background have been elected in the 1999 elections. Of them, two belong to the BJP, three to the SP and two to the BSP. (*Maharashtra Times*, 13 Oct 1999). Of the 180 MLAs elected to the Gujarat assembly in December 2002, as many as 36 (20 per cent) have a criminal background.

It would be wrong to blame the political parties entirely for the entry of criminals into politics. Criminals have often fought elections as independent candidates and people have voted for them with open eyes. Pappu Yadav, who is facing a murder charge, fought the Lok Sabha poll in 1999 from Purnia jail as an independent candidate, and managed to get 66.3 per cent votes, the highest in the state of Bihar. (*Times of India*, 6 Nov 1999). The fact that Yadav was elected with a lead of over two lakh votes shows that the influence of caste continues to dominate in Bihar, as well as in several other parts of the country. For once, Bal Thackeray is right when he says, 'In India, people don't cast their vote, they vote their caste.' (*Outlook*, 8 Nov 1999). Pappu Kalani, a noted criminal in Maharashtra, who won as an independent candidate in the assembly polls held in 1999, was detained in the Yeravada jail, where he enjoyed five star facilities. In a surprise raid on his prison cell, Rs 27,500 in cash, a charger for a mobile phone and some cassettes were confiscated by prison authorities. (*Sakal*, 6 Nov 1999).

According to the provisions of the Representation of People Act, only a person convicted in a criminal case for a minimum stipulated period is barred from contesting elections for a period of six years. The EC, by its order in August 1997, has decided that a person will not be eligible to contest an election if he is convicted by a court and his appeal against such conviction is pending in the higher court. The EC has also made it compulsory for each candidate to give necessary information regarding his antecedents while filing his nomination.

The Law Commission has recommended that a person against whom a charge has been framed under certain sections of the IPC, the Unlawful Activities (Prevention) Act, 1967, the Narcotic Drugs and Psychotropic Substances Act, 1985, or any other offence punishable with imprisonment for life or death under any law, 'shall be disqualified for a period of five years from the date of framing the charge, provided he is not acquitted of the said charge before the date of scrutiny notified under section 36 of this [RP] Act.'[20] This is in order so far as it goes. But the question still remains whether all this is adequate to meet the requirements of the situation. The time limit of five years, from the date of framing of charges, proposed by the Law Commission for disqualification of a candidate will serve little purpose considering the inordinate delays in deciding criminal cases. There is also no reason why the disqualification should be restricted to charges framed only under certain sections of certain criminal laws.

Ideally, no law-breaker should be a law-maker. With this objective in view, the citizens' panel established by *Outlook* magazine had laid down, in February 1998, the following criteria for identifying candidates with a criminal background and making an appeal to the voters to reject them:

(i) Those persons who have been convicted by a criminal court regardless of whether an appeal is pending with a higher court.

[20]Law Commission of India, *op cit.*, pp. 133–134.

(ii) Persons who have been chargesheeted by a judicial court in a criminal case.
(iii) Persons against whom there are *prima facie* findings by an investigating agency on the basis of which a challan has been filed in a court.
(iv) Persons who are absconding from the law, although they may not have been challaned; persons who are in jail, under preventive laws, on economic or criminal grounds, after approval by the advisory board; and persons who have a long history of crime in their area and who have been in and out of the police net several times.

Two recent developments in this regard merit mention. In a judgment delivered in the writ petition by the Association for Democratic Reforms and the People's Union for Civil Liberties, the Supreme Court has underlined that votes cast by uninformed voters in favour of a candidate would be meaningless. The court, therefore, ruled that candidates for the Lok Sabha or legislative assemblies would have to disclose their antecedents, assets and educational qualifications, if any, to help the electorate in making the right choice. Some may doubt whether this will serve any purpose, considering that persons such as Jayalalitha, Laloo Prasad Yadav and scores of others have been elected by the people with a thumping majority in spite of their convictions by the court or their involvement in a large number of criminal cases. But, this only brings to the fore the need for creating better awareness and consciousness among the voters. The Bill for the amendment of RPA which is based on all party consensus falls considerably short of what the Supreme Court had suggested. This is in spite of the fact that the President had returned the Bill for reconsideration. This one again shows how far removed are the law-givers from the progressive thinking in the country. The second development is the recommendation of the NCRWC that the RPA be amended to disqualify and debar a person who is charged with an offence punishable with imprisonment for a maximum term of five years or more, on the expiry of a period of one year from the date the charges were framed, till the conclusion of the trial. In case of conviction, the bar should apply during the period he is undergoing the sentence and for a period of six years after completion of the sentence. A person should be permanently debarred if convicted for any heinous crime. In the case of corrupt practices, the position prevailing before the 1975 amendment of the RPA should be relevant.

In drafting a law to keep criminals away from legislatures and other forums of governance, it is necessary to adopt these principles. After all, the right to contest an election is not a fundamental right. A set of reasonable restrictions should be laid down to ensure the purity and integrity of the system.

### Reducing the Number of Non-Serious Candidates

Looking at the rapidly increasing cost of holding elections, it is necessary to lay down some reasonable restrictions on non-serious candidates contesting the elections. In the elections in 1980, there were as many as 39 candidates in one constituency,. Several constituencies had 25 to 30 candidates. In some constituencies in Karnataka and Tamil Nadu, elections had to be postponed to make special arrangements for printing ballot papers the size and thickness of notebooks and a larger number of bigger ballot-boxes for casting these notebooks! This situation has improved to some extent over the years but the number of candidates in some constituencies is large enough to cause concern. Most of these are independent candidates. The number of candidates contesting the elections has come down sharply from the elections in 1998 after the deposit to be paid by a candidate was increased.

The percentage of independent candidates forfeiting their deposits went up steeply from 60.1 per cent in the 1957 elections to 99.7 per cent in 1996 but came down slightly to 99.1 per cent in 1998.

In spite of the declining number of independent candidates getting elected in each election, the presence of independents has complicated the question of stability of governments at the centre and the states. Horse-trading of independent candidates has become a matter for serious concern. Often such independent candidates supporting a government had to be given ministerial berths. In the long run, the country must move towards a two party or at least a multi-party system, rather than having to cope with the problem of managing independents.

A reference may be made in this context to the judgement of the division bench of the Bombay high court in March 1997 by which the court had held that independent candidates cannot come together after elections to form a new grouping or give up the platform on which they had contested the election. In a case pertaining to the Mahabaleshwar *Giristhan Nagar Parishad*, the high court has disqualified the concerned councillors for non-adherence to this principle under the anti-defection law and has cancelled their election. The appeal is now pending in the Supreme Court. The final decision in this case will be of considerable significance to the future of independent candidates and their role in India's increasingly fractious polity.

It is often suggested that there should be a total ban on independent candidates contesting elections. In the Law Commission's view, the time is now ripe for debarring independent candidates from contesting Lok Sabha and legislative assembly elections.[21] The NCRWC very rightly feels that independent candidates need to be discouraged from contesting elections. But the steps it proposed are barely workable and appear to be too harsh. The commission has suggested that independents should be nominated by at least 20 elected members of panchayats, municipalities or other local bodies in the area of the proposed constituency to qualify for contesting an election; the security deposit for such candidates should be doubled and it should be progressively increased for those who are defeated and want to recontest. If an independent candidate fails to get at least five per cent of the total votes cast, he should not be allowed to contest as an independent for at least six years, and if he loses the election three times consecutively for the same office, he should be debarred permanently.

[21]*Ibid.*, p. 186.

It would be unjustified to altogether ban independent candidates or to put unreasonable restrictions on them, particularly since Indian party politics seldom allows persons who are not professional politicians an opportunity to contest elections as party candidates. It cannot be denied that there is a need for the induction of eminent persons from various fields into politics. Often a large number of independent candidates are those who have been denied tickets by their own parties. It should also be noted that after the state funding scheme is introduced, the fact that such funding will not be available to independent candidates will itself be a factor which will discourage such candidates from contesting elections. Against this background, there need be no explicit bar to independents contesting the elections. However, to further reduce the number of non-serious candidates, the deposit payable by candidates should be further increased. Yet another safeguard could be introduced by way of a stipulation that any independent candidate getting less than 5 per cent of the total votes polled should be disqualified from contesting election again from the same constituency for a certain number of years.

## Bar on Contesting from More than One Constituency

In 1980, one candidate stood for election from 13 parliamentary constituencies and several others from three to four constituencies. Finally, in 1996, the RPA was amended so that a person could contest, at the most, from two constituencies. Even stalwarts such as Indira Gandhi, L.K. Advani, Mulayam Singh Yadav and Sonia Gandhi have contested from more than one constituency at a time. There have been cases where a candidate has been elected from more than one constituency. In such a case, he has to resign from one of the constituencies, leading to fresh elections there. Though the number of such cases has gone down over the years, it is still avoidable public expenditure which the country can ill afford. It is high time that the electoral law is amended to prohibit a candidate from contesting an election from more than one parliamentary/assembly constituency or simultaneously from a parliamentary and an assembly constituency.

### Punishment for Electoral Offences

As emphasised by the Law Commission, there is an urgent need to enhance the punishment for various electoral offences mentioned in the RPA as well as in the IPC. These offences seriously interfere with a fair electoral process. The punishments provided at present are totally inadequate and ridiculously low.[22]

A reference must be made in this context to the punishment of disqualification and disenfranchisement imposed by the President of India on Shiv Sena Chief Bal Thackeray. Of particular concern was the punishment which barred Thackeray from casting his vote in any election for a period of six years up to 10 December 2001. The punishment was announced eleven years after he committed the electoral malpractice. Rather than being seen as a deterrent, the punishment brought the electoral law and its implementation into public ridicule.

It was the first time that such a punishment had been imposed on any one, and that too the chief of a political party. The wisdom of such a course of action can be seriously challenged. The ends of justice could have been met by disqualifying Thackeray from contesting any election for a certain period. But, how can anyone be divested of his right to vote? In a democracy, it makes no sense to deprive anyone of his right to vote. If a more stringent punishment than mere disqualification is considered necessary, the law could be amended to bar such a person from holding any office in any political party for a certain number of years. Clearly, the existing provisions of law in this regard need to be looked into.

### Full Five-Year Term for Lok Sabha and State Assemblies

The Atal Behari Vajpayee government, sworn in after the Lok Sabha elections in 1999, has declared its intention to introduce legislation to ensure a full five-year term for the Lok Sabha and state assemblies. This is clearly a short-sighted response to the instability witnessed at the centre during

---

[22]*Ibid.*, p. 134.

recent years when the country had to go to the polls on three occasions. The fear is that the cure could turn out to be worse than the disease.

It must be appreciated that the stability of government cannot be assured by such subterfuges. The legislators must be prepared to face the electorate at any time and should be in no doubt that if they do not deliver, they can and will have to face rejection by the voters.

Fixing a term for the legislature will not necessarily lead to the stability of the government. In fact, it is quite likely that the effect may be quite the opposite. India has witnessed the nightmare of the Emergency in 1975–77. No one would care to go through the same experience again. The fixing of a tenure for legislatures may have the effect of making the legislators as well as the government complacent. It would also imply that legislators will be free to play their games of defection with the full confidence that the House cannot be dissolved on the ground that no stable government can be formed.

It must be noted that such a proposal will appeal to legislators since they will not have to face the electorate at frequent intervals. The MPLADS and similar schemes for MLAs are other attractions which place at the disposal of legislators huge funds for discretionary expenditure, thereby consolidating their hold over their respective constituencies. Yet another attraction is the monthly pension whose quantum is dependent on their term as legislators because the longer the term, the larger the pension. Thus, the dice is fully loaded in favour of passage of the Bill immediately after it is introduced by the government. In fact, one should not be surprised if it is passed without any discussion, as in previous cases of Bills pertaining to the pay and allowances of legislators. This brings out the importance of rallying public opinion against the measure and forcing the government to abandon the move.

The purpose of ensuring the stability of the government, as opposed to a fixed term for the House, can be achieved to some extent by laying down that the leader of the House should be elected by the House as a whole as opposed to party/parties forming the government, and that when a no-confidence motion is moved, the name of the alternate person who should head the government should also be put to the vote in parliament or the state legislature. However, in the current fractious political situation, this is hardly likely to find acceptance among political parties.

### Caretaker Government in the Period Leading to Elections

M.S. Gill, then the CEC, had suggested that chief ministers should demit office six months before elections are held in their states. While the sentiment behind this suggestion will be universally shared, it is doubtful if the suggestion itself can and should be implemented. At the outset, it has to be accepted that governments, both in the states and the centre, have been remiss in observing ethical proprieties in the period preceding the polls. Even after five decades of democracy, political parties in power have been conducting themselves without regard for democratic norms. The fact that the words 'caretaker government' have not been mentioned in the Constitution has been made much of in this debate. The media is also responsible, in no small measure, in encouraging the governments to take all decisions during this period as if they are firmly in the saddle. This 'business as usual' literally becomes 'business' most unusual. It goes without saying that the conventions, guidelines, norms and proprieties in a democracy are as important, if not more important, than the written word of the Constitution, particularly where ethical standards are involved. Successive governments at the centre have thrown all norms to the winds in taking decisions which appease one section of the voters or the other, enable the making of as much money as possible during the remaining time in office or enable the party in power to raise funds for elections. This also applies to the governments in the states.

But, the question is whether imposition of President's rule is the answer to the problem. First, there is no provision in the Constitution for the imposition of President's rule at the centre. This would mean treating the centre differently from the states. This can hardly be justified. Second, President's rule will mean rule by the central government. It is quite likely that the centre will be as partisan, if not more partisan, in its dealings, particularly if the political party in power at the centre is different from that in the state. Third, President's rule implies putting the Governor in charge of the state. Judging by the manner in which active party functionaries, belonging to the political party in power at the centre, are being appointed as Governors, this will again mean central rule via the back door.

The more reasonable solution will, therefore, lie in the President/Governor keeping a close watch on the decisions of the government at the centre and in the state respectively in the period preceding the elections. Whenever any undue favours are shown to any person, industrial house or a section of society with an eye on elections, the President/Governor should direct the government not to implement the said decision till the new government comes to power. Second, the media must play its role in vigilantly giving publicity to such uncalled for and partisan decisions. Third, as a matter of normal practice, the incoming government should review all decisions taken by the earlier government six months before the elections. Once everyone knows that all decisions will be reviewed in this manner, both officers and politicians will be more careful in taking partisan decisions. The concerned parties will also not be keen on getting decisions from outgoing governments which may be reversed by the new government.

### Infructuous Expenditure by the EC

A number of decisions of the EC, which have cost the country crores of rupees, have gone unquestioned by public or parliament. In due course, these items find mention in routine audit paras by the Comptroller and Auditor-General but if any lessons are to be learnt for the future, the present decision-making processes within the EC need to be subjected to a fresh review and close scrutiny. Reference may be made to just two cases to drive home this point.

The scheme of voter identity cards was introduced by the EC

without adequate thought. A number of points raised by the state governments, media and members of the public were imperiously overruled by the then CEC, T.N. Seshan. In one press conference in Delhi, he had termed as 'rubbish' the explanation given at the chief ministers' conference that the scheme would be phenomenally costly. In a typical Seshan turn of phrase which had captivated the middle class citizenry and the media, he said that he had written to prime minister P.V. Narasimha Rao in 1992 about the multi-purpose identity card scheme, but the government 'sat on it, snored on it and slumbered on it for 20 months.'[23]

After the initial thrust, the scheme has been held in abeyance since January 1998. No new cards have been issued since then. In the elections in 1998 and 1999, even those who had been issued the identity cards were not asked to produce them at the polling stations. As a result, the expenditure of over Rs 75 crore incurred on the scheme has been totally wasted but no heads have rolled for putting the country to this colossal infructuous expenditure.

There has been a persistent demand for the issue of citizen identity cards. Such a scheme has been long in the offing but has not been taken up for want of funds. There has been a proposal to issue identity cards to the residents of the border areas in the north-east, Jammu and Kashmir, Rajasthan, Punjab and Gujarat. The income tax department is issuing photo identity cards to income tax payers. All such requirements could have been taken care of by one multi-purpose identity card. But this would have required a lot of patience which the EC did not have. The country has paid dearly for the impatience of one of its own Constitutional authorities.

The same is also true of electronic voting machines. These machines have been lying in the warehouses of the EC for years at a stretch. An expenditure of Rs 11 crore was incurred on them without adequate forethought as to their use and without

[23]Lok Sabha Secretariat, *Diary of Political Events*, Vol. 21, Nos. 1–12, 1994, p. 3.

consultations with state governments and political parties. It was only during the elections in 1999 that some of these machines were finally put to use in some constituencies on an experimental basis. It was only in the Gujarat assembly elections in 2002 that full use was made of these machines. No one can question the need for the introduction of electronic voting in India. The question is whether adequate homework was done by the EC before taking a decision to purchase the machines.

Unfortunately, any attempt at financial scrutiny of proposals of such Constitutional authorities is resisted on the ground that it is an interference with and dilution of their autonomy. The fact that their expenditure is 'charged' and not 'voted', as in the case of other expenditure of the government, is often given as an excuse by these authorities for declining to submit themselves to any financial scrutiny. It is time for this practice to be discontinued. A system of concurrent audit must be introduced in the EC. Its financial proposals must be scrutinised closely and thoroughly at a sufficiently high level. A suitable mechanism needs to be set up for the purpose. An example which comes to mind is that of the department of space and the department of atomic energy where the secretary, department of economic affairs, works as the ex-officio financial advisor to both these departments. This is meant to safeguard the secrecy of the proposals and to ensure that they are examined at the seniormost level in the ministry of finance. A similar arrangement could be evolved for the EC to avoid infructuous expenditure in the future.

### Size of Legislatures and Redrawing of Constituencies

The Constitution (Forty Second Amendment) Act, 1976, froze the boundaries of constituencies demarcated on the basis of the 1971 census and deferred further delimitation and statewise reallocation of seats until after the census scheduled for the year 2001. The first question for consideration is whether the size of the Lok Sabha and state assemblies needs be increased.

The same argument for which the above Constitutional amendment was passed in 1976 holds good even today and will continue to be relevant in the medium term. The rate of growth of population in the BIMARU states (Bihar, Madhya Pradesh, Rajasthan and Uttar Pradesh) is much higher than in the other states and they will, therefore, take that much longer to stabilise their population. To increase the number of seats in parliament on the basis of revised figures of population would mean giving much larger representation than at present to these and some other states. This is likely to create new tensions and anxieties. Increasing the number of seats in state assemblies will also create difficulties in respect of the election of the President of India, and the size and composition of the Rajya Sabha.

Though no leaders of political parties are prepared to accept it, India, with its population crossing a billion mark, is faced with the serious problem of a population explosion. According to some estimates, India's population is expected to continue to grow till it reaches the 1.5 billion mark. It is true that while parliamentarians in the US or Russia represent about 30,000 to 50,000 people, in India each MP represents about 3 lakh people. Several constituencies are even larger. But, if the seats in parliament and the state assemblies are to be increased on the basis of population, the sessions of these bodies will have to be held in Olympic size indoor stadiums! We cannot afford to have such large, unwieldy and unmanageable legislative forums. Conducting any meaningful business in such mass meetings will be almost impossible.

Looking at the subject from this perspective, it is difficult to agree with the recommendations of the Law Commission of India to increase the size of the Lok Sabha and state assemblies.[24] We will have to make do with the present number of seats in these bodies. Their number should be frozen till the population declines perceptibly at some future date. Fortunately, the population policy announced by the centre in the year 2000 makes a categorical pronouncement to freeze the number of constituencies for a long time to come.

But, due to the large and unjustifiable discrepancies in the size

---

[24] Law Commission of India, *op cit.*, pp. 167–169.

of the constituencies—the number of voters in some constituencies is more than twice that in some other constituencies—it is necessary to redraw their boundaries. For example, while the Outer Delhi constituency has 20 lakh voters, Chandni Chowk has only 3.75 lakh voters. It is imperative that in redrawing the constituencies, as far as possible, their size, in terms of the number of voters, is brought on par, except in cases where the population is widely dispersed or geographical considerations militate against this. The central government has taken a decision to set up a delimitation commission for the purpose.

**Election Petitions**

The delays in court decisions in election petitions have become a matter for serious concern. Thus, for example, the Supreme Court annulled the election of an Orissa Congress MLA from the Bhanjangar assembly constituency, held in 1995, only in September 1999. (*Indian Express*, 23 Sep 1999). There are several cases in which election petitions have been finally decided long after the term of the House, to which the person was elected, had expired. The most shocking case of its kind was the punishment imposed in July 1999 on Bal Thackeray, referred to earlier, almost eleven years after the offence was committed. This should be an excellent case-study for all students of political science, political analysts, thinkers and policy makers. Such inordinate delays make a mockery of the provisions of law.

The NCRWC has suggested that special courts and benches of the high courts are set up to hear election petitions. From past experience, this is unlikely to serve any useful purpose. It, therefore, needs to be considered whether powers to decide such cases should be given to the EC. During the off-election period, the commission has the time to devote to deciding such petitions. Since the EC is now a multi-member body, full use must be made of its time and expertise. Since the members of the commission have the rank of a Supreme Court judge, only one appeal may be provided against the decision of the EC and that too only to the division bench of the Supreme Court.

### Minimum Educational Qualifications for a Legislator

India took a revolutionary step by accepting the concept of universal suffrage in its Constitution. Even in the constituent assembly, there was a demand that some minimum educational qualification be prescribed as eligibility for contesting elections to the Lok Sabha or state legislative assembly. In retrospect, it must be admitted that the founding fathers wisely decided against any such step at that time, considering the level of literacy in the country and the need for building up a united country and creating social cohesion in which all citizens are treated as equal.

After 55 years of Independence, it is, however, time to consider whether such a minimum qualification should be prescribed now. This is particularly relevant in view of the fact that the educational qualifications of MPs have been going up steadily over the years. In the twelfth Lok Sabha, 419 of the 545 MPs (77 per cent) were graduates and above.

Looking to the complexity of the issues of governance which come before legislatures, it is only appropriate that legislators should be able to comprehend the issues and contribute to the deliberations in the House. The same is true of legislative proposals which come before parliament and the state legislatures. Earlier in this chapter, we have dealt with the importance of strengthening the committee system. In such smaller forums, it is all the more necessary that MPs/MLAs understand the finer details of the subjects under discussion and are able to keep the government on its toes. Further, it is difficult to argue that while it is necessary to have minimum educational qualifications for the post of a peon, messenger or clerk, no such qualifications need be prescribed for a legislator who is to be a law-giver of the land. Against this background, it is necessary to lay down that a degree should be the minimum educational qualification for contesting an election as an MP/MLA. There should be no dearth of suitable persons with such qualifications even in tribal areas, let alone rural areas.

## Number of Children: Another Minimum Qualification for a Legislator

It is time we take some significant and striking initiatives to show our resolve to deal with the Herculean problem of population explosion. There has been a lack of consensus on this important subject so far. The policy statement on population made during the Emergency in 1975 remained unaltered for over two decades. The 1994 report of the group of experts chaired by M.S. Swaminathan languished without any action for nearly six years. The new policy announced in the year 2000 has little to offer. After the debacle of the compulsory family planning campaign foisted on the country by Sanjay Gandhi during the Emergency, no political party is prepared to strongly advocate the family planning programme. In fact, even the words 'family planning' are taboo. It is now euphemistically called 'family welfare'.

In a democracy, leaders have to set an example for others to follow. Just as the moral tone of a society is set by its leaders, a lead in family planning too has to be provided by its leaders. It is therefore time that a legislation be passed to lay down that an aspiring legislator will have to satisfy the condition of having not more than two children. Such a requirement can be considered quite reasonable.

A Constitution amendment Bill for this purpose has been languishing since 1992. This is in keeping with the general lack of seriousness on this subject among all political parties. The Bill needs to be resurrected and passed without further delay.

## First-Past-The-Post *vs* List System

The Law Commission has recommended that the Lok Sabha shall, in addition to its members as at present, consist of not more than 138 members chosen according to the list system in such manner as parliament may by law provide. In the case of state legislative assemblies, twenty five per cent of the enlarged membership of the assemblies will be chosen according to the list system.

We have earlier discussed the inadvisability of increasing the strength of the legislatures. That apart, the list system will further increase the hold of the leadership of a political party on the organisation. As has been seen from the experience of the Rajya Sabha and the state legislative councils, the list system is likely to lead to the induction of only professional politicians, who are not likely to get elected directly, in the lists of nominees by respective parties. It would thus be inadvisable to adopt the list system.

The Law Commission has also recommended that to be declared elected a person must get more than 50 per cent plus one vote of the total valid votes. The NCRWC has expressed the same view but it has suggested that its feasibility should be examined. *Prima facie*, the proposal seems unworkable, at least for the present, since even without such an innovation, the election process is spread over a period of nearly six weeks. Further, unless the electronic voting system is fully implemented, the printing of fresh ballot papers and other requirements will delay the declaration of final results considerably. Currently, there is a considerable time gap between the polling in a constituency and the counting of votes. A run-off or second round of voting can take place only after the counting of votes of the first round is completed. Such delays are likely to be resented by the people as it would stretch their patience beyond reasonable limits. Thus, while there is much to commend in the concept, its workability, feasibility and the time-frame for its implementation will have to be examined carefully.

**Representation of Women in the Lok Sabha**

The representation of women in the Lok Sabha continues to be dismal. The highest number of women members (44) was in the eighth Lok Sabha, followed by the twelfth (43) and eleventh Lok Sabha (40). As a percentage of the total number of seats, women's representation has never exceeded 8.1 per cent, a far cry from the reservation of 33 per cent which is proposed by most parties. This is in stark contrast with Scandinavia where women's representation has been over 40 per cent. In the recent elections to the South African National Assembly there were 120 women out of a total of 400, crossing the 30 per cent threshold. The African National Congress alone has 97 women constituting 36.47 per cent of its 226 members in the National Assembly.[25]

Female literacy in India is a mere 50 per cent, well below the 73 per cent for men. Female infanticide, child marriage, dowry deaths and other atrocities against women are rampant. We have earlier referred to the continuing high rate of growth of population, particularly in the BIMARU states. Giving women a place in the sun will go a long way to hasten overdue social sector reforms and improving the situation. One of the most important steps in this direction is the reservation of seats for women in legislatures. Strictly speaking, considering their percentage of the total population, 50 per cent of seats must be earmarked for women. However, in view of the resistance to the reservation of 33 per cent of seats all at once, it is suggested that reservation may be progressively stepped up. It could start with 15 per cent in the next Lok Sabha/state legislative assembly elections, and thereafter be raised by 5 percentage points in each of the succeeding elections till the reservation of 33 per cent is reached. It should be further provided that the reservation of 33 per cent will continue for 25 years, in the first instance. Until such a Constitutional amendment is made, political parties must take the initiative and give 33 per cent of their tickets to women candidates.

## Muslim Representation in the Lok Sabha

We must be prepared to face the truth about the present grossly inadequate representation of Muslims in parliament and state legislatures. The maximum number of Muslim members (46) was in the seventh Lok Sabha, followed by the eighth Lok Sabha (41). The percentage, in terms of total membership, declined

[25]Sushila Ramaswamy, Women in Politics, *Hindustan Times*, 14 September 1999.

steeply from 7.27 in the first Lok Sabha and 8.5 in the seventh Lok Sabha to 4.99 in the twelfth Lok Sabha. As compared with the percentage of Muslims (13) in the total population, this is undeniably too low, suggesting that democratic processes in India are not truly inclusive of minority groups.

For the first time since Independence, there are just two junior Muslim ministers in the Atal Behari Vajpayee ministry formed after the 1999 elections. This kind of insensitivity and short-sightedness certainly send a wrong message to the Muslim community. It cannot be denied that, except for a few elite Muslim families, the ordinary Muslim has largely remained outside the mainstream of national life. The levels of literacy among Muslims (men and women) continue to be much lower than in other sections of society. By and large, their primary and secondary education is restricted to religious institutions (*madrasas*), away from the liberal education stream. Their share in organised sector employment is miserably low. Their percentage of employment in government and public sector is negligible. This is equally true of the police and security forces. One crucial element in addressing these urgent problems is to give adequate representation to minorities in the Lok Sabha and state legislatures. If this aspect continues to be neglected, India will, sooner rather than later, be faced with the demand for reservation of seats for Muslims. Such a demand will have big and unmistakable political overtones, bring back memories of Partition and militate against the principle of secularism which is an integral part of the basic structure of the Constitution. It is high time all political parties listen to and, more importantly, act upon this message.

Opinion and Exit Polls

Preceding the 1999 Lok Sabha and legislative assembly polls, the election waters had been muddied by a number of controversies. One of the more enduring of which pertained to the publication of the results of the opinion and exit polls. The unreliability of opinion polls was brought home once again in the elections held for the UP and Uttaranchal legislative assemblies in February 2002. The vote percentage predicted for the BJP in different polls varied from 27 per cent to 38 per cent. The question as to whether exit polls should be given publicity till the completion of voting in the whole state once again came into focus, as these polls projected very divergent outcomes. There was something amiss about the polls in terms of the methods employed and the challenges of predicting the outcome of multi-cornered contests. (*Times of India*, 15 Feb 2002). This was further underlined in the Gujarat assembly elections in December 2002, and earlier in the assembly elections in Bihar and J&K.

M.S. Gill, then the CEC, commented that this is also a topic of debate in other democracies. New Zealand made the conducting of opinion polls related to elections an offence in 1993. In the US, the result of an exit poll on the east coast is not allowed to be revealed until the last vote is cast on the west coast.[26]

The problem would have been much less intractable if the polling had been over a much shorter period of three days to one week as in the past. But now the polling process takes over five weeks to complete all over the country. Unless some dramatic amendments are made in the electoral laws and the punishment for electoral offences made much more stringent, it is unlikely that the election process will be smooth or even peaceful in the near future. This may therefore mean an even longer polling period in different states. This factor must be borne in mind before coming to any final view on the manner in which opinion and exit polls should be dealt with.

Equally relevant is the question of the impartiality and credibility of the agencies conducting such polls. It is no secret that the sponsors of these polls often have an axe to grind and a goal to achieve. It is not therefore surprising that the result of the poll can often be predicted on the basis of the political leanings of the sponsors of the polls and/or the agency conducting the polls. As Bhaskar Rao, founder chairman of the

[26]Interview with M.S. Gill, 'I Refuse to be a Thanedar', *Outlook*, 11 October 1999, p. 22.

Centre for Media Studies, has observed, 'The concerns about poll surveys today arise for different reasons. They include, proliferation of poll surveys by all kinds of known and unknown agencies often without transparency about the poll itself and the methodology used, the use of such surveys by political parties in their campaign, the way the media itself has been using poll surveys, giving them authenticity and prominence; so much so that I came out with a paid advertisement two years ago cautioning the public that the results of my survey were not the accurate results.'[27]

The debate as to whether such polls influence the voter is meaningless. If they do not, there is no reason to conduct such polls at such cost and publish their results with so much fanfare. Clearly, such polls are sponsored and published because they influence the voter subtly but significantly. This is particularly true in the case of exit polls conducted in areas where polling has ended. If the trend of voting is in favour of any party or political front, the voters in other areas which are yet to go to polls are unlikely to buck the trend. The importance of these polls cannot therefore be minimised or overlooked.

There is no mechanism at present to conduct a rating of the agencies conducting the polls. It may be noted that the credit rating agencies which do the credit rating of companies are officially recognised by RBI for rating commercial paper and SEBI for debentures. It is time the agencies conducting opinion and exit polls are brought under the overall supervision of the EC. The methodology adopted by these agencies to conduct polls, the manner of sample selection, the nature of questions asked and so on are matters which merit a closer look. It should be mandatory for these agencies to publish all this information from time to time. The EC may appoint a standing panel of experts, whose impartiality and objectivity is beyond doubt, to go into these and other related matters and advise the EC. The EC's findings thereon may be published from time to time so

[27] Vrinda Gopinath, Polls, Pollsters and Politicians, *Indian Express*, 25 September 1999.

as to enable people to evaluate the poll forecasts and reach to informed judgments thereon.

It is interesting to note that the Press Council of India (PCI) had also issued guidelines that newspapers should not give publicity to the results of such polls before voting in all constituencies has been completed. The chairman of PCI had expressed an apprehension that if this was not done 'democracy would become mediacracy'. (*Sakal*, 24 Sep 1999).

The orders issued by the EC banning the publication of the results of such polls were struck down by the Supreme Court on the preliminary ground that there was no mechanism for their enforcement. The court is reported to have observed, 'Your [EC's] guideline will remain a guideline... At the end of the day you (EC) may go home with a perception that you have far less powers than the public perception of it'. (*Indian Express*, 15 Sep 1999). This is a far more damaging observation of the court than the mere striking down of the ban orders and was perhaps unwarranted.

The Supreme Court had not gone into the substantive issues pertaining to the merits of such polls, their impact on the voters or the implication of the ban on publication on the fundamental right of freedom of speech and expression guaranteed under Article 19 of the Constitution. After all, freedom of speech and expression is not unlimited and is subject to reasonable restrictions. These issues need to be argued before the Supreme Court again very early. There is clearly a need to take a fresh look at the advisability of publishing of the results of opinion and exit polls. In the meanwhile, as discussed earlier, it is necessary that the Constitution be amended to put the question of the powers of the EC, to conduct elections in a free, fair and credible manner and to take all reasonable steps towards that end, beyond any shadow of doubt.

## Issues Pertaining to Rajya Sabha Elections

The Rajya Sabha was conceived as the House of Elders and was meant to be a sobering influence on the House of the People.

Over a period of time, the complexion of the Rajya Sabha has changed perceptibly. Now, there is nothing much to distinguish it from the Lower House in so far as its functioning is concerned, except for its composition—indirect election and some nominated members. The Rajya Sabha is as noisy as the Lok Sabha. It has its own 'shouting brigades'. It is the same House in which a former Chairman, Shankar Dayal Sharma, was so insulted that he wept in the Chair.

One issue which requires urgent consideration on the part of all political parties relates to the criteria to be applied for selecting candidates for Rajya Sabha elections. By and large, professional politicians, who are unsuccessful in Lok Sabha elections or lack public support to contest the Lok Sabha elections get nominated to the Rajya Sabha. Since election to the Rajya Sabha is indirect, those who are lucky enough to be so selected are well provided for, for a period of six years. It is very rarely that political parties have adopted talented and accomplished persons from other fields as their candidates for the Rajya Sabha. As a result, the respect which the House of Elders should command has declined perceptibly. The only two categories of professionals that have been treated favourably are the journalists who wield a lot of clout among politicians because to their capacity to do considerable harm or good to them, and industrialists, largely due to their money power. In some cases, candidates who had lost Lok Sabha elections were immediately brought into the Rajya Sabha, thereby completely undoing the public mandate. This is a mockery of democracy.

The Rajya Sabha was supposed to represent the states. This was the main justification for the second chamber. Though not explicitly stated anywhere, it was expected that the members representing a particular state would belong to that state. This was how the selection of candidates took place in the initial years. However, later, the Rajya Sabha was largely used by some political parties to accommodate the favourite candidates of the leadership of the parties, irrespective of the state to which they belonged. These persons had no qualms in knowingly giving incorrect information as to their place of residence etc. in their nomination papers. The EC had ordered an inquiry into 25 of such cases among the sitting members during 1994–95. Manmohan Singh, former union finance minister, was one of them. The actual number of such members may be considerably larger. Interestingly, seven of them were union ministers. The decision of the Supreme Court in the case of Manmohan Singh to quash the proceedings started by the CEC and the Electoral Registration Officer, on purely technical grounds, was indeed unfortunate as the case involved a major constitutional issue. (*Hindu*, 2 Dec 1999). It is imperative that the matter be pursued further through appropriate constitutional amendment. The NCRWC has rightly recommended that the domiciliary requirement should be made essential in the case of membership of the Rajya Sabha.

There is no evidence to show that the Rajya Sabha has done anything notable to safeguard the interests of the states. It is therefore time to go into these issues and to seriously examine whether such a second chamber is needed at all. (This is equally true in the case of the upper Houses of the state legislatures.) It does not seem to serve any purpose except to duplicate the discussions in the Lower House and to delay the transaction of business. Five decades of record of work done by the Rajya Sabha should be adequate for such an examination in this golden jubilee year of parliament.

Another matter of some concern is the composition of the Rajya Sabha. Since one-third of its members retire every two years, it takes a long time for the Rajya Sabha to reflect the changed composition of the Lok Sabha. And, by that time, the composition of the Lok Sabha itself may change! This often means a deadlock with one party or political front enjoying a majority in the Lok Sabha, and the parties in the opposition in the Lok Sabha having a majority in the Rajya Sabha. As the experience of the past few years has shown, this is becoming a hurdle in the speedy transaction of legislative business in parliament as a whole. The country has often seen the sorry spectacle of parties in majority in the Rajya Sabha holding to ransom the government elected by a direct mandate of the people. A case in point was the threat given by the Congress party that it would hold up important legislative Bills for speeding up economic reforms if Rajiv Gandhi's name was not removed from the list of accused in the charge-sheet in the Bofors case. This has also been the experience in regard to the passage of a number of important Bills. This situation was clearly not visualised by the founding fathers of the Constitution. It is time for this issue also to be addressed with some urgency. More importantly, there is a good case for the abolishing the Rajya Sabha itself. This will be a strong signal for the downsizing of the government and the legislatutre.

### Nominated Members in the Rajya Sabha

Under Article 80(1) of the Constitution of India, twelve members are to be nominated by the President in accordance with the provisions of clause (3) thereof. The members to be nominated are expected to have special knowledge or practical experience in respect of such matters as the following, namely, literature, science, art and social service.

In spite of this explicit provision, the government has, from time to time, recommended for nomination persons who are professional politicians by grossly misusing the category 'social service'. Any politician can claim to have practical experience of social service. One wonders whether this category was deliberately included in Article 80 to accommodate such cases. According to newsreports, in a few cases, the President has resisted such proposals though not always successfully. In such a tug-of-war, at times, the vacancies in this category have remained unfilled for months at a time and finally the President has had to yield. But, in most other cases, the President has signed on the dotted line. One such recent nomination was that of Chaudhari Harmohan Singh Yadav, a professional politician, who was nominated to the Rajya Sabha during the days of the United Front Government in 1997. (*Loksatta*, 29 Aug 1997). In the same category is the nomination of Nanaji Deshmukh, senior leader of the RSS who had been an MP in 1977, made by the President, on the recommendation of the Atal Behari Vajpayee government, in November 1999. This has also been the experience in respect of nominations to the upper Houses in the state legislatures. In most of these cases, the Governors have failed to apply their minds and have not even taken the trouble to refer the proposals to the state government for reconsideration, before approving them. The most preposterous case of this kind was the nomination by the Governor of Maharashtra, in February 2002, of twelve active politicians to the upper House of the state legislature. This has led to the filing of three PILs in the Bombay high court.

The provision pertaining to nominations in Article 80 of the Constitution looks good on paper. But, it is time to assess carefully and objectively, the impact of this provision on the deliberations in the Rajya Sabha. This is particularly so because from 1952 to 1999, as many as 98 persons have been nominated under this Article. Some of them have added glamour to the otherwise staid and somewhat dull and drab setting in the Rajya Sabha but a handful of these nominated members, have contributed anything significant to the deliberations. Several of these nominated members did not utter a single word in the House during their entire tenure. The Rajya Sabha itself has expressed its displeasure in November 2002 over the long absences of Lata Mangeshkar, one of the nominated members, from the House. Is there then a need to continue the present system of nominations in its present form? It will be useful to go into this issue at some length whenever the future of the Rajya Sabha is reconsidered.

### Democratic Decentralisation—A Non-Starter

While bilateral and multilateral institutions started looking into the issues pertaining to democratic decentralisation and advocating its virtues only in the 1990s, pioneering work done in this field in India dates back to the early 1950s. Article 40 of the Constitution, contained in Part IV pertaining to the

Directive Principles of Sate Policy, casts an obligation that, 'the State shall take steps to organise village panchayats and endow them with such powers and authority as may be necessary to enable them to function as units of self-government'. This provision was acted upon faithfully by states such as Gujarat, Karnataka and Maharashtra. The community development programme was launched in October 1952. In 1957 the Balwantrai Mehta Committee was set up. This was followed by the Ashok Mehta Committee in 1978. The committees appointed by the centre and the states thereafter have examined in depth the various facets of democratic decentralisation.

Unfortunately, for want of political and administrative will, local governments have continued to languish except in a few states. They are the children of lesser gods. The task force appointed by the Planning Commission, under the chairmanship of Raja Chelliah, reported that local expenditures as a percentage of all expenditures by the central, state and local governments had fallen to 4.5 per cent in 1980–81 as compared to 8 per cent in 1960–61. During 1970s and 1980s, about half of the municipal councils and corporations were under supersession at any given time. The Chennai Corporation was superseded in 1973 and continued in that state for 24 years! Elections to gram panchayats in Bihar were not held for 22 years.

A more significant milestone in democratic decentralisation was the passage of the Constitution (Seventy-third Amendment) Act, 1992, and the Constitution (Seventy-fourth Amendment) Act, 1992, which gave extensive new powers and functions to the village panchayats and municipal bodies, respectively. In a sense, for the first time, the Indian federal structure became (at least on paper) five-tiered: panchayats constituted at the village, intermediate and district levels, the state governments and the central government. For the urban areas, a provision was made for the organisation of nagar panchayats, municipal councils and municipal corporations, depending on the size of the urban area.

Among other provisions, the Amendment Acts provided for: mandatory elections, ordinarily once in five years; supercession of local bodies only in exceptional circumstances and for a period

## Indian Democracy: The Unfinished Agenda

not exceeding six months; one third of seats to be reserved for women; reservation for SCs/STs in proportion to their population; setting up of state finance commissions (SFCs) every five years to consider the devolution of funds and delegation of taxation powers to these bodies; setting up of district planning committees (DPCs), and the establishment of a state election commission.

The seventy-third amendment introduced a new schedule (Eleventh Schedule) in the Constitution under which any of the 29 subjects, specified therein, could be given to the panchayats by the state government 'to enable them to function as institutions of self-government' by passing a law to that effect. The Twelfth Schedule introduced in the Constitution by the seventy-fourth amendment similarly enabled the state legislature to give any of the powers, specified therein, to municipal bodies. Even a cursory look at the list of functions to be given to the local bodies shows that the intention was to take the government to the people in the real sense of the term.

Yet another striking change made in the Constitution pertained to Article 280 on the central finance commission (CFC). By the seventy-third and seventy-fourth amendments of the Constitution, the matters on which the CFC is to make recommendation to the President were expanded to include:

> '(b) the measures needed to augment the Consolidated Fund of a State to supplement the resources of the Panchayats in the State on the basis of the recommendations made by the Finance Commission of the State;
> (c) the measures needed to augment the Consolidated Fund of a State to supplement the resources of the Municipalities in the State on the basis of the recommendations made by the Finance Commission of the State'.

Unfortunately, even after ten years of the coming into effect of these Constitutional amendments, there has hardly been any real follow-up action by the states on these path-breaking amendments which were meant to empower nearly 29.2 lakh elected representatives of panchayats (of whom 10 lakh are women, and 3.65 lakh and 2.5 lakh are scheduled castes and scheduled tribes respectively) at various levels. While elections to local bodies have been held in almost all states, and the SFCs have submitted their reports, the crucial task of empowering the local bodies, through the transfer of financial and administrative powers, remains to be achieved. Salient provisions pertaining to reservation of office-bearers of these bodies, by turn, for women and persons belonging to SCs/STs are being subverted. According to a news report, in Rajasthan, during a period of one year, as many as 75 persons belonging to these categories were removed from office by passing a vote of no confidence and their places were taken by persons belonging to upper castes. (*Maharashtra Times*, 14 Aug 1998).

Of the 20 reports submitted by the SFCs, only thirteen have been acted upon in any significant manner. The ATRs submitted to the legislatures indicate that, in most cases, acceptance has been limited to a few items while other recommendations are reported to be under consideration.[28] Due to the serious constraint of resources faced by the government of Tamil Nadu, for example, local bodies had not received funds from the state government for more than a year. Reportedly, only 25 per cent of the Rs 517.32 crore SFC grant had been released. The total amount earmarked itself was lower than the previous year's allocation of Rs 577.80 crore. (*Frontline*, 29 March 2002). The situation is the same in a number of other states.

It will be interesting to take a look at the study made by the National Institute of Public Finance and Policy of the reports of some SFCs in so far as they relate to municipal bodies. As the study brings out, there is no clarity in respect of the functions and responsibilities of municipalities, particularly those that are enumerated in the Constitution (Seventy-fourth) Amendment Act, 1992. This is most disconcerting. The study comes to the conclusion that the adequacy of the recommendations of the

---

[28]K.C. Sivaramakrishnan, *Sub-State Level Governments*, Paper written for the Workshop on Constitution of India: A Case of Rethinking, 11–13 December 1999, New Delhi, Mimeo.

SFCs for projecting the financial requirements of municipalities appears to be questionable for several reasons: (a) lack of clarity about the financial responsibilities of the municipalities, (b) absence of a rationale in specifying the shares of municipalities in the state budget, and (c) the difficulty in assessing the overall impact of the recommendations on the state budget.[29]

As the Eleventh Finance Commission has brought out, in 1997–98, the revenue generated by village level panchayats was just 10.43 per cent of their total revenue as compared to the corresponding figure of 16.26 per cent in 1990–91. Similarly deterioration is seen in respect of the district level panchayats with the figure of 0.77 per cent in 1997–98 as compared to 1.26 per cent in 1990–91. The position is the same in regard to the urban local bodies with the corresponding figures of 67.81 per cent and 69.60 per cent respectively.[30]

A study by the Planning Commission in November 2001 shows the tardy rate of the progress of implementation of the 73rd and 74th amendments of the Constitution.[31] Among the major states, in only five namely, Karnataka, Kerala, Tamil Nadu, Rajasthan and West Bengal have all the 29 functions been transferred to panchayats. In some states such as Orissa (25), and Himachal Pradesh, Madhya Pradesh and Chhatisgarh (23 each), a large number of functions have been transferred. But in other states such as Andhra Pradesh (13), Haryana (16), Maharashtra (18), Punjab (7), Uttar Pradesh and Uttaranchal (13 each), the performance is far from satisfactory. In regard to transfer of funds as also the functionaries, Karnataka tops the list with having transferred the funds and functionaries of all the 29

[29]O.P. Mathur, *Reports of State Finance Commissions (Summary of Recommendations)*, National Institute of Public Finance and Policy, New Delhi, July 1997, and *Extending the Recommendations of the Finance Commissions of States into the Future*, Mimeo.

[30]Government of India, *Report of the Eleventh Finance Commission*, pp. 232–236.

[31]Government of India, Planning Commission, *Report of the Working Group on Decentralised Planning and Panchayat Raj Institutions for the Tenth Five Year Plan*, November 2001, pp. 61–62.

functions given to the panchayats. The performance of most other states is far from satisfactory. States such as Assam, Bihar, Jharkhand, Goa and Gujarat have not taken any steps to transfer either the functions, funds or functionaries to panchayats. Among the smaller states, Sikkim tops the list with the transfer of all the 29 functions along with the funds and functionaries. In respect of the establishment of the district planning committees (DPCs), Kerala, Orissa, Rajasthan and West Bengal top the list with the setting up of these committees in all districts with the chairperson of the district panchayat as the chairperson of DPC, closely followed by Karnataka (17 districts). In almost all other states, there has been no action.

A brief case study of Maharashtra is interesting. In Maharashtra, the three tier panchayat raj system was introduced following the Bombay Village Panchayat Act, 1958 and the Maharashtra Zilla Parishad and Panchayat Samitis Act, 1961. Under these enactments, the state government transferred a number of subjects, practically along the lines of those in the seventy-third amendment of the Constitution, to the zilla parishads, panchayat samitis and village panchayats. Maharashtra has had the distinction of having some all-women village panchayats. As far back as 1979 there were already 320 women members at the panchayat samiti and zilla parishad levels. In 1992, the state legislature made a provision in the Zilla Parishad Act for 30 per cent reservation of seats for women at all levels of panchayat raj institutions. In fact, it went one step further by framing a policy for women and establishing statutory committees in each zilla parishad for the development of women and children, comprising 70 per cent of women members and chaired by women.

Unfortunately, simultaneously, the government of Maharashtra was taking steps to withdraw a number of powers and subjects given earlier to the panchayat raj institutions. This was done by successive governments, clearly signifying that they did not subscribe to the ideology of democratic decentralisation. Parallel organisations were set up in the state government to handle subjects and schemes which were transferred to the zilla parishads. The provisions for appointment of associate and co-

## Indian Democracy: The Unfinished Agenda

opted members were deleted. The provisions permitting the president and vice president of the zilla parishad and chairmen of panchayat samitis to carry on the current administrative duties until their successor entered upon the office were deleted as the elections to these bodies were delayed inordinately. There was a long gap of thirteen years after which elections to these bodies were held in 1992.

This trend of benign neglect gathered strength during the regime of the Shiv Sena-BJP government during 1995-1999. The term of office of the elected office-bearers was reduced from five years to one year, in February 1997, thereby making a mockery of the whole concept of self-government. No office-bearer can acquire any worthwhile understanding or get a grasp of the work in such a short period. A PIL had to be filed against this decision of the government before the Aurangabad bench of the Bombay high court. The other equally questionable amendment made by the Shiv Sena-BJP government was to do away with the requirement of two-thirds majority for the passage of a vote of no-confidence in any office-bearer and to lay down that a simple majority was adequate for the purpose. This severely affected the stability of the term of elected office-bearers of these institutions. Both these important amendments were clearly short-sighted and counter-productive. Since a number of panchayat raj institutions were being controlled by the Congress party which was in the opposition in the state legislature, the aim of the Shiv Sena-BJP government was to weaken these bodies for the advancement of their own political prospects in the state. Fortunately, the democratic front government reversed these decisions in February 2000 and fixed the term of office at two and a half years.

This neglect of democratic decentralisation was further borne out by the shocking manner in which the government of Maharashtra dealt with the report of the SFC appointed on 23 April 1994. The chairman of the SFC was changed twice and the members were changed three times before its deliberations could be completed. Finally, the SFC presented its report to the state government on 31 January 1997. The quality of the report and the depth of analysis of the problems facing the local bodies leave a great deal to be desired. It is distressing to see that the report does not do justice to the local bodies in a state which has had such a long history of local self-government and is one of the most urbanised states in the country. In view of the precarious condition of state finances, the state government clearly wanted to delay taking action on the report of the SFC. The state cabinet, after going through the pretence of deliberating on the report in a cabinet sub-committee, finally took decisions on its recommendations on 22 February 1999, a full two years after the already delayed submission of the report. The report of the commission, along with the action taken statement, was placed on the table of the legislature on 17 March 1999! Even this would not have happened had a PIL not been filed in the Bombay high court to force the government to take an early decision. As a result of these cumulative delays, the recommendations of the SFC have come into effect two years later i.e. from the financial year 1999–2000 instead of 1997–98. The action taken statement is so badly prepared that no one is any wiser about the extent to which the finances of the local bodies will stand to benefit by the decisions of the government. Even the total financial resources transferred to the local bodies cannot be assessed from the statement of action taken.

The state government had also not taken any action to consider the transfer of subjects as in the Eleventh and the Twelfth Schedules of the Constitution to the local bodies. Like in several other matters, this issue too was raised in a PIL filed before the Bombay high court. It is significant to note that the conference of office-bearers of zilla parishads held at Kolhapur in December 1998 passed as many as 54 resolutions expressing their grievances and seeking more powers and functions. The democratic front government, comprising the two Congress parties and several other parties, which came to power in October 1999 promised to review the decisions of the previous government and, once again, to breathe new life into the panchayat raj institutions in the state. Accordingly, the state government took a momentous decision to transfer 116 schemes, along with the budget provisions and staff of 25,000, to the zilla parishads from 2 October 2000. However, in June 2002, the state government has curtailed the powers of zilla parishads even to carry out maintenance work.

A reference may be made to the experiment conducted by Maharashtra to strengthen democratic decentralisation in large urban areas. This was by introducing the Mayor-in-Council (MIC) system, in April 1998, on a pilot basis in Mumbai and Nagpur, to begin with. This meant reducing the powers of the municipal commissioner and instead giving greater powers to the mayor and the chairmen of various committees. The idea was that the MIC should function as a cabinet form of government. One would have expected the political parties and the people to welcome such a move but there was such persistent criticism of the functioning of MIC from all these quarters as also the media, that the state government decided to scrap the MIC, within a year of launching it, and revert to the earlier regime under which the municipal commissioner enjoyed wide powers.

The position was equally disconcerting in a number of other states. The most notable is the case of Karnataka, which in the 1960s, was in the forefront of democratic decentralisation, along with Gujarat and Maharashtra. As Marina Pinto has observed, 'With the return of the Congress party to power in 1989, the democratic decentralisation [in Karnataka] is in reverse gear. These local bodies have been re-centralised, some dissolved and even placed under administrators. The new statute of 1993 replaces the Act of 1983...The zilla parishad's composition continues as before, but its functions are reduced, since it has just supervisory and coordinating roles. There is also a diminution of the administrative powers of the chairman and an increase in those of the CEO [chief executive officer]... The state government's powers of supervision and control over the panchayat bodies has (*sic*) been substantially increased under the new Act... In sum, the new Act seems to turn the clock back in that with increase in the powers of the state government there is reduction in the autonomy of panchayat raj institutions. With increase in powers of the CEO and executive officers, there is greater bureaucratisation.'[32] However, since then, as brought out earlier, Karnataka has taken rapid strides and now tops the list of states in giving effect to the seventy-third amendment of the Constitution.

The Andhra Pradesh legislative assembly has, on 16 November 1999, passed a resolution to request the government of India to amend the Constitution to give more freedom to the state legislature to decide the manner in which the elections of chairpersons at various levels were to be held and some other matters.

The seventy-third and seventy-fourth amendments of the Constitution do not apply to the state of Jammu and Kashmir. It is interesting to note that the local bodies in Jammu and Kashmir have been defunct for years. The urban local bodies have never been permitted to impose taxes on land and buildings, trade or professions, water, street lighting, vehicles and entertainment. The only tax they were authorised to impose was octroi which was abolished in 1987. So they have no tax revenue at all. The powers of the municipal bodies for taxation under the Municipal Act, 1951, have been concurrently taken over by the state government under various enactments. Most of the municipal functions assigned to the urban local bodies no longer belong to them because they have been taken over by the state government. The state government had appointed a Municipal Finance Commission in 1988. Its report was received in 1991. The recommendations of the commission are still under consideration by the state government.[33]

In June 2002, the Bihar high court, in a *suo moto* action, has castigated the state government for not transferring due powers to the panchayats. In July 2002, several zilla parishad chiefs in Andhra Pradesh have filed a PIL to force the state government to implement the seventy-third amendment of the Constitution.

[32]Marina Pinto, What Ails Panchayat Raj?, Panchayat Raj and People's Aspirations, *The Public Administrator*, The Indian Institute of Public Administration, Maharashtra Branch, Special Issue 1995–96, pp. 33–34.

[33]Government of Jammu and Kashmir, *Report of the Committee on Economic Reforms for Jammu and Kashmir*, August 1998, pp. 40–41.

The two exceptions to the marked setback to democratic decentralisation in the states are Kerala and West Bengal in which Communist parties have held sway for a long time. These parties are firm believers in democratic decentralisation, given their ideology. The decentralisation of powers and functions has helped these parties to build their party cadres down to the village level and enabled them to keep a tight grip on state politics.

In July 1996, the Government of Kerala decided to devolve 40 per cent of the state's ninth plan resources to panchayats. It initiated a process of empowering gram panchayats to assume responsibility for determining the use of these funds. The state planning board began a people's campaign 'to break the atmosphere of cynicism that exists among the people today and instill in them a new sense of optimism and direction so that the mobilisation of resources for the ninth plan goes beyond the traditional confines'. In 1997–98, nearly Rs 400 crores was distributed to the gram panchayats, block panchayats and district panchayats in the ratio of 70:15:15. The inter-panchayat plan outlay was made on the basis of the population within the jurisdiction of the panchayats. The Conformity Acts of 1994 for panchayats and municipalities were amended into a new Act in February 1999. This Act made far-reaching institutional and legal changes to facilitate functional, financial and administrative autonomy. Forty-four state legislations were amended to broaden the entitlements of local bodies, increase their powers, and create institutions like the ombudsman with a high court judge as the chairperson, appellate tribunals, audit commission, state development council and the People's Plan to assign the rightful Constitutional role to the district planning committees.[34] The People's Plan, produced through a process of local level interaction, has resulted in the formulation of nearly 150,000 projects. All 990 gram panchayats in the state know the exact allocations for projects in their area. Panchayats now have a

[34] M.A. Oommen, Eleventh Finance Commission (EFC) Transfer System and the Local Bodies: A Critique, *The Radical Humanist*, July 2001, p. 28.

greater sense of ownership, having prepared their own action plan.[35]

An issue which has come up prominently in some states, and particularly in Gujarat, is whether voluntary agencies and stakeholders' organisations in areas such as soil and water conservation, watershed development, prohibition, and amelioration of the condition of backward classes should be left to do the work or whether these activities should also be entrusted to village panchayats. There could be a distinct advantage in leaving these functions to stakeholders' organisations.

Note must be made of a number of points in the working of local bodies which have become matters of concern and must be addressed if their role is to be expanded in the future. Some of these are listed below:

- It needs to be seriously examined why the panchayati raj system has failed in states such as Gujarat and Maharashtra and why there is so much reluctance to take energetic follow-up action on the seventy-third and seventy-fourth amendments. A recent example of this is the recommendation of the committee of the Maharashtra legislature that the implementation of the prime minister's rural roads scheme should be withdrawn from the zilla parishads and entrusted to the state public works department.[36] Equally significant is the decision of the state government to entrust the subject of agriculture to zilla parishads on an agency basis and not to transfer it along with all the funds and functionaries. After all, these states were in the vanguard of this movement in the sixties. Such introspection will go a long way in hastening the process of change over to the new regime envisaged by these Constitutional amendments.
- Convening *Gram Sabhas* (meetings of the whole village), at least twice a year, has to be made an integral part of

[35]United Nations Development Programme, *Diversity and Disparities in Development—Key Challenges for India*, New Delhi, January 1999, pp. 35–36.
[36]Maharashtra Legislature Secretariat, *Report of the Irrigation and PWD Standing Committee on Budget Demands 2002–03*, April 2002, p. 18.

democratic decentralisation. This alone will give local people a chance to take part in governance at the local level. Unfortunately, this has not happened in most states. Most often, *gram sabhas* are held as a ritual to complete the formalities on paper.

- The expenditure on salaries and allowances of a number of these bodies is increasing rapidly. In most states, the pay scales of the employees of local bodies are on par with those of state government employees whose salaries, in turn, are equated with those of central government employees. The impact of the fifth pay commission, in particular, has been sizeable. The Bruhanmumbai Municipal Corporation (BMC) incurs over 70 per cent of its total expenditure on staff salaries and allowances. Its pay scales and emoluments for certain categories of employees are higher than those at the corresponding level in the state government. The deficit in the budget of the BMC has gone up rapidly over the years. It is now even attempting to temporarily tap the provident fund of its employees to bridge the deficit. As a result of such runaway revenue expenditure, the development expenditure of local bodies has come down steeply.
- Except for a few honourable exceptions, the local bodies, particularly in the rural areas, are dependent on grants from the state governments to cover 90 per cent of their total expenditure. In other cases, these bodies merely implement the schemes of the state government on an agency basis. Their own sources of revenue are negligible. The recovery of taxes and levies is minimal and there are large arrears. The rates of taxes and levies have not been revised for years.
- There is practically no cost recovery in the services provided by these bodies. As a result, there are large arrears due by these bodies to the state electricity boards and water supply and sewerage boards.
- There are thousands of encroachments on public and private properties. These bodies have not been able to get such encroachments vacated and have had to regularise them from time to time, making a mockery of town planning.

- The move to give certain activities of municipal bodies on a contract basis to the private sector has received a setback in recent years. A division bench of the Madhya Pradesh high court is reported to have decided that octroi collection through private contractors is unconstitutional. The Bombay high court has decided that the BMC should regularise all conservancy staff appointed on contract basis, thereby putting a huge financial burden on the corporation.
- The electoral results in these bodies are as fractious as those at the state and national level, resulting in defections from one political party to another. Added to this are the complications arising from a number of independents getting elected to these bodies.
- The criminalisation of politics gives serious cause for worry in the elections of local bodies. It is imperative to amend the relevant laws to safeguard against this evil so as to restore the confidence of people in these institutions of self-government.
- The present arrangements for auditing the expenditures of local bodies are too weak to inspire confidence. These bodies are not afraid of an audit and often treat it in a casual manner. Audit paras, even those pertaining to misappropriation and defalcation of funds, remain unattended for years. The report of the local fund audit in Maharashtra for the year 1998–99 shows that there was a delay in reporting compliance by panchayat raj bodies in 71,263 cases and the total amount of expenditure which was in question was Rs 1,259.26 crore. In 90,692 cases of audit objections involving expenditure of Rs 1,087.46 crore, the final compliance was still pending. It is imperative that the C&AG lays down the audit standards for all these institutions and also conducts a test audit to ensure adherence to certain minimum auditing standards. The C&AG must be given the overall responsibility for supervision of the audit of local bodies though the audit itself may be entrusted to local fund auditors and/or chartered accountants. This is particularly important if larger and larger expenditures are to flow through these institutions.

- Right to information is much more relevant at this level of administration. It is essential that this statutory right is conferred on citizens as soon as possible.
- By and large, the State Finance Commissions have not made much difference to the precarious financial position of local bodies. State governments have been reluctant to share their dwindling revenues with these bodies. As a result, several local bodies seem to be giving up the functions they had undertaken earlier. Regrettably, city public transport seems to be the first casualty of such cut-backs in expenditure. Curtailment of public transport services, without permitting private buses to operate, is leading to an ever-rising number of personal vehicles on the road. The quality of several civic services has also suffered, thereby increasing the privations of the people.
- To cope with this situation, some comparatively better-off and forward-looking municipal bodies have begun exploring the possibility of tapping the capital market by floating bonds. This move will inevitably require the credit rating of these bodies. This should hopefully bring some financial and managerial discipline into their working.
- Whether democratic decentralisation can lead to reduction in corruption is still an open question. There is no convincing evidence either way. Perhaps it is safest to say that corruption in a local body comes more easily and quickly into the limelight. To that extent, there is a greater possibility of it being brought under control by the public action. Clearly, democratic decentralisation is not a magic wand for eradicating corruption, unless, simultaneously, the series of steps discussed in this book are taken.
- We have earlier referred to the MPLADS under which Rs 2 crore is placed at the disposal of each MP for undertaking development work in his constituency. This contagion has now afflicted local bodies in some states and members of zilla parishads and municipal councillors are also being given discretionary funds, of varying amounts, each year. This is contrary to the spirit of the Constitution. It also tends to

perpetuate, through such largesse, the influence of the sitting member of an area at the expense of the public exchequer. As stated earlier, it is imperative that this scheme be abolished forthwith. Failing this, at least the Supreme Court ought to expedite its decision on the PIL pending on the subject.

A note must be made of the two main hurdles slowing down the process of democratic decentralisation. The first is the bureaucracy which often resists the transfer of schemes, programmes and budget of the state government to local bodies. The relations between elected members and office-bearers of these institutions and employees have deteriorated considerably over a period of time. There are frequent reports of physical attacks and insulting treatment of employees by the representatives of the people. As a result, officers and staff working in the state sector are reluctant to work in these institutions. There is stiff resistance to the formation of district cadres as this would increase the stranglehold of the office-bearers of these institutions on the services. Employees are also opposed to their annual work assessment being entrusted to the office-bearers of these bodies.

The other equally forceful opposition to decentralisation comes from MPs, MLAs and state ministers who fear the curtailment of their influence. This has led to the very questionable practice in some states of making MLAs and MPs ex-officio members of the local bodies. The enabling provisions in this behalf in the seventy-third and seventy-fourth Constitution Amendment Acts need to be deleted as they result in stultifying the new leadership emerging in these institutions. The ministers who find their power getting curtailed as a result of the decentralisation of powers and functions try every possible method of delaying and even opposing the transfer of powers and functions to local bodies.

The central government too has not set a particularly good example for the states. The central government refuses to part with powers and functions in a number of important subjects. For example, there is no reason for having such huge ministries of agriculture and education at the centre, since these subjects are largely handled at the state level. The central government had tried to increase its hold on a number of subjects in the State and Concurrent Lists of the Constitution by holding out the lure of centrally sponsored schemes. Since the states are perpetually starved of funds, they are willing to tolerate the interference of the centre in the hope of getting larger central assistance. If democratic decentralisation has to proceed at a fast pace, it must begin at the central government level.

Before we conclude, it may be interesting to note, how one of the oldest municipal bodies in the country, the BMC, has been concentrating on peripherals and neglecting its core civic functions. As many as 2,500 roads and *chowks* (intersections) have been given new names in Mumbai and fresh proposals are continuing to pour in. Unwittingly or otherwise, a precious part of old Mumbai and the history associated with the names of streets also continues to be wiped out. (*Indian Express*, 23 Aug 1999). Now, there is only one area (Khar) left in Mumbai, and perhaps in the whole country, where roads have numbers. One does not know how long the residents will be able to resist the pressure to rename these roads. Having changed the names of roads and their small side-roads several times, now efforts are being made to name even footpaths! This should open a new and lucrative avenue for corruption.

Despite these aberrations, it has to be admitted that decentralisation is the key to the empowerment of the common man. Top-down, 'command and control' policies have proved to be inefficient and ineffective. The new economic policies for liberalisation, in effect, decentralise economic decision-making to individuals and firms, reducing the scope for distortions and inefficiencies inherent in a regime of administered prices and a controlled, closed economy.[37]

The NCRWC has made some very valuable recommendations to strengthen the institutions of self government. These include the creation of a separate fiscal domain for panchayats and municipalities; giving them full administrative and functional

[37] *Ibid.*, p. 34.

control over their staff by enacting suitable legislation at the state level; setting up a state panchayat council; laying down the requirement that whenever a municipality is superseded, a report is placed before the state legislature; and empowering C&AG to audit or at least lay down accounting standards for panchayats. The commission has also suggested a series of further Constitutional amendments to subserve the larger objectives underlying the seventy-third and seventy-fourth amendments of the Constitution. At the conference of panchayati raj institutions held in Delhi in March 2002, the prime minister as also the leader of the opposition in parliament had expressed their dissatisfaction at the slow pace of progress in this field and had even suggested convening a special session of parliament to discuss the relevant issues. This once again underlines the urgency of the task.

For a country as large and diverse as India, decentralised governance alone can deliver results. The principle of 'subsidiarity' —whatever can be done at the lower level need not be done at the higher level—should be the guide-post in our search for decentralised administration. Since democratic norms and institutions have taken firm root in the country, it should not be difficult to build on these foundations a superstructure in the form of a pyramid which will have a strong and resilient legal framework and institutions of self-governance. This will, however, require purposeful and committed political and administrative action to push through the many reforms which are imperative for democratic decentralisation. Unfortunately, there are no such hopeful signs visible.

# 3

# Reinventing the Government

**Rule of Law**

The Supreme Court, in the contempt petition involving H. Borobabu Singh, Speaker of the Manipur assembly, observed on 5 February 1993 that, 'It is our constitutional duty which requires us to make this order, to uphold the majesty of law and justify the confidence of the people, that no one in the country is above the law and the governance is not of men but of the "rule of law".' This principle has been emphasised by the higher courts time and again—Be you ever so high the law is above you. However, the first question is rule of what kind of law? This is particularly relevant in India with so many old and outdated laws, rules and regulations.

In a letter to the union home minister, the then chairman of the national human rights commission (NHRC), M.N. Venkatachaliah, had underlined that, 'the provisions of the 102 year old Prison Act were totally outdated to cater to the modern requirements of purposeful custody, reformation and treatment of prisoners'. (*Times of India*, 12 May 1997). The Indian police are still governed by the antiquated Police Act of 1861. Under the Prohibition of Prostitution and Immoral Traffic Act, 1950, a penalty of Rs 50 has been prescribed. The Bombay high court very rightly asked the government advocate why the state government could not issue an ordinance to step up the minimum fine to Rs 5,000. (*Sakal*, 9 Sep 1998). It was only in July 1999 that the 128-year old Coroner's Act was abolished by the government of Maharashtra through an ordinance. A reinterpretation by the Bombay high court of the Muslim Women's Act provided that a husband would have to provide for his wife's 'entire future' within the *iddat* period. With this judgement, Muslim women, deserted by their husbands, will now also be able to obtain a lumpsum amount as settlement without having to depend on section 125 of the Criminal Procedure Code which provides for a maximum of Rs 500 as monthly maintenance for life. This amount was fixed by the Criminal Procedure Code decades ago. Though the Law Commission has submitted a proposal suggesting that the limit be fixed and maintenance decided on the paying capacity of the husband and the need of the petitioner, it is yet to be acted upon by the government. (*Hindustan Times*, 11 May 1999). The Land Acquisition Act is of 1894 vintage and is hardly suited to present requirements.

As Rakesh Bhatnagar explains, all hotels including five star establishments in Delhi, are still governed by the Sarai Act of 1860! In those days, the concept of a hotel was unheard of; there were only inns for travellers. The Act makes it mandatory for every inn owner to serve cold water and provide other basic amenities free of cost to the travellers. Hoteliers are expected to comply with this 137-year old statute, but it is anybody's guess whether such a condition makes sense when even drinking water comes at a price. Another century old statute, the Epidemic Diseases Act, continues to guide civic authorities. According to a legal researcher, the inspiration behind this Act was a Bombay legislation meant to help sick cattle.[1] Such instances abound.

As H.D. Shourie has stated, 'As many as approximately 40

---

[1] Rakesh Bhatnagar, Legal System Needs Spring-Cleaning, *Times of India*, 10 June 1997.

per cent of the presently operative laws date to the 1800's and early 1900's [vintage].' These include the Telegraph Act of 1885, Wireless Telegraph Act of 1933, Railways Act of 1890, and Electricity Act of 1910. These Acts are supposed to regulate presently existing matters and processes some of which were not dreamt of in those days...I have come across two laws, Admiralty of Offences (Colonial) Act, 1849 and Admiralty Jurisdiction Act of 1860, which even lay down the words, 'Act to provide for prosecution and trial of Admiralty of Offences in Her Majesty's territories in India'.[2]

The Government of India had appointed a Commission on Review of Administrative Laws (COROAL) which submitted its report in September 1999. The commission was, *inter alia*, asked to identify proposals for amendment of laws and regulations having inter-sectoral impact, and to make recommendations for repeal/amendment of laws, regulations and procedures. Some of the more important recommendations of the commission are:

- The repeal of over 1,300 central laws of different categories out of about 2,500 laws in force. These include, among others, 166 central Acts, 11 British statutes still in force, 17 War-time permanent ordinances, and 114 central Acts relating to state subjects for repeal by state governments. The commission recommends their repeal on the ground that these laws have become either irrelevant or dysfunctional. In this context, review of all pre-Constitution laws should be taken up to bring them in line with present day requirements. Sunset provisions similar to those in the USA should be introduced in laws wherever possible.
- Expeditious amendments should be considered in respect of a critical list of about 110 laws including those regarding which action has been initiated.
- All ministries/departments should compile up to date

[2] Review of Laws, Regulations and Procedures, *Common Cause*, October-December 1997.

information about rules, regulations, orders and procedures under different central laws administered by them including manuals in respect of areas which are important from the point of view of the general public. These should be disseminated to the electronic media with periodical updating. Similar efforts should be made by state governments also, since the regulatory framework in the states has an impact on the working of the economic and social sectors.
- There is a need to study the entire complex of laws, regulations and procedures affecting the quality of life of the poor and disadvantaged sectors of society in a focused manner.
- There is a need to unify and harmonise statutes, laws and regulations with reference to the perspective of domestic and foreign investors, trade and industry, consumers, builders, exporters and importers. In this process the government should simplify the language used in all regulations, rules and orders. The unification exercise should also address the centre-state interface and the issues can be remitted to the Inter-State Council.
- Specific proposals have been formulated on the regulatory frameworks relating to 13 sectors, including housing and urban development, land acquisition, sick industrial companies, company law, non-banking financial companies, foreign investment, Essential Commodities Act, health, environment, industry, labour, direct and indirect taxation, consumer protection, import and export, administration of justice, and alternate disputes resolution. In these recommendations, the effort has been to focus on the problems and needs of the user groups, apart from the administrative requirements of efficiency, co-ordination and economy.
- The commission has drawn attention to the accumulation of a huge backlog of about 28 million cases. Apart from the improvement of judicial administration, the recommendation is for expanding the system of alternate disputes resolution, its more effective use by extending the establishment of legal

services authority to all states and districts, and use of a self-regulatory mechanism by industry and trade.[3]

According to newsreports, 435 laws have been repealed by parliament. The Repealing and Amending Act, 2001, came into force on 3 September 2001. (*Economic Times*, 26 Apr 2002). During the conference of chief ministers on effective and responsive government held in May 1997 the chief ministers decided to review the laws, regulations and procedures with a view to simplifying them and bringing them up to date. However, in most states, the problem has not even been looked into so far. There are also no reports of any action taken though the Committee on Economic Reforms appointed by the Government of Jammu and Kashmir, under the chairmanship of this author, had recommended such a review by setting up a state law commission. It is to the credit of government of Karnataka that, of the 1760 laws in the state, as many as 1038 have been repealed.[4]

It is rightly said that ignorance of law is no excuse. Very often, though, Acts, rules and regulations are not available in the market on the ground that they are out of print. The Commission on Review of Administrative Laws (COROAL) too has underlined the need for the documentation of a complete set of subordinate legislation and has recommended, 'It is desirable that all information about laws, regulations, procedures, circulars and activities of different departments are made available through the electronic media as well as documented compilations to keep the public and various users fully informed of the latest instructions on various subjects'. The COROAL had also noted that most ministries did not have any information about the rules and regulations issued by state governments by virtue of the authority vested under central laws such as various legislations on labour, Prevention of Food Adulteration Act, Drugs and Cosmetics Act, etc. The COROAL has, therefore,

---

[3] See *Press Note* dated 30 September 1998 issued by the Department of Administrative Reforms, Government of India, New Delhi.
[4] Government of Karnataka, *Karnataka Administrative Reforms Commission, Interim Report*, January 2001, p. 88.

recommended that ministries/departments centrally compile information about all the rules and regulations issued by them and state governments by virtue of the authority vested under central laws.

The non-availability of Acts, rules and regulations was opposed by way of a PIL in the Bombay high court.[5] The petitioners argued that: (i) The state government be directed to make available by publishing and printing adequate number of authenticated copies of the bare Acts, legislations, rules and other statutory instruments having force of law at a reasonable price to the public at large throughout the state. (ii) Respondents be directed to make available adequate number of authenticated copies of the bare Acts, legislations, rules, regulations and other statutory instruments having force of law in the state to all the three benches of the high court of judicature as well as to all the moffusil courts in the state immediately. No affidavit was filed on behalf of the state government. The court observed that if ignorance of law is no excuse, it presupposes that a citizen is able to know the law. The elementary requirement in the country is that the citizen is able to obtain an authenticated copy of the Act, rules, and regulations. The prayer was made absolute. It is not known what follow-up action has been taken by the state government. Perhaps, only a fresh contempt petition will make this clear!

B.K. Nehru has invited attention to yet another facet of the problem. This pertains to the objective of establishing the rule of law in the country. He has said: 'There is no shortage of laws in this country. Every session of parliament adds a dozen or more to them. The British government in India passed no more than a little over 400 laws in the ninety years of their rule between 1857 and 1947. The independent government of India has passed in the forty-four years since Independence almost 5,000 Acts at the centre alone; only a small fraction of them that are

---

[5] *Sanjeev M. Gorwadkar and Another, Petitioners* v. *State of Maharashtra, Union of India, and Others,* Respondents, writ petition No. 5396 of 1996, AIR 1997 Bombay 303.

actually implemented. Every single one of the British laws was implemented; one of the major considerations in enacting a piece of legislation was whether it was possible, given the limitations of the administrative apparatus, to enforce it. If a proposal was such that it would be impossible to enforce it, it was considered preferable not to have it, no matter how desirable, than to bring the whole system of law into disrepute by laws being violated with impunity.'[6]

The existing laws also need to be reviewed from yet another angle. In some laws, such as the Maharashtra Town Planning Act, appellate powers over the decisions of the field officers vest in the ministers. Giving such powers to ministers has politicised the question of removal of encroachments and unauthorised constructions in municipal areas. A minister is expected to give a hearing to the parties concerned and, if considered necessary, to visit the site before giving his decision. The provision to give appellate powers to ministers is archaic and needs to be amended so as to give these powers to senior officers. Thereafter, further appeals must be to the civil courts.

It needs to be examined whether certain kinds of conduct need not be categorised as a crime. In the five decades since Independence, only a few penal laws have been permitted to lapse or been repealed by the government. These include the Terrorist and Disruptive Activities Act (TADA), the Whipping Act and the Criminal Tribes Act. On the other hand, scores of new laws have been enacted which have added immensely to the workload of the police. Though cases under certain Acts such as the Gambling Act, Prohibition Act or Immoral Traffic (Prevention) Act take inordinate amount of police time, the conviction rate is very low and the punishment awarded is negligible. It is necessary to consider whether these activities need be made punishable under law.[7] More reliance will have to be

---

[6] B.K. Nehru, A Fresh Look At the Constitution, in C.K. Jain (ed.), *Constitution of India—In Precept and Practice*, p. 404.

[7] Report by a group of retired police officers on *How To Speed up Police Investigations and Court Trials*, Mimeo, 1998.

placed on community action, public education and social sanctions to eradicate these evils.

Yet another disconcerting fact is that laws are often passed without adequate thought or discussion. The controversial Urban Land Ceiling and Regulation Bill was introduced in the Lok Sabha on 29 January 1976. The Bill was passed by the Lok Sabha on 2 February 1976 and by the Rajya Sabha on 5 February 1976. Within ten days, it was ratified by state legislatures and became a major stumbling block for housing and a goldmine for corruption at all administrative and political levels for decades thereafter!

The other equally worrying aspect is the delay in notifying the laws passed by parliament. The longest delay has been in the notification of the Prasar Bharati Act which was passed by parliament in 1990 and came into effect only in 1997. There has also been a delay in bringing into effect the Family Courts Act. A PIL had to be filed in the Delhi high court to seek the intervention of the court to bring into effect the Delhi Rent Act. The history of the Hire Purchase Act is even more interesting. The government notified on 13 April 1973 that the Act would come into force from 1 June 1973. Another notification was issued that the Act would come into force from 1 August 1973. The government issued yet another notification dated 30 August 1973 rescinding the operation of the Act from 1 September 1973. Thus the Act remained in force for only one month![8]

Amnesty schemes declared under various laws have become counter-productive and tended to encourage people to break the law with impunity. The classic case is that of the amnesty schemes declared under the Income Tax Act. Considering the vast amount of black money in the system and nearly $100 to $200 billion stashed abroad in illegal bank accounts, the response to the amnesty schemes has been negligible. But each successive scheme is made more lenient than the previous one. These schemes have created an attitude of taking the law for granted

---

[8]The Never-never Act, interview with Justice B.P. Jeevan Reddy, Chairman, Law Commission of India, *Times of India*, 23 November 1999.

and breaking the law in a brazen manner. In the process, the rule of law has been seriously undermined. This is evident from the fact that there are only 70,000 assessees who are in the income bracket of Rs 5 lakh to 10 lakh and only 3,000 assessees with an income of over Rs 10 lakh per annum in this country!

The withdrawal of criminal cases is another reason why the rule of law has suffered a set-back. During the regime of the Shiv Sena-BJP (1995–1999), the government of Maharashtra withdrew a number of cases which were pending against Bal Thackeray, the chief of the Shiv Sena. No reasons were assigned in any of these cases. In a PIL filed in the Bombay high court, the advocate general took the position that it was not incumbent on the government to give the reasons for withdrawal of cases. By another decision, the government of Maharashtra withdrew over eleven hundred cases filed under the Scheduled Castes and Scheduled Tribes (Prevention of Atrocities) Act against persons who launched an agitation in connection with the change of the name of the Marathwada University to Babasaheb Ambedkar University. In the same league was the decision of the Kalyan Singh government in the UP to withdraw all cases against those who participated in the Ram Janmabhoomi-Babri Masjid agitation in 1990. The question which needs to be asked is: why have laws at all if they are to be flouted in such a flagrant manner? How can any government be expected to govern if it has no respect for the rule of law?

The mindset of demeaning the law is further strengthened by the extraordinary provision in section 438 of the Criminal Procedure Code regarding anticipatory bail. This provision was inserted in 1973 to prevent influential and rich persons from trying to implicate their rivals in false cases with a view to disgrace them by getting them arrested. This objective of assisting the rich and the powerful preferentially can itself be questioned in a democracy. Provision for anticipatory bail does not exist in advanced and more mature democracies such as the UK and US. The provision of anticipatory bail has many adverse effects on the investigation of important cases. When anticipatory bail is granted, the psychological impact of arrest and interrogation in police custody is lost. A full bench of the Punjab and Haryana high court in the *Gurubaksh Singh* v. *State of Punjab* case had observed that the very purpose of arrest and remand in police custody is to allow the investigating officer to interrogate the accused in isolation, a delicate and expert job in which relative isolation of the accused is one of the most important contributing factors. It is only rich and influential people who have been taking advantage of this provision to avoid arrest and frustrate successful investigation. It is therefore in the public interest to delete this provision altogether.[9]

The scant respect for law is seen again and again in the pronouncements and actions of certain sections of society. Bal Thackeray, Shiv Sena chief, has publicly and repeatedly warned that Maharashtra will be in flames if any action was taken to implement the recommendations of the Srikrishna Commission of Inquiry into the Mumbai riots in 1992–93. In a public speech in November 1997 he encouraged people to kill the dacoits and assured them that they should not worry about any action by the police as there would be none. (*Sakal*, 21 Nov 1997). Taxi operators and transporters have repeatedly gone on strike to deter the government from taking any action against polluting vehicles. Milk vendors have resorted to mass action and have poured their milk on the road in protest against government action to stop milk adulteration. Petrol pump owners have resorted to strikes to pressurise the government not to take any action against them for adulteration of petrol, diesel and other products. Government employees have taken to the streets to protest against the launching of cases under the Prevention of Corruption Act against some of them.

This contagion has caught on even at higher levels of the bureaucracy. The municipal commissioners in Maharashtra have suggested to the state government that, wherever possible, encroachments in municipal areas should be regularised by the levy of a suitable fine rather than by the demolition of unauthorised structures. In such a social milieu, the rule of law

---

[9] Report by a group of retired police officers, *op cit.*, pp. 13–14.

has been the first casualty. How to reverse this trend is one of the most serious challenges facing the country. Unless the rule of law is re-established in the country, the very survival of a civilised society is in danger.

## World Shrouded in Secrecy

Sir Arnold Robinson, fictional cabinet secretary in the television series *Yes Minister* says, 'Open government is a contradiction in terms. You can be open or you can have government'. James Callaghan, former British home secretary, had observed in his evidence before the Franks committee, 'You know the difference between leaking and briefing. Briefing is what I do and leaking is what you do'. A Russian diplomat is reported to have commented, 'In India, there are three kinds of secrets—secret, top secret and open secret'. These statements, though made in a lighter vein, aptly sum up how the government works under the rigorous regime of the Official Secrets Act.

The Official Secrets Act, 1923, has held sway over the functioning of the government since colonial days. The 'catch-all' section 5 of the Act has not been invoked too often but 'its deterrent effect is pervasive and it is invoked no sooner skeletons in the official cupboard are disturbed. Secrecy is an inseparable companion of abuse of power and indeed of repression'.[10] Quoting Justice Polak, Justice K.K. Mathew stated in a Supreme Court case (1979(3) SCC), 'The secrecy system has become much less a means by which government protects national security than a means by which government safeguards its reputation, dissembles its purpose, buries its mistakes, manipulates its citizens, maximises its power and corrupts itself'.

Repeated suggestions have been made to amend, if not repeal, the Act altogether. The Press Council of India (PCI) had, *inter alia*, recommended that 'the Act should be repealed in toto. Amending or remodelling section 5 will not serve the purpose. It is no use amending the bad law. It is better to start on a clean

[10] A.G. Noorani, Secrets Act: An Anachronism, *Indian Express*, 31 July 1987.

slate. The psychological implication of having an Official Secrets Act is that secrecy in the functioning of the government is a rule... The Act is thus repugnant to the concept of open government and also militates against the ethos of the Constitutional guarantee of freedom of speech and expression enshrined in Article 19(1)(a).' The PCI had further recommended that, 'The provisions regarding espionage such as those contained in sections 3, 4, etc. of the existing Official Secrets Act, 1923 should be re-enacted with necessary adaptations to changed circumstances, as a separate legislation'.[11] However, even the traditionally accepted, much more restrictive, ambit of an official secrets legislation needs to be looked into carefully as it goes to the heart of governance. Otherwise, as rightly warned by K. Subrahmanyam, it may become a ritualistic exercise.[12] This is worthy of some serious thought.

Even in matters pertaining to defence, there must be limits to secrecy. Thus, for example, there is no reason why the procedures followed in making defence purchases need be kept secret. The purchases of defence equipment by any country do not remain secret any longer as all this information is readily available in various well known international defence journals and publications. While the information pertaining to the deployment of weapons and equipment must be kept a secret, their purchase, and particularly the manner in which this was effected should not be permitted to be treated as a secret. This is amply clear after the scandals associated with almost all high value defence purchases over the years.

The circumstances leading to the loss of a large number of Indian Air Force fighter planes in accidents is a scandal which has been kept from the people in the name of official secrecy. According to some reports, since 1991, as many as 190 aircraft, involving thousands of crores of rupees, have been lost due to accidents. More than 85 pilots have lost their lives in these

[11] Press Council of India, *Annual Report (April 1, 1990–March 31, 1991)*, New Delhi, p. 329.

[12] K. Subrahmanyam, For A Transparent India, *Economic Times*, 15 May 1997.

accidents. From 6 May 2001 to 3 May 2002 itself, twelve MiG 21 planes were involved in accidents leading to the death of five pilots. If this had happened in the civilian sector, all hell would have broken loose. But, in the name of defence secrets, all this has been kept away from public scrutiny. Finally, a PIL has been fited in Rajasthan high court to phase out these planes.

Secrecy in matters pertaining to the peaceful use of nuclear energy must similarly be put on a different footing as it concerns the safety of civilian lives. This is particularly important in the context of the declaration by the government to produce 20,000 MW of power from nuclear power plants by the year 2020. This issue came to the forefront in the context of the serious apprehensions regarding the safety of the nuclear installations expressed by A. Gopalkrishnan, former chairman of the atomic energy regulatory board (AERB). The annual report of AERB for 1995 had listed 130 safety violations in various nuclear installations. Two PILs were filed in this behalf in the Bombay high court. The petitions, *inter alia*, urged the court to quash section 18 of the Nuclear Energy Act which gives a shield of secrecy to all information regarding nuclear installations. The government of India took the position that this information was secret and that a committee was being appointed to look into the matter. Unfortunately, this contention was upheld by the court and the PILs were dismissed. (*Times of India*, 2 Feb 1997). It is significant to note that Gopalakrishnan has reiterated that excessive secrecy in the department of atomic energy (DAE) and the inability of AERB to function independently compromised the safety of nuclear installations in India. 'With a captive AERB from which the DAE can, in effect, withhold information as they wish, coupled with the shelter the DAE enjoys through invoking "national security" bogey and the Official Secrets Act, we are likely to face a serious nuclear accident in the not-too-distant future', (*sic*) he has warned. (*Times of India*, 22 Oct 1999). Unfortunately, even this warning has made no difference regarding greater transparency and accountability in the nuclear energy field.

The former Chief of Army Staff, General V.N. Sharma and

other retired senior officers of the defence services have criticised the government for continuing to keep secret records of past army operations, which are due for declassification, saying this would harm future battle preparedness. Thus the records of the 1962, 1965 and 1971 operations continue to be secret. The K. Subrahmanyam committee which was appointed to go into what went wrong in dealing with the Kargil situation submitted its report in January 2000. It was a refreshing change to see the government placing a summary of the report before parliament at its very next session. Unfortunately, the reports of the four task forces, appointed as a follow up of the Kargil committee report, which were submitted to the government in August 2000 have been kept secret. This is in spite of the fact that the task forces on internal security, border management and the defence set up had made a categorical recommendation that their reports be made public.[13] However, it is to the credit of the government that the report of the group of ministers on the recommendations of the four task forces was placed before parliament in February 2001.

As S.L. Rao has brought out, unlike in the United States, the details of Indian defence expenditure are a secret... It would be logical to evaluate the efficiency of the expenditure, and the relative efficiencies of the different expenditure items. But it is impossible to do so. Expenditure details are not available, nor are the performance evaluations of the various items on which it is spent.[14] As brought out in chapter 2, the defence ministry and the parliamentary standing committee on defence are involved in a tug of war over disclosure of the report of the committee on defence expenditure said to contain 'sensitive and controversial recommendations'. (*Business Standard*, 9 Sep 1995). This frustration is also shared by S.S. Gill who has observed, 'It is a pity that in India it has become taboo to criticise the armed forces even on vital matters of national interest. This has not only distorted the civil-military perspective,

---

[13]This author was the chairman of the task force on border management.
[14]S.L. Rao, Defence in the Economy, *Economic Times*, 5 October 1998.

but also enabled the defence forces to evade parliamentary scrutiny and get away with colossal waste'.[15] This universal concern (outside the defence establishment) was also expressed in an editorial in the *Economic Times*, which has noted, 'India already spends over Rs 50,000 crore on its armed forces, much of it inefficiently. Instead of shovelling out more money, the new government should increase the efficiency of defence spending'.[16]

The secrecy issue came to the fore in the case pertaining to the dismissal of Naval Chief, Admiral Vishnu Bhagwat, in December 1998. This was the first time that the chief of any of the armed forces of the country had been so summarily sent home by the government. Even in such an important matter which concerned the morale and the prestige and position of the services, the government took refuge behind the Official Secrets Act, and in the process severely undermined its own credibility. The PILs filed on the subject were also dismissed by the Delhi and Bombay high courts. It is disheartening to see that, in all cases involving defence and the security of the country, the inclination of the courts, generally, is to give the benefit of the doubt to the government rather than independently arrive at a judgement on the basis of tenable evidence.

The other holy cow, which is generally treated as a legitimate subject of any official secrets, is the intelligence apparatus. It is time even this were reviewed. As V. Balachandran, former special secretary of the research and analysis wing (RAW), has brought out, anything connected with intelligence, even the postal address of their offices, is taboo in India...Most of our intelligence agencies operate without any well-defined charter, much less by way of legal sanction, often poaching on other's turf. There is no oversight worth the name and consequently no accountability. We are yet to know why our intelligence agencies could not prevent the Rajiv Gandhi assassination despite having some electronic intercepts in their possession earlier.[17]

[15]S.S. Gill, *The Dynasty—A Political Biography of the Premier Ruling Family of Modern India*, Harper Collins, New Delhi, 1996, p. 479.

[16]The editorial, 'Foresight, please!', *Economic Times*, 12 October 1999.

[17]V. Balachandran, Intelligence Reform, *Pioneer*, 27 April 1998.

In yet another perceptive article, V. Balachandran has underlined that since 1947, US intelligence agencies have been investigated by 12 commissions, five presidential and seven congressional, the last being the 1995–96 Harold Brown Congressional Commission. [After the 9/11 terrorist attack, committees of Congress and Senate are going into the role and inadequacies of the US intelligence agencies.] As against this, anything to do with the government in India is 'restricted' either in the 'public interest' or on 'security considerations'.[18]

Interestingly, a retired secretary of RAW, A.K. Verma, has expressed similar reservations regarding the present state of affairs. He has rightly emphasised that the intelligence [agency] itself should not be left to set its own agenda and priorities... Ideally, intelligence has always enjoyed a great deal of autonomy. But implicit in that feature is the need for self-regulation and self-accountability. What checks exist to ensure that such a demanding code of conduct is adhered to?[19]

In such a milieu, it is not surprising that these agencies are brazenly used by the ruling party for its own purposes. A shocking instance of this is brought out, in his characteristically forthright manner, by B.K. Nehru during his term as Governor of Jammu and Kashmir: 'The funds [to bring down the government of chief minister Farooq Abdullah] were provided by my friend Tirath Ram Amla, a staunch and tried Congress worker, and were supplied to him in cash from Congress party money in Delhi, transported in mail pouches of the Intelligence Bureau. The use of official machinery for party purposes had by then become so commonplace that it did not call for any eyebrows to be even slightly raised.'[20]

Understandably, there is widespread suspicion that the intelligence agencies are used by the government to keep a watch

---

[18] V. Balachandran, Perils of Government Secrecy, *Economic and Political Weekly*, 25 September 1999, p. 2793.

[19] A.K. Verma, Lift the iron curtain on the intelligence agencies, *Times of India*, 6 May 1997.

[20] B.K. Nehru, *op cit.*, p. 627.

on its political opponents. In fact, the very creation of RAW is ascribed to the desire of then prime minister Indira Gandhi to have an intelligence set-up directly under her charge. The Shah Commission of Enquiry in its report on Emergency excesses has brought out how intelligence agencies were misused by the then Congress government. This is corroborated by the account given by Vengala Rao, former chief minister of Andhra Pradesh, in his autobiography where he tells how a letter written by an MLA to Sanjeeva Reddy, then President of India, was intercepted by the intelligence agencies.[21]

The country has never been taken into confidence even in a case such as that of Rattan Sehgal, then Additional Director of Intelligence Bureau (IB), who was asked to resign in November 1996 for his unauthorised contacts with American intelligence operatives. Commenting on the episode, T.S. Kasturi has highlighted that the nation deserves an explanation for the conduct of a government agency that spends most of its time keeping tabs on political opponents of the government in office.[22] As *Frontline* magazine had brought out, the real implications of the Sehgal affair go beyond diplomacy. They have a crucial bearing on the state of health of the IB and on India's intelligence apparatus...There is an urgent need for public and parliamentary scrutiny of the IB's working.[23]

B.N. Mullick, the longest serving Director of the Intelligence Bureau has, in his memoirs, revealed some of the ways in which secret funds of the IB were spent. Writing about the arrest and detention of Sheikh Abdullah, Mullick writes, 'The leading accused like Sheikh Abdullah and Afzal Beg were enjoying all the facilities in the special jail. Their families were paid

---

[21]Review of the book, Naa Jeevitha Katha (Telugu) by Jalagam Vengala Rao, An Account of A.P. Politics from J. Vengala Rao's Autobiography, *Frontline*, 4 October 1996, p. 75.

[22]T.S. Kasturi, Wheels Within Wheels, *Financial Express*, 26 January 1997.

[23]Praveen Swami, The Rattan Sehgal Affair, Questions Over India's Intelligence Apparatus, *Frontline*, 21 March 1997, pp. 49–51.

handsome allowance; all the educational expenses of their sons in colleges were met and they lived like Nawab's sons...'[24]

The brief account of the issues pertaining to intelligence agencies shows how wrong it would be to continue to keep these agencies outside the scrutiny of parliament and the public. Even in advanced Western democracies these agencies no longer enjoy such protection. The same is also true of external relations. India's involvement in Sri Lanka's ethnic strife proved to be its 'Vietnam'. It is best that the sordid story of our training of LTTE cadres, and provision of arms, ammunition and financial help to them is forgotten but not without learning lessons for the future. Thus even traditionally accepted subjects such as defence, national security, intelligence agencies or external relations must not be permitted to escape parliamentary and public scrutiny in the name of 'national interest' or 'public interest'. While formulating a new law on official secrets this must be the bottom line.

It is not just the above areas which are considered top secret in common government parlance. In India, there is an obsession with secrecy regarding anything pertaining to the government and its functionaries. Not surprisingly, during the field visits of Balasaheb Desai, the home minister of Maharashtra in the early 1960s, police wireless messages marked secret were sent regarding the menu for his meals. The government of India manual which deals with classification of papers lays down that anything which is likely to cause embarrassment to the government should be marked secret. *Nyaya Vyavahar Kosh*, a glossary of legal terms in Marathi compiled by the government of Maharashtra, is classified 'confidential'.

Lal Bahadur Shastri's letters to US President Lyndon Johnson are easily available in American archives but they are still treated as secret in India. Recently declassified US State Department papers of the Kennedy era reveal official confirmation of the tacit acceptance by both India and Pakistan of the de-facto partition

---

[24]B.N. Mullick, *My Years With Nehru—Kashmir*, Allied Publishers, Bombay, 1971, p. 94.

of Kashmir along the line of control. The corresponding papers in India are still secret. Arun Shourie had to rely on the India Office Library and the Public Records Office in London to write some portions of his book *Worshipping False Gods*.[25] According to a newsreport, Jawaharlal Nehru, as prime minister, had refused the offer of permanent membership of the UN Security Council for India in 1955. (*Sakal*, 26 Nov 2001). After nearly fifty years, the people have a right to know how this decision was made, whether the matter went to the cabinet and whether the far-reaching implications thereof were analysed and appreciated fully by the decision-makers then.

Even matters which are extremely relevant to the public interest are treated as secret and a privilege is claimed by the government in court proceedings. The most scandalous instance of its kind was the plea by the government of Maharashtra, in a PIL, to treat as secret the official findings in respect of the death of nearly 4,000 tribal children due to malnutrition in Melghat. Fortunately, the high court overruled the plea and made the report available to the petitioners.

It is absurd that the state and central government have refused to share secret information even with the judicial commissions appointed by it. This was seen in the case of the Jain Commission appointed by the centre to look into the assassination of Rajiv Gandhi. This was also true in respect of the Srikrishna Commission appointed to inquire into the Mumbai riots in December 1992–January 1993, following the demolition of the Babri Masjid. It was the same in the case of the Gundewar Commission appointed by the government of Maharashtra to inquire into the riots and public firing following the desecration of the statue of Babasaheb Ambedkar in Mumbai. If judicial commissions are to be denied information in this manner, why appoint them at all? Is this stand in keeping with the Official Secrets Act?

Irfan Habib, former chairman, Indian Council of Historical

---

[25]See Acknowledgements in Arun Shourie, *Worshipping False Gods, Ambedkar and the Facts which have been Erased*, ASA Publications, New Delhi, 1997.

Research, has revealed that the home ministry rejected his request, made at the behest of Professor S. Gopal, that the full text of the pre-1947 intelligence reports be made available to the editors of the 'Towards Freedom' volumes. 'We were asked to be satisfied with the official (and doubtless sanitised) summaries provided to the National Archives of India', he states.[26] The Reserve Bank of India (RBI) is one of the most opaque institutions in the country. While a certain amount of secrecy in a central bank is understandable, the RBI is excessively so. This is also true of banks in India. The non-performing assets of banks which have crossed Rs 100,000 crore led to sharp divisions regarding the future course of action. The Verma committee appointed by the RBI as also the task force appointed by the CII have, in their reports, suggested a series of steps including closure of some banks (recommended by the task force), reduction in staff, freeze on wages and so on. This led to the demand by employees unions that the lists of defaulters of bank loans of over Rs 10 lakh each be published so as to bring moral pressure on the defaulters to pay their dues promptly. At long last, the parliament has passed the Securitisation and Reconstruction of Financial Assets and Enforcement of Security Interest Act, 2002.

Railway accidents have become a matter of serious concern in recent years. According to some reports, during the 1990s nearly 4,000 persons lost their lives in such accidents as compared to nearly 2,500 persons in the 1980s. According to some estimates, a train derails somewhere in the country six days a week. The 25,000 unmanned railway crossings see at least one accident every fifth day. Over two-thirds of the accidents are caused by human failure. More than 400 accidents took place in 1998–99 but the report of the Railway Safety Review Committee said that the number is manipulated, and it is actually over 1,000 (*Indian Express*, 16 Sep 1999). Against this background, it is shocking to see that there has been no discussion in parliament and the media on the reports of the enquiries into these accidents.

[26] See 'Letters' in *Frontline*, 3 October 1997, pp. 109–110.

Clearly, wide publicity needs to be given to the findings of these reports and particularly the remedial actions suggested therein.

A newsreport brings out that upset over media reports on various decisions taken by then railway minister Mamata Banerjee and her differences with bureaucrats, the railway ministry tried to muzzle the media. A circular was issued to officers in the ministry cautioning them that they would be liable to imprisonment of up to three years or fine, or both, under section 5 of the Official Secrets Act of 1923 if they 'unauthorisedly' parted with information. (*Times of India*, 25 Feb 2000).

The World Bank has charged that India treats data like state secrets. 'Access to existing data remains highly restricted. For example, few researchers have received permission to analyse national sample survey organisation data at the unit-record level. There are an enormous number of urgent questions which could be investigated if such data were accessible, and there is certainly no shortage of well-qualified researchers in India who could undertake such studies'. (*Economic Times*, 27 Aug 1997). In a sense, all these problems arise only because of the sheer volume of data. In the 1960s, when Britain was plagued by balance of payment problems, a journalist asked the chancellor of the exchequer why the nation had fared so much better in the days of Queen Victoria, 'Ah', he replied, 'back then, we didn't have any statistics'!

The government keeps secrets not only from the public but also from the President of the country in whose name technically government business is carried out. This is exposed in the memoirs of Giani Zail Singh, former President of India. Referring to the anti-Sikh riots in Delhi following the assassination of Indira Gandhi, he writes, 'It is strange that after the evening of 1 November, I did not receive any call from the victims, nor could I contact anyone. The telephone lines had been doctored by the authorities. I came to know later that there was a spate of calls from persons under attack, but they could not reach me. Their desperate cries for help were falling in wilderness. (pp. 208–209)... The government chose to withhold

the reports of the commissions of inquiry from the President...
I drew the Prime Minister's attention to the fact that lately
certain reports of commissions of inquiry received by the
government had not been furnished to me even though my
secretariat had written to the home ministry on three occasions
to convey my desire for perusal of the reports...I told the Prime
Minister that I wanted these reports in the discharge of the
obligations cast on me by the Constitution...No action was
taken by anyone in the government to send me the reports...I
often thought that if they could treat the President in such a
manner, what would be the fate of a common citizen. It caused
me hurt when the Prime Minister said that my request was being
examined. (pp. 232–233)...I asked him [Prime Minister] about
the reports of the IB, which had suddenly stopped being sent to
me. Though the supply of weekly reports had been resumed after
I had insisted on it, the daily reports were still a casualty...I drew
his attention to the reports received from our ambassadors in
other countries which used to be made available to the President
for his persual, the flow of which had also been stopped. The
Prime Minister said these were secret reports which could not
be sent... Rajiv Gandhi's observations about the Thakkar
Commission's Report were quite upsetting. Even the Cabinet
had not seen the report of Justice Thakkar, he claimed, and thus
it was not necessary to show it to the President. I told PM that
I differed from this perception... When I asked the Prime
Minister for some intelligence reports for my persual and
information, he had minuted on my communication that the
matter would be examined'. (pp. 249–251).[27] It is well known
that there were serious differences between the first President of
India, Rajendra Prasad and prime minister Jawaharlal Nehru
regarding powers of the President. The President was to deliver
a major speech on the subject in the Indian Law Institute in
Delhi. An advance copy of the speech was seen by the prime
minister who was upset on reading it and decided to attend the

[27]*Memoirs of Giani Zail Singh, The Seventh President of India*, Har-Anand Publicatons Pvt. Ltd., New Delhi, 1997.

function personally. Mysteriously, copies of the speech were never distributed to the audience. Nor were any copies kept on record. (*Sakal*, 26 Jan 1997). What a way to write history!

The rulers often believe that they alone know what is in the public interest. This is attested to by the statement of the then Kerala chief minister E.K. Nayanar that he had been deliberately giving doctored information to the media regarding the law and order situation in the state and that he would continue to do so in the future as well!

In yet another strange case, even the national crime investigating agency, namely, the CBI has been refused access to certain papers pertaining to investigation in the Bofors case on the ground that they are secret! According to newsreports, the CBI has asked for declassification of defence ministry files relating to the Bofors gun deal as many of the witnesses and suspects parried vital questions during their examination, advancing the excuse that the information was classified. (*Times of India*, 5 May 1997). According to yet another report, the CBI has planned to approach the Lok Sabha speaker for permission to gain access to the documents at the disposal the joint parliamentary committee on Bofors. (*Times of India*, 9 May 1997).

The practice of secrecy has now afflicted even the private sector in this country. It was shocking to see the cricket control board of India keeping the Chandrachud committee report on match-fixing a secret! The report was finally released by the board only after persistent public demand made the central government ask the board to release the report.

Finally, we lack a clear policy on the release of old government records for the information of the public. There is no obligation on the government to release all records at the expiry of thirty years. A huge number of records still remain locked up in government record rooms on the grounds that they are sensitive, secret or top secret. Several records of the freedom movement have still not been released. In the absence of access to authentic information, what kind of history are we going to write? Even records available to a researcher in London, Tokyo or USA are not available to a researcher in India.

It is necessary that the time limit of thirty years for the release of records is reduced to fifteen or twenty years. An institutionalised arrangement is needed for the declassification and release of records every five years so that as much as possible is released for public persual soon after the relevant file is closed. There is also a need to set up a standing high-level records commission to carefully examine the records which need to be kept confidential after the stipulated period. Such a commission must comprise respected people in various walks of life, apart from senior government officers. Fortunately, for the first time in the country, a lead in this matter has been taken by the government of Maharashtra in the ordinance on the right to information issued on 23 September 2002.

Finally, apart from repealing the Official Secrets Act and substituting it with a much more restrictive law, it is also necessary to amend the Third Schedule of the Constitution which, *inter alia*, lays down the format for the oath or affirmation of secrecy. It says, '...I will not directly or indirectly communicate or reveal to any person or persons any matter which shall be brought under my consideration or shall become known to me as a minister for the Union except as may be required for the due discharge of my duties as such minister.' It is necessary to restrict the oath of secrecy only in such matters as defence and national security which may fall within the purview of the new Official Secrets Act. In all other matters, a minister must be duty bound to give all information to the people. Government servants' conduct rules also need to be amended accordingly.

### Right to Information: Unending Struggle[28]

After dithering for years, the parliament finally passed the Freedom of Information Bill, in December 2002. This will have to be considered an achievement in itself! But, the struggle is far

---

[28] Partly based on the article written by this author in the *Economic and Political Weekly*, August 12–18, 2000, p. 2899.

from over. In fact, it has just started as the Bill, presented in parliament, hardly did justice to the cause. Some of the major deficiencies are given below.

The very title of the Bill is questionable. It is well established that the right to information is a fundamental right. The statement of objects and reasons (SOR) enclosed with the Bill states that 'the proposed Bill is in accord with both article 19 of the Constitution as well as article 19 of the Universal Declaration of Human Rights'. The NCRWC has, in fact, recommended that Article 19(1) of the Constitution is amended to make the right to information explicit. There is therefore no question of watering it down to mere freedom of information given at the whim and fancy of a government functionary. What is given by the Constitution cannot be diluted by a statute. The objective of the Bill should be to operationalise the right to information given by the Constitution. The Bill should, therefore, more appropriately be titled the Right to Information Bill and not the Freedom of Information Bill, as proposed by the government.

Paragraph 5 of the SOR states that the Freedom of Information Act will be consistent with the objective of having a stable, honest, transparent and efficient government. It is not clear how the Act is expected to contribute to the stability of the government. The word 'stable' in the second last line of paragraph 5 of the SOR should therefore be deleted.

The next question is to whom should the proposed Act apply? Ideally, it should apply to all sections of society and not just the governmental sector as provided in the Bill. The private sector, registered societies, charitable and other trusts, and other organisations which are registered under any state or central law must be covered by the provisions of the proposed Act because the right to information needs to be exercised with reference to all such entities. This is particularly relevant in the context of the expanding role of the private sector and the impending downsizing of the government. It is not just governmental bureaucracy which is impervious and unresponsive to people's grievances. The private sector is as much, if not more wooden-headed and lethargic. There is no reason why non-governmental organisations (NGOs), charitable trusts or trade unions should not be as accountable and transparent as the government in a democracy. The ambit of the Bill therefore needs to be expanded to cover all sections of society.

In the very preamble of the Bill, it is stated that freedom of information has to be 'consistent with public interest'. The concept of public interest can prove to be a dangerous one in the hands of the government. Why should it be left to the government to decide what is in the public interest? It is worth noting that all denial of information so far and the rigours of the secrecy law in force have also been justified by the government in 'public interest'. Once it is accepted that the right to information is a fundamental right, the question of it being in the public interest or otherwise does not arise. It is therefore suggested that the words, 'consistent with the public interest' appearing in the preamble of the Bill be deleted.

Considering the resistance to the enactment of a law on the subject so far, it is necessary to ensure that the Bill will be brought into force as soon as possible after it is passed by parliament. A explained earlier, this urgency amply springs from the experience of unconscionable delays in the past in issuing requisite gazette notifications to give effect to a number of Acts passed by parliament. It is therefore necessary to provide explicitly in section 5(3) of the Bill that the Act shall come into force on the expiry of three months from the date of its passage by parliament.

The construction in section 3, 'Subject to the provisions of this Act, all citizens shall have freedom of information' is clumsy and meaningless. As stated earlier, the Constitution itself recognises the right to information as one of the fundamental rights. There is therefore no need to provide for freedom of information separately. The Bill should instead recognise the Constitutional sanctity of the right to information and should state that it is meant to operationalise that right.

Section 4 deals with the obligations of public authorities to furnish certain information *suo motu* periodically. As compared to the earlier drafts circulated for soliciting informal reactions as also the recommendations of the Shourie Committee, the provision is much more restrictive and needs to be liberalised to give freedom to various offices to review their own interactions with the public and to provide *suo motu* as much additional information as they deem necessary from time to time. The whole objective must be to make the Act, by and large, redundant in terms of the need for a person to approach government offices for information.

Section 4(e) states that certain information pertaining to the proposed projects may be made available to the persons affected or likely to be affected by the project, in particular, 'in the best interest of maintenance of democratic principles'. It is suggested that the words, 'and the canons of natural justice' may be added at the end of the sub-section after the word 'principles'. It is also proposed that the word 'maintenance' be substituted by 'promotion'.

Section 6 contains a welcome new provision to enable making requests for information through the electronic media. It may be provided that in such cases, wherever feasible, replies, including intimation regarding the quantum of fees to be remitted by the applicant, may also be sent by the electronic media. This will save considerable time and effort in transmitting of information.

Section 8 of the Bill relates to exemption from disclosure of information. This section deserves the most careful scrutiny. It contains exemptions marked (a) to (g). Most of these sub-clauses contain several exemptions lumped together under one sub-clause. Thus, in effect, there are very many more exemptions than may appear at first glance. Each one of these exemptions needs to be discussed and analysed fully to understand all the implications. Just a few of them are discussed below.

The proposed exemption regarding 'conduct of international relations' contained in 8(a) looks innocuous on the face of it but, as past experience shows, excessive secrecy in such matters may be against the national interest. This was amply borne out by our ill-advised involvement in Sri Lankan affairs during the regimes of Indira Gandhi and Rajiv Gandhi. Section 8(c) refers to 'information, the disclosure of which would prejudicially affect the conduct of Centre-State relations'. It is not clear what kind of information is proposed to be covered in this provision and why these matters need to be held back from the public at all. This is particularly so in a country with a federal structure. Sub-sections (d) and (e) refer to cabinet papers, internal notings on a file, advice tendered by ministers and officers and so on. There is no justification for keeping these matters under wraps once a decision is reached on any matter. The public should have a right to know the basis on which a decision has been reached. There should be no reason to keep the advice given by anyone and noted on files a secret. If such matters are to be kept secret, the whole purpose of passing the legislation will be defeated. It is necessary to note that there are generally two kinds of officers in the bureaucracy. The first category, which is now an endangered species, comprises officers who are objective, fearless, apolitical and upright and are not afraid to give their free and frank advice dispassionately. Such officers will be happy if their advice is made public. But, a great many others, who are prone to crawl when asked to bend and are happy to give advice as suits the requirements of their political masters, obviously would not like their advice to become public at any time. If administration is to be made accountable and transparent, undue secrecy in these matters has to be ended. For obvious reasons, both the bureaucracy and the ruling political elite find it convenient to perpetuate the existing culture of secrecy.

Similarly, the provision pertaining to commercial secrets contained in section 8(f) appears innocuous. It will be recalled that this very justification was invoked to keep back from the people the power purchase agreement between the government of Maharashtra and Enron. The disastrous consequences of this are well known and have become a major talking point against India.

Thus, in all matters pertaining to exemptions, the overriding concern must be to safeguard national and public interest. It will be dangerous to ignore our past experience in these matters and all exemptions proposed in the Bill deserve to be looked into afresh in this light. Substantial changes are necessary in this section if the basic purpose of the proposed Act is not to be frustrated.

It is also necessary to make an overriding provision in the Bill that any information which cannot be denied to parliament and state legislature will have to be made available under the proposed Act.

Section 8(2) contains a welcome provision that, 'Any information relating to any occurrence, event or matter which has taken place, occurred or happened twenty-five years before the date on which any request is made under section 6 shall be provided to any person making a request under that section'. This automatically provides protection from public disclosure to all secret and confidential papers for a period of twenty-five years. First, this period is too long and needs to be reduced to fifteen years. Second, there should also be reviews of such papers every five years so as to release those which need not be retained for a longer period. Third, there should a Records Commission comprising eminent public figures, academics and senior government officers to review such matters and the decision of the commission should be final, unless it is set aside by the minister in charge of the subject concerned for reasons to be recorded in writing. Fourth, all powers retained by the government under the proviso to this sub-section—'Provided that where any question arises as to the date from which the said period of twenty-five years has to be computed, the decision of the Central Government shall be final'—should be entrusted to the Records Commission.

Section 9 relates to the grounds for refusal to access to information in certain cases. Sub-section (d) thereof pertains to requests [which] 'relate to information which would cause unwarranted invasion of the privacy of any person'. A reference may be made in this context to the proviso to section 11 which states that, 'Provided that except in the case of trade or commercial secrets protected by law, disclosure may be allowed if the public interest in disclosure outweighs in importance any possible harm or injury to the interests of such third party'. A proviso along similar lines needs to be incorporated into section 9 to ensure that public interest is not compromised.

Section 11 pertains to third party information. It provides for calling for representation, if any, from the third party against furnishing of any information. The time period proposed to be given to the third party to make such a representation is fifty days. This is too long and needs to be reduced to thirty days.

As brought out in section 12, appeal is to be preferred to such authority as may be prescribed by rules separately. This is all very well but it is necessary to note that appeals must be to authorities nearest to the applicant's home. It is hoped that appeals will not have to be filed to the state government. It will be difficult for individual applicants to visit state headquarters to pursue their appeals.

Section 14 states that, 'The Provisions of Official Secrets Act, 1923, and every other Act in force shall cease to be operative to the extent to which they are inconsistent with the provisions of this Act'. This is fine but it is necessary to add the words, 'Rules and Manuals' after the words 'every other Act' to ensure that even if no action is taken expeditiously by the government to amend the rules and manuals which are in contravention of the provisions of the Freedom of Information Act, such provisions will cease to have any effect from the date the Act comes into effect.

Section 15 states that, 'No court shall entertain any suit, application or other proceedings in respect of any order made under this Act and no such order shall be called in question otherwise than by way of an appeal under this Act'. The purpose of this provision is not clear. It would seem to imply that a citizen will be only left with the remedy of writ petitions to the high court. Such a course of action is costly. Section 15 therefore needs to be deleted. It should be left to the discretion of a court to admit any civil suit, keeping in mind the fact that the law provides for its own separate appellate procedure.

The Shourie Committee report as also the earlier draft Bills prepared by the government contained a provision for setting up freedom of information councils at the centre and in each state to oversee the implementation of the Act. This very worthwhile provision has been deleted in the Bill introduced in parliament. As a result, there will be no institutional mechanisms or forums for periodically reviewing the implementation of the Act. This is a retrograde step. Such councils need to be set up not only at the central and state level but also at district levels to push the speedy implementation of the Act.

Reference must be made to two other deficiencies in the Bill. It does not contain any provision for imposing penalty on employees for contravention of its provisions. This casts serious doubts on the efficacy of the proposed legislation. Second, both appeals provided in the Bill are only to the higher officers. At least the final appeal should to be an outside, independent agency.

It is interesting to note that during the last five years of extensive discussions on the Bill, the position of the central government has remained unaltered, in so far as the basic features of the Bill are concerned, irrespective of which political party/parties were in power. During this period, the centre was ruled by two United Front governments as well as the BJP and its allies. It is even more interesting to note that it seems to make no difference to the fortunes of the legislation on right to information no matter which political party is in power in a state government. It is not therefore surprising that the Act on the subject passed in Tamil Nadu governed by DMK and its allies has hardly anything to commend itself. The same was true of the Act passed in Maharashtra in July–August 2000 which is ruled by a coalition of two Congress parties and several other parties. It is disconcerting to see that in this important area of governance, the interests of bureaucracy and the ruling political elite seem to converge against the empowerment of the common man. After fifty years of Independence, there can be no more eloquent commentary on our democracy!

The Bill as above was introduced in parliament and considered by the standing committee. While the committee, in its report submitted in July 2001, accepted a few of the above points made before it by this author and some others it had remitted back a number of major issues to the ministry of personnel for consideration.[29] Unfortunately, the Bill, as passed by parliament, suffers from a number of these weaknesses and shows how superficial is the commitment of the political parties in the country to the empowerment of the people. Reference must be made in this context to the Maharashtra Right to Information Ordinance referred to earlier. It was credible that, in response to persistent criticism, the government of Maharashtra agreed to repeal its earlier very retrograde law on the subject and set up a committee under the law minister to redraft the law. This author was also a member of the committee. The government has accepted all the recommendations of the committee except for one point. The committee had recommended that the administrative wings of the legislature, judiciary and the Governor's office should also be covered by the proposed Bill. However, all these three institutions objected and as a result, these institutions have been omitted in the ordinance. This is indeed a big setback and a major disappointment but, except for this one point, the ordinance passed by the government of Maharashtra can be called a model and contains all the features which one would look for in such a legislation.

### Good Governance—A Distant Dream?[30]

At the outset, it needs to be appreciated that the concept of good governance covers more than mere administrative reforms in the conventional sense of the term. Good governance has much to do with ethical grounding and firm adherence to certain moral values and principles. It essentially looks at the government from the point of view of its acknowledged stakeholders, beneficiaries

---

[29]Rajya Sabha Secretariat, *Department-Related Parliamentary Standing Committee on Home Affairs, Seventy-Eighth Report on Freedom of Information Bill, 2000*, New Delhi, July 2001.

[30]For more detailed discussion, see Madhav Godbole, *Report of the One Man Committee on Good Governance*, Government of Maharshtra, Mumbai, July 2001.

and customers. As a result, a mission statement of good governance will read quite differently from a mission statement of administrative reforms.

There is widespread disenchantment with the functioning of both central and state governments. In the perception of the common man, the government is seen as an exploitative arm of the state. From the viewpoint of the citizens, the government epitomises corruption, inordinate delays, long-winded procedures, lack of transparency, and extreme rudeness and insensitivity, often bordering on callousness. Experience suggests that an attempt to reform this corrupt apparatus will not be easy. For any perceptible result to be achieved, political and administrative will of the highest order, apart from ingenuity, innovativeness and persistence, are required. The following discussion will illustrate the magnitude of this task. This section is divided into three parts, namely, public policy, civil service reforms, and citizen-friendly, open and accountable government.

**Public Policy**

Some of the most important issues of public policy pertain to the enactment of a law on good governance, and legislation on fiscal responsibility and budget management referred to in chapter 1, legislation on protection of whistle-blowers who bring to light scams, corruption and wrong-doings in their offices in the public interest, and the compilation of an annual index of good governance. Considerable ground work will be required to prepare specific proposals on these subjects and create a consensus on the need for these reforms. Some of the other points are given very tersely so as to immediately highlight the points for action.

*Incorporation of 'Sun-Set Provision' in All New Legislation*: Almost all our laws are meant to continue for eternity. But, laws also need to keep in step with the changes in the economic, social and cultural environment in a society. What is perceived as an important legislation at one point of time may no longer be viewed as such at a later time. It would, therefore, be reasonable to lay down a specific time limit for any law to remain in force. Thereafter, it may be continued only with a fresh mandate from the legislature. Standing instructions should be given to the law department of the central and state governments to incorporate a sun-set provision in all new legislations. Whenever old and outdated laws are revised, as suggested earlier, a sun-set provision may be included in each of them. Similar provision may be made in all laws in force by introducing a comprehensive bill for this purpose in the legislature.

*'Sun-Set' Provision for All Schemes and Programmes*: All government schemes and programmes are generally meant to continue in effect indefinitely, howsoever the world may have changed in the meantime. This has meant large and infructuous expenditure. There is considerable overlap and duplication in a number of state and central sector and centrally sponsored schemes and programmes. This is particularly true in the case of schemes for rural development, land development and employment generation.

The government should announce that all existing schemes and programmes shall lapse on a given date unless a specific decision is taken, in the meanwhile, at the level of the cabinet to continue them in the same or modified form. This will enable the government to discard deadwood and use scarce financial and managerial resources efficiently, productively and diligently.

*Social Audit*: It is necessary to emphasise that the only justification for any government activity is that it subserves the interests of society. In this light, it is necessary that the work of all wings of the government be reviewed periodically and audited by the stakeholders themselves. As discussed in a later section, it is obvious that this function is not performed adequately by the audit of the comptroller and auditor general of India (C&AG). The government should announce its intention of conducting a social audit of some of its main spending departments through well respected, knowledgeable and non-political individuals.

Special care will have to be taken to see that the members of the social audit committees command universal respect and are above party politics. It is suggested that to begin with, such audits be undertaken on an experimental basis in a few departments.

*Setting up of Autonomous Regulatory Commissions*: Ideally, the government should not be in the business of providing services such as electricity, water, milk, transport and so on. Though it may take some time to give up these activities or cease to be a dominant player in the field, at least the government should not be in the business of fixing charges for the sale of these services. It is everyday experience that if a private sector producer/distributor or a co-operative society increases the prices of any goods or services, there is no outcry or public agitation. But the government is held to ransom for similar action. This is partly because, in the past, the government has shown that it bows to public pressure. Vote-bank politics also plays its part in such decisions as does the fact that the process of fixing of prices by the government is shrouded in secrecy and is hardly ever transparent. It is seen that the techniques and methodology for computation of costs incurred by government in providing various services leave a great deal to be desired. It is necessary to standardise this exercise by commissioning special studies for the purpose.

One way out of the present impasse in cost recovery is to set up statutory autonomous regulatory commissions to fix the prices of all goods and services in the governmental sector. In the case of public utilities, their jurisdiction will have to extend to the private sector as well. This would imply giving the opportunity to all interested parties to present their point of view in open hearings of these bodies. It would also mean that these bodies pass 'speaking orders' and appeals over the orders of these bodies will lie only to the high court. The decision of the regulatory commission will be binding on all parties, including the state government. In arriving at its decisions, the commission will take into account the capacity of various consumer groups to pay the proposed tariff. The commission may also provide for a reasonable cross-subsidy ststem among consumer groups. If the state government would like a lower tariff to be charged to any group or category of consumers, it will have to provide an explicit subsidy in its annual budget for disbursement to the concerned agency and give an undertaking to the commission to discharge such an obligation in suitable instalments each year during the pendency of the award.

Another noteworthy advantage of such regulatory commissions is that it is expected to go into the question of whether the cost of providing the service estimated by the concerned department is reasonable or whether there is scope for reducing it. In the open hearings of a commission, various interested parties such as consumers groups and others will get an opportunity to comment on it and make suitable recommendations for the consideration of the commission.

It is equally important to note that a regulatory commission will also lay down the standards of service to be provided by the department/organisation concerned. If the service is not up to specified standards, a consumer can approach the commission for redressal of his grievance. This will compel the concerned government department or undertaking to show greater efficiency and productivity in its work. Thus, the setting up of regulatory commissions will further the objective of good governance. It is gratifying to note that steps have been taken in a number of states to set up state electricity regulatory commissions (SERCs).

*Cutting Down the Citizen's Interface with Government:* One of the prime reasons for the harassment of citizens by government agencies is the need of the people to approach these agencies for various requirements from time to time. It is not uncommon to hear people complain about harassment, wastage of time and money, repeated visits to offices and institutionalised systems of informal payments (often called speed money) which have to be made for getting stamp paper, VII–XII extracts of land records, non-encumbrance certificates, driving licenses, and, believe it or not, even to pay dues to the government! A great deal of corruption and harassment can be reduced if these requirements can become available, bypassing government departments, through single-window stations, such as the TWINS in Hyderabad, funded in the course of time by the private sector. Payment of all government dues through banks and even post offices could be another way to deal with this problem. The state government should announce that cutting down the citizen's interface with government agencies will be one of the main instruments in the programme for good governance.

*Primary Responsibilities of the Government*: In view of the serious financial constraints facing central and state governments, the time has come to give serious thought to the question of the primary responsibilities of the government. Spreading resources thinly, as in the past, will be counter- productive. A 'Christmas tree' or 'hold-all' approach under which small outlays are provided for a large number of schemes and programmes in all sectors of the economy, adopted so far, will have to be abandoned.

The primary responsibilities of the government can be briefly stated as law and order and police, a system for adequate and timely civil and criminal justice, and protection of the interests of the economically and socially weaker sections of society. The government will also have to take the responsibility for providing primary education, public health, and water supply, particularly in rural and semi-urban areas. If these are fully taken care of, a number of the remaining activities can be left to the private or co-operative sectors. The state may step in to fill the gap only in sectors and activities which cannot be catered for by the private and co-operative sectors. Once this is accepted, the efforts for good governance can be more focused and properly targeted. It is recommended that each state government should prepare a working paper on this subject and publish it to elicit the views of the public.

*Segregation of Information Technology (IT) and Non-IT Streams*: The Andhra Pradesh government has the distinction of being in the forefront not only among the other state governments but also the central government in the propagation of IT culture in government. Some other states have also taken such steps though they are confined to specific offices. It is, however, necessary to realise that if this lead has to be maintained and even improved on further, the government will have to create conditions in which private sector capital can be invited to participate in these endeavours. Otherwise, there are limits to which the state government can set aside funds not only for the initial capital expenditure but also for the recurrent expenditure as also the eventual replacement of these facilities by new state-of-the-art technology. It is imperative to encourage private sector investment to speed up the process of bringing IT into the diverse fields of governmental activities. This will imply acceptance of the following prerequisites:

- Identification of areas in which private sector participation, either wholly or in a joint venture with the government, can be invited;
- Working out the estimates of initial capital investment as well as the recurrent costs;
- Providing a reasonable rate of return on this investment;
- Examining the extent to which cost recovery is feasible;
- Exploring the extent of cross-subsidies which could be reasonably provided for to give relief to the weaker sections of society; and
- Deciding the extent of the burden of subsidy which the state budget will be able to shoulder from year to year till these schemes are able to stand on their own.

It is only by making such an assessment department by department that a realistic medium term phased programme for introduction of IT in governmental activities can be evolved and adopted.

Even after such an exercise, it will be seen that for some time to come, certain activities will continue to be handled as at present, without computerisation. Regarding these activities, more conventional and well accepted, but hardly ever implemented, techniques of good governance, as below, will have to be followed in a time-bound manner.

*Declaring NGOs as Partners in Development*: It is increasingly accepted all over the world that NGOs need to be brought into the mainstream of development efforts by government agencies. The present adversarial relationship between government agencies and NGOs, based on mutual suspicion and distrust, needs to give way to constructive partnership and healthy respect for each other's concerns. The mindset that the government knows best is often at the root of this dysfunctional relationship. NGOs too will have to change their current attitude of looking down on anything that has to do with the government. A symbiotic relationship between government and NGOs can go a long way towards building bridges of understanding and speeding up the process of development and improving its content and impact.

*Media and Government*: The present dictum of keeping the media at arm's length has been largely responsible for the disenchantment of citizens with government. Currently, at best, a bureaucrat listlessly, and mostly disinterestedly, reacts to adverse reports and criticism of the functioning of the government in the print and electronic media. At worst, he simply turns a blind eye to such criticism and even refuses to take notice till the matter is raised in the legislature or parliament. This is mainly due to the mutual distrust and suspicion between the media and the government.

It is time to put this relationship on a new footing. This would imply changing government servants' conduct rules so as to cast an obligation on officers to supply factual information on all matters to the citizens and the media. A state government should permit all heads of offices in the field and the designated senior officers in the offices of heads of departments and state secretariat to interact with the media, in so far as their own work/jurisdiction is concerned. This means that officers will take the initiative to give background briefings on important decisions of the government. The accessibility of officers to the media will also help to project the correct position on any matter to the media and avoid, to a considerable extent, publication of reports based on incomplete or wrong information. Thus, a pro-active role by the bureaucracy *vis-a-vis* the media has to be an intrinsic part of any strategy for good governance.

At times, senior officers are subjected to unjustified criticism in the media. In some cases, this extends to motivated and scurrilous attacks against officers by the media. Needless to say, this demoralises upright officers, and lowers the image of the government. It is imperative that, in such cases, the chief secretary takes the initiative to issue a clarification on behalf of the government at the earliest opportunity. It is also necessary that the concerned officer be given all the assistance needed to file a complaint to the Press Council of India.

*Zero Tolerance for Corruption*: While a series of steps as outlined above would go a long way in lowering the level of corruption in the government, it is imperative that the government is seen to be firm and ruthless in dealing with corruption. It must proclaim that it will have zero tolerance for corruption.

The government should come down heavily on those who are found indulging in corrupt practices. A law should be passed to empower the government to confiscate the property of not only those public servants who have unaccounted wealth but also the property standing the name of their dependants. This will be fully in keeping with the observations of the Supreme Court in a number of cases.

### Civil Service Reforms

*Going Back to Basics*: The civil service which we inherited from the British and accepted consciously after Independence is based on some cardinal principles. These include absolute honesty and integrity, total apolitical dealings, giving free, frank and objective advice to the political masters in position from time to time, and complete independence from political interference. In several ways it is difficult to see any similarity between the present civil service in India and its role model of the pre-Independence days. Each one of its distinguishing characteristics has come under a cloud. The two latest developments in this regard deserve mention. The first pertains to the move by the Central Vigilance Commission to publicise the names of officers against whom it has recommended prosecution or the holding of a departmental enquiry on charges of corruption. In view of the rampant corruption in the civil services, there is no reason why this information need be treated as secret. It is only by bringing public shame and creating social sanctions that the menace of corruption can be effectively countered. The second was the move by the government of Gujarat to permit its state government employees to join the *Rashtriya Swayamsevak Sangh*. It was amazing to see prime minister Atal Behari Vajpayee and deputy prime minister L.K. Advani defending this action of the state government. It was only the pressure inside and outside parliament that forced the Gujarat government to finally relent and withdraw the orders. The influence of large industrial and commercial houses, influence peddlers and lobbyists on the civil services has increased perceptibly. These developments, coupled with the politicisation and communalisation of the civil service, raise the basic question whether permanent civil service on the British pattern is likely to survive in India for very long. This question deserves serious introspection on the part of all political parties, social activists and thinkers in the country. It is clear that if the rules of the game cannot be observed by all players, it is best that we look for a suitable alternative to the permanent civil service in the country.

*Setting Up Statutory Civil Service Boards*: Transfers, postings, promotions, and disciplinary and other personnel matters, pertaining to the higher civil services, are dealt with, at present, in an *ad-hoc* and secretive manner. It is necessary that all such matters are handled in a non-political, open and transparent manner so as to improve the morale of the services by setting up statutory civil service boards. The recommendations of the board should be binding on the state government. If the state government decides to reject the recommendation on any point, it should be required to lay a statement on the table of the legislature at its very next session.

The board may consist of five members, namely, a retired judge of the high court, two retired officers of the rank of chief secretary in the state or secretary to government of India, a serving chief secretary, and a senior secretary nominated by the state government. The secretary of the general administration department may serve as the secretary of the board. The secretary and the head of the department of each department may be permanent invitees at the meetings of the board at which their proposals are to be considered.

*Transfer Policy*: Transfer *melas* and auctioning of posts are now rampant in almost all states. In UP, during his tenure in 1993–94, Chief Minister Mulayam Singh Yadav, transferred 323 IAS and IPS officers. Kalyan Singh tried to outdo him by transferring 485 IAS and 665 IPS officers. Mayawati, in her earlier two terms of four and six months each as chief minister created a record by transferring 568 IAS and 787 IPS officers. Her current term promises to be even worse with the transfer of 100 IAS and IPS officers within just 100 hours of her taking over as the chief minister. (*Sakal*, 10 May 2002). The UPIAS Association has decided to approach the prime minister and deputy prime minister about large scale transfers and suspension of officers though this is unlikely to serve any purpose. With the efforts of the opposition parties to destabilise the government gathering momentum in June 2002, the democratic front government in Maharashtra has announced that a government servant will now be considered eligible for transfer even after completion of one year in a post. This was meant to satisfy the demands of MLAs of ruling political parties! In Andhra Pradesh and Tamil Nadu, even chief secretaries have been summarily transferred in 2002.

Frequent and untimely transfers cause a host of problems for employees: finding suitable and affordable residential accommodation; admission of children in schools and colleges, particularly in the middle of the academic year; difficulties in getting permission for transfer of children studying in professional institutions; spouses in full time employment not being able to move to the new location. This often means keeping establishments at two places, causing a lot of financial and other worries for the employees. All this affects efficiency. Frequent transfers also mean considerable avoidable expenditure for the government. Interference in transfers by non-officials also compromises the discipline of the services and leads to their politicisation.

Against this background, it is recommended that the government undertake legislation on transfers incorporating the following principles among others:

- The transfer of an employee will not be ordered as a punishment. If an employee is found remiss in his duties, he will be proceeded against departmentally.
- All employees with a good record will be transferred, by rotation, to remote, inaccessible and tribal areas for a period of three years. Wherever educational and other facilities are not available, the place of posting will be treated as a non-family station and the employee will be eligible to retain government accommodation at the previous place of posting or will be given house rent allowance if he chooses to keep his family elsewhere.
- Every transferable employee will be retained at one station for a minimum period of three years.
- No employee will be retained at any station for more than six years comprising two postings of three years each in two offices located in the same station.
- If an employee is transferred within a period shorter than three years, it will be for special reasons such as his promotion, commencement of a departmental inquiry against him and so on. These reasons will be communicated in writing to the employee before effecting his transfer and he will be given a reasonable opportunity to respond.
- All transfers will be effected only during the summer vacations of academic institutions.

*Extension and Re-employment:* Ad hoc extension in service or re-employment of a few favourite officers cause considerable demoralisation due to the limited promotion opportunities available at higher levels. This also leads to officers adopting a policy of not displeasing their political masters. If an officer is expected to be objective, fearless and non-political, he should have no allurements of any kind. Whatever is due to him must come in its turn, provided he deserves it on the basis of his work and merit. It is, therefore, recommended that state governments make an unambiguous policy announcement that no extension in service or re-employment will be allowed in any case, at any level.

*Amendment of Civil Service Rules:* We have earlier recommended a number of steps for ushering in good government. In this context, we have briefly dealt with issues pertaining to the larger involvement of NGOs, social audit, and the need for putting the relationship with the media on a new footing. All this will be possible only if the civil service rules and regulations make it obligatory for a government employee to give factual information to the citizens, media, NGOs and so on. The present mindset of the bureaucracy to treat all information as secret will have to be changed and a new culture of openness will have to permeate government offices. Towards this end, it is recommended that the relevant rules and regulations be amended to make it obligatory on the part of every government employee to give out all information except what is confidential, or top secret. While the legislation on the right to information will help deal with the issue, a beginning should be made with the amendment of civil service rules as above.

*Publication of Annual Property Returns:* At present, the reports of annual property returns filed by officers are treated as confidential and accessed only if and when an anti-corruption enquiry is started against an officer. This policy needs to be changed so as to make public annual property returns filed by an officer in respect of himself and his dependents. This information could also be put on the internet.

## Citizen-Friendly, Open and Accountable Government

The prime mover in the effort to make the government citizen-friendly, open, transparent, sensitive and accountable will be the passing of the law on the right to information. It is, however, necessary to realise that this, by itself, will not be a magic wand unless simultaneous efforts are made in a number of areas to radically change the functioning of the government. In this section, parallel action is proposed on a number of points which need not await the passage of the legislation on right to information in a state. Most of these actions, in fact, will go a long way towards enhancing the impact of empowering citizens through the right to information.

*Upkeep and Maintenance of Government Offices*: A reference must be made to the fact that most government offices present a shoddy, dusty and neglected look. Even the name boards of several offices are rusted and badly painted. Thus, from the moment a citizen enters a government office, he is dismayed by its appearance, even before he comes in contact with the staff. Working in such an environment also adversely affects the efficiency, productivity and motivation of the staff. While this is partly due to the lack of interest of the head of the office, it will have to be admitted that it is also because of inadequate provision for the maintenance of government buildings year after year. In several cases, this has meant criminal neglect of buildings of historical or heritage interest. Provisions for the proper maintenance of all government offices and their compounds will go a long way towards creating a congenial atmosphere.

*Office Discipline*: There is a widespread feeling among the public that government does not function any longer for the common person. It may seem harsh but some go to the extent of describing the government as 'of the employees, by the employees and for the employees'. It will be wrong to brush aside this public perception. Closer introspection will show that it is not too far from the reality. To an objective observer, the employees do not seem to be accountable to anyone. They arrive and leave the office as and when they please. Officers and staff are away for a long time, often without adequate justification. All this will have to change if good governance is to become a reality.

It is suggested that all employees, including the secretaries to government, should wear name tags while on duty in their offices. This will be one major step forward in inculcating a sense of accountability in administration. This is already done in a few offices and now needs to be universalised. The wearing of name tags is standard practice in both the public and private sectors in some other countries.

*Inspection of Subordinate Offices*: The system of inspection of subordinate offices by officers at various levels was an intrinsic part of office management in the pre-independence period and was scrupulously followed for a few years thereafter. It kept the officers and staff on their toes for they knew that their annual confidential reports would largely depend on the inspection notes drawn on their work. District and taluka level officers had to do inspections right up to village level. Unfortunately, this system has fallen into disuse. Hardly any offices are inspected any longer on the plea that there is just no time to do so. This needs to be corrected and a rigid time schedule for monthly inspections needs to be drawn up and adhered to by each officer. But this will be possible only if some discipline, such as leaving the first and third week of each month free for inspections, is introduced in drawing up the tour programmes of ministers and in meetings convened by ministers and senior officers.

*Unproductive Meetings*: It will not be wrong to say that the day of a government officer begins and ends with one meeting or the other. There is hardly any time to think. The system of holding meetings was meant to speed up decisions and reduce lengthy, clerical and fruitless notings on files. But, in a typically Indian way, we have made a mockery of the system. There are just too many meetings scheduled each day. Often participants do not even have the time to read agenda papers and they attend the meetings without any forethought or preparation. Officers have to rush from one meeting to another. Several of these meetings are called at short notice. Meetings have also become a device to evade responsibility by everyone as it is supposed to be a decision by a group. With too many meetings each day at which their presence is insisted upon, officers are unable to go on tour or inspect field offices. It is time all this is changed.

*Proliferation of Useless Information*: It is generally believed that information is power. But, it is rarely recognised that too much information can become a drag on the system. This is particularly important in the age of information technology. It must be realised that the collection and collation of information is time-consuming. Every bit of information sought from the lower echelons must be scrutinised using the criteria of the use to which it is going to be put. Reduction of man-hours spent in collection of unnecessary information can lead to considerable enhancement of efficiency and productivity in an organisation. It is recommended that all information which is being presently collected should be scrutinised on this basis to curtail the collection and collation of information wherever possible.

The other corollary in this regard is equally important. Information should not be unnecessarily permitted to be transmitted to levels where it is unlikely to be used meaningfully. Present information-gathering practices should also be examined on this basis.

*Delegation of Power*: The excessive concentration of power has been the bane of the governmental system through the ages. There is not only a resistance at the higher levels to delegate power, but there is also reluctance, if not resistance, to use the delegated power. It is not, therefore, unusual to see files marked to senior officers with remarks, 'may see before issue', 'may see after issue', or just 'for information'! It is necessary to ensure that power is not only delegated but is actually used by those to whom it is delegated. Orders need to be issued that adverse note will be taken in the confidential record of an officer if he is found not to be using the delegated power. Similarly, officers who show reluctance to delegate power also need to be identified in their confidential records.

With the spread of IT, there is a real danger of decision-making getting concentrated at higher levels in administration. Scrupulous effort will have to be made to avoid this as it will sap initiative at the lower levels. This aspect may be specifically brought out while issuing orders of delegation of power.

It is normally laid down that delegation of power may be 'periodically' reviewed. In practice, this is found to be ineffective and unworkable. It is necessary to institutionalise the practice by laying down that delegation of power will be reviewed by all departments of the government in a particular month every two years. The administrative reforms department may be entrusted with the responsibility of ensuring compliance on a state-wide basis.

It has been seen that, in most cases, orders of delegation are not based on any detailed analysis of cases received in various offices with the intention of reducing unnecessary references to higher officers. It is also noticed that suggestions regarding delegation of power are hardly ever called for from lower offices. This needs to be rectified. In future, the exercise of delegation of power should be initiated at least three months prior to the month in which the final orders are to be issued, i.e. in the month of January of the year in which orders are to be issued.

It should be possible to issue clear guidelines in complicated cases where powers are to be delegated. It could be laid down that only where a case cannot be decided on the basis of the guidelines that a reference need be made to the higher office.

The powers must be exercised at the level at which they are delegated. No higher officer or minister should usurp the powers in any way. This will be the only way to take the government to the people where they can approach the empowered officer easily.

The delegation must separately cover both administrative and financial power. The delegation of power as above must be given wide publicity with a request that the citizens need approach only the concerned officer and no one else.

*Suo-Motu Publication of Information*: Each office should set apart a room as a public concourse where people can have easy access. It should have all basic facilities such as proper seating arrangements, drinking water, fans, a notice board, an intercom telephone connection to the officers, etc. There should be a facilitation officer available in the public concourse for guiding the public. In the case of smaller offices, this responsibility can be entrusted to one of the officers/senior staff members on a part-time basis.

As a general rule, it may be stated that every six months, or as often as necessary, each office should update and make available the following information to the public: organisational structure, names of officers and work looked after by each office, telephone numbers, fax numbers, e-mail addresses etc., services offered and responsibilities dealt with by the office, activities which require licences and approvals, and other such information that would be relevant to the public and facilitate easy access to the service provided. Each office should identify the kind of information pertaining to its activities which is of interest to people at large and arrange to publish it on its notice board and by a communication to the media and NGOs operating in the concerned field, at regular intervals, as may be prescribed. Thus, for example, every municipal body should periodically make public all the building permissions granted, along with relaxations, if any, permitted. Details of property tax levied in each case could also be published on the notice board for people to see. Such an experiment by the Vijayawada municipal corporation led to a large increase in its revenue. A village panchayat should make available, on its notice board, a list of workers engaged on employment programmes such as *Jawahar Rojgar Yojana*, for people to see. The whole idea should be to transact all work in any given office in as open, transparent and accountable a manner as possible.

It is suggested that a time frame of three months laid down for all offices to set up public concourses and to identify, with the approval of their higher offices, the kind of information which will be published *suo motu* and the intervals at which it will be so published.

*Publication of Standing Orders, Guard Files and Guidelines*: A great deal of government work is transacted on the basis of standing orders and guidelines laid down from time to time. Guard files act as beacons for functionaries in government offices. It is necessary that citizens know the basis on which a certain decision is likely to be taken by the government. Like the laws, rules and regulations, guidelines also ought to be in the public domain, available for anyone to see, though they have never been treated as such in government offices. In fact, the tendency in government offices is to treat them as top secret. As a result, the working of the government is shrouded in mystery It is time steps were taken to demystify the government.

All offices/heads of departments/secretariat departments should publish within a period of three months all standing order files, guard files and guidelines and to make a copy thereof available for people to read. It will be equally important to publish, from time to time, any new standing orders or guidelines issued by the government.

*Reduction of Paperwork*: Government offices are repositories of tons and tons of paper. As someone has observed, the red-tape used in files in government offices can girdle the earth several times over. This is partly due to the tendency to hold a government employee responsible for anything done by him years ago and even up to four years after his retirement. There is, therefore, a tendency to put everything in writing. This phenomenon is also largely due to the tendency to look at everyone with suspicion, unless he is proved to be honest! As a result, age-old systems of maintenance of accounts, files and registers have continued without any significant change, let alone any radical reform.

In many Western countries, people are talking about the paperless office. The United States has a law—Paperwork Reduction Act —to address this problem. But, in India, this is easier said than done. In fact, even the suggestion is likely to be dismissed outright.

Information technology is also not a complete answer to the problem, otherwise a country like the US, which is so advanced in computerisation in government offices, would not have been serious about strict adherence to the Paperwork Reduction Act. As stated earlier, it will take quite some time to bring in IT in all departments of the government, at all levels, unless the private sector is brought in on a large scale. This would imply making all these efforts self-supporting. This again poses a number of challenges, including those of cost recovery. Thus, in the intervening period, there is no escape from looking at systemic changes which can be introduced in a time-bound manner. These efforts will have to concentrate on paperwork reduction. It is necessary to underline that merely issuing a government *fiat* in this regard will not serve any purpose, unless the functioning of departments is gone into minutely to identify the areas for effecting a change, not only in the procedures but also the rules, regulations, and so on.

As a part of this effort, all government and local body offices may be asked to scrutinise carefully, within a period of three months, all existing forms prescribed by them so as to combine, revise and simplify them, wherever possible. The best way to go about it is to ask the office staff itself to sit down and fill up some of these forms to enable them to appreciate how unintelligible and confusing they can be! It will be interesting to note in this context that all government offices in the United States are required under the Paperwork Reduction Act to explain, before any new form is prescribed or additional information is called for from the public, as to why it is necessary to do so. The public also has the right to raise objections to the proposed steps.

In respect of departments and organisations in which it may not be possible to introduce IT in the immediate future, studies of existing rules, regulations, procedures and conventions may be undertaken to attend to the task of paperwork reduction. A pilot study of two departments may be started immediately and completed within three months. Thereafter, efforts can be made to replicate the results in other departments.

*Exit Polls in Government Offices*: We have earlier drawn attention to the need for reducing the interface of members of the public with government offices. Towards this end, it may be useful to undertake periodical exit polls of all government offices which have a large scale interface with the public. During the polls, questions could be asked to gather information on points such as the following: Why did a person go to that office?; How long did it take to have his work attended to?; Did he receive courteous and helpful treatment?; Was any illicit gratification asked for?; How many forms did he have to fill?; Did he think any information asked for was unnecessary or excessive or overlapping?; How many times were incomplete back queries raised on his application?; Was he a resident of the same place or did he have to come from out of town? This is just an example of the kind of feedback which will have to be sought to change the ways in which government functions.

*Payment of Government Dues through Banks and Post Offices*: It is not uncommon to see members of the public wasting a lot of time and energy in paying the dues in government/municipal/ zilla parishad offices. The procedures for such payment continue to be out-dated and time-consuming, with receipts prepared in duplicate/triplicate with the use of carbonpaper. A 'time and motion study' of all these transactions can indeed be revealing. Often, the person accepting payment at the window is unhelpful and ill-mannered. There is never a smile or a thank you.

One way to deal with the problem is to decentralise the responsibility for collection of government dues/bills for electricity, water and so on. It should be possible to persuade banks (private, public sector and co-operative) and post offices to take over this work on payment of a suitable commission. Extending common courtesies is not a common trait in most work places in India, so this may not necessarily mean getting better treatment at the payment window at these places, but at least the citizen will be able to choose where he wants to make the payment and save time in the process.

There is no reason at all why payments need to be in cash. Orders may be issued for acceptance of payment by cheque and credit cards. In the case of out-station cheques, suitable additional charges may be levied. In case a cheque bounces, a criminal case may promptly be filed against the concerned person.

Some citizens may prefer to pay their bills in advance by giving a deposit, to avoid having to deal with the bills from month to month. A system could be introduced wherein a customer would receive reasonable interest, as may be fixed from time to time, on the declining balance of his deposit, with the bills being adjusted against his deposit. This will save time, manpower and hassles for all concerned. All government departments and local bodies need to introduce arrangements along these lines.

*Sale of Stamp Paper through Banks and Post Offices:* The old system of sale of stamps through authorised stamp vendors, for example, has become problematic leading to harassment and corruption, apart from several other malpractices. There is no reason why stamp paper cannot be made available through banks and post offices. This example is given only as an illustration. The idea should be to increase and diversify the outlets for supply of all items dealt with by the government to meet the convenience of the customers.

*Increasing the Validity Period of Licenses and Permits:* State government departments and local bodies issue licenses, permits and permissions in a number of cases. They have a certain validity period after which they have to be issued afresh or renewed. A case-by-case review may be undertaken to examine the extent to which the period of the licenses, permits and permissions can be lengthened so as to reduce the harassment and inconvenience caused to the citizens.

The statutory powers for issue of sanctions, plans and so on should continue to vest only in government or local bodies which are answerable for their actions through the representatives of the people. The experiment undertaken by the Delhi municipal corporation to entrust certain powers of the corporation for sanction of building plans to architects was, on review, not found to be particularly successful. Cases where certain architects had misused their power were reported to the council of architecture which failed to take any deterrent action against such architects. The experience has been the same with certain other professional bodies such as associations of doctors and chartered accountants. Until there is a perceptible improvement in the public accountability of these professional bodies, it is difficult to suggest the delegation of government powers to them.

*Single Window Approach*: This concept has often been grossly misused and has, therefore, fallen into disrepute. But, there are some outstanding examples of well-conceived ideas such as the TWINS in Hyderabad. Yet another version of the single window approach could also be attempted. Under this, wherever possible, applications could be accepted in each office at certain designated times, only after due scrutiny in the presence of the applicant. If the application is found to be incomplete, the applicant can be asked to complete it, provide the missing supporting documents and so on. Once the completed application is received, he will be given a receipt with a specific date on which he could collect the requisite certificate, permit and so on, or the date by which it will be posted. Obviously, this will be feasible only in the case of those who would like to present the application in person. To begin with, this scheme may be implemented on a pilot basis in selected offices.

*More Purposeful Use of Telephones*: The telephones in government offices are invariably engaged or off the hook. It is not uncommon to see the telephones being used for private calls by the staff. One cannot expect to telephone a government office and get a sensible and helpful reply. The instance of a government official returning a telephone call from a member of the public is unheard of! This is hardly conducive to the increasingly fast pace of life. It also does not help those citizens who would like to avoid unnecessary travelling to and from government offices. Providing telephones in the villages, other remote areas and 'on demand' in urban areas will be meaningless if they are not put to any worthwhile use.

But, this will call for a 'cultural change'. Expenditure on telephones should no longer be looked upon as unproductive and unnecessary expenditure to which economy orders are applied year after year. More intensive and productive use of telephones in government offices will avoid over-crowding in these offices and improve the work environment. It will also mean a massive saving of time. Towards this end, PBX facilities maybe provided in all government offices which interface with the public. These telephone numbers should be widely advertised. People should be encouraged to seek information on all matters by telephone. Government officers and staff should be asked to diligently return calls from members of the public and provide all assistance and help over the telephone. Wide publicity should be given to the installation of these facilities in selected offices, to begin with, and the new instructions issued to the staff therein on dealing with the members of the public.

*Codification of Discretionary Powers*: It is inevitable that in all legislations, considerable discretionary powers are given to the executive. But, this does not mean that these can be used in an unguided manner as largesse, whether by officers or ministers. Wherever possible, guidelines must be framed as to how these powers are to be used. It is equally important that these guidelines are not kept confidential/secret/for restricted circulation. In fact, they must be widely publicised so that members of the public know how the powers will be used by any competent authority. Unfortunately, at present, there are no guidelines in respect of most of the discretionary powers. In the light of the above, the state government should ask all departments/heads of offices/field offices to identify all areas of discretion available to them and to formulate the guidelines for the use of such discretion. All such guidelines should be widely published with copies sent to the media, concerned NGOs and so on. Copies of these guidelines should also be kept in the public concourse of each office for the information of citizens.

Having said the above, it will have to be accepted that there will be cases so unique that no general guidelines can be framed to decide them. In such cases, the state government should issue standing orders that any officer or minister deciding such a case should pass a 'speaking order' which will, in a self-contained manner, explain why and how the discretion was used.

*Time Limits on Stays*: Often a stay given to the actions in a case continues for months and even years. In such cases, the person who has managed to get a stay has no interest in getting it vacated and the government, being totally disinterested, has no interest in vacating it either. Often, such stays cause large losses of revenue to government. In some other cases, the stays cause a great deal of hardship to the other parties. It is therefore suggested that formal orders should be issued that no stay will remain in force for more than three months at the latest and if it is not vacated within that period, will automatically lapse.

*Passing Self-Contained Orders*: What is true in the case of use of discretion is equally true in other cases. If the government has to be open, transparent and accountable, it is necessary that the people should know why a particular order was passed in a particular case. But, this will be possible only when a 'speaking' or self-contained order is passed by the competent authority in each case. The actual experience is, however, quite the opposite. Often cryptic, one-line orders are passed agreeing to the request or rejecting it. At times, palpably wrong, illegal orders are passed without going into the legality of issues involved. In any system of good governance, this must end. Standing orders should be issued making it obligatory for officers and ministers to pass self-contained orders in each case.

*Spelling Out Criteria for Selection of Beneficiaries*: It is noticed that in a number of schemes, the selection of beneficiaries is made on an *ad hoc* basis. This has given rise to the quota system for various office-holders, MLAs, MPs, and so on. This is nothing but largesse and is hardly conducive to bringing about transparency in administration. It is therefore imperative that, while sanctioning a scheme, the criteria for the selection of each category of beneficiaries under each scheme are spelt out by the government as unambiguously as possible. Wide publicity should be given to the selection criteria by the officer implementing the scheme, while calling for applications. The selection of beneficiaries should be done strictly according to the prescribed criteria in a transparent manner. Where the number of persons fulfilling the criteria is more than the number to be selected, the beneficiaries should be selected by drawing lots in an open forum. The intention must be to make the process of selection as transparent and accountable as possible.

*Redressal of Public Grievances*: This is one of the most neglected items of work in government offices. It is a rare occasion, calling for celebration, when a citizen receives a prompt, polite and helpful reply to any of his communications addressed to a government office. Repeated instructions issued by the government for the redressal of grievances have fallen on deaf ears. Keeping this in view, a number of recommendations have been made to make the government more open, accountable and sensitive to the needs of the public. This should go a long way in reducing public grievances.

Reference must be made in this context to the excellent consumer redressal system put in place by the Hyderabad metropolitan water supply and sewerage board. It includes some interesting features such as the display of supply timings, advance intimation of planned disruptions, 24 hour service of a helpline on telephone number 1916, water line service, and so on. This is perhaps the first public utility in the country to compensate a consumer for the breach of a customer service assured in its citizen's charter. This example needs to be followed by all departments and agencies.

*Citizen's Charter:* A number of organisations and departments of state governments have formulated citizen's charters (CCs). It is, however, seen that if the CCs are to serve their purpose, the following pre-requisites are necessary:

- Before a CC is framed, the existing systems and procedures need to be fully studied. The items on which improvements are considered necessary must be shortlisted along with the timeframe for each of the proposed improvements.
- The CC must lay down clear and unambiguous targets which will be met within a given timeframe.
- The CC must be the product of discussions at various levels of the organisation.
- Representatives of consumer organisations and NGOs working in the given sector should also be consulted before finalising the CC.
- The CC must be widely published for the information of the public. Copies of the CC must be available on the payment of a nominal price to any member of the public. Copies of the CC must be made available in the public concourse of each office.
- The progress made in the implementation of the CC, particularly the fulfilment of targets laid down therein must be monitored carefully and results thereof given periodical and wide publicity.
- There must be some provision to compensate the citizen monetarily for non-fulfilment of the time limits laid down and assurances given in the CC.

Looked at in this light, much remains to be done and steps need to be initiated immediately.

*Big Brother is Watching:* All systems and procedures in the government are based on distrust. It is not, therefore, unusual to have institutions which are specially set up for watching over the work of others. But, at times this is overdone as seems to be the case in Andhra Pradesh where there are four organisations acting as 'big brothers'. These are the Lok Ayukta, the vigilance department with a staff of over 500, the anti-corruption bureau, and the consultants appointed for quality control of works executed by government departments. In spite of this supervision, the government continues to function the way it does raising the question of whether there is any scope for reducing this overlap and duplication of functions. Apart from instilling a greater sense of responsibility in the administrative secretaries and heads of departments, this should mean curtailment of the large and bloated bureaucracy. A series of actions, as above, for ushering in more open, transparent, accountable and sensitive governance would make the government less prone to corrupt practices and curb *ad hoc* and questionable decision-making practices. This will reduce the scope for the proliferation of such organisations dealing with anti-corruption.

*Good Governance and Quarterly Meetings*: In keeping with the practice followed in some private sector companies for promoting quality consciousness among their employees, it may be laid down that, during the first month of each quarter, a meeting of all officers and staff of each office will be held to review the steps taken for good governance by the office. A middle level officer may be made responsible for convening these meetings to promote a sense of involvement in the concept of good governance among all incumbents working in that office. These meetings may be attended by all senior officers, including the head of the office and all officers and other employees.

# 4

# Governance—Some Major Concerns

**Downsizing the Government**

The state and its functions are being reviewed all over the world. What functions the state must perform is a question that is being debated, though the perception of what a state ought to do differs from country to country.

At one end of the spectrum is France where the civil service continues to be all-powerful. In most other European countries, the number of people working for the state has declined. But in France it has grown—by no less than 20 per cent over the past two decades. One in four French workers is now on the public payroll, compared with one in six in Germany and the US and one in seven in Britain. Small wonder that France has one of the highest tax burdens among the world's rich countries—46 per cent of GDP, compared with 30 per cent in the US, 36 per cent in Britain and 39 per cent in Germany. A report commissioned by Alain Juppe, a conservative who was prime minister from 1995–1997, suggested that France's bloated public sector should shed some 500,000 workers, or 10 per cent of the total. Juppe half-heartedly proposed to make a start by abolising some 5,000 jobs a year. But Lionel Jospin's socialist government, which replaced Juppe's, froze numbers at near-record levels.[1] However, this position also seems to be changing. A recent newsreport shows that the number of civil service jobs available for the over-35 year-olds has declined enormously because of privatisation and the diminished role of the state. (*Time*, 22 Apr 2002).

Speaking at the Rajiv Gandhi memorial lecture on 21 August 1995, Margaret Thatcher, underlined that countries were not rich in proportion to their natural resources; if that were so Russia would be the richest country in the world; it had everything, oil, gas, diamonds, platinum, gold, silver, industrial metals, timber and a rich soil. Countries are rich when governments have policies which encourage the essential creativity of people, granting them a congenial atmosphere to produce goods and services that people choose to buy. So Japan, Switzerland, Hong Kong, Taiwan, Singapore and others have no natural resources but are now among the most prosperous countries in the world... The state must be the servant not the master. There must be no drift into paternalism. Paternalism is the enemy of freedom and responsibility...It is quite wrong to say, as some do, that this model—of small government, low taxes, limited regulation, a wide distribution of private property, and a rule of law—is something which only suits wealthy Western countries. It is in large part because countries like the US adopted that model that they became wealthy. And it is because others did not adopt it that they remained less developed.[2]

Under the current market-centred policies, several countries are trying to streamline the public sector and reduce the workforce. For instance, in the UK, since 1979, the government has reduced the number of public sector employees by 25 per cent, transferred over 930,000 public employees to the private sector, and announced a 25 per cent cutback in senior positions...From time to time, the central government introduced measures to reduce public employment by 2 per cent annually in Australia, by 15,000 persons a year in Canada, by 20,000 jobs

---

[1] France: A Civil Self-Service, *The Economist*, 1 May 1999, pp. 49–50.
[2] *Economic Times*, 28 August 1995.

in the Netherlands, by 10 per cent in Sweden, and by 252,000 positions in the US. Similarly, the intention to freeze or reduce public sector employment has been announced in Greece, Italy, Finland, and Japan. Another barrier to the performance of the public service, of course, is its growing financial constraints as a result of the overall budget cut and the transfer of resources from various social programmes to market-oriented initiatives such as divestment and contracting out.[3]

The rate of growth of state-spending in the US has been declining in recent years. Downsizing state government has become both a political and economic imperative in a number of states. Oklahoma has a better track record at downsizing than several other states according to the 1995 issue of *State Policy Reports*. Oklahoma was one of the eight states nationally that reduced employment in the period November 1990 to November 1995. Oklahoma state employment decreased by 0.3 per cent in the period studied according to *State Policy Reports*.

The process of simplifying unnecessary or burdensome government regulations has been continuing in the US. The new reforms cover the departments of treasury, labour, health and human services and transportation and other agencies, and with previous actions will eliminate some 16,000 pages of regulations and streamline another 31,000 pages. The reforms have already saved taxpayers $63 billion. (*Economic Times*, 8 Sep 1995). The success of reinventing the government launched under the leadership of the then vice president of the US, Al Gore, can be debated but the fact that it was able to achieve some remarkable successes in this difficult area cannot be doubted. For example, the first national performance review (NPR) report had reduced a four-hundred page construction manual to four pages and cut eighteen different sets of housing regulations to one.[4] It is interesting to note that early in the

---

[3] M. Shamsul Haque, Legitimisation Crisis: A Challenge for Public Service in the Next Century, *International Review of Administrative Sciences* [0020-8523 (199803) 64:1], 1998.

[4] Bob Zelnick, *Gore—A Political Life*, Regnery Publishing Inc., Washington D.C., 1999, p. 234.

process, the leaders of key government unions decided not to fight the idea of reinventing government concentrating instead on protecting union jobs and making sure unions were involved if major changes were made in how jobs were to be done. Thus building a partnership with the unions became central to the NPR. This led to the establishment of a new national partnership council (NPC). One of the criticisms of the programme is that it essentially concentrated on middle manager civilians rather than unionised employees. As is the case in any other programme, a great deal was found wanting in this programme but it cannot be denied that it was the first novel effort of its kind in totally uncharted waters.

Peter Drucker sounded what would become the dominant theme of most critics of Gore's effort, namely, to ask fundamental questions about the role of government in society. 'Every agency, every policy, every programme, every activity should be confronted with these questions: What is your mission? Is it still worth doing? If we were not already doing this, would we go into it now?' For a time, at the beginning of 1995, Gore himself raised such questions.

Gary Sturgess rightly argues that the size of government—large or small—should not be a matter of ideology...The state will probably grow in terms of its power or leverage in society but it will get much smaller as a percentage of workforce...The relevant question is not how small the government can get. The more useful question is, what does the state need to undertake to add value to society, and how can we construct more meaningful partnerships between the many components of the public and private sector?[5]

A similar trend exists in other parts of the world. In 1965, Japan had a total of 8,34,391 persons in the civil service. By 1970, the number had decreased to 1,92,793 and by 1991, it decreased still further to 1,80,700. The Singapore civil service

[5] Gary Sturgess, Virtual Government: What Will Remain Inside the Public Sector?, *Australian Journal of Public Administration*, 55(3): 59–73, September 1996.

has just 70,000 persons. In New Zealand, when the civil service reforms began, there were 88,000 civil servants. After the reforms, only 36,000 remained and most of them were employed in the departments of welfare, justice and revenue. The New Zealand government was able to effect such drastic reduction because departments were restructured, jobs redefined and accountability fixed. Along with downsizing, a number of other steps were taken by these countries to restructure and reform the civil services.[6]

These winds of change have not touched Indian shores. The growth in the number of central government employees since Independence has been phenomenal. It has gone up from 14.4 lakh in 1948 to 42 lakh in 1999. In just 1999–2000, the number of employees went up by 81,000. This number was expected to further rise by 28,000 in 2000–2001. The number of ministries and departments has gone up from 35 to 81. According to a reply given to a Lok Sabha question, from 1 Jan 1998 to 1 Oct 2001, the posts of secretaries in the central government have gone up from 117 on 137, additional secretaries from 99 to 110, joint secretaries from 389 to 489, directors from 453 to 645, deputy secretaries from 395 to 636 and under secretaries from 555 to 1372! And all this was during the period when the centre was making claims about downsizing the bureaucracy. This is particularly disturbing as central government finances have deteriorated sharply during this period. The latest estimate of fiscal deficit to GDP for the year 2001–02 (5.94 per cent) is the highest since 1994–95. The position is equally alarming in the states. There is such a surfeit of employees in Bihar that it made no difference to the working of the government when its 7.5 lakh non-gazetted employees and teachers went on a seven-month-long strike! (*Hindustan Times*, 30 Apr 1999). In Maharashtra, there are 58 secretary level posts with a full time secretary for the Maharashtra-Karnataka border dispute which has been in cold storage for decades! The number of senior level

---

[6]Government of Karnataka, *Karnataka Administrative Reforms Commission, Interim Report*, January 2001, pp. 63–66.

posts in the IPS in the states is difficult to justify by any stretch of the imagination. According to World Bank estimates, the surplus staff in the railways is over half a million. In spite of this, successive railway ministers have declared that there would be no ban on new recruitment in the railways. Due to no other reason than political expediency, the railway ministry has decided to create several new zones which will cost the exchequer Rs 700 to Rs 1000 crore.

The popular British television serial, *Yes Minister*, featured an episode where the bureaucracy described a state-run hospital, functioning for years without patients, as an exemplary, hard-working one. The staff, they pityingly explained to the minister, was working hard at personnel management, materials management, financial management, cleanliness drives and so forth. And patients would 'only clutter up the place'! The government gave a similar explanation to the Lok Sabha for paying full emoluments to 1,510 employees of Hindustan Fertiliser Limited, Haldia, where nothing had been produced for sale in the 10-odd years since it was established in October 1986. (*Times of India*, 11 Mar 1996).

Such examples are legion in this country. According to the committee presided over by N.R. Narayanmurthy, former Infosys chief, the staff count in Doordarshan and All India Radio is in excess by 75 per cent. (*Hindustan Times*, N.D., 9 Oct 2000). More than half the budgetary provision of the tourism ministry is spent on maintaining tourist offices in 18 countries. One such tourist office was opened in Argentina. Since the opening of the office, only 17 tourists from that country had visited India! (*Maharashtra Times*, 23 Sep 1999).

The post of commissioner for linguistic minorities (CLM) was created in July 1957 in pursuance of the provision of Article 350-B of the Constitution, which came into existence as a result of the recommendations of the states reorganisation commission. The headquarters of this office is in Allahabad with regional offices at Calcutta, Belgaum and Chennai. In the Eleventh Report (1 Apr 1988 to 31 Mar 1989), the minorities commission has stated, 'When the minorities commission was set up, it was envisaged that the commissioner for linguistic minorities organisation would be absorbed in the commission after necessary amendment of the Constitution. But, the proposed amendment did not materialise. But the work of linguistic minorities continued to be looked after by the commission...It is recommended that the commissioner for linguistic minorities be brought within the purview of the commission'. No action has been taken on this so far. In fact, the work of linguistic minorities has lost much of its earlier relevance or significance and the office of CLM needs to be abolished altogether!

In spite of all the talk about downsizing, the government continues to shower benefits on the bureaucracy. According to the Rakesh Mohan committee, which examined railway finances, concessions given to railway employees probably cost the exchequer Rs 500 crore every year. The most shocking instance of its kind pertained to the fifth pay commission. The then united front government implemented only that part of the report of the commission which related to upward revision of pay scales, allowances and pension of employees. All other recommendations which were meant to reduce the size of the bureaucracy, and increase its efficiency and productivity were effectively shelved. The ministers who negotiated with the employees acted more like trade union representatives than ministers! The huge financial implications of the fifth pay commission's recommendations totalling over Rs 100,000 crore for revision of pay-scales and allowances of employees at various levels upto panchayats as also the grant-in-aid institutions were conveniently overlooked. This has created a financial crisis for not only the state governments but also for municipal and panchayat raj bodies all over the country. In a further move, the central government upgraded posts in more than twenty central services in Group A in July 1999. (*Financial Express*, 4 Jul 1999). The government has also accepted the policy of two time-bound promotions for its 42 lakh employees. (*Indian Express*, 6 Aug 1999). This is bound to have a cascading effect all over the country. The wage bill of central and state governments taken together in 1999–2000 was more than 80 per cent higher than just three years before in 1996–97, while pension payments have soared to a level almost 150 per cent higher. As a percentage of GDP, pay and allowances have gone up from 5.6 per cent in 1993–94 to 6.8 per cent in 1999–2000. The corresponding figures for pensions were 1 per cent and 1.9 per cent respectively.[7]

Reference was made earlier to the large council of ministers in the centre and the states. To accommodate this many ministers, new departments and ministries have been created. Many of these departments and ministries in the centre pertain to subjects such as poverty eradication, drinking water supply, tribal development and rural development which fall within the purview of the states. There is a proliferation of political appointees. There are now four information advisors to the prime minister, when for decades in the past, there used to be just one. (*Indian Express*, 14 Nov 1999).

Recruitment to government services is largesse which no politician wants to let go. In several states, government jobs are for sale. The price ranges anywhere from Rs 50,000 to over Rs 500,000. Even state public service commissions are not immune to such influences. The latest scandals in this regard pertain to the Punjab, Maharashtra and Orissa public service commission. The recruitment rules are often revised arbitrarily, without any regard for the efficiency and productivity of the services, to suit the political exigencies of the situation from time to time. In one such move, the government of Haryana has raised the recruitment age to 40 years. (*Indian Express*, 19 Sep 1999).

If downsizing the government is to be a reality, as brought out earlier, serious thought must be given to the question of the primary responsibilities of government. There is need to have a wider debate on these matters in society. Only by developing a consensus on the subject will the government be able to redefine its role. If one has to go in this direction, privatisation and

---

[7]Shankar Acharya, Paying for Pay Commission, *Economic Times*, 5/7/2001.

co-operativisation of several government functions will be needed. 'Out-sourcing' and 'contracting-out' must be practised as widely as possible. This will imply a change in relevant laws such as those dealing with contract labour. These decisions will be possible only if there is a ground-swell of public opinion in favour of such actions. This will call for conscious efforts to educate public opinion. Unfortunately, no political party is prepared to bell the cat. There is a total disinclination to displease any of the organised sections of society. Thus, it is the vested interests of organised labour and white collar workers which are holding society's interests to ransom.

An eminent example of what can be achieved with political courage and statemanship is to be seen in the Andhra Pradesh (Regulation of Appointments to Public Services and Rationalisation of Staff Pattern and Pay Structure) Act, 1994. A forbidding title indeed and a truly forbidding Act! This is perhaps the only enactment in the country which prohibits the appointment of staff on daily wages and regulation of temporary appointments without proper sanctions. Such appointments are often back-door entries for regular government jobs. To reduce such recruitment can, therefore, be the surest way of holding new employment in government in check. Contravention of the provisions of the Act has, therefore, rightly been made a criminal offence punishable with imprisonment for a term which shall not be less than six months and which may extend up to two years and also a fine which shall not be less than five thousand rupees but which may extend up to ten thousand rupees. Abettors are also liable to the same punishment as provided in the Act for such an offence.

For a brief period of about two and a half years during 1986–1989 when zero base budgeting (ZBB) was being implemented rigorously in Maharashtra, during this author's term as principal finance secretary, there was a total ban on new recruitment. All posts falling vacant as a result of retirement, death or resignation of employees were kept vacant. Only those vacancies could be filled which were approved by the cabinet. New posts could be created only with the approval of the cabinet. Unfortunately, this political and administrative resolve was short-lived and soon the situation went back to normal when ZBB was abolished.

There is a common belief in India that government cannot go bankrupt. The experience of Argentina and some south east Asian countries shows that this is not true. In India itself, several states have not been able to honour their financial obligations and failed to make timely payments on their debt service obligations resulting in the downgrading of their credit rating. It is not uncommon to see state government treasuries being kept closed for want of funds. It is a travesty that in spite of this, central and state governments as well as local bodies are looked upon as avenues of employment. There has been no effort to change public perception in this regard. Looking at the experience so far, it would not be wrong to say that downsizing government will be the single most difficult challenge for the government. As of now, no political party seems to be even remotely prepared to accept the challenge. One of the few exceptions has been the government of Kerala which launched a 'rescue operation' in March 2002 to save the state from an unprecedented financial crisis. (*Frontline*, 29 Mar 2002). It remains to be seen how many of these decisions get implemented faithfully. Unfortunately, the record of several state governments in this regard is exceedingly tardy.

## Police Reforms and Human Rights

Public accountability of the police is tested everyday on a number of scores. These include the protection of weaker sections of society, enforcement of the rule of law and upholding of human rights. In a sense, the last criterion encompasses the others. The recent data on violations of human rights is unnerving. The number of such cases registered in the national human rights commission (NHRC) has gone up from 40,713 in 1998–99 to 50,634 in 1999–2000 and 71,553 in 2000–01. The cases of alleged illegal detention reported to the NHRC have increased from 436 in 1998–99 to 1157 in 1999–2000 and 1257 in 2000–01. Complaints received against the armed forces and para- military forces have gone up from 69 in 1998–99 and 61 in 1999–2000 to 486 in 2000–01. The number of under-trial prisoners, at the end of 1999, was as high as 2,04,480. As on 30 June 2001 there were 2,90,065 inmates in the jails while their authorised capacity was 2,19,880, resulting in over-crowding of 31.2 per cent. The number of cases reported to the national minorities commission has nearly doubled from 388 in 1997–98 to 697 in 2000–01. Custodial deaths were 1286 in 1998–99, 1093 in 1999–2000 and 1037 in 2000–01. According to the reply given to a parliament question on 26 February 2002, during 1999–2001, crimes against women totalled 3,73,269. Shockingly, these included five cases of *sati*. According to the reply given to another question on 24 April 2002, during 1998–2001, atrocities against scheduled castes and scheduled tribes totalled 25,651 and 4,473 respectively.

Against this background, it is a matter of some satisfaction that the NCRWC has recommended that Article 21 of the Constitution pertaining to the fundamental right of protection of life and personal liberty should be amplified and amended to say that, 'No one shall be subjected to torture or to cruel, inhuman or degrading treatment or punishment', and 'every person who has been illegally deprived of his right to life or liberty shall have an enforceable right to compensation'. It is also significant that the freedom of information Act passed by parliament as also the Maharashtra right to information ordinance, referred to in the previous chapter, make a specific provision, that, while other information asked for may be supplied within 30/15 days respectively, any information sought in relation to the life and liberty of a person shall be made available to the applicant within a period of 48 hours. These are pointers of the new sense of importance attached by society to the cause of human rights. The urgency and the contents of police reforms need to be examined from this perspective. This section is divided into three parts, namely, police reforms; secessionist movements, terrorism and human rights; and summing up.

## Police Reforms

It would be wrong to defend violations of human rights by the police as being in the interest of the maintenance of peace, security and law and order. A civilised society ought to deal with these matters in a civilised way. Crime prevention, investigation and prosecution must not degenerate into violence against the suspect or the accused, as is customary in India. But, to address these issues, we must go back to the basics. There is a great deal that is wrong with the manner in which we have attempted to deal with the violations of human rights. While each such case has to be investigated and the guilty brought to book, if lasting solutions to the problems in the field are to be found, institutional and other reforms will have to be pursued vigorously.

At the outset, it must be noted that the real size of the problem of human rights violations is largely unknown because a great deal of crime in the country goes unreported. Whatever crime is reported, it is hardly ever registered. And even if it is registered, its real gravity is hardly ever recorded and, more often, a much watered down version appears in the police records. It is not, therefore, surprising that in the all India crime figures, states like Maharashtra, Madhya Pradesh and Tamil Nadu figure at the top while UP and Bihar are way down in the list! As is borne out by the reports of the national commissions for women, scheduled castes and scheduled tribes, and minorities, this is particularly true where crime against weaker sections of society is concerned. If the problem of human rights violations is to be addressed in earnest, this situation will have to be rectified by making it compulsory for the police to register the crime, without sending the members of the public from pillar to post.

Institutional changes will have to begin with the very process of recruitment of police constables and subordinate officers. The minimum educational qualification for recruitment as police constable prescribed in most states is the passing of the VIIth standard. This is adequate as far as the policing of remote tribal and other rural areas is concerned. In other areas of the country, the minimum educational standards need to be up-graded to SSC in so far as mofussil areas are concerned and graduates in towns and cities. This will also mean providing three different pay scales for the police in the three areas.

Psychological tests ought to be an important ingredient at the recruitment stage to ensure that a person with violent tendencies, one who is quick tempered and has an 'attitude problem' is not recruited at this cutting-edge level of administration.

Human rights must form an integral part of the training programme of police personnel at all levels. Regrettably, this is either lacking altogether or is given minimum importance in the syllabus. This subject must also figure prominently in the periodical refresher courses organised for police personnel at various levels. In such programmes, persons who have been victims of human rights violations by the police and other sections of society, as also representatives of various sections of society should be invited to talk to the police. It may also be useful to familiarise them with the important judgements on human rights pronounced by courts and the investigations and assessment made by the national and state human rights commissions and commissions for SCs, STs, minorities and women, from time to time. Thus, sensitising the police to the importance of human rights has to be the cornerstone of the efforts to improve the present situation.

It is equally important to improve the public image of the police. The present over-bearing attitude of the police is largely because the police do not get any respect in society. The policeman is feared but not respected or looked upon as a friend. In this context, the image of the London Bobby has a great deal to commend itself. Partly, this is also due to the style of policing practised by the British police. They spend a great deal of time on foot-patrol and in the process come in close contact with common people on a daily basis. In contrast, one hardly finds a policeman patrolling our streets.

This will be facilitated if the responsibilities of the police for VIP security and looking after the *bandobast* during the visits of ministers are reduced. In no other country does one find the police devoting such a disproportionately large amount of their time to these duties. In India, VIP security has become a status symbol. It is time the police are permitted to do their normal police duties faithfully and diligently.

A related reform which is long overdue is to segregate the law and order duties from the work of criminal investigation. A policeman may be entrusted with one of these duties at a time and he should be permitted to do it uninterruptedly for three to five years. This will help him concentrate on his given duties, develop expertise, get insights, and improve his efficiency, productivity and morale at the same time. The persons entrusted with crime investigation could take on law and order duties if there is a serious emergency but they should revert back to the work of crime investigation as soon as the emergency is over.

Related to this reform is the imperative need to upgrade the investigative skills of the police by special training and by providing modern aids to investigation. This will, *inter alia*, mean providing greater mobility, upgradation of communication facilities, modernisation of hand-writing and finger-printing bureaus, setting up of DNA testing facilities, upgrading chemical testing facilities, computerisation, and networking at inter-state and national levels. This will call for much larger budgetary outlays. Fortunately, the central government has increased the allocation for modernisation of the police substantially. However, to avail of the funds under this scheme, the states will have to provide a matching contribution. With the upgradation of the infrastructure, interrogation and investigation will move away from physical abuses and beating of the accused to the adoption of a scientific approach to these matters and the development of a scientific temper.

Human rights abuses are, in no small measure, due to the unholy nexus between the police, politicians, the well-to-do and influential sections of society, and criminals. This has led to a crisis of confidence especially among the weaker sections of society such as women, children, scheduled castes and scheduled tribes, landless labour and bonded labour. People belonging to these sections see the police as an exploitative arm of the government. This situation must change.

Note must be taken of yet another significant factor. The police force in the country does not have representation from all sections of society. The representation of women in the police is less than one per cent of the total police strength. There is a preponderant representation of the majority community and in this category too, the largest representation goes to the dominant castes. The scheduled castes, scheduled tribes, religious and linguistic minorities, and those belonging to other weaker sections such as landless labour hardly find any worthwhile representation in the police force. A conscious effort was made by the centre to remedy these deficiencies while constituting the Rapid Action Force of the Central Reserve Police which is meant to deal with communal situations in the country. Similar efforts must be made by states if the police are to inspire confidence in all sections of society.

The communalisation of the police is yet another factor causing concern. A number of reports of the commissions appointed by state governments to look into communal riots have invited attention to this matter. The latest commission to do so was the Srikrishna Commission on the Mumbai riots in 1992–93. The minorities commissions at the centre and in the states have cautioned against the spread of communalism among the police and its larger implications for human rights violations. The gravity of this problem was once again brought home starkly during the communal riots in Gujarat in 2002. It is time this issue is addressed with some urgency.

In this light, the most important of the pending reforms is to give autonomy to the police to discharge their responsibilities under the various enactments fearlessly, objectively and in a forthright manner. The police owe their responsibilities under any law to the courts and the people at large. The executive cannot be permitted to interfere in the discharge of these responsibilities. The concept of police autonomy has been upheld in a number of countries. One of the earliest of these decisions was in 1861 in the Supreme Court of Massachusetts in *Buttrick v. The City of Lowell* in which it was ruled that police officers were not agents or officers of the city and that their powers were derived from the law. The city or the town could not be held liable for the mode in which they exercised their powers. They were exercising a function of government delegated by the legislature. In Canada, there emerged a different notion that the police were in theory neither agents nor servants of the Crown, nor servants of the municipality, but persons owing a duty to the public. In the Australian case of *Attorney General for New South Wales v. Perpetual Trustee Company*, it was held that some police duties were statutory and some were derived from the common law, but all were of a public character, and although a constable is bound to obey the lawful orders of his superiors, 'neither they nor the Crown itself can lawfully require him to abstain from performing the duties which the law imposes upon him with respect to the preservation of the peace and the apprehension of the offenders'. In recent times, in *R. v. Metropolitan Police Commissioner, ex parte Blackburn*, Lord Denning said, 'I hold it to be the duty of the Commissioner of Police, as it is of every Chief Constable, to enforce the law of the land...he is not the servant of any one, save of the law itself. No Minister of the Crown can tell him that he must or must not keep observation on this place or that; or that he must or must not prosecute this man or that one. Nor can any public authority tell him so. He is answerable to the law and the law alone'.[8] One can imagine how different the outcome would have been in such notorious cases as Bofors, *Havala*, H.D.W. submarines, St. Kitts, and scores of others, which have shaken the confidence of the people in the rule of law, if police in India too had enjoyed similar autonomy. This was also underlined by the judgment of the Delhi high court in the Bofors case, quashing the chargesheet against Hindujas, when the court observed, 'I cannot be unmindful of the fact that the CBI has been under a cloud. It has been accused of being a political shield or a whip of the government of the day.' (*Times of India*, 11 Jun 2002).

[8] Jeffrey Jowell and Dawn Oliver (ed.), *The Changing Constitution*, Third Edition, Clarendon Press, Oxford, 1994, pp. 296–300.

The political executive exerts influence on the police through the mechanism of interference in personnel matters such as recruitment, postings, transfers, departmental enquiries, foreign postings and foreign training. Even in a state like Maharashtra, the IPS officers' Association passed a resolution in November 2002 condemning the extra-departmental and questionable means adopted by some officers to further their own prospects. If the police are to be made answerable only to the law and the courts fully and effectively, this interference must cease. It is therefore necessary that a *statutory* state security commission (SSSC) is set up in each state and at the centre. The SSSC may comprise independent persons of repute and standing in society and the chief secretary, home secretary and the director general of police of the state and the corresponding officers at the centre. The composition as above is distinctly different from what was recommended by the national police commission (NPC), keeping in view the experience since the submission of the report of the commission. Thus, it will frustrate the objective of the commission if the chief minister, home minister and the leader of opposition are to be on the SSSC. Inclusion of the leader of opposition on the SSSC will also further politicise the police. The recommendations of SSSC must be binding on the government. If, for any reason, the government does not wish to accept its recommendation, the government must lay a statement on the floor of the legislature/ parliament explaining its reasons.

A reference must, in this context, be made to the report of the committee appointed by the ministry of home affairs (MHA) under the chairmanship of J.F. Rebeiro to review and suggest ways and means for the implementation of the pending recommendations of the NPC, the Law Commission, the NHRC and the Vohra committee. This committee had the opportunity to give a fillip to the long pending issues pertaining to police reforms. Unfortunately, the committee failed to take advantage of its opportunity. Thus, on an important question of follow-up action on the recommendations of the Vohra committee on the nexus between criminals, politicians and bureaucrats, the Rebeiro committee limited itself to the observation, 'It is learnt that a cell is already operative [in MHA], but how far it has succeeded in its endeavours is not known to our committee'. The committee has come to the surprising conclusion that the procedures adopted to select the chiefs and senior officers of the central police organisations do not call for any changes. Even a cursory acquaintance with the functioning of the central government can show how this faith is misplaced, how arbitrary and opaque the system is, and how the selection procedures need to be reviewed and replaced by a more transparent and accountable system. On the important question of setting up a SSSC in each state, it is amazing to read the conclusion of the committee, 'Taking all these considerations into account, we veered round to the view that the commission should be a non-statutory, advisory and recommendatory body for the present as recommended by the NHRC...Our committee feels that this would be largely acceptable to state governments as it will not impinge on Government's overall control and superintendence over the police'. With this one recommendation, the committee has demolished the whole foundation for the reform of the police. Yet another ill-conceived recommendation is that 'the *deliberations* of the security commission should be released to the press *after every sitting*' (italics mine). This will, in fact, deter free and frank discussion in the commission. Nowhere in the world do such discussions become public knowledge. The SSSC's recommendation only, and not the deliberations, should be made public, and that too only if the recommendation is not accepted by the government. The composition of the commission recommended by the committee is also open to serious objections. The question of *sitting* judges of high courts sitting on such a commission along with the home minister and leader of opposition will go against the separation of executive and judiciary. The recent trend of sitting judges involving themselves in executive functions has long term implications for the governance of the country and needs to be reversed firmly. For the same reason, associating the leader of the opposition with such a commission, which is to look after the personnel matters of the police, also requires careful thought. Further, making the minister in charge of the home portfolio the chairman of the security commission undercuts the whole purpose of the exercise. The proposal to give authority to the NHRC to nominate the members of the security commission is similarly difficult to understand. Acceptance of these and several other recommendations of the committee would be counter-productive and largely a façade. It is hoped that these recommendations will not form the basis for the decisions of the apex court in the PIL before it. The above discussion admittedly makes depressing reading. Police reforms appear to be a mirage, constantly elusive.[9]

For a long time it was believed that opening all-women police stations would help in addressing the problems of atrocities against women better. A reference must be invited in this context to an interesting news item published in the *Hindu* (12 Feb 2000). It stated that, according to the state human rights commission (SHRC), in Madhya Pradesh, women police officers had allegedly surpassed their male counterparts in abuse and atrocities. The SHRC was reportedly unhappy with the functioning of the *'mahila thanas'* (police stations run by women constables). The commission chairman said that, 'either the government should improve the functioning of the *thanas* or take a serious decision to close them down and post the women officers in regular police stations'. Thus, it is wrong to think in simplistic terms regarding conventional gender biases and prejudices while addressing issues in this complex field. What matters is the capacity to make systemic changes with an open mind.

Specific mention may be made of how some of the existing provisions of law need another look in the interest of interrogation of the accused in custody which is often of considerable significance to the success of a police investigation. A reference was made earlier to the archaic provision of dubious merit pertaining to the grant of anticipatory bail. The Law Commission had recommended that section 25 of the Indian

---

[9]Madhav Godbole, Mirage of Reforms, *Seminar, Police Speak*, November 1999, pp. 53–58.

Evidence Act, 1872, may be amended and police officers of and above the rank of deputy superintendent of police should be empowered to record confessions of the accused. It is indeed strange that 130 years after the Act was originally passed, even senior, well educated, experienced and responsible police officers are not regarded as persons fit to be entrusted with this responsibility.[10] It is interesting to note in this context that statements given to the officers of the enforcement directorate can be used as evidence under the Indian Evidence Act, unlike those recorded before police officers. Necessary amendment will help in speedy trials and bringing the guilty to book.

The Law Commission of India, in its One Hundred and Fifty Fourth Report on the Code of Criminal Procedure, 1973, submitted in 1996 made several recommendations for speedy justice in criminal cases. Some of the significant proposed changes include the creation of a separate and exclusive cadre of investigators to investigate grave offences in every district subject to supervision by the higher authorities, the establishment of the directorate of prosecution, making a provision for compounding more offences than at present, allowing plea bargaining in respect of a variety of offences punishable with imprisonment of less than seven years, etc. Some of these recommendations have been endorsed by the NCRWC. It is necessary that further action to amend the law is expedited.

Any discussion on police reforms cannot be complete without reference to custodial crimes. Year after year, such cases are reported by NHRC in its annual reports. International human rights groups give wide publicity to these atrocities. Significantly, such cases are reported not only from India's 'Wild West' i.e. the states of UP and Bihar. Maharashtra, Delhi and West Bengal are often at the top of the list of states reporting such atrocities. The second significant factor is that there are more such crimes in judicial custody than even in police custody!

Here the term custody needs to be interpreted in the widest

---

[10]Recommendations by a Group of Retired Senior Police Officers to Speed Up Police Investigations and Court Trials, 1998, pp. 12–13.

possible sense and should include all authorities who hold any one in custody—police, armed forces, security agencies, intelligence agencies, other agencies such as the enforcement directorate or the narcotics directorate, remand homes for children, women's homes for destitute women and so on. Such persons in charge of the custody are morally and legally responsible for looking after the safety of the protectees. Unfortunately, often these custodians themselves commit atrocities of an unmentionable kind. In some recent cases, the courts have awarded compensation to the victims of such crimes or their dependents. But, there are no central or state laws on the subject.

An effort was made by this author when he was the union home secretary in 1992 to draft such an all India legislation. For this purpose, a draft Bill, containing the following basic principles, was prepared: the person holding custody of a person will be personally held responsible for his safety and well-being and, if there is any custodial crime, it will be presumed that the custodian is responsible for it unless he proves his innocence; in every case of custodial crime, full medical examination will be got done at the earliest opportunity; in each case of custodial crime, an enquiry by a judicial magistrate will be ordered; the report of medical examination and judicial enquiry will be published and copies made available to the victim, and in the case of his death, to his dependents and the media; the victim of such crime and, in the case of his death, his dependents will be given interim compensation according to a pre-determined scale; the final compensation will be decided by the court while deciding the criminal case; and, in the event of conviction of the person in whose custody the victim was lodged, the compensation so paid will be recoverable from him. The Law Commission in its 113th report had also suggested the introduction of a rebuttable presumption in the Indian Evidence Act that injuries sustained by a person in police custody may be presumed to have been caused by a police officer. Passing such a central law, which could have had uniform application all over the country, would have shown the country's seriousness of purpose in dealing with the shameful events of custodial crimes.

Unfortunately, the proposal met with stiff resistance at both the official and political levels in state governments. The central government did not have the political courage or will to push through this long over-due reform. This is a sad commentary on our commitment to human rights.

With their enormous powers, authority and lack of accountability, the police often become the ugly face of the government. This is so in a number of countries. A member of the Mexican Institute of Organised Crime Studies, commenting on the corruption and violence among police officers in Mexico, is reported to have observed, 'The borderline between cops and criminals is now unclear'. (*Newsweek*, 10 Aug 1998). The report of the parliamentary standing committee brings out that during the one year from 1 Jul 1995 to 30 Jun 1996, 200 Delhi police officials had been arrested in 160 criminal cases. The rankwise break-up is also revealing: inspectors-5; sub-inspectors-22; assistant sub-inspectors-19; head constables-47; constables-106; and class IV-1.[11] The committee felt that, 'an image building exercise needs to be taken up urgently by Delhi police so that women and weaker sections who have been victims look to them [the police] as their saviours and not tormentors'. It will be interesting to see similar statistics for the police belonging to other states, because, this is not just the question of improving the 'image' of the police. It shows a deep malaise in the system which cannot be remedied without institutional and systemic reforms.

There are two other areas which require action at the national level. The first of these pertains to the passing of a central law for the CBI which currently works under the tenuous provisions of the Delhi Special Police Establishment Act. Under this arrangement, the CBI works under several handicaps and is often faced with the unhelpful and recalcitrant attitude of state governments. It is imperative that a central law be passed to enable the CBI to operate all over the country with full

[11] Rajya Sabha Secretariat, *Department Related Parliamentary Standing Committee on Home Affairs (1996–97), Thirty Second Report on Demands for Grants 1996–97*, August 1996, pp. 12–13.

authority. The second matter is equally urgent. It relates to the enactment of a central law for dealing with crimes of such a scale as to have multi-state and international ramifications. India is one of the few countries which does not have such a national crime agency. Both these issues have been under the examination of the centre for decades but the states are reluctant to give such powers to the centre due to the fear that these will be misused by the ruling political party at the centre against states ruled by other political parties. It is unlikely that there will be any concrete action on either of these points in the near future.

Unfortunately, police reforms, like many other matters crucial for the establishment of the rule of law and good governance, have been relegated to the backburner by successive governments at the centre and the states, irrespective of the political party to which they belonged. The police has become the instrument used by every government to consolidate its hold over the power structure.

**Secessionist Movements, Terrorism and Human Rights**

Any discussion on human rights is incomplete without reference to the security and terrorist threats facing the country. Several parts of the country have been rocked by violence, terrorism, secessionist movements and insurgency. The police as also the armed forces are facing an uphill task in containing these violent activities and maintaining peace and order. An important issue which has come up in this context relates to the need for special legislation such as the Prevention of Terrorism Act (POTA) enacted by parliament and similar other enactments passed in states like Maharashtra, Karnataka, Delhi and Tamil Nadu to cope with the situation and to empower the police to deal with threats effectively. It must be appreciated that there is an imperative need for such special legislations as the normal laws are not adequate to deal with the situation.

Such legislation is often criticised as being harsh, draconian and in violation of the human rights of the accused. It is necessary to underline that the human rights of the victims of violence and terrorism are as important, if not more important than of those who take the law into their own hands. Several parts of the country have been rocked by violence, terrorism, secessionist movements and insurgency in which over 75,000 people have lost their lives since 1990. But, we, as a society, have become insensitive to all this. It is possible to glamorise a terrorist by saying that one man's terrorist is another man's freedom fighter. But, no country can tolerate such secessionist movements. These movements are mostly assisted actively by forces from across the borders who are bent on dismembering the country. There is no point in calling the persons involved in terrorism 'misguided youth' as is the fashion among some of our politicians. First, a number of such persons are not in the category of youths and are mature and sometimes elderly persons. Second, it is not correct to treat them as 'misguided' as they are properly guided by forces inimical to India.

Having said the above, it is necessary to underline that it will be wrong to treat all such violent movements as pure law and order problems. Often, their origin is in socio-economic causes such as neglect of land reforms, lack of employment opportunities, economic exploitation by well-to-do and landed classes etc. Any strategy to deal with the problem of naxalite violence, for example, will be futile if these basic realities are not kept prominently in view and efforts not made to address the underlying causes. In the final analysis, the main cause of the disaffection of the masses is their alienation and honest efforts must be made to identify the factors leading to alienation. In certain situations, violations of human rights by the police and the armed forces themselves could be the cause. The sooner this is realised and acted upon the better it would be for all concerned.

In taking a holistic view of the situation it must be borne in mind that, by their training, neither the police nor the armed forces, are equipped to deal with insurgency and acts of terrorism. It is therefore necessary to have laws on the statute book which will deter people from taking the law into their hands. In the ultimate analysis, only the fear of law will help in reducing violence and terrorism. Seen from this angle, the Terrorist and Disruptive Activities (Prevention) Act, 1987 (TADA) had a great deal to commend itself. Unfortunately, this Act was permitted to lapse on 23 May 1995. It is true that certain provisions of the Act were grossly misused by the police. Instead of applying TADA in cases such as of the Jammu and Kashmir Liberation Front (JKLF) chief Mohammad Yaseen Malik and Hurriyat Conference leader Gilani for using clandestine and terrorist funds from abroad (which finally led to their arrest under POTA in 2002), the Act was used against common criminals and others on a large scale. This inevitably led to a sharp public reaction. But, it was wrong to throw out the baby with the bath water. The Supreme Court had upheld the Constitutional validity of the Act. Certain proposals for amending the Act to plug the loopholes and take action on the lines suggested by the Supreme Court were under consideration by the ministry of home affairs. In spite of this, a political campaign was launched by a section of the then ruling Congress party itself, led by Rajesh Pilot, then minister for internal security, for the repeal of the Act on the ground that it was anti-Muslim. To argue that any law is against the practitioners of any religion, and that too in a secular state like India, is ludicrous, to say the least. But, in the interest of vote bank politics, all the so called secular parties in the country joined the bandwagon to scrap the TADA. Amazingly, the NHRC joined the campaign with its chairman writing letters to all members of parliament seeking their support for the cause. All this finally resulted in the scrapping of TADA. Admittedly, the police forces in the country were perceptibly weakened in their fight against terrorism by taking away the weapon of TADA.[12]

Such was the political fallout that none of the political parties which have come to power at the centre since 1995 (and this was a wide spectrum of parties) had the political courage to move

[12]Madhav Godbole, *Increasing Internal Security Concerns and Human Rights*, Yeshwantrao Chavan Memorial Lecture 1995–96, The Indian Institute of Public Administration, Maharashtra Regional Branch, 21 November 1995, Mumbai.

## Governance—Some Major Concerns

a Bill for an alternate law on the subject till POTA was enacted in 2002 after an historic joint session of parliament. Unfortunately, soon after its enactment, fears have again been expressed (as in the case of erstwhile TADA) about the misuse of POTA with actions taken by the police in 432 cases in Jammu and Kashmir and 36 cases in Jharkhand (*Outlook*, 22 Apr 2002), and the dismissal of the case by the court in Mumbai against Mohammad Afroz in March 2002. Unless scrupulous and vigilant steps are taken to guard against its misuse, POTA will meet the same fate as TADA.

An attack is similarly being orchestrated against the Armed Forces (Special Powers) Act, 1958, though, in November 1997, the Supreme Court upheld the Constitutional validity of the Act and declared that the powers given to the armed forces were not unreasonable or arbitrary. Once again, the NHRC was taking a leading role in asking for the repeal of the Act. The commission took a decision to seek to be impleaded in the proceedings before the Supreme Court and to assist the court by placing the commission's views before it on this issue.[13] It would be indeed unfortunate if the NHRC takes such a partisan and one-sided view on matters concerning national security. It would not therefore be surprising if one of these days this Act too is repealed, leaving our armed forces to do a job, for which they are not equipped, without any special powers. This is also true of some of the other state and central laws which are meant to deal with the special situations arising from secessionist movements and terrorism in certain parts of the country.

It speaks volumes for the demoralisation of the political parties and their leadership that none of the political parties has been prepared to take a firm stand on these matters. It is necessary to remember that the situations leading to secessionist movements and terrorism are largely the creation of political, social and economic mismanagement of the concerned states by politicians who are time-servers and more interested in remaining in power than in giving good governance.

[13] National Human Rights Commission, *Annual Report 1996–97*, p. 33.

It must be realised that in this fight against terrorism and secessionism, India will have to go it alone. The international community will not come to its assistance. This has been seen in the last decade when India was rocked by violence and paid a heavy price. It was seen again in the case of the hijacking of the Indian Airlines plane to Kandahar in Afghanistan, terrorist attacks on the Indian parliament and the Jammu and Kashmir legislative assembly, and the killing of innocent civilians and armed forces personnel and their families during the spate of incidents in Jammu and Kashmir in 2001 and the beginning of 2002. The demand for the extradition of twenty dreaded terrorists involved in crimes in India and based in Pakistan has not received any support from the international community. In the final analysis, this is a low intensity proxy war which is less expensive for the adversary but which will bleed this country for years till there is a war weariness and fatigue. This is what the adversary is hoping for. Let us not go into this war with all our weapons surrendered. It must be remembered that the insurgency in Punjab was over only when the police and armed forces got an upper hand over the terrorists and the people of Punjab started extending support to the fight against insurgency. Let the talk of human rights not dull our resolve to wage a war against secessionism and terrorism.

Over the years, there has been a qualitative change in that international human rights groups have come to accept these challenges facing India. This is borne out by references to these challenges in their reports and publications. It should not, however, be forgotten that this is only a moral vindication of our position. It must help us to argue more forcefully for action to meet these challenges. There is no reason to be on the defensive in talking about the steps taken by the government to deal with insurgency and terrorism.

A word of caution is necessary in respect of the role of the media in dealing with human rights issues. It has been seen, particularly in the insurgency affected areas, that the media comes under pressure from terrorist groups to report the news in one way or the other. Often, the news itself is fabricated to sway public opinion. As brought out in chapter 6 (section II), in Punjab, Jammu and Kashmir, Assam and other north-eastern states, the media, under pressure, often became a handmaiden of terrorists and secessionists in reporting the so called human rights violations. Such reports often targeted security forces and the police so as to demoralise them and to sully their image. It is necessary that all responsible sections of society bear this in mind before coming to hasty conclusions about violations of human rights.

### Summing Up

The canvas of human rights is as large as life itself. There are so many connotations of human rights—social, political, economic, cultural, regional, linguistic, religious and so on. Upholding human rights in all these spheres is a challenge which every civilised society has to accept. It will be necessary to ensure that there is a continuous movement forward, howsoever small it may be. This will call for perpetual vigilance. In all such endeavours, the world is a small village, with a great deal to be learned from each other in upholding human rights. We learn from the experiences of others. And the course of communication of our successes and failures must be free of obstacles.

## Making State Budgets Transparent and User-Friendly[14]

A movement towards greater transparency in government operations is now sweeping many parts of the world. The grim financial situation at the centre and in the states in India has imparted a new sense of urgency to strengthening financial accountability. Strict budget constraints are now inevitable. There are no soft options left. These compulsions give rise to difficult choices. Unless public opinion is created in favour of

---

[14]Baed on the report submitted by the one-man committee of the author to the Government of Maharashtra in September 2000. For more details, see Madhav Golbole, Making State Budgets Transparent and User-Friendly, *Economic and Political Weekly*, Vol. XXXVI, No. 16, 21 April 2001, pp. 1349–1358.

these hard decisions, people will be disinclined to support any efforts of the government to put its financial house in order. It is, therefore, imperative that people are taken into confidence regarding the true state of affairs and the restructuring of state finances which would be necessary to sustain these efforts.

The demystification of the budget is also important from the point of view of empowerment of the people. It is only by making the budget and budget-related documents transparent and user-friendly that a real participatory democracy will be brought about in which the government will be answerable to the people for its actions and inactions. People must know, in the real sense of the term, where each rupee in the budget comes from and where it 'goes'.

The budget of the government of Maharashtra for 2000–2001 consisted of 46 publications, comprising 352 'demands', running into about 6,336 pages. In addition there were the supplementary demands presented during each of the three sessions of the legislature. These total, on an average, about 500 in a year. This is still not the end of the story. Each department presents its performance budget. Fifty-seven such performance budgets, running into about 5,000 pages, are presented. Thus, each year, on an average, budget/budget-related documents running into nearly 12,000 pages are made available to the legislature. The question is what impact, if any, do these tomes of paper have and how effective are they in the demystification of the budget.

At the outset, it has to be accepted that most of these budget publications comprise pages and pages of tabular material that an average person finds unreadable. It takes a Herculean effort to find the information one may be looking for. In the maze of details, the bigger and more important issues are lost sight of. There are hardly any analytical write-ups which can enlighten a person on the critical issues in a sector. It is distressing to see that there is hardly ever any incisive or in-depth discussion in the legislature on financial and fiscal issues. This is clearly brought out by the fact that hardly any use is made by the legislatures of the huge bulk of budget/budget-related documentation made available to them. The government will be alert only if it knows that it would be questioned in the legislature for its wrong doings. This is important in the context of the short time horizon of each successive government. The general tendency is to look at problems which are likely to arise in the immediate future and not to bother about those which may have to be addressed by the successor government. This is particularly true in respect of matters in the financial field.

Attention may be invited to yet another facet of the budgets in India. Budget-making is inextricably shrouded in secrecy. One could understand if taxation proposals were treated as secret but, under the present system which is a legacy of the British era, everything pertaining to the formulation of a budget is treated as secret. This is in stark contrast with the open budget-making process in a country like the United States. Countries like Canada, Australia, Poland, Vietnam and the US prepare and present mid-year reviews to highlight the performance of the economy and the required policy responses. There is no reason why the present secrecy surrounding the budget need be continued, particularly in respect of state government budgets. It is time a total review is undertaken of what needs to be retained as secret in the process of budget formulation.

In the British form of parliamentary democracy which we have adopted, approval of a cut motion, howsoever justified it may be, is treated as a defeat for the government, leading to its resignation. There is no reason why the budget should be treated as sacrosanct. In a democracy, there has to be room for give and take and the mutual acceptance of ideas which would serve the larger public interest.

**Road Map for the Future**

Seen from the point of view of openness and transparency, the present system of budget-making and its presentation leave a great deal to be desired. If the legislature and the people at large are to be taken into confidence on matters pertaining to the financial health of a state government, a fresh view will need to be taken on disclosure norms pertaining to a large number of issues. The objective of such an exercise must be to restructure state finances and to enunciate and implement a sustainable medium term fiscal policy which would, *inter alia*, aim at achieving revenue surplus, compressing establishment expenditure and adopting prudent fiscal and debt management practices. Such a framework should, *inter alia*, lay down targets for phased reduction in fiscal and revenue deficits and other quantifiable performance norms. As of now, there is no such explicit targeting of such indicators.

Once the fiscal objectives are determined and budget proposals framed on that basis, it would be useful to prepare medium term projections for a 3–5 year period pertaining to both revenue and expenditure. Disaggregated projections pertaining to major items would help in assessing the sustainability of the budgetary framework. An important advantage of medium term forecasting is that it helps to link the capital and revenue budgets by projection of revenue surpluses or deficits. The recommendations in the following paragraphs, though made in the context of Maharashtra, should be equally valid in the case of most other states.

*Pre-Budget Consultations:* The system of pre-budget consultations needs to be institutionalised by drawing up a list of eminent persons, organisations and interest groups who could be invited for such consultations on a regular basis. This list could include chambers of commerce and industry, consumer groups, academics and heads of research institutions, representatives of urban and panchayat raj bodies, labour unions, media, and eminent citizens in various walks of life.

*Do Away with Budget Secrecy:* The state government should announce, as a matter of policy, that there would be no secrecy in budget formulation except in regard to taxation proposals. All other estimates and projections of revenue and expenditure should be a matter of public knowledge. The government of Andhra Pradesh made a beginning in this direction with its budget for 2002–03.

*Documents to be Circulated before Presentation of the Budget:* The following three documents should be placed on the table of the legislature before presentation of the budget each year to provide the backdrop against which the budget may be assessed: (i) Economic Survey, (ii) Subsidies, and (iii) Performance of PSUs. Of these, publication (iii) above is being taken out since 1988 and does not require any change. However, the first two publications need to be reviewed and revamped completely.

The Economic Survey of the state needs to be recast along the lines of the Economic Survey of the government of India in so far as it relates to Maharashtra. At present, it is a mere descriptive publication with hardly any analytical content. There is no discussion of the issues facing the diverse development sectors in the state, available policy options and so on. Clearly, this publication would benefit by inputs from experts, academics, researchers and others. It is necessary that an editorial board of such persons is formed to advise the directorate of economics and statistics in the preparation of the survey. The coverage, chapter scheme and contents of the survey could be recast on the advice of such a board.

The methodology for the computation of subsidies adopted in Maharashtra needs a fresh look. The present coverage of subsidies is not exhaustive. At present, subsidies are also not divided between merit and non-merit subsidies. Due to the difference in methodology adopted in Maharashtra as compared to that adopted on an all-India basis, it is not possible to compare the subsidies in Maharashtra with those in other states and on an all-India basis. For all these reasons, Maharashtra should change over to the methodology developed by the National Institute of Public Finance and Policy (NIPFP).

*Budget at a Glance*: This one page document, brought out by the government of India as a part of its budget documentation, is very useful in capturing the highlights of the budget. Budget At A Glance should be prepared by the state government in the same format as that of the government of India, but suitably modified to suit the requirements of the state budget.

*Revised Format For Budget in Brief*: This publication is at present given along with the budget documents. However, a detailed examination shows that it has many defects. The information contained in various tabular statements cannot be cross-checked. The nomenclatures used in different tables are not uniform. The tables are not self-contained. Graphs do not convey much information. It was, therefore, recast altogether in a new format. Considerable additional information was added, both by way of graphs and tabular statements. Ratio analysis was incorporated to bring out the major features of the budget. Additional charts added to the format include, among others, percentage of revenue deficit to fiscal deficit, trends of revenue receipts and revenue and capital expenditures, percentage of development expenditure to total expenditure, percentage of borrowing used for capital expenditure, components of expenditure vs. components of receipts, and so on.

*Finances of Government of Maharashtra—Some Significant Pointers (FOGOMSSP)*: This new publication is meant to provide information on a series of points which are relevant for the proper understanding of the financial health of the state. One of its intrinsic elements is the enunciation of a medium term fiscal policy for the state. This publication will help to fill in the gaps in information and assist in a better understanding of the budget. It will provide summarised information on all critical points that one may seek in a budget through its detailed study. There will be a distinct advantage in giving all relevant information in one booklet rather than placing it on the table of the House separately for each item. This will facilitate easy and consolidated accessibility and ready reference.

*Reduction in Number of Grants*: At the instance of this committee, the finance department of the state government has prepared a list of 156 demands for grants by retaining the distinction between the revenue and capital sections departmentwise. The demands are as per the functions and as per the controlling officer executing the functions, as the main purpose of obtaining the demand is to ensure the accountability of the executive to the legislature. Even this will mean substantial reduction in demands as compared to the number of demands (352) in the budget for the year 2000–2001. It is recommended that this list should be finalised after detailed consultations with all departments.

*Quarterly Trends of Receipts, Expenditures and Deficit*. The comptroller general of accounts, government of India, brings out a publication of monthly trends called *Accounts At A Glance*. It comprises revenue receipts, non-debt capital receipts, total receipts, non-pan expenditure, plan expenditure and total expenditure, fiscal deficit, revenue deficit and primary deficit. It may not be possible for the state government to give such information on a monthly basis to begin with. However, it is important that this information be made available periodically for monitoring the finances of the state government. It is, therefore, recommended that, to begin with, such information be published on a quarterly basis. Later, efforts should be made to do this on a monthly basis.

*Classification of Outstanding Debt*. The debt of the state may be classified on the basis of its maturity profile. Such categorisation may be under three headings, namely, short term debt (to be repaid within one year), medium term (to be repaid within 1–3 years) and long term (to be repaid after 3 years). The maturity profile of the debt raised in the last one year may be stated separately. Interest rates payable on various bond issues may also be shown separately.

*Profile of the Debt*. At present, the budget documents give only the stock of debt of the state government at the end of the preceding year. It does not give a repayment profile of the debt spread over a ten year period. As a result, it is not possible to assess the impact of bunching of repayments, if any. It is suggested that in future such a debt repayment profile for a ten year period, on a roll-on basis, may be placed on the table of the House through the FOGOMSSP.

*Contingent Liability*. It is necessary that the details of various outstanding contingent liabilities such as guarantees, disputed liabilities, litigation and other claims on the state government are clearly brought out in the FOGOMSSP. At present, a comprehensive statement of such liability is not presented to the legislature. It is recommended that an annual statement of the total contingent repayment liabilities of the state government should be included in the FOGOMSSP. It would also be useful to include there in details of the beneficiaries of the guarantees such as banks, financial institutions, bondholders and so on. Since all guaranteed obligations are not due in any given year, it is necessary to give a break up of the guarantee liabilities in terms of the years in which these contingent liabilities might become real liabilities. Another important input will be of the past track record of the government in terms of guarantees invoked, honoured and the time taken to honour the guarantee obligation.

*Marksmanship*: The success of the budget must be assessed with reference to its marksmanship *vis-a-vis* elements such as revenue targets, expenditure estimates, revenue surplus/deficit and so on. At present, often, the tendency is to over-estimate the revenues and under-estimate the expenditures at the time of budget formulation to either balance the books or to keep the deficit within reasonable limits. It is seen that the variations in revenue deficit have been quite striking in recent years.

It is necessary for the assumptions underlying the estimates of revenues and expenditures to be clearly brought out in the budget document. This will enable a person to arrive at a judgement regarding their accuracy and reliability. It is further necessary that the reasons for the variations are explained as fully as possible. The cryptic, one-line reasons that are given in the Green Book are often not adequate.

*Multi-Year Budgeting*: The present system of budgeting for a year at a time suffers from a number of weaknesses. The most important is that the full financial implications of projects which are to be implemented over a period of years are not brought out fully. A government decision may entail only a nominal expenditure in year one but may call for sizeable expenditure in the following years. With the one-year budgeting system, the full implications of incomplete works are not fully realised. It is, therefore, necessary that government shifts to multi-year budgeting and gives the estimates of revenue and expenditure for a period of four years in addition to the year to which the budget pertains, on a roll-on basis. This will enable better appreciation of the fund requirements of the on-going schemes, programmes and projects and inculcate a greater sense of realism in budgeting. It is suggested that a study of two or three large departments may be undertaken to finalise the methodology for this purpose.

*Works in Progress*: In the light of the severe problem of a large number of incomplete works, it is recommended that consolidated figures of works in progress, the original cost and the revised cost thereof and the balance investment which remains to be made for their completion may be provided in the FOGOMSSP each year both by department and by category of work.

*Decisions with Prospective Effect*: It is necessary to invite the special attention of the legislature and the people at large to the decisions of the government such as grant-in-aid for schools which are to have prospective effect. These may be reflected in the FOGOMSSP.

*Devolution to Local Bodies*: At present the figures of total devolution to urban local bodies and panchayat raj bodies are not easily available at one place in the budget. It is recommended that this deficiency is corrected by exhibiting consolidated devolution under Major Head 3604—compensation and assignments to local bodies and panchayat raj institutions—for these two broad categories of local bodies separately. The detailed break-up of the devolution may continue to be shown under the respective departments. Requisite minor heads may be opened as suggested by the Eleventh Finance Commission. This information should be specifically brought out in FOGOMSSP.

*Burden of Salaries and Allowances:* Apart from the employees in the government, zilla parishads and nagar parishads, government has also taken on the responsibility for the salaries and allowances of the employees of a large and increasing number of aided institutions. Unfortunately, the data regarding such aided institutions is currently not compiled on an annual basis. It is recommended that time series data of the number of employees in government, zilla parishads, nagar parishads, municipal corporations (other than bruhan mumbai municipal corporation), agricultural universities, and aided institutions whose salary and/or allowances are paid by the state government should be compiled each year and placed before the legislature by incorporating the same, along with a projection for the next five year period, on a roll-on basis, in the FOGOMSSP. A separate statement regarding employees of PSUs whose burden is borne by the government may also be incorporated as time series data in the FOGOMSSP.

*Pension Liability:* It is necessary to compile data of the pension burden for each category of pensioners separately. It is further necessary to give a time series data as also a five-year projection of this burden based on actuarial calculations and other suitable assumptions.

The rapidly growing pension burden of pensioners of aided institutions and other pensioners will have large policy implications for the finances of the government. It is necessary to start thinking seriously in terms of introducing a contributory pension scheme as opposed to the present scheme funded entirely by the government. A study in this behalf should be entrusted to a consultancy firm.

It is recommended that the burden of pension payments be brought out as a time series data, along with projections for a five-year period on a roll-on basis, and be placed on the table of the legislature each year by incorporation in the FOGOMSSP. If there are any employees of PSUs whose pension liability, whether wholly or partly, falls on the government, the information pertaining to the them may also be included in the FOGOMSSP.

*Tax Expenditures*: Reduction in every rupee foregone by way of tax expenditures has to be made good by a corresponding increase in revenue. This simple proposition is often forgotten. It is necessary that important tax expenditure each year is incorporated in the FOGOMSSP along with the economic benefits that accrue to the state on account of this.

*Overdrafts and Ways and Means Advances*: These are important pointers of the financial health of the state government. It is imperative that information in this behalf pertaining to the preceding year is included in the FOGOMSSP.

*Maintenance of Assets*: It is recommended that the budget provisions made for the maintenance of various categories of capital assets along with the provisions which ought to have been made according to the all India norms should be given as time series data in the FOGOMSSP. It will also be useful to give a break-up of this provision showing salaries, wages and allowances and the works component. This will help pinpoint the critical problem of excess labour which is the bane of the system operating in the public works department.

*Off Budget Transactions*: Off-budget transactions such as borrowing by PSUs and statutory corporations which cast a burden on the finances of the state government are important for making an assessment of the financial health of the state. It is imperative that all such transactions are fully brought out in the FOGOMSSP.

*Performance Budgets*: The formats of these budgets have become out of date. These budgets need to be recast *de-novo* to bring out the impact of the government programmes, output which is targeted and achieved, the efficiency and productivity of expenditures, time and cost over-run of projects and so on. Impact studies need to be commissioned by non-governmental organisations working in the field. Verification is necessary to check whether the conclusions of these studies have been taken into account while recasting schemes and programmes. Programmes which have out-lived their utility need to be identified so that they can be abolished, redesigned or merged with other on-going programmes. The performance budgets must contain an analysis of important problems facing the department and how they are proposed to be addressed. All this will imply redesigning the performance budgets in concise formats not exceeding 50 pages each. It is suggested that a separate study be commissioned for the purpose.

*Release of Share Capital to PSUs*: All expenditure should be classified in terms of its final nature. The debt service liability shown in the budget often does not cover the interest on bonds because a part of it is given as share capital contribution to the irrigation corporations. In a large number of cases the share capital released by the state government to PSUs is not used for the purpose for which it was released. Instead it gets used for administrative expenses or meeting the cash losses of the PSUs or for paying interest on loans taken by the PSUs. It is necessary that the purpose for which the amount is proposed to be used is ascertained carefully from PSUs before release of share capital contribution. In cases where it is not to be used for capital expenditure, the amount should be released as a loan and treated as revenue expenditure rather than as share capital contribution.

*Accounting of Debt Service Liability*: At present there is no uniformity as regards the funds released by the government to the PSUs for payment of interest on the bonds/loans raised by them. While funds are given to the five irrigation corporations as share capital contribution, they are given to the Maharashtra *jeevan pradhikaran* as grant and to the MSEB and the Maharashtra police housing corporation as a loan. The terms of the loan are also not uniform. It is recommended that in future such amounts are released so as to reflect accurately the nature of fund transfer.

*Information on Resources of PSUs*: Currently, this information is not easily available in the budget, neither is it available for budgetary support to PSUs with demarcation between loan, equity and subsidy components of such financing. It is imperative that this information is given each year in the FOGOMSSP. It would also be useful to provide an itemwise and yearwise information of the accumulated arrears of amounts due from the PSUs to the state government.

*Accounts of Departmental Commercial Undertakings*: There are several departmental commercial undertakings whose accounts are currently in the budget. In these cases, the total sale proceeds are shown as non-tax revenue and the expenses are booked under departmental revenue expenditure. It is necessary to separate these undertakings from the government and convert them into corporate entities.

*Book Adjustment vs. Cash Flow*: Book adjustments made vis-a-vis the PSUs need to be brought out clearly, particularly when it involves adjustment between capital and revenue account. Thus, for example, amounts may be due to the state government from PSUs towards recoveries made by them on behalf of the state government. Often, these amounts are adjusted against amounts which are due to be paid by the government to the PSUs as share capital contribution. In 2000–2001, the government agreed to convert loans amounting to Rs 1,986 crore given to MSEB into equity. The government also agreed to release subsidy due to MSEB to attain a rate of return of 4.5 per cent on assets in operation from 1997–98 to 1999–2000. The state government has also agreed to adjust the dues to MSEB from municipalities and other local bodies from the grants to be released to such bodies and to give the same to MSEB. Each such transaction must be made transparent with suitable explanatory notes.

*Reserve Funds*: There are some items of expenditure that do not reflect the true nature of the underlying expenditure. For example, transfers are made from tax receipts under the tax head itself to specified reserve funds that are then utilised to finance a wide range of expenditure, both revenue and capital. Even if it is felt that earmarking of taxes should continue, the budget presentation must reveal the final outcome of the expenditure process. This also implies the need to adhere faithfully to the transfer of funds to the reserve funds as are mandated and to make sure that the amounts in the funds are used for the purpose for which they are meant. Any deviation must be specifically brought to the notice of the legislature.

The reserve funds are a legacy of the past and the need for the continuance of these funds needs to be examined afresh. Reserve funds make accounting opaque. They also lead to the islanding of revenues. It is, therefore, recommended that the state government should abolish the reserve funds altogether in the interest of greater transparency in budgeting.

*Sinking Fund*: The government of Maharashtra created a sinking fund in 1999–2000 for the redemption of loans. This was a long overdue step and needs to be welcomed but the contributions to the sinking fund need to be increased substantially each year. It is suggested that the latest position regarding the sinking fund and the extent to which it may be able to meet the liabilities each year be given in the FOGOMSSP.

*Freedom of Legislators to Decide*: An increasingly large proportion of the total budgetable outlay is now getting classified as 'committed' expenditure each year. The full implications of this need to be brought home to legislators by bringing out the details in the FOGOMSSP.

*Policies Likely to Impact on the Budget*: Past experience shows that certain decisions of the government cast a long shadow on the state budget though these decisions relate to agencies which do not have a direct connection with the government budget. One such scheme is the monopoly procurement of cotton scheme. Decisions taken by government, which have been totally contrary to the provisions of the relevant Act, have cast on the state government a burden of recoupment of loss of nearly Rs 4,500 crore incurred by the scheme over the years. It is necessary that such decisions, with their full financial implications, are brought to the notice of the legislature through the FOGOMSSP.

*Credit Rating of PSUs:* The five irrigation development corporations in Maharashtra are credit rated for their bond issues. Increasingly, they have all seen their credit rating declining steeply. This is also the position in regard to the road development corporation and the state government itself. Any upward or downward change in credit rating is an important development which must be brought to the notice of the legislature and the people at large. In future, information pertaining to credit rating should be brought out in the FOGOMSSP each year.

*Budget Manual:* The Maharashtra Budget Manual was last revised in June 1977. There have been several major developments since then, including the new accounting classification introduced in 1988. Several new points have also been brought out in this report. In the light of these developments, it is recommended that a comprehensive revision of the budget manual should be taken up.

*Summary of Centrally-Sponsored Schemes:* It is recommended that a summary of centrally-sponsored schemes may be provided with each white book of departmentwise demands for easy reference.

*Risk Analysis:* The state government should attempt an analysis of risks associated with the transactions of the government as far as the finances of the state government are concerned. For example, the state government has given large guarantees to private power generation projects and has undertaken to pay for the power drawn by MSEB if the latter fails to discharge its obligations. It will be useful if the state government makes a realistic assessment of the risks of invocation of these guarantees. The state government has also given a large number of guarantees to cooperative and other institutions. Here the state government should make an analysis of the data available to it regarding the working results of these institutions to make an assessment of the risks associated with such guarantees. Similar analysis will be necessary regarding guarantees extended to the bonds of irrigation and road development corporations. The fiscal risk analysis should also cover the quantitative impact of variations in assumptions on fiscal forecasts as also other major uncertainties about the costs of certain programmes in the budget. Such a risk analysis should be incorporated in the FOGOMSSP. In the light of the above, the following course of action is recommended:

- The state government should sponsor legislation to put a ceiling on guarantees to be given at any point of time. The law should provide that whenever the prescribed ceiling is reached, it should be incumbent on the government to seek the approval of the legislature for a higher ceiling.
- The guarantee fees to be charged in each case should have some relation to the assessed risk involved in the guarantee.
- All cases in which a guarantee fee is fixed at a lower rate than that warranted should be specifically brought out in the FOGOMSSP.
- Receipts from guarantee fees should be accounted for separately. The intention must be to pay for any guarantees invoked, from time to time, through the guarantee fund. In the interim period, till an adequate corpus is built up, suitable provision should be made in the budget each year for contribution to the guarantee fund.
- The risk analysis of guarantees given by the state government should be done, once every three years, by an independent outside expert agency and its report must be placed on the table of the legislature through the FOGOMSSP, and
- Similar risk analysis studies should be commissioned by expert agencies in respect of various other fiscal risks involved in the transactions of the state government. The reports of such studies should also be placed on the table of the legislature through the FOGOMSSP.

*Aided Institutions*: The financial burden of supporting the activities of private institutions in sectors such as education, social welfare, tribal welfare and others has been going up steeply over the years. The full implications of this are hardly apparent, on the face of it, in the budget. In 2000–2001, of the total budgetable outlay of the government of Maharashtra, as much as 27 per cent was to be incurred on aided institutions. It is recommended that a write-up on the full implications of this increasing burden should be given in the FOGOMSSP. It should provide not only the time series data for the past ten years but also give projections for the coming five years with a break-up of expenditure such as salary grants, non-salary grants, burden of pension and gratuity, grants for capital expenditure, and so on.

*Wider Dissemination of Budget Documents*: It is necessary to ensure that the budget/budget-related documents are made available to as large a cross-section of interested readers as possible. For this purpose, all data relating to the budget should be put on the internet. In addition, a comprehensive mailing list of all research and educational institutions, prominent intellectuals and public persons, NGOs and print and electronic media should be prepared and all documents should be sent to them from time to time, after they are placed on the table of the legislature. A list of documents put on the internet may also be furnished to them periodically.

It is gratifying that the government of Maharashtra has initiated follow up action on a number of the above recommendations and has also introduced a budget management and fiscal responsibility Bill in the state legislature in December 2002.

## Auditing the Auditors

In a number of countries, steps have been taken to strengthen the financial control of parliament over the executive. Two prominent examples should suffice to bring home this point. The National Audit Act (NAA), introduced as a private member's Bill, was passed in England in 1983 despite initial government opposition. However, the strength of support for the Bill in the House was such that the government was forced to compromise and the Bill was passed. It is one of the few cases in which a major legislative and institutional change of far reaching significance has been brought about through a private member's Bill.

The NAA has several significant features. As the preamble of the Act states, it is an Act meant to strengthen parliamentary control and supervision of expenditure of public money by making a new provision for the appointment and status of the comptroller and auditor general (C&AG), establishing a public accounts commission and a national audit office (NAO) and making new provisions for promoting economy, efficiency and effectiveness in the use of such money by government departments and other authorities and bodies.[15]

Section 1(2) states that the C&AG shall by virtue of his office be an officer of the House of Commons. No longer is he to be the equivalent of an 'in-house auditor' for the treasury. His independence is ensured by the terms of his appointment by prime ministerial motion for an address by the House of Commons, with the agreement of the chairman of the public accounts committee, and by the complete discretion conferred upon him in the discharge of his functions.

The Act creates the public accounts commission which consists of: (a) the member of the House of Commons who is for the time being the chairman of the committee of public accounts; (b) the leader of the House of Commons; and (c) seven other members of the House of Commons appointed by the House, none of whom shall be a minister of the Crown. The Act also created the NAO consisting of (a) the C&AG, who shall be the head of the office; and (b) the staff appointed by him under this section.

Section 6 casts the responsibility on the C&AG to carry out examinations into the *economy, efficiency and effectiveness with which any department, authority or other body to which this section applies has used its resources in discharging its functions.* (italics mine). This is opposed to the audit based on legality, regularity and propriety laid down under section 13 of the Indian C&AG

[15] National Audit Act, 1983.

Act. Section 6(2) clarifies that subsection (1) above shall not be construed as entitling the C&AG to question the merits of the policy objectives of any department, authority or body in respect of which an examinations is carried out.

Section 7(1) states that if the C&AG has reasonable cause to believe that any authority or body to which this section applies has in any of its financial years received more than half its income from public funds he may carry out an examination into the economy, efficiency and effectiveness with which it has in that year used its resources in discharging its functions. This is in contrast with the provision in the Indian C&AG Act in which the floor is higher (75 per cent). A substantial portion of public expenditure is now subject to investigation by C&AG in the UK, thereby increasing openness and accountability to parliament and the public.[16]

Section 8 gives the C&AG the right to obtain documents and information. Section 8(1) states that subject to subsection (2) below, the C&AG shall have a right of access at all reasonable times to all such documents as he may reasonably require for carrying out any examination under section 6 or 7 above and shall be entitled to require from any person holding or accountable for any such document such information and explanation as are reasonably necessary for that purpose.

In yet another significant provision (section 9), the C&AG has been given freedom to report to the House of Commons the result of any examination carried out by him under section 6 or 7 above.

The NAO undertakes two forms of auditing: certification audit and value for money (VFM) audit. The VFM examinations are potentially more far-reaching as a means of audit. At least 20 per cent of NAO staff and consultants are engaged in VFM examinations which are a significant proportion of its activity. Some of the most important VFM studies have been into the major privatisations and are carried out at the C&AG's

---

[16] Jeffrey Jowell and Dawn Oliver (eds.), *The Changing Constitution*, Third Edition, Clarendon Press, Oxford, 1994, p. 424.

discretion and are subject to the important restraint that the merits of the policy are outside the jurisdiction of the C&AG.[17]

Evaluating efficiency and effectiveness has been a common theme in recent years. The NAO defines economy, efficiency and effectiveness as follows:

Economy is concerned with minimising the cost of resources acquired with regard to appropriate quality. Efficiency is concerned with the relationship between output of goods, services or other results and the resources used, and effectiveness is concerned with the relationship between intended results and the actual results of targets.

The most fundamental criticism of the NAO is that it has failed to set out future directions to be followed by departments. It is pointed out that one handicap in the NAO's role in developing efficiency and effectiveness measures has been the basic accounting systems of government departments. It is said that the NAO may find the data provided by a focus on departmental accounts inadequate to the task of VFM examination. This criticism has to some extent been overtaken by the changes introduced in the late 1980s with the preparation of departmental spending White Papers.[18]

The second striking example is that of Germany where the reform of budget law has subjected not only the federation's accounts but its entire management of public finances to control by the federal court of audit (FCA).[19] At the outset, a reference may be made to the manner in which the president and vice-president of FCA are appointed to ensure their complete independence. Section 5(1) of the Federal Audit Court Act of 11 July 1985 provides: 'Upon the proposal of the Federal Government, the Bundestag and the Bundesrat shall elect the

[17] *Ibid.*, p. 199.

[18] *Ibid.*, p. 201.

[19] The discussion pertaining to the German system of audit and financial control is drawn from Heinz Gunter Zavelberg, Partners in Financial Control—The Federal Court of Audit, the Budget Committee, and the Audit Committee in Josef Thesing and Wilhelm Hofmeister (eds.), *Financial Control in a Democracy*, Konrad Adenauer Stiftung, 1995, pp. 75–83.

President and the Vice-President without debate by majority vote in secret ballot. Appointments shall subsequently be made by the Federal President. Neither officer shall be re-elected'.

This innovation of the FCA truly broke new ground: Not only the figures given in the accounts, not only revenue or expenditure items, but also the measures associated with them now form the subject of audits. Whole new fields of auditing opened up to financial control that were not connected in any way to individual budget items; these included organisation and staff-management investigations, achievement control, efficiency checks, and analysis of the risks associated with the facts on which decisions are based.

Another benefit is that the FCA's work is now almost contemporaneous with events, for it is no longer necessary to wait until accounts have been drawn up and related transactions entered. It is true to say that the FCA must not share in the responsibility for or in the making of decisions taken by the executive branch, for that would impair its capacity to criticise—a danger about which parliament in its capacity as controlling organ needs to be aware. But, the FCA may now come in much earlier, and its auditing activity may be parallel with the programmes and long-term procurement actions. There is not even any need for payment obligations to have arisen; for the FCA to become active, it is enough if decisions have been taken that may have a potential financial effect; thus, in a construction project, such a decision might concern the commencement of planning. In other words, the FCA is entitled to take action 'before the horse has bolted'.

The budget law reform of 1969 gave the FCA direct access to parliament. It is now in a position to report immediately to the legislative body and not required to make a detour via the ministry of finance, which until then decided when the FCA's reports should be presented to parliament.

Next to auditing, the FCA has now taken on counselling. As an independent financial-control function, counselling supplements auditing as it makes audit findings available to the decision-making process. The advice of the FCA is of particular importance in conjunction with the annual discussion of the budget, when each budget item is given its allocation.

In section 1 of the Federal Audit Court Act, the main concern of the law is clearly expressed—to ensure concurrent support by the FCA of the decisions of the German Federal Diet, the Federal Council, and the federal government.

The closeness of parliament and the FCA is exemplified by the fact that both the Federal Diet and the Federal Council share in the nomination of the Court's leaders. Its President and Vice-President are no longer appointed by the government alone. There is a tacit agreement to the effect that nominations will only be made by the government after consultation with the Budget Committee.

After two decades of experience in auditing, on the basis of the new budget law, it appears that financial control is making increasingly comprehensive use of its options and opportunities. Today, all the manifold aspects of cost-effective auditing—reviews of organisation and personnel management, achievement, efficiency, and risks—form part of the routine work of the FCA. This necessarily affects the annual reports submitted to parliament and the federal government under the name of 'Observations'. Till the early 1970s, these Observations dealt mainly with past transactions, today they contain investigations of complex matters, of weaknesses and defects in the implementation of programmes and laws which affect the future.

Implementing the resolutions of the audit committee is made easier by the fact that its members also sit on the budget committee, so that feedback between budget control and budget decision-making is as brisk as it can be. While such double membership implies a great deal of work for all committee members, their personal influence is also enhanced to considerable extent. This is one of the mainsprings of the efficacy of financial control.

The esteem in which the audit committee is held is exemplified by the fact that, unlike in previous years, it is a matter of course nowadays for government departments to be represented at the FCA's deliberations by high-ranking political officers such as under-secretaries or parliamentary secretaries of state. Even an appearance by a minister is no longer rare or exceptional. This goes to show that government departments are greatly interested in the FCA's future-oriented observations and subsequent deliberations and decisions of the audit committee.

Not only does the FCA submit annual reports in the form of Observations, it is empowered to inform the Federal Diet, the Federal Council and the federal government at any time about matters of outstanding importance. The institution of such unscheduled reports is yet another way of meeting the demand for concurrent auditing.

The Bali Declaration of June 1988 on the role of audit in promoting reforms for efficient public administration and corporate management adopted by the Asian organisation of supreme audit institutions underlines, *inter alia*, that public auditors have [increasingly] taken on responsibilities, in addition to their normal functions, of evaluating government adequacy in terms of management, performance and results. These responsibilities include evaluation of operations in terms of economy, efficiency and effectiveness.

It is against this broad-brush presentation that the auditing of public expenditures in India needs to be looked into. Speaking in the Constituent Assembly, Dr. B.R. Ambedkar had unambiguously underlined the importance of the C&AG: 'Personally, speaking for myself, I am of the opinion that this dignitary or officer is probably the most important officer in the Constitution of India. He is the one man who is going to see that the expenses voted by parliament are not exceeded, or varied from what has been laid down by parliament in what is called the Appropriation Act. If this functionary is to carry out the duties—and his duties, I submit, are far more important than the duties even of the judiciary—he should have been certainly as independent as the judiciary. But, comparing the articles about the Supreme Court and the articles relating to the auditor general, I cannot help saying that we have not given him the same independence which we have given the judiciary, although

I personally feel that he ought to have far greater independence than the judiciary itself'.[20] This deficiency has not been rectified though the Constitution has been amended over eighty times since then.

The C&AG's (Duties, Powers and Conditions of Service) Act, 1971, as revised from time to time, needs to be considered afresh in the light of developments in auditing in a number of other countries. The effort must be to incorporate the best and most progressive provisions in the enactments of other countries with suitable modifications. The manner in which the C&AG is appointed has become controversial in recent years. There is a feeling that the claims of all those who are qualified to hold the post are not considered objectively. It is necessary to avoid such a situation by having the selection of the incumbent made in a more broad-based and transparent manner. Considering the importance and sensitivity of the post, it is necessary that the selection committee should comprise the prime minister as chairman, the chief justice of India, the speaker of Lok Sabha and vice chairman of Rajya Sabha, leaders of opposition in Lok Sabha and Rajya Sabha and the finance minister, as members.

It is high time the C&AG is declared an officer of parliament. This will put him on a special footing and provide him with the necessary stature to carry out his responsibilities more effectively.

As a follow up of this, he should be entitled to place his reports directly before parliament and the state legislatures, without going through the central and state governments. This will curtail the delays which are so common at present in the presentation of the reports of the C&AG to these bodies and also enable him to make special reports, from time to time, to these bodies.

The provisions of section 13 of the Act relating to audit are rather restrictive. The examination of expenditures is mainly to 'ascertain whether the moneys shown in the accounts as having been disbursed were legally available for and applicable to the

[20]Constituent Assembly Debates, Vol. VIII, 16 May–16 June 1949, pp. 407–408.

service or purpose to which they have been applied or charged and whether the expenditure confirms to the authority which governs it'. As can be seen, the scope of examination is much less than that in the two illustrative case studies of the UK and Germany given earlier.

The report of the sub-committee constituted by the conference of the chairmen of the public accounts committees has invited attention to some very pertinent points. One of the observations was that in some states, there were extreme cases where audit has been denied the benefit of looking into the relevant files (A classic understatement!). The report laments that, 'Audit reports are neither taken cognisance of nor are they studied in depth by the vigilance departments including the anti-corruption bureau and the central bureau of investigation'. The committee has recommended that if necessary, a suitable amendment in the Criminal Procedure Code be made to obviate the necessity of examining the first informant by drawing a statutory presumption in favour of the correctness of the audit para. This is to be applicable to only such of the audit paras where loss of public funds is made out. The very fact that audit paras can provoke instantaneous investigation by the vigilance will have a salutary effect on the departments concerned.[21] It is necessary that very early follow-up action is taken on this recommendation.

A provision may also be made in the C&AG's (DPC) Act by which the CBI/CVC would be required to specifically incorporate in their report to parliament the action taken by them on such audit recommendations/findings where a vigilance angle or indulgence of officers in corrupt practices was indicated.

As brought out in chapter 2, local fund audit has emerged as one of the weakest areas of audit in India. As compared to earlier years, now huge funds flow directly from the centre to the

---

[21]Lok Sabha Secretariat, *Accountability in Administration*, Report of the Sub-Committee Constituted by the Conference of the Chairmen of the Public Accounts Committees held in September 1986, New Delhi, February 1987, pp. 7–8.

panchayat raj institutions and municipal bodies. This trend will be further strengthened in view of the seventy-third and seventy-fourth amendments of the Constitution. It is therefore vital that the expenditures of these bodies are looked into closely by independent and qualified auditors who will not be amenable to local pressure and political and other influences. Ideally, the question of entrusting the audit of local bodies to the C&AG needs to be examined. Even if it is not possible for the C&AG to take over the entire responsibility for audit, he should at least be made responsible for the overall supervision, laying down of guidelines and carrying out of test audit to bring in some semblance of discipline and order into the system.

The provision in the Constitution pertaining to the declaration of financial emergency as contained in Article 360 has not been used so far. The Article, *inter alia*, states that, 'If the President is satisfied that a situation has arisen whereby the financial stability or credit of India or of any part of the territory thereof is threatened, he may by a proclamation make a declaration to that effect...During the period of any such proclamation..., the executive authority of the Union shall extend to the giving of directions to any state to observe such canons of financial propriety as may be specified in the directions, and to the giving of such other directions as the President may deem necessary and adequate for the purpose'. In Bihar, during the period 1990–1995, the conditions were eminently suitable for the declaration of financial emergency. In the case of the monumental fodder scam, there was a total break-down of financial discipline in the state. The audit done by C&AG during this period and in the initial years of the scam left a great deal to be desired. The C&AG also failed to make appropriate recommendations for the declaration of financial emergency in the state.

The explanation to section 14(1) of the C&AG's (DPC) Act, 1971 lays down that when the grant or loan to a body or authority from the consolidated fund of India or of any state or of any union territory having a legislative assembly in a financial year is not less than Rs 25 lakh *and* the amount of such grant or loan is not less than seventy five per cent of the total expenditure of that body or authority, such body or authority shall be deemed for the purposes of this sub-section, to be substantially financed by such grants or loans as the case may be. It is suggested that the floor may be brought down to fifty per cent of total expenditure by the concerned body as has been done in the United Kingdom. It is proposed that the C&AG audit may become operative if the loan or grant is Rs 25 lakh or 50 per cent of the total expenditure of a body, whichever is less.

To curtail the delays in placing the reports of the C&AG before parliament and state legislatures, it is suggested that the C&AG's (DPC) Act should be amended to provide that the audit report would be laid before the concerned legislature within a month of its submission to the government, or at the latest, by the first week of the following session if the report had been submitted when the legislature was not in session.

The Serious Fraud Office in the U.K. functions under the Attorney General and has a legislative backing under the Criminal Justice Act, 1987, with wide ranging powers. The investigation is done by a multi-disciplinary team consisting of lawyers, police officers, accountants and other experts. The main advantage of the U.K. Serious Fraud Office is that all the powers of investigating and prosecuting agencies are combined in one institution and therefore they are able to investigate frauds quickly, launch prosecution and secure conviction in many cases. However, their work is restricted to major frauds. The C&AG may be given powers to direct the CVC to take similar action, based on its audit findings.

It is interesting to note that the Auditors General of New Zealand and Canada have the power to examine a person under oath. In Canada, under section 13(4) of the Act it is stated that the Auditor General may examine any person on oath on any matter pertaining to any account subject to audit by him and for the purposes of any such examination the Auditor General may exercise all the powers of a Commissioner under Part I of the Inquiries Act. In New Zealand, the Act states that the Auditor General may, for the purpose of fulfilling any function or duty lawfully conferred or imposed on him or the Audit Office, by notice in writing, require any person to attend and give evidence before him or before any officer of the audit department authorised by him. The implications of giving this kind of power to the C&AG in India need to be examined. Anything which can strengthen his hands to stem the rot in current financial management should be whole-heartedly supported as a step in the right direction.

Reference may be made to two of the recommendations of the NCRWC. These pertain to the setting up of an audit board and the institution of a system of external audit for the C&AG's organisation. Both these are well conceived and deserve to be accepted.

The audit scrutiny by the C&AG in politically sensitive cases involving misuse of large funds or of political office has often brought the office of C&AG in conflict with the ruling political elite at the centre as well as in the states. The larger implications of this can be neglected only at the peril of the institution of C&AG. For example, the whole process of audit and its efficacy came into serious question in Bihar during the fodder scam. The intemperate and immature comments of Laloo Prasad Yadav, then chief minister, that the C&AG and the Bihar AG should be jailed for dereliction of their duties (*Times of India*, 5 Mar 1997) was the lowest point in the public debate on the subject which cannot be overlooked when writing the history of this supreme audit institution in the country. It is unfortunate that there was no public outcry against and condemnation of this outburst, in parliament and outside. In yet another case, Nagaland chief minister, S.C. Jamir, sought a probe against the C&AG for leaking official documents pertaining to the audit of the lotteries of the state to the Press before they could be presented to the state legislature. The union law minister, Arun Jaitley, while addressing a public meeting in Mumbai in December 2001 stated, in connection with the controversy regarding purchase of aluminium coffins by the Army at exorbitant prices, that he had greater faith in a General in the Army than in the C&AG. George Fernandes, defence minister, went to the extent of charging the C&AG with unethical conduct and termed the C&AG's report 'false and baseless'. With such irresponsible pronouncements made by ministers, the public image of the C&AG is bound to suffer irreparable damage.

The audit of personal ledger accounts maintained without authorisation by officers at various levels in the West Bengal government involving amounts of Rs 2,500 crore created a political storm and led to the filing of a PIL in the Calcutta high court. It was the same when certain contracts in the petroleum sector were awarded by the government led to PILs in the Delhi high court. Dozens of PILs have been filed against the government in recent years in various high courts and the Supreme Court based on the audit paras of the C&AG. Thus, while parliament and state legislatures have, by and large, been passive or silent observers of the efforts of the C&AG to keep the government on its toes, the people are becoming increasingly conscious of their rights and duties where audit of government expenditure is involved. This is highly gratifying and brings out the importance and urgency of strengthening the institution of C&AG.

### Lok Ayukta—A Toothless Tiger

The idea of establishing an independent office to redress people's grievances is quite old. The word 'ombudsman' was originally a Swedish word. Like the concept of the right to information, the idea of ombudsman also originated in Sweden. In 1919, Finland became the second country to create an ombudsman, followed by Denmark in 1955. In 1963, Norway set up a parliamentary ombudsman for civil administration. The Danish ombudsman was the model for the New Zealand ombudsman which was created in 1962. The growth of the concept of an ombudsman in both the public and private sectors in UK came about in the 1960s and 1970s. Since then a number of other Commonwealth countries have set up such institutions.

Four key criteria were identified by a working party set up by the U.K. Ombudsman Conference (1991): independence from those investigated, effectiveness, fairness and public accountability. The ombudsman should be accessible; the complainant should have the right to complain free of charge. There should be a reasonable expectation that the decisions of the ombudsman will be complied with, and, where they are not enforced, the ombudsman should have the power to publicise this at the expense of those investigated. As for accountability, an ombudsman should publish an annual report and be entitled to publish reports of investigation.[22]

The VIth international conference of the international ombudsman institute held in October 1996 was attended by 121 ombudsmen from 86 countries. It adopted a declaration which, *inter alia*, reaffirmed the essential characteristics of these institutions, namely, independence, accessibility, flexibility and credibility.

In 1984, in Canada, Justice Dickson, delivering the unanimous decision of the Supreme Court of Canada in *British Columbia Development Corporation and another* v. *Friedman* [1984] 2 RCS 447, 460, 463, made the following statement concerning the nature and efficacy of the role of the ombudsman: 'The limitation of the courts are also well known. Litigation can be costly and slow. Only the most serious cases of administrative abuse are therefore likely to find their way into the courts. More importantly, there is simply no remedy at law available in a great many cases... Read as a whole, the Ombudsman Act of British Columbia provides an efficient procedure through which complaints may be investigated, bureaucratic errors and abuses brought to light and corrective action initiated. It should therefore receive a broad purposive interpretation consistent with the unique role the ombudsman is intended to fulfil.'[23]

Former Australian commonwealth ombudsman, Dennis

[22]S. C. Vajpayi, *Some Issues Regarding Public Grievances*, paper read at the colloquium on Ombudsmen: India and the World Community, 8–10 March 1995 at the Indian Institute of Public Administration, New Delhi.

[23]Republic of Mauritius, *Twenty Third Annual Report of the Ombudsman, January–December 1996, No. 9 of 1997.*

## Governance—Some Major Concerns 253

Pearce, wrote in his final report in 1990 that the objectives of the ombudsman are to improve the quality of administration and to provide a mechanism for individuals to obtain redress by:

- identifying instances of defective administration through independent investigations;
- encouraging agencies to provide remedies for members of the public affected by defective administration;
- identifying legislative, policy and procedural deficiencies, and encouraging systemic improvements to overcome those deficiencies; and
- contributing to advice to the government on the adequacy, effectiveness and efficiency of the various means of review of administrative actions.

It is interesting to note that in a number of countries, the ombudsman has also been assigned a role under the Right to Information Act and the Archives Act to investigate the refusal by the government to release requested information. In some countries, the ombudsman is an independent authority, while in some others he is an agent of the legislative assembly/parliament.

The Hongkong ombudsman has instituted an award system to encourage better response from government departments and organisations to his investigations. The awards are assessed by the degree of co-operation of complainee organisations to the ombudsman investigations and by their commitment to improve the quality of their services. Their positive approach in accepting and implementing the ombudsman's recommendations is an indication of their commitment.

The local government ombudsman in England has significantly noted in the annual report for 1996/97 that, 'More and more services have been contracted out to the private sector and voluntary bodies. The commission [for local administration] will continue to monitor what effects, if any, contracting out is having on the incidence of maladministration causing injustice... Since the contractors act on behalf of councils, their actions are open to investigation by ombudsmen and, if fault is found, it is the council who will be called on to provide redress. Councils will want to keep this is mind in making contracts with the service providers.'[24] The commission has published a new Digest of Cases which illustrate lessons for good administrative practices. Here a reference may be made to an interesting practice followed by the commission to get compliance from local councils on the suggestions made by the commission. If a council fails to satisfy the commission by taking appropriate action following a report, the commission issues a further report. If it still fails to take any action, the commission requires the council to issue a statement in the press, at its own expense, explaining why it has refused to comply with its recommendations.

As the ombudsman of Ontario has stressed in the annual report for 1997/98, 'The fundamental issue, as I see it, is the challenge of keeping government accountable to the people. In particular, this means ensuring that fair and equitable service is provided by all public institutions and the right to independent resolution of complaints is preserved and enhanced.'

This concept of ombudsman in Scandinavian countries and parliamentary commissioners in the Commonwealth countries was recommended for adoption in India by the administrative reforms commission (ARC). The ARC, in its report submitted in October 1966, had recommended the creation of the two institutions, namely, Lokpal for dealing with the complaints against administrative acts of ministers or secretaries to government at the centre and in the states, and another authority to be designated as Lok Ayukta in each state and at the centre for dealing with the complaints against administrative acts of other officials. The ARC was of the view that for the Lok Pal and Lok Ayukta to be fully effective, and for them to acquire power without conflicting with the other functionaries under the Constitution, it would be necessary to give Constitutional status to their offices, their powers, functions etc. In view of the urgency of setting up the institutions, the ARC had, however, recommended that pending Constitutional amendment, the

[24]The Commission for Local Administration in England, *Local Government Ombudsman—Annual Report 1996/97*.

government may take steps to establish these institutions by passing necessary legislation. Accordingly, fourteen states—Assam, Andhra Pradesh, Bihar, Gujarat, Haryana, Himachal Pradesh, Karnataka, Kerala, Madhya Pradesh, Maharashtra, Orissa, Punjab, Rajasthan and Uttar Pradesh—have taken steps to establish Lok Ayuktas. A public interest litigation has been filed in the Supreme Court by *Common Cause* to speed up the appointment of Lok Ayuktas in the remaining states.

There is no uniformity in the provisions of the state enactments on the subject. While in some states, grievances against the administration can be remedied by the Lok Ayukta, in some others, grievances are not within his purview. In some enactments, there is a wide range of functionaries covered including vice-chancellors and registrars of universities. In some states, the chief minister is brought within the purview of the Act while in some others, he is not. This is also the case with members of the state legislature. There is no uniformity as regards the qualifications of the persons to be appointed as Lok Ayukta/Upa Lok Ayukta, their emoluments, allowances, status and powers. In some of the Acts, the power of search and seizure is not provided. Some Acts provide for exercise of *suo motu* power by the Lok Ayukta/Upa Lok Ayukta. In some states, the administrative expenses of the Lok Ayukta are made chargeable on the Consolidated Fund of the state. Power to punish for contempt is conferred on the Lok Ayukta in some states. There are several other matters also on which there is no uniformity in the Acts.

The all India Lok Ayuktas conference held, from time to time, has passed unanimous resolutions that there should be a Lok Ayukta in each state, that Constitutional status should be given to the institution, and that there should be uniformity in the provisions of the state Acts. The conference also took the initiative of drafting a model Bill for the purpose.[25] The model Bill aims not only at uniformity, but also at making the various

---

[25] The model Lok Ayukta Bill presented by the Implementation Committee constituted by the Third All India Lok Ayuktas Conference held at Hyderabad, 1991.

provisions comprehensive. The more important provisions of the draft model Bill are brought out briefly hereafter. The scope of the definition of various terms such as allegation, maladministration has been widened to include more matters for investigation. The definition of public functionary is made more broad-based and includes the chief minister, ministers, members of state legislature, vice-chancellors etc. The criteria of merit, eminence and suitability of the person to be appointed as Lok Ayukta are sought to be assured by providing for consultation with the chief justice of the high court and the leader of the opposition in the legislative assembly. A provision is made for the administrative expenses of the institution of Lok Ayukta to be charged on the consolidated fund of the state. Discretion is given to the Lok Ayukta to dispense with the requirement of filing an affidavit along with the complaint. While providing for comprehensive powers to the Lok Ayukta to take up investigations, whether on complaint or self-motivated, into allegations of corruption or grievances of maladministration against public functionaries, the model Bill provides for:

- empowering the Lok Ayukta to recommend to the competent authority 'stay' on implementation of the order or action complained against so as to take such mandatory or preventive action as may be specified;
- taking such action as is necessary including suspension of the public functionary complained against; and
- grant of the interim relief to the complainant.

Powers of search and seizure, summoning of witnesses and documents, inspection of any office of the state government, and review, revision, restoration and granting of permission for withdrawal of the complaint have been provided for in the Bill.

A provision is also made for initiation of prosecution of any public functionary, if the Lok Ayukta is satisfied that the public functionary has committed an offence. An independent investigating agency to function under the exclusive administrative control and direction of Lok Ayukta is also provided. A provision is also made for the utilisation of the services of any person or agency of the state or central government to assist the Lok Ayukta in his functions. It has also been provided for the submission of property statements by certain public functionaries to the Lok Ayukta.

The proceedings before the Lok Ayukta are categorised as judicial proceedings. Jurisdiction, powers and authority are conferred on him in respect of contempt of itself as a high court under the provisions of the Contempt of Courts Act. Another statutory provision analogous to the Canadian statutes relating to ombudsman incorporated in the model Bill is the vesting of discretion in the Lok Ayukta to publish reports in the public interest relating to the exercise and performance of his functions and duties or any particulars of a case investigated by him.

The implementation committee of the conference of Lok Ayuktas has reiterated that it is necessary to give Constitutional status to the office, powers and functions etc. of Lok Ayukta as is available to the judges of the high courts. The committee also proposed that amendments to other laws such as the Representation of People Act etc. may also be necessary for the effective implementation of the model Bill.

The NCRWC has recommended that the Constitution should be amended to incorporate a provision obliging the states to establish the institution of Lok Ayukta.

The above discussion should provide a useful backdrop for an assessment of the functioning of the Lok Ayukta. Maharashtra was the first state to establish the institution of Lok Ayukta in 1972 but it is by no means the most effective among such institutions in the country. Orissa was the first state to pass a legislation for establishing a Lok Ayukta but the institution could not come into being in that state till 1983. Orissa also has the questionable distinction of having abolished the institution in 1992. The same fate befell the Haryana Lok Pal where the institution was abolished overnight through an ordinance. This was in spite of the fact that explicit protection was given to the serving high court judge appointed as the Lok Pal against such summary dismissal, but to get over the legal difficulty, the government abolished the institution itself! The matter was brought before the high court. The state legislature has passed a new law on the subject. According to newsreports, the Haryana Congress urged the Governor to withhold his assent to the Bill on the ground that it aimed at appointing a person close to the chief minister 'for the persecution of his political opponents'. (*Times of India*, 20 Nov 1999). The Punjab government repealed the Lok Pal Act in 1996 by issuing an ordinance. Reportedly, the outgoing Lok Pal had received eight complaints during his tenure and at least three were against former ministers in the late Beant Singh ministry. The repeal of the Act would give a reprieve to those against whom the complaints were pending with the Lok Pal. (*Times of India*, 13 Dec 1996). Appointment of a Lok Pal in Punjab has become equally controversial. The question whether there was effective consultation before appointment of the Lok Pal has became a subject matter of dispute before the high court of Punjab and Haryana (*Times of India*, 6 Nov 1999). There have been frequent changes in the policy on whether the Lok Pal should be a single member or multi-member body. The appointment of a Lok Pal became controversial once again in Orissa in 1997 when it was alleged that it was a ploy by the then chief minister to exercise control over this vital post. The matter was also brought before the Orissa High Court. (*Sunday*, 19–25 January 1997). In Maharashtra, the then Lok Ayukta H.N. Kantharia did not resign though he was physically incapacitated from performing his duties for several months. Finally, when a PIL was filed in the Bombay high court, he tendered his resignation. With politicisation and such actions, the institution has lost its public credibility.

The disenchantment of the Lok Ayuktas themselves with the present state of affairs is brought out from time to time in their pronouncements. Justice Mahender Bhushan Sharma, former Lok Ayukta of Rajasthan, is of the opinion that the Rajasthan government should wind up the institution of Lok Ayukta as it would serve no purpose unless it was empowered to initiate disciplinary action against corrupt bureaucrats and make it into an independent investigating agency to hold inquiry.

Justice Sharma admitted that he could not deliver the goods during his five-year tenure which could be attributed to the cosmetic structure of the institution. He felt it was simply a waste of his judicial background and efficiency as none of the recommendations made by him to the state government was accepted. All his predecessors faced this situation and it has been continuing since the inception of Lok Ayukta in 1973. Justice Sharma added that he had clearly recommended to the state government in his annual report in 1996 that there was no use of continuation of Lok Ayukta... The government has spent crores of rupees during the past 23 years on Lok Ayukta but the outcome was nil. (*Hindustan Times*, 8 Jul 1999).

The Madhya Pradesh Lok Ayukta had indicted two ministers in the state council of ministers in a land deal. Certain other ministers were also held responsible in the past for wrong decisions. Unfortunately, hardly any action was ever taken against them. The then Madhya Pradesh Lok Ayukta, Justice Faizanuddin, had expressed regret that the state government was not giving much-needed powers of prosecution to the Lok Ayukta. 'The government thus uses its own powers of not allowing prosecution to save the corrupt'. In his 16th annual report (1997–98) tabled in the Assembly, the Lok Ayukta has again demanded adequate powers and said that, 'if this is not done by the government there is no point in just formally keeping the anti-corruption organisation alive'. Since March 31, 1998, the state government has not granted permission for prosecution of 48 persons. Justice Faizanuddin says that the nexus between politicians, bureaucrats and criminals is resulting in the growing number of corruption cases in M.P. Because of the nexus, the big fish were let off the hook and the small fry were booked. (*Hindustan Times*, 9 Jul 1999).

The Himachal Pradesh Lok Ayukta has sought *suo motu* powers to take cognisance of complaints against politicians and other public servants. The present Act provides for action only on the basis of complaints on a sworn affidavit. Further, he should be empowered to take cognisance of grievances by way of complaints and not just the allegations as at present. It was suggested that the Lok Ayukta should be authorised to treat as complaint a letter written by a person in police custody, jail or any asylum. Provision should also be made for sending an interim report to government, when necessary. Such an interim report could contain recommendations for the suspension of a civil servant.[26]

The Karnataka Lok Ayukta Act provides that each year all MLAs and ministers, including the chief minister, have to submit property returns to the Lok Ayukta before the end of June. However, no MLA or minister had submitted such returns to the Lok Ayukta. Though the Lok Ayukta submitted to the government a list of all those who had not filed the returns, no action was taken against any one of them. (*Sakal*, 27 Feb 1997). The matter had to be raised in the high court.

In spite of repeated demands, the question of amendment of the Lok Ayukta Act in Maharashtra has been pending for years on end. The committee on good governance, referred to earlier, has recommended that the Lok Ayukta Act be amended to provide for the following:

- Entrusting the Lok Ayukta with the overall responsibilities of overseeing the vigilance work in the state and putting the director general, anti-corruption, under his charge.
- Placing a special investigation team of police officers at the disposal of the Lok Ayukta, as in Karnataka and Madhya Pradesh.
- Empowering the Lok Ayukta to release his reports to the general public as soon as they are presented to the government.
- Giving financial autonomy to the Lok Ayukta and to make the expenditure of the office of Lok Ayukta a 'charged' item.
- Treating the recommendation of the Lok Ayukta to sanction procution as mandatory.
- Deleting the provision of the Act to keep the name of the complainant and the officer complained against as confidential. Instead, it be provided that every enquiry by Lok

[26]Lok Ayukta Seeks More Teeth, *Tribune*, Chandigarh, 6 February 1996.

Ayukta shall be public, unless, for reasons recorded in writing, the Lok Ayukta decides to hold it in camera.
- Continuing the enquiries even after the persons complained against has demitted office.
- Bringing the state electricity board and the state road transport corporation within the purview of Lok Ayukta, and
- Giving effect to the other recommendations contained in the model Bill prepared by the conference of Lok Ayuktas.[27]

It needs to be noted that the government of Maharashtra has decided to make the Lok Ayukta the final appellate authority under the ordinance on right to information.

It can be seen how the institution of Lok Ayukta has failed to make any perceptible impact except in a few states. This is also evident from the fact that the workload of the Lok Ayuktas differs a great deal from state to state. In some states, the number of complaints is very small though the institution of Lok Ayukta has been functioning for a number of years. It may be useful to refer briefly to the observations, as under, made by Lok Ayuktas in their annual reports which bring out their institutional concerns over the years:

*Himachal Pradesh*: Competent authorities to whom recommendations are conveyed do not strictly adhere to the time schedule as prescribed in the Act. There are inordinate delays on the part of the authorities to whom complaints are referred for preliminary enquiry or for giving background of the case.[28]

*Andhra Pradesh*: A number of amendments have been proposed by the Lok Ayukta in the A.P. Lok Ayukta and Upa-Lok Ayukta Act and Rules. Important among these are:

---

[27]Madhav Godbole, *Report of the One Man Committee on Good Governance*, Government of Maharashtra, Mumbai, July 2001, pp. 13–14.
[28]Government of Himachal Pradesh, Home (Vigilance) Department, *Fourteenth Annual Consolidated Report of the Lok Ayukta of Himachal Pradesh for the period from 1/1/1996 to 31/12/1996.*

- to enlarge the scope of investigations by incorporating 'grievance' after the word 'allegation' under section 7; to provide for jurisdiction over officers drawing scales of pay lower than the minimum prescribed when they are found to be conjointly responsible with senior officers drawing higher scales of pay; to provide for jurisdiction over retired officers also for their actions while holding the posts.
- to bar jurisdiction of other agencies when the Lok Ayukta or Upa-Lok Ayukta has initiated proceedings against a public servant from carrying out collateral proceedings or disciplinary action, except prosecution for an offence under the Indian Penal Code or Prevention of Corruption Act.
- to authorise any police officer, not below the rank of an inspector of police of this institution, by a search warrant to enter and search any building or place for seizing incriminating material evidence required in any inquiry or other proceedings to be conducted by Lok Ayukta.
- to provide for payment of compensation by the state government to the complainant in appropriate cases and to direct that such compensation or any part thereof shall be paid by such officer or public servant.
- to forward an interim report to the competent authority for suspension of the public servant pending enquiry; to prevent further acts of misconduct of the public servant; to prevent the public servant from secreting the assets earned by him suspected to be by corrupt means; to safeguard against wastage of or damage to public property or public revenue by the administrative acts of the public servant; to advance public interest in any other manner; and to try summarily any person appearing in any proceeding before the Lok Ayukta for giving or fabricating false evidence.

These and other amendments are pending with the state government.[29]

[29]Government of Andhra Pradesh, *The Tenth Consolidated Report of the Institution of A.P. Lok Ayukta and Upa Lok Ayukta for the period from 1 January 1994 to 31 December 1994.*

According to a single judge judgement of the A.P. high court delivered in writ petition Nos. 2396/93 and 2397/93, it was declared that the Lok Ayukta has no jurisdiction over all-India service officers. A careful examination of the judgement of the learned judge indicates that the learned judge never tried to consider the scheme and scope of Act 11 of 1983. It should be remembered that the Lok Ayukta and Upa Lok Ayukta Act is not an Act dealing with the conditions of service. In the Fifth All India Lok Ayuktas' conference held at Gandhinagar, it was the unanimous opinion of all the Lok Ayuktas who attended that the single judge judgement of the A.P. high court is totally wrong and it is a misconceived judgement. Lok Ayuktas in other states such as Karnataka and Rajasthan are investigating into actions of all India service officers and action is being taken against them by the state government. Clearly, the Lok Ayukta has jurisdiction over the all-India service officers working in connection with the affairs of the state. The model Bill makes this position clear.[30]

*Gujarat*: The Lok Ayukta in Gujarat has no powers to look into complaints of maladministration. This deficiency in the Act needs to be rectified. The question of substituting the present Act by a new Act on the lines of the model Bill referred to earlier needs to be expedited. In this context, the definition of public grievance also needs to be widened. Thus, an act should also include failure to take action. The jurisdiction of the Lok Ayukta in Gujarat is very much truncated making the institution ineffective to deal with large number of public grievances. Many more public functionaries ought to be brought within the purview of the Lok Ayukta than at present. The Lok Ayukta should have the power to recommend to the competent authority concerned with such injustice or undue hardship, the steps to be taken to remedy or redress in such manner and within

---

[30] Government of Andhra Pradesh, *The Eleventh Consolidated report of the Institution of A.P. Lok Ayukta and Upa Lok Ayukta for the period from 1 January 1995 to 13 December 1995.*

such time as he deems fit. Where action taken is not satisfactory, the Lok Ayukta should have the power to make a special report.[31]

The annual report for the year ending 31 March 1997 again highlights the need to make amendments in the Act on the lines of the model Bill if the Lok Ayukta is not to remain a toothless tiger. The Act should, *inter alia*, vest the Lok Ayukta with the necessary authority to find out whether a public power has been used properly, misused or abused. In the Gujarat Act, there is no provision for the Lok Ayukta to make any specific recommendation or to specify the period within which action suggested by him is required to be taken. This needs to be rectified.[32]

*Bihar.* Some amendments have been made in the Bihar Lok Ayukta Act which have increased his powers and functions. The Lok Ayukta has suggested further amendments on the lines of the model Bill prepared by the conference of Lok Ayuktas. He has also suggested that a special investigation cell may be established in his office. He has also proposed that the expenditure of his office should be charged on the consolidated fund of the state.[33]

In another annual report, the Lok Ayukta has bitterly complained about the functioning of the government of Bihar. 'Because of callous negligence on the part of the departments concerned, there have been a few cases of grievances which could not be resolved for more than a decade despite the best efforts of this institution. Claims for pension, provident fund and gratuity etc. made by certain petitioners could not be settled even after issuance of 20 to 50 reminders by the Lok Ayukta to the respective departments. In certain cases I was compelled to make a special report to the Governor under section 12(5) of the Bihar

[31]Government of Gujarat, *Eighth Annual Consolidated Report of Lok Ayukta, Gujarat State, for the period from 1 April 1995 to 31 March 1996.*

[32]Government of Gujarat, *Ninth Annual Consolidated Report of Lok Ayukta, Gujarat State, for the period from 1 April 1996 to 31 March 1997.*

[33]Government of Bihar, *Annual Report 1989 of the Lok Ayukta, Bihar, for the period from 1 January 1989 to 31 December 1989,* 1991.

Lokayukta Act; but that did not help the complainants because of the dilatory procedure of submission of these special reports to the legislature... I repeat that if the Lok Ayukta has to be effective in the prevention of corruption and maladministration, he must have an independent investigating agency and his letters must receive prompt attention by the officers concerned and the head of departments must take stern action against those employees who were found to have caused delay and hindrances in the redressal of grievances'.[34]

*Punjab*: The Punjab Act needs to be amended on the lines of the Haryana Act. This will give larger powers and functions to the Punjab Lok Pal. Presently, the Lok Pal does not have sufficient workload. The Lok Pal should be the supreme vigilance body in the state and there would be no need to have a separate vigilance department.[35]

*Rajasthan*: The anti-corruption department should be placed under the direct control and supervision of Lok Ayukta and the sanction given by the Lok Ayukta to prosecute a person should be deemed to have been given by the competent authority. The necessary changes in the law to implement the above suggestions should be made. The Lok Ayukta has suggested a number of other amendments in the Act. These include: The definition of the word 'allegation' may be further extended so as to include the failure to act in accordance with the norms of integrity and conduct, abuse of position, and loss caused to the exchequer or property, not only of the state but also of the statutory local authorities, nationalised banks, etc.[36]

The Lok Ayukta has suggested the extension of his jurisdiction to former public servants including former ministers. As Lok

---

[34] Government of Bihar, *Annual Report 1990 of the Lok Ayukta, Bihar, for the period from 1 January 1990 to 31 December 1990*, 1991.

[35] Government of Punjab, *Consolidated Report on the Administration of Punjab Lokpal Act*, 1998.

[36] Government of Rajasthan, *Twelfth Report of Justice Shri Mohan Lall Shrimal, Lok Ayukta, Rajasthan, for the period from 1 July 1989 to 31 December 1989*.

Ayuktas in several other states have demanded, he has also asked for an independent investigating agency under Lok Ayukta. The other suggestion made by him pertains to the inclusion of complaints of public grievances about maladministration within the jurisdiction of the Lok Ayukta. He has suggested that powers be conferred on the Lok Ayukta to send for, from the state government, statements of property acquired by public servants.[37]

*Karnataka*: The Lok Ayukta has suggested that he should have the power to start an investigation on his own initiative. He has reiterated the suggestion made by the conference of Lok Ayuktas that the expression 'court' and 'judge' should mean only high court, civil and criminal courts and their presiding officers as the case may be. Clause (d) of the Second Schedule to the Act should be so amended as to enable investigation under the Act to be held in regard to claims for arrears of pay and revised pay scales. The Act should be amended on the lines of the draft model Bill formulated by the conference of Lok Ayuktas.[38]

This brief survey of the annual reports of Lok Ayuktas in several states brings out how the institution of Lok Ayukta in most states lacks powers or teeth to address the tasks for which the office was created. Even in a state such as Maharashtra, where the institution has been in existence for over twenty five years, it has failed to make any impact. The need for such an institution in the Indian context cannot be over-emphasised but there is no political will to make it a success. In any scheme of good governance, a grievance redressal institution such as the Lok Ayukta must find a prime place. But, this would mean starting afresh with the requisite Constitutional amendment and a uniform central law on the subject. Looking at past experience, this is a tall order indeed.

---

[37]Lokayukta Sachivalaya, Rajasthan, *Thirteenth Annual Report, 1993*.
[38]Government of Karnataka, *Tenth Annual Consolidated Report of Karnataka Lokayukta for the period from 1 April 1995 to 31 March 1996*.

# 5

# Corporate and Co-operative Governance

## Corporate Governance

### Introduction

Michel Camdessus, former Managing Director of the IMF, has emphasised that, 'Anyone who takes the need for transparency seriously will profoundly change the course of events. Such reforms will require a vast change in domestic business practices, corporate culture, and government behaviour. Obviously, this will be a long-term process.[1] This statement provides a useful framework for discussion in this chapter. At the outset, a major difference between the government and the corporate sector must be noted. Government at various levels, is accountable to the people. Its functioning comes up for scrutiny in parliament, state legislatures, zilla parishads, municipal councils and their committees. The government is also held accountable by the

---

[1] Michel Camdessus, Good Governance Has Become Essential in Promoting Growth and Stability (edited excerpts of an address at the meeting of Transparency International in Paris on 21 January 1998), *Southern Economist*, 15 March 1998, p. 22.

courts. This level of accountability and transparency is absent as as far as the corporate sector is concerned. While each shareholder is an owner of the company, it is only in name. Most shareholders do not hold shares of a company on a long term basis. Their aim is to obtain capital appreciation and then exit to greener pastures. Thus, in a large number of cases, shareholders are more investors than owners. As a result, shareholders hardly ever pay close attention to the functioning of companies. Often, shareholders prefer to off-load the shares of a company doing badly, rather than ask questions at the annual general body meetings. In a sense, this is the most effective weapon for ensuring good corporate behaviour, but in all such cases, the employees and the small investor are the losers. Shareholders abandoning a company should therefore be considered only as a remedy or last resort for bringing its management to book. Ways have to be found for setting up close and continuous systemic surveillance mechanisms and early warning signals of any wrong-doing. It is, therefore, surprising that the governance of companies has become a subject matter of discussion only during the last decade. Even rudimentary things like rules of transaction of business, which are a part of the working of any government, are being debated now as a part of the code of best practices and corporate governance.

Any discussion on corporate governance must necessarily begin with the Cadbury committee report in the UK in the early 1990s. The circumstances in which the Cadbury committee was set up deserve special mention as they are relevant to the conditions prevailing in India even today. First, there was concern at the low level of financial reporting and the inability of auditors to provide safeguards that the users of financial information expected. The underlying factors were seen as the looseness of accounting standards which provided too many options, the absence of a clear framework for ensuring that the directors kept the controls in their business under review, and the competitive pressures both on companies and auditors which made it difficult for the auditors to stand up to demanding boards. Second, there had been unexpected failures of major companies in the UK. There was a feeling that annual reports had failed to provide forewarning of companies which subsequently failed. Third, there was criticism as far as boards of management were concerned that the directors of the board were being paid excessive salaries or remuneration that was unlinked to their actual corporate performance. For the first time this committee gave corporate governance a form and substance and more importantly gave it a definition to say, 'corporate governance is the system by which the companies are directed and controlled'. Other efforts in this regard include, among others, corporate governance principles adopted by the OECD (Organisation of Economic Co-operation and Development), and in the US, UK (London Stock Exchange Combined Code), and European and other countries. The latest in the series in the set of reforms proposed by the New York Stock Exchange in May 2002.

The studies on this subject in India are of comparatively recent origin and include the reports of the task force of the Confederation of Indian Industry (CII) in April 1997, committee of the Securities and Exchange Board of India (SEBI) in 1999, advisory group of RBI in March 2001, the RBI consultative group of directors of banks/financial institutions in April 2002 and the Naresh Chandra committee on corporate audit and governance (December 2002). While there are some variations and change of emphasis, the ground covered in these reports largely overlaps. The areas covered include, among others, size, composition, charter, responsibilities and meetings of the board of directors; tenure of directors; age limit for appointment as directors; liability of directors; accountability to shareholders and stakeholders; access of information; nominee directors and their remuneration; committee on grievances of shareholders; executive vs. non-executive chairman of the board; audit committee; remuneration committee; nomination committee; board procedures; accounting standards and financial reporting; disclosure and transparency; auditor independence; audit firm rotation; responsibilities of individual and institutional shareholders; and matters relating to the implementation of canons of corporate governance.

## International Experience

A basic survey of international experience given hereafter shows that corporate governance leaves a great deal to be desired even in advanced Western democracies in spite of a fairly well developed legal, regulatory and institutional framework, and much greater activism on the part of shareholders and institutional investors. The collapse of the mighty and all powerful Enron Corporation in 2001 has shown how important it is that a code of best practices and the tenets of corporate governance be scrupulously adhered to even by corporate giants to avoid exemplary punishment by the market. Before it went under, in November 2001, Enron announced that it would restate all its annual financial statements from 1997 to 2000, resulting in a cumulative profit reduction of $591 million and an increase in debt of $628 million. The stories doing the rounds since the collapse of Enron are legion including the one about the make-believe trading hall built at a cost of half a million dollars to create a frenzy among gullible investors which could provide material for dozens of Hollywood (and Bollywood) suspense thrillers!

In 1998, Comroad, a navigation technology company in Germany, invented two-thirds of its revenue in the name of a non-existent client in Hongkong. The auditor, KPMG, did not bother to verify this. Renowned companies like Waste Management, Cendant, and Xerox too have lied to investors. As *The Economist* (4 May 2002) has brought out, 'Business leaders are being knocked off their pedestals faster than Communist heroes after the fall of Berlin Wall'. Bernie Ebbers, a deal maker from Mississippi whose creation, Worldcom, the epitome of telecom excitement, was forced out in April 2002 and had to file the largest bankruptcy suit in US history in July 2002. Diana 'DeDe' Brooks, a forceful former chief executive of Sotheby's, was sentenced to house arrest and narrowly escaped being jailed—the fate handed out to her former chairman, Alfred Taubman. Even Jack Welch, the former chief executive officer (CEO) of General Electric (GE) (the world's most admired company according to *Fortune* magazine) who was perhaps the best-known celebrity CEO of them all (the most successful manager of the past quarter century, according to *The Economist*), has seen his reputation dive. In August 2000, GE's shares were fetching $60 each. On 24 April 2002, GE's shares had fallen to $33, valuing the company at $268 billion less than its worth at its peak. Dynegy CEO, Chuck Watson, had to step down after it emerged that like Enron, his company had used special purpose entities to disguise debt. A recent survey shows that Americans now think more highly of politicians than they do of business executives! The vehemence of today's reaction against business leaders is partly a reflection of how far their company's shares have fallen, and also the extent of their personal greed. *Business Week* has called it 'CEO credibility crisis', while *Fortune* magazine speaks of it as a 'systemic breakdown'.

Americans are not the only ones turning against their former corporate heroes. In Europe too, Jean-Marie Messier of Vivendi Universal has seen investors turning against him due to poor results, much publicised infighting and a 40 per cent fall in the share price in 2002. This is also true of Percy Barnevik, the Swede once described by *Fortune* as 'Europe's answer to Jack Welch'.

These cases have raised some important questions pertaining to the auditing profession, its own corporate governance and institutional arrangements for its regulation. All accounting firms which audit listed companies in the US are subject to self-regulation by the American Institute of Certified Public Accountants (AICPA). According to the London *Financial Times*, peer reviews in 1999–2000 covered 441 firms, 67 of which were asked to initiate action to improve their performance. Action was taken against a number of firms charged with audit failure, with neither the firms nor the individuals being spared. Over and above this self-regulation, there is another body known as the Public Oversight Board.[2] In spite of this elaborate system, several gaping holes and not just

[2] Mythili Bhusnurmath, 'Ensuring "Best Practice" in Letter and Spirit', *Economic Times*, 24/12/2001.

chinks have come to light in the armour of audit. Warren Buffett was right when he said that the basic problem is that auditors feel they are working for the management and not for shareholders. The Enron scandal has led to Arthur Andersen, one of the 'Big Five' accounting firms in the world, established in 1913, losing its own independent identity. Andersen, described by the prosecution as a 'lapdog rather than a watchdog' of Enron is now facing several civil and criminal suits in American courts. A guilty verdict by the jury in a criminal case pertaining to obstruction of justice in June 2002 has shaken the normally sedate accounting profession in the US. The Texas State Board of Public Accountancy has underlined that, 'Andersen's failure to comply with professional standards was not due to the actions of one "rogue" partner or "out-of-control" office, but the structure and corporate climate that created a lack of integrity and objectivity'. (*Times of India*, 25 Feb 2002). The question of larger significance is the breakdown of the Chinese Walls separating different financial activities. The first question which requires serious consideration is whether audit firms should be permitted to provide other services such as consultancy to their clients. Andersen, for instance, earned $25 million as audit fee, $2 million less than what it earned from its consultancy work. According to a newsreport, the Securities and Exchange Commission (SEC) has said that Ernst & Young, another of the 'Big Five' accounting firms, was auditing the books of People Soft at the same time it was developing and marketing a software product with the company. (*Economic Times*, 22 May 2002). The second question is of conflict of interest. For example, a large number of former employees of Andersen held top financial jobs in Enron. According to one report, blacklists have circulated round the City of London and Wall Street. One of them listed all companies whose chief financial officers had been recruited from one of the 'Big Five' accounting firms. The third question is whether, the present practice of each company appointing its auditor should be superceded and, the appointment made by an independent public agency so that the auditor will have greater independence in his work. The payment to the auditor could also be made by such an agency. The fourth is the proposal before the US federal regulators that the chief executive officer of a company should be made personally responsible for satisfying himself about and certifying the correctness of his company's quarterly and annual financial statements. It is also proposed to reduce the time limits for submission of such reports. The US Senate has already approved legislation to create an accounting oversight board to set standards and discipline wayward auditors. A demand is also being voiced that publicly traded companies should be required to make their tax returns public. The Sorbanes-Oxley Act (Sox), which is a sweeping corporate reform law passed in 2002, lays down several stringent requirements. As a result, CEOs and CFOs of companies will have to certify financial statements, stock options will have to be deducted to arrive at the final profit figure and auditors will have to submit themselves to the discipline of the new public overright board. The Act also lays down stringent jail terms for top officials knowingly defrauding investors. The Sox will lead to SEC adopting new rules at least on 24 different areas of its supervision.

In spite of these recent setbacks to the cause of corporate governance, note must be taken of some of the major developments in this field during the past few years. Wharton professor Michael Useem has underlined that, 'Fifteen years ago, a chief executive probably could not even name who his major shareholders were. Now, they are on first name basis with all the fund managers. There is increasing willingness on the part of big money managers to go for the CEO's head if he does not get results.[3] A growing number of bold European CEOs are also putting shareholders first in their scheme of things. As Janet Guyon has brought out, 'In the 1970s and 1980s, shareholders were mostly ignored as government coddled major industries to preserve jobs. Some companies got bigger, of course, but often they focused on increasing revenue at the expense of profits. "Shareholder value was put on the shelf" says Jorma Ollila, who took over as CEO of Finland's Nokia in 1992. Ollila recalls that

[3]Ronald B Lieber, Who Owns The 500?, *Fortune 500*.

in the 1980s, when Nokia ignored its shareholders—they were hardly mentioned at board meetings—the company made some bad acquisitions that could not have been justified under a more rigorous system of accountability.'[4]

At the same time, it is widely recognised that Europe Inc. must find its own way to increase returns to shareholders. Europe (like India) still has a number of laws and attitudes that protect employees and companies from the brutalities of the market. But companies that have embraced shareholder value see it as an essential tool for global competition. As some one has said, the returns can be mind-bending. Daimler-Benz used the discipline of Wall Street's demands to cut costs, sell divisions, and boost its stock value so high that it was able to swallow Chrysler in a deal that at the time was the biggest industrial takeover ever.

Note must also be taken of the fact that in the US anyone who contravenes the law of the land is quickly brought to book. This is as true of affluent corporate executives as it is of common criminals. One such jailed CEO, Barry Minkow, of ZZZZ Bet, said when sentenced in 1989, 'Today is a great day for this country. The system works. They got the right guy.'

Azhar Kazmi has underlined that ethics and values became an important concern in the U.S. in the 1980s. In the US, there are about 500 courses, 25 textbooks and three academic journals devoted to business ethics (Stark, 1993). In the wake of mounting scandals, corporations all over the world are adopting a code of ethics, business management schools are developing ethics courses and consultants are hired to put 'integrity' into corporate culture (Sullivan and Brown, 1994). S.R. Shad states in the *New York Times*, 'I have been very disturbed most recently with the large number of graduates of leading business and law schools who have become convincted felons'. (Gavin and Klinefelter, 1988). He went on to provide the Harvard Business School an endowment of US$30 million in 1987 to focus on the interest of teaching business ethics to management students.

---

[4]Janet Guyon, Rebels with a Cause, *Fortune*, December 21, 1998.

This seems to coincide with the initial wave of current interest in teaching ethics in the US (Macdonald and Dunleavy, 1995).[5]

Spirituality is the latest corporate buzzword in the US. What is new is that it has just entered the mainstream. Corporate America is in the midst of a 'Damascus Conversion'. The Davos agenda in 1999 included confabulations on 'spiritual anchors for the new millennium' and 'the future of meditation in a networked economy'. Thirty MBA programmes now offer courses on the subject. It is also the focus of a recent Harvard Business School Bulletin.[6]

In the US, it is not uncommon to see a chief executive being forced to leave due to the poor results of the company he is heading—something unheard of in India. In April 1999, Compaq Computer Corporation stunned the technology world by ousting its chief executive Eckhard Pfeiffer because the first quarter profits were half those expected. Pfeiffer resigned when the board of directors told him that it wanted new leadership for the company.

A reference must also be made to Fortune 500's second annual listing of America's worst boards of directors.[7] Colvin says, directors are no longer 'the parsley [herb used for flavouring] on the fish' as a US Steel CEO memorably described them more than fifty years ago. By hiring, paying, or firing the CEO and approving strategy, they create or destroy masses of wealth, which is why major institutional investors like pension funds and mutual funds increasingly vote against directors who are not performing—something almost unheard of just a few years ago. The author explains, 'for our second annual roster of America's worst boards, we canvassed institutional investors, corporate governance experts, investor advisory firms, and shareholder rights activists for nominations. We made the final selection'.

[5]Azhar Kazmi, Ethics and Professional Values in Business and Industry in India, *Paradigm*, Vol. I, No. 2, January 1998, pp. 86–93.

[6]Marci Mcdonald, 'Shush, The Guy in the Cubicle is Meditating', *US News & World Report*, May 3, 1999, p. 46.

[7]Geoffrey Colvin, Bad Boards, Bad Boards—Whatcha Gonna Do?, *Fortune 500*, Vol. 139, No. 8, April 26, 1999, p. 411.

The excessive and exorbitant compensation packages of CEOs in the US has become a matter of serious concern in that country. According to *Business Week*, the average CEO of a major corporation made 42 times the pay of a typical American factory worker in 1980. By 1990, that ratio had more than doubled to 85 times the average factory wage and almost quintupled again to 419 times more in 1998. If that rate of exponential growth were to continue, the average CEO would make the salary equivalent of more than 150,000 American factory workers in 2050.[8]

A recent research report by London-based economic advisor Smithers & Co. recalculated the profits of the 100 largest US companies by adjusting for the value of their executives' stock options. The study found that 11 firms went from profit to loss, and another 13 had their profits cut in half. In addition, the Investor Responsibility Research Centre has found the average potential dilution of shareholder value from stock option plans is 9.2 per cent for S&P 500 companies.

The question to be considered is whether American companies have to pay exorbitant CEO salaries just because there are not enough capable executives in the United States? Corporations in other countries do not seem to have trouble motivating their CEOs with less stratospheric pay packages. According to the international human resources company Towers Perrin, the average CEO in the United Kingdom makes $645,540; in Japan, $420,855; and in Germany, $398,430—far less than the average American CEO. When Germany's Daimler-Benz acquired the substantially smaller American car producer Chrysler, Chrysler CEO Robert Eaton was making eight times the salary of Daimler-Benz CEO Juergen Schrempp.[9] AFL-CIO, the apex trade union organisation, has, in fact, established a web site called executive pay watch. One of its news analyses gives six ways to fight the menace of runaway CEO pay: get inside the

---

[8] Executive Pay Watch: Runaway CEO Pay, http://www.aflcio.org/paywatch/ceopay.htm
[9] *Ibid.*

boardroom, use your shareholder clout, rally your co-workers and the community, take it to the IRS (Internal Revenue Service), call on the regulators, namely, SEC, and organise campaigns.

As regards emoluments to be paid to the non-executive directors, the original practice was to pay them only the sitting fees which were nominal. This position has undergone a change in recent years with the sitting fees being stepped up considerably. In addition, they are also given a share in the net profit of the company subject to certain upper limits. It is of some advantage to make such payments partly by way of company stocks and partly by way of stock options. The first would create a stake for the directors in the company. The second will be an incentive for them to make sure that the company continues to do well on the stock exchange.

Two other innovations have been attempted in some companies in the US: the first is to hold some meetings of the board without the presence of the CEO. This encourages more independent views to emerge on several crucial matters. The second is to periodically evaluate the work of the CEO when he is absent from the meeting. This fosters a healthy respect for the position of the board and establishes its primacy *vis-a-vis* the CEO.

*The Economist* cites the case of Campbell Soup to show what good governance means. In 1990, this food company, which had been in the doldrums for years, appointed a new chief executive, David Johnson. Johnson believes that accountable bosses are better bosses. Since taking over, he—not the shareholders—has persuaded the board to transform the firm into a model of active corporate governance. The pay of top managers is closely linked to performance. The performance criteria are tough, requiring the firm to outdo its closest competitors. Board members are independent, and are paid in company shares. Senior managers are required to hold shares worth three times their annual salary. The firm has no poison pills or anti-take-over devices. It talks often with institutional shareholders—and actively votes the proxies of shares held by its pension fund in other firms. And the pay-off? Since Johnson took charge, Campbell Soup's profits have soared. So has Mr Johnson's pay. So, too, has the firm's share price. It can be done.[10]

Looking at the way ahead, *The Economist* underlines that, 'one striking thing about each different national system of corporate governance is that market forces have been prevented from seeking out the most efficient relationship between shareholders and managers. Politics, law, organisational incentives, culture and historical chance have wielded enormous influence... Such differences suggest that though each country's corporate governance may evolve in a similar direction, they will do so in distinct ways.'[11]

### Nearer Home

It is against this background that one must assess the corporate governance scene in India. The brief discussion above has brought out the innovations made, initiatives taken and the close attention paid to corporate governance by stakeholders in these countries. In comparison, the realities in India are far removed from the precepts of corporate governance advocated by the committees. In fact, they highlight the gap between preaching and practice.

It will be totally wrong to assume that, in a competitive market (if there is one), what is good for the Tatas or the Ambanis is good for India, as was asserted in an article in a national daily. This is as preposterous as the once celebrated statement, 'Indira (Gandhi) is India and India is Indira'. The question to be considered is whether it would be correct to equate the private sector in India with that in advanced Western countries in terms of its efficiency and productivity, and whether there is a framework of strong institutions and safeguards to protect society at large from the unscrupulous and exploitative traits of the private sector which seem to extend to even subverting national interests.[12]

[10]Corporate Governance, *The Economist*, 29 January 1994.
[11]*Ibid.*
[12]Madhav Godbole, Corporate Democracy and Responsibility, *Hindu*, 15 November 1996, *The Changing Times—A Commentary on Current Affairs*, Orient Longman, 2000, p. 278.

Gone are the days when the nexus between politicians and top business tycoons used to be kept hidden from public view. Now there is a new boldness in flaunting the connection. In this connection, a joke doing the rounds in Indonesian President Suharto's days may be recounted because, in terms of crony capitalism, India and Indonesia have a great deal in common —Suharto is chatting with his Chinese businessman friend Liem Sioe Liong. 'Who owns Indofood?' the president asks. 'I do'. 'Indomobile?', 'I do'. 'Indomilk?', 'I do'. Finally Suharto asks, 'Who owns Indonesia?' and Liam answers, 'That's a joint venture'.[13] This could as well have been a dialogue between a prime minister (with some honourable exceptions) and Dhirubhai Ambani in India.

The investigations by the CBI, the Enforcement Directorate and other agencies into the involvement of some of the large industrial houses in shady and illegal activities, such as violations of the foreign exchange regulations or making clandestine payments in the Jharkhand case, gave rise to an astonishing response from the leaders of industry. Various apex industry organisations have reacted sharply to the so-called 'human rights violations' and 'excesses' by the investigating agencies. An ingenious argument has been put forth that a differentiation must be made between criminal charges and alleged economic irregularities, as also between technical violations of outmoded and obsolete laws and offences involving common and hard criminals. It is argued that it is wrong to arrest persons involved in economic crimes or to put them in prison before they are convicted. These apex bodies asserted that the actions of investigating agencies could lead to a fear psychosis, slowing down industrial growth and eroding the confidence of people in economic liberalisation. It was asserted that such actions were against the principles of a free market. They hoped that 'at this critical stage of globalisation, the overseas investors should not

---

[13]Indonesia: Ethnic Hot Zone, *Newsweek*, February 10, 1997, p. 25.

be scared away'.[14] This was again brought out by the lobbying of the CII with the government for companies caught in the final list of FERA violations before the expiry of the Act. (*Economic Times*, 16 Oct 2002).

It has been recognised all over the world that a free market does not mean a free-for-all market. Propagating the highly misleading and self-serving view that economic liberalisation gives freedom to flout the laws of the land with impunity, in fact, weakens the case for liberalisation and economic reforms. There is a large cross- section of public opinion in this country which firmly believes that foreign investment must be accepted on our own terms and we should not compromise our sovereignty and integrity in any way. The arguments now put forth by the captains of industry are quite contrary to this. No one can countenance permitting foreign firms to flout our laws, rules and regulations, howsoever irksome or cumbersome they may be.

It is pertinent to underline that a number of industry and trade delegations from abroad have repeatedly and publicly urged this country to follow open and transparent policies and procedures in deciding matters pertaining to new investments. No one has asked for unlimited liberties. All that they have requested is that the rules of the game be made clear. But, how can anyone ask for immunity or exemption from law? Even Indian industry setting up ventures abroad cannot expect such dispensation from the host country.

This debate also raises another important issue regarding the differentiation between economic crimes and other crimes. In the eyes of law, there can be no such distinction. If any distinction has to be made, persons indulging in economic crimes must be treated more harshly than common criminals, keeping in view their financial and political clout, education, family background, motivation and so on.

---

[14] Madhav Godbole, Economic Crimes and Corporate Sector: No Scope for Leniency, *Indian Express*, 5 December 1996, *The Changing Times—A Commentary on Current Affairs*, Orient Longman, p. 282.

Thus, we have a long way to go in creating a socially conscious, responsible and responsive corporate sector in the country. When this happens, such unconscionable demands from leaders of industry for a permissive dispensation will cease. For, if a choice has to be made between the rule of law and economic liberalisation, we as a country will have to opt for the rule of law.

.It is necessary to remember that shareholders are only one of the stakeholders. Increasing shareholder value can be only one of the objectives of corporate governance. The other equally important stakeholders are employees, creditors, customers and last, but not least, the community. Looked at in this perceptive, it is clear that corporate governance in India is in its infancy.

Mrityunjay Athreya has brought out a three-step process for transforming corporate governance comprising laws for minimum good governance; competent entrepreneurs, professional managers and their dedicated leadership for better governance; and business values and ethics for superior governance.[15] In the Indian context, the last one is of particular significance as it has rarely been given the recognition it deserves.

K.B. Dadiseth was right when he said that corporate governance in its widest sense is almost like a trusteeship. He cautioned that we in India therefore cannot confine our model of corporate governance to only the hardware of rules and regulations like committees and number of non-executive directors. More crucial is the software—creating a corporate conscience and consciousness, the culture of transparency and openness in the organisation; the confidence that every person in the corporation will know and do on his own, what is right... The ultimate purpose of governance should be to create a self-driven, self-assessed and self-regulated organisation. This is the principle which corporate governance models the world over

---

[15]Mrityunjay Athreya, Transforming Corporate Governance, *Paradigm*, Vol. I, No. 2, January 1998, p. 10.

underscore and this is what companies in India will need to imbibe, whether in strategy or implementation.[16]

Against the background, it is interesting to see that a large number of companies have overstated their profits while reporting their accounts in 2000–01. A study showed that of the 639 companies covered, 139 companies overstated their profits. The degree of overstating was widest at well over 1000 per cent from the CRISIL norm.

One of the ingredients of corporate governance is the appointment of independent directors on the boards of companies. A note needs to be taken, in this context, of the findings of a study by Omkar Goswami of the boards of the top 100 listed private companies. It reveals that most of them are numerically dominated by executive directors or are packed with retired corporate executives, bureaucrats, family members and well-wishers who wish to have no say in the companies or by executives of other group companies so that there are hardly any de facto non-executive directors. The report states that it is incredible that a country with such a large talent of professionals does not have a larger pool of committed non-executive directors. The fact that such a pool has not come into play in the corporate world is because Indian companies do not search for such people and choose the comfortable riskless option of selecting non- executive directors from a small coterie. (*Economic Times*, 3 Feb 1997).

*Business Today* carried out an exercise in 1997 to identify the best boards of directors in the country.[17] The criteria adopted for evaluation were: (a) accountability to shareholders, (b) transparency of disclosures,[18] (c) quality of disclosures, and (d) independence of decision-making.

[16]K.B. Dadiseth, *Corporate Governance in India*, 32nd A.D. Shroff Memorial Lecture delivered under the auspices of the Forum of Free Enterprise on 24 October 1997 in Mumbai.

[17]The Best Boards, *Business Today*, May 7, 1997.

[18]This is particularly relevant. As a humorist has commented, balance sheets of companies, like bikinis, conceal vital portions but reveal interesting features.

In this field the examples to follow will necessarily have to be of those who have either tapped foreign capital markets or who are leaders of the corporate world in this country. Infosys Technologies Limited of Bangalore, one of India's leading information technology companies, was the first Indian company to obtain a direct listing on the US market by registering on the Nasdaq Stock Exchange on March 11, 1999. Infosys financial statements are prepared in compliance with the US General Audit and Accounting Practices (GAPP) and SEC (Securities and Exchange Commission) accounting standards and disclosure norms, the most stringent set of accounting standards in the world. Its annual reports have redefined standards in financial transparency. Material disclosures are instantly communicated to stakeholders. It is the first Indian company to value intangibles on the balance sheet, like human resources, brand, etc. The company also brings out quarterly audited reports. It was the first Indian company to offer stock options to its employees. It was one of the first few companies to have a planned investor relation strategy in the form of analyst conferences, conference calls after every result, results in audio/video posted over the Web, etc.

A reference may be made to yet another aspect of corporate governance. This pertains to appointment by a company of a social audit committee for a detailed review of its performance. Unfortunately, there have been very few instances of corporates submitting themselves to such a social audit. One such example was that of the Unit Trust of India. The report of the social audit committee, under the chairmanship of M.H. Kania, former chief justice of India, submitted in October 1994 makes interesting reading.[19] With all its limitations, this is a welcome initiative and needs to be encouraged.

It will be instructive to refer to the shocking case of lack of public accountability and transparency in respect of accumulation of so-called non-performing assets (NPAs), which were more appropriately called bad debts earlier, in the public sector banks. The union finance minister has rightly called it the loot of the financial sector. The NPAs account for over

[19]Unit Trust of India, *Report of the Social Audit Committee*, October 1994.

Rs 100,000 crore. The report of the parliamentary standing committee on finance which went into the matter is revealing.[20] The report states that the RBI had reviewed the top 300 NPAs of public sector banks in 1996 to identify whether staff lapses were responsible for the incidence of NPAs and if so whether action to identify staff accountability has been taken/was being taken by banks. It was noticed that staff lapses leading to accounts turning into NPAs were very few and banks had initiated appropriate action where necessary. The review further revealed that a majority of NPAs had arisen in the normal course of business and the failure of a venture due to various reasons. This is yet another example, in the bank scam tradition, of ascribing everything to systemic failures and not holding anyone responsible. The lending institutions are as culpable as the corporate sector for this day-light robbery.

Debashis Basu rightly seems to get exasperated with so much talk of corporate governance in the country and so little action. To him, corporate governance simply means the social responsibility of business, and any discussion on this subject must take the bull of family ownership and control by the horns. 'In India, good corporate governance would mean not siphoning off money. How can we even talk of governance when there has hardly been any change in the attitude of the families towards minority shareholders, an attitude that has been the cause of so much of destruction of shareholder wealth'. As Basu underlines, corporate governance will come into place if there is a little more activism and far less of committees, closed-door meetings and pompous code of conduct.[21]

The CII is right when it says that the financial institutions have not done well as board-level monitors. In fact, the net worth of many firms, where banks and financial institutions have exposures and where they have appointed nominee directors, have been negative. Calpers, the largest pension fund in the US

---

[20]Lok Sabha Secretariat, *Report of the Standing Comittee of Finance (1998–99), Twelfth Lok Sabha, Demands for Grants (1997–98)*, July 1998, pp. 10–12.

[21]Debashis Basu, Second Opinion/Forced Governance, *Economic Times Online*, 16 June 1999.

and the third largest in the world, says that it refuses directorships because directorships align a fund with a company's management. Instead, it uses its voting rights to remove non-perfoming directors and sends recommendations on proxies to block reappointment of directors with a poor record and bad resolutions. In India, the system of nominee directors has been very unsatisfactory. This system came into being in the wake of the socialistic policies promulgated by Indira Gandhi after the split of the Congress party in the late 1960s and early 1970s. As a part of these policies, the government gave directives to the financial institutions to convert their loans into equity in suitable cases. The idea of social responsibility of the private sector, in fact, was brought to the fore during this period though Mahatma Gandhi had talked of trusteeship earlier. The practice of appointing nominee directors came into being as a part of the policies enunciated by Indira Gandhi. Unfortunately, the institution of nominee directors was used more to bring pressure on industries to do certain things or to desist from doing certain things as per the wishes of the ruling political party rather than exercising independent judgment about the working of the company. Nominee directors have been supporting existing managements on the ground that it is necessary to provide stability. They have also served as protection against hostile take-overs. It will be recalled that Swaraj Paul's bid to take over Escorts and DCM in the 1980s was stymied by the nominees of FIs on the boards of these companies. Though the financial institutions owned 38 per cent of the company, nominee directors ignored the findings of the special audit of ITC which had sounded the first warning about FERA violations within the company. Talking of the role of FIs in ITC, Subir Ray has rightly said, 'The institutions have looked after the interests of neither the country nor the company. In fact, they have looked after no interests, not even of themselves, except those of their political masters of the day'.[22] Nominee directors, except for

[22]Subir Ray, ITC Mess Highlights FI Dilemma, *Business Standard*, 15 November 1996.

honourable exceptions, have been silent spectators of the goings on in the board and have sought government instructions on all sensitive and critical points instead of using their independent judgement. As has been seen, the nominee directors do not intervene even in matters involving larger public interests. For example, when the Ambanis were making a clandestine bid to take over Larson and Toubro some years ago, the nominee directors as one newspaper put it 'were not heard to be even breathing, leave aside opposing the move'. If nominee directors had been effective in their work on the boards, the banks and financial institutions would have had far less NPAs than they presently have.

The manner of selection of nominee directors is far from satisfactory. It is not, therefore, surprising that the RBI consultative group of directors of banks/financial institutions has recommended (April 2002) that due diligence of the directors of all banks should be done in regard to their suitability for the post, and the government, while nominating directors on the boards of public sector banks, should be guided by certain broad 'fit and proper' norms for the directors. Such is the low level of transparency and accountability that the criteria for selection of nominee directors have remained a mystery. Even a composite list of the names of nominee directors is not put out by the banks and financial institutions periodically for people to see. In view of this past experience, it is best that the system of nominee directors is abolished, except in cases in which a borrower is in imminent danger of or in actual default in repayment of loan or payment of interest. Even in a case where a FI holds equity shares in a company, it will be much more effective if it votes with its feet. The best way to exercise control over the assisted companies is to leave them in no doubt that the FI will disinvest if the company does not do well, a criterion which has hardly ever been applied by the FIs in India diligently and uniformly.

While a number of recommendations contained in the reports on corporate governance are unexceptional, there can be a difference of opinion on a few of them. For example, the recommendation pertaining to the maximum number of companies (10) on which a person may be permitted to accept directorship is seriously open to question. If a person is to be permitted to hold directorship on ten companies excluding their subsidiaries and associate companies, he would hardly be able to do justice to the job and pay the kind of close attention to the working of the company that is expected of him. This is particularly important as he may have to work on a number of committees of the board. Similarly, the Naresh Chandra committee's recommendations that there is no need for any statutory rotation of audit firms or public accounting oversight boards are difficult to understand. The recent controversy pertaining to the AF Ferguson report on Tata Finance Limited brings out the seriousness of the relevant issues.

The corporate sector in India chants the new *mantra* of economic liberalisation and globalisation incessantly and is not averse to preaching to the government and, for that matter, all other sections of society to set their houses in order to meet these new challenges. But, when it comes to their own affairs, they find it difficult to change their old mindset. A reference may be invited in this context to only two of the recommendations of the report of the working group on the companies Act, 1956. These are difficult to fathom, particularly with all the talk of good governance which is heard at the five star hotel seminars organised by the CII and the other apex chambers of commerce and industry.[23] The first of these pertains to the voluntary appointments of audit committees. The working group has recommended that, 'At this juncture, the requirement for audit committees and nomination or remuneration committees should not be mandated by the Companies Act. Instead, it should be voluntary, with the three apex industry associations—CII, FICCI and ASSOCHAM—playing a catalytic role.' It is interesting to see that this is being recommended at a time when stringent measures have been placed in position in a number of countries on these matters. The audit committee format has been in vogue in the US since July 1978 when it became mandatory

[23]Taxman, *Report of Working Group on Companies Act, 1956*, 1997.

for the companies listed on the New York Stock Exchange to establish such committees comprising solely independent directors. A survey by the United States General Accounting Office in 1996 of *Fortune 1000* publicly traded companies revealed that at least 90 per cent of these companies required an independent audit committee as a matter of policy. The Cadbury committee indicated that over half of the top 250 UK listed companies in *Times 1000* had audit committees.[24] In another recommendation, the working group has proposed that the provisions under section 233B concerning mandatory cost audit at the directives of the department of company affairs should be removed. However, the requirement to maintain cost records should continue as before. Both these are retrograde recommendations. Their significance and importance in the Indian context cannot be over-emphasised if corporate governance is to have any meaning.

A few other issues have come to the fore in the Indian context. The first relates to the need for credible and strong regulatory mechanisms. Unfortunately, the record here is far from satisfactory. The powers given to SEBI have been insignificant as compared to its counterpart, SEC, in the US. With its limited investigative and penal powers, SEBI had been ineffective as a market regulator. It did not have even the powers of search and seizure. The maximum penalty that the SEBI could impose on a market manipulator was a paltry Rs 5 lakh. Corporates had even offered to make this payment upfront. This has now been remedied to some extent with the amendment of the SEBI Act. But, the other equally worrisome factor is the hostile attitude of corporate houses to any regulation at all. As D.R. Mehta, the former chairman of SEBI, said candidly, 'corporates don't want a strong regulator. They are working overtime to attack SEBI and even resort to personal attacks on senior officials. The moment you try to take action against any powerful corporates

---

[24]R. Narayanswamy, Round Table: Auditing Reforms and Better Corporate Governance, *Management Review*, Institute of Management, Bangalore, July-September 1996, October-December 1996.

then you should see how they try to browbeat you through various means...When I took action against HLL [Hindustan Lever Limited] in the insider trading case they tried to put all kinds of pressure.'[25] Delays in the finalisation of court cases are as important. The insider trading case against HLL is pending for over 5 years and SEBI had to approach the high court to get it expedited. The travails of the telephone regulatory authority of India (TRAI) have been equally distressing with the government abolishing the erstwhile authority altogether when it found that it was too independent, and enacting a new law for its reconstitution. In the process, TRAI's powers were also whittled down. The electricity regulatory commissions (ERCs) established in the centre and the states have fared no better with a large number of them giving vent to their frustration at the inaction and apathy on the part of power utilities, both in the public and private sector, and the state governments.[26] In some states, leaders of political parties have also criticised the ERCs in intemperate language. It is significant to note that, in the ERC Act, the government has taken powers to give directives to the ERCs in matters of public policy. So much for the independence of these bodies!

The acquisition of Indian Petro Chemical Corporation (IPCL) by Reliance Industries Limited (RIL) has raised strong fears about a monopoly in the petrochemical sector. RIL now has a stranglehold with its share of about 67 per cent of the market for most such products. For some products like paraxylene (PX) it will have 98 per cent share of the local market. Particularly worrisome is the fact that though import duties on most other products have been reduced substantially, with the political clout of RIL, the average protection level on most petrochemical products is absurdly high. For ethylene, propylene, PVC and polypropylene, it is as high as 35 per cent. Amazingly, import duty on PX, in which RIL has a 98 per cent market share, was

[25]Tuesday Interview: No Scam, Just Price Movements on a Global Trend, *The Economic Times*, 19/2/2002.

[26]Madhav Godbole, Electricity Regulatory Commissions: The Jury Is Still Out, *Economic and Political Weekly*, 8–14 June 2002, pp. 2195–2200.

hiked in 2002. For some other products, the duty is 25 per cent. This shows the government's of concern for the ordinary consumer. In fact, the import duties on all petrochemical products must be brought down to 10–15 per cent. While the government has brazenly permitted the monopoly of RIL to emerge in the petrochemical sector, it decided not to permit the Indian Oil Corporation (IOC) to bid for Bharat Petroleum Corporation Limited (BPCL) and Hindustan Petroleum Corporation Limited (HPCL) on the ground that it would lead to an excessively large share of IOC in the market. The underlying intention is clearly to help RIL in further strengthening its position in the oil sector. Thus while one rule is applied to the private sector, quite another is applied to the public sector. If acquisitions and mergers are good for the private sector, there is no reason why they should not be permitted for the cash rich oil and petrochemical companies in the public sector. It is a travesty that now a demand for a level playing field has to be made for the public sector in the country. The specious and ingenious argument being advanced by the government is that monopoly by itself is not bad. What is bad is its abuse! The new Competition Act, directs the Competition Commission of India to take into account many factors for the purpose of determining whether there would be an appreciably adverse effect on competition. Among the listed factors are the level of competition through imports in the market, the extent of barriers to market entry, the extent of effective competition in the market, the extent to which substitutes are available, and the nature and extent of innovation.[27] However, the proposal to enact a competition law had been kept pending by the government for more than two years due to pressure from the corporate sector and the large industrial houses. It will be recalled that similar pressure had delayed the enactment of the law on SEBI for several years. Clearly, apex chambers of commerce and industry such as the CII have *de facto* veto power in major economic and

[27] S. Chakravarthy, Need For a Good Competition Law, *Economic Times*, 31/5/2002.

financial legislation by their position as the third chamber of parliament! This certainly does not augur well for ensuring good corporate governance in the country.

We had referred earlier to the major issues which have come into prominence regarding the audit of companies. Equally relevant are the matters pertaining to the credit rating agencies, their accountability and the transparency of their operations, brought out by R. Viswanathan.[28] The Credit Rating Information Services India Limited (Crisil) has downgraded BPL's non-convertible debenture issue by a full 12 stages from A to D or default category at one go. Obviously, the earlier rating was highly defective. The Industrial Credit Rating Agency (ICRA) downgraded 1.4 per cent of instruments rated by it as high safety to junk bond status within one year. As in the case of statutory auditors, the management of the company getting itself credit rated pays the credit rating agency whereas the rating is for the benefit of the investors. This often affects the independence and judgment of the agency. It is necessary that proper regulatory mechanisms are evolved by the RBI and SEBI to ensure that credit rating agencies do not let down the investors.

The issue of excessive salaries in the corporate sector is becoming as relevant in India as in some other countries. Dhirubhai Ambani of RIL drew a salary of Rs 11.7 crore per annum in 2001–02, followed by his son Mukesh with Rs 9.5 crore. Anji Reddy drew a salary of almost Rs 10 crore. In spite of industrial recession the corporate heads gave themselves unconscionable increases in salary. The lone voice in wilderness was that of M.R. Narayana Murthy who suggested that CEOs should get 15 times the salary of their lowest-paid employee.. India now counts its millionaires and billionaires as proudly as the US. The only difference is that India is a poor country inhabited by rich people. As opposed to the US and other countries, there is no public outcry by shareholders and other stakeholders against such exorbitant salaries.

[28] R. Viswanathan, Rating Agencies: Are They Credit Worthy, *Economic Times*, 12/6/2002.

It will be in the fitness of things to conclude this chapter on a sombre note. As the *Times of India* brought out editorially, 'The recent spate of *exposes* involving well known companies or business groups like ITC, Shaw Wallace, Reliance, Videocon, Essar, Jindal, Bindal, Torrent and so on [and Tatas are no exception] have once again brought into focus the issue of corporate governance...(At the same time) when every institution is coming under scrutiny for lack of ethics and transparency, the corporate sector cannot hope to remain untouched...Most of the corporate *exposes* have occurred because one or another player in the game has squealed... Indeed, the spate of recent *exposes* can only be the tip of an enormous iceberg of wrong-doing and corporate misgovernance. Reliance's Mukesh Ambani was not off the mark when he recently drew attention to what he called 'systemic corruption', as opposed to 'petty corruption'. 'For every fall from virtue', said Mr Ambani, 'there is a seducer. Millions can be offered only when billions can be made'. While deregulation and liberalisation are necessary conditions for reducing corporate crime, they are not sufficient conditions. These will have to be accompanied by a more vigilant, if less intrusive, regulatory system. In the few cases of white collar crime that have surfaced recently, the punishment should be such that corporates learn to play by the rules, even as they campaign for more business-friendly rules.'[29]

This brings us to the question, where do we go from here? Greater activism by shareholders and other stakeholders alone would bring about better corporate governance. In the ultimate analysis, punishment by the market is the most effective instrument for disciplining a company. But, there is still a long way to go before this become a routine reality. Companies need to look at corporate governance not as an irritant or impediment but as an essential mechanism for their very survival in the new environment of economic liberalisation and globalisation, with increasing competition both at home and from abroad. As compared to the apathy of the Indian financial institutions, the

[29]Editorial, Corporate Citizens, *Times of India*, 12 November 1996.

increasing number of foreign portfolio investors are bound to raise the demands for better corporate governance, more transparency, and timely disclosures. There is no reason why Indian investors and shareholders should be denied the same level of transparency and disclosures which are acceded to by Indian companies when they float American Depository Receipts (ADRs) or resort to external commercial borrowing. Public accountability and transparency is as important for the corporate sector as it is to any other sector of the economy. The Indian corporate sector has escaped this responsibility for too long a time. But, as Sir Adrian Cadbury perceptively observed, a company would behave according to the accepted norms of society. It is essentially society at large which will have to set the tone for the quality of corporate governance.

## Co-operative Governance

**Introduction**

Some sectors of the economy have remained untouched by the winds of economic liberalisation and globalisation which have been sweeping over the country for more a decade. The co-operative sector is prominent among these. This is particularly worrying since co-operatives play an important role in the economies of a number of states. The total number of co-operatives in India, at all levels, is 4,11,123 of which 3,96,175 are primary co-operatives. The total membership at all levels covers 19.78 crore of which membership of primaries accounts for 18.65 crore. The share capital is around Rs 9,350.18 crore and the participation of the government (credit plus non-credit) is 20.68 per cent. The total working capital of co-operatives is Rs 1,31,384.38 crore. The total assets are around Rs 39,103.10 crore. The co-operative movement covers 99.5 per cent of the villages and 67 per cent of rural households. The share of co-operative enterprises in the development of the economy is quite substantial. Co-operatives contribute 58.97 per cent of the total agricultural credit and 30.50 per cent of the total disbursement of credit for fertilisers. In sugar production, they account for 60 per cent. In wheat procurement, the contribution of co-operatives is 36 per cent. In retail fair price shops, their share is 17 per cent. In milk procurement, their share is approximately 6.59 per cent. In the oil market (branded), they account for 50 per cent. Cotton yarn production by co-operatives is around 16.5 per cent and in cotton marketed/procurement, they account for 55 per cent. Co-operatives account for 8 per cent of cotton yarn exports and 21 per cent of total handloom fabrics production. The co-operative network generates self-employment for 12.5 million persons.[30] Co-operative governance is therefore no less important than corporate governance.

Unfortunately, as in the case of corporate governance, in the co-operatives sector also, lofty principles and philosophy, are bandied about, but the reality is quite the opposite. Hardly any thought has been given to the operationalisation of these principles. There is no universally accepted code of best practices. There are no norms, as in the case of corporate governance, against which the performance of individual co-operative enterprises can be judged. Inevitably, questions have, therefore, arisen about the social and economic relevance of co-operatives as an instrument of development and a viable form of organisation. The experience so far has also underlined the urgency of a comprehensive review of policies governing the sector and the regulatory framework for ensuring its accountability.

Co-operative Philosophy

It will be useful to begin this discussion with the statement on co-operative identity issued by the International Co-operative Alliance (ICA) at its meeting in Manchester on 23 September 1995. This will help put the issues in perspective and also enable an assessment to be made as to how far the real world of

[30] Sanjeev Chopra (ed.), *Co-operatives: Policy Issues for the SAARC Region*, Book World, Dehra Dun, 1998, p. 188.

co-operatives is removed from the ideals underlying the movement. The statement defines a co-operative as an autonomous association of persons united voluntarily to meet their common economic, social and cultural needs and aspirations through a jointly-owned and democratically-controlled enterprise. Co-operatives are based on the values of self-help, self-responsibility, democracy, equality, equity, and solidarity. The members of a co-operative believe in the ethical values of honesty, openness, social responsibility and caring for others. Concern for the community which was added as a new principle by the ICA is germane to the theme of this book.

The Fifth Asia-Pacific Co-operative Ministers' Conference held in Beijing in October 1999 highlighted some major issues facing the co-operative movement in the region.[31] As regards autonomy and independence, the conference noted that much of Asia still uses the argument that co-operatives are weak and therefore need continued external (government) support. This is a self-fulfilling argument and compelling evidence suggests that co-operatives remain weak precisely because of continued government intervention. The two key ingredients for the success of co-operatives (good management and effective member control) are clearly ignored by this argument. The conference stressed that co-operatives have to be recognised for what they are— self-help, member-controlled institutions whose strength comes from within. Co-operatives are economic enterprises with a distinct social purpose because they are established by people or entities to gain the market leverage they would not have if they had acted individually. Thus, co-operatives are instruments of members to improve their economic and social situation. This is their unique contribution to development. And this is where government can utilise the advantage of co-operatives while pursuing their development objectives. Institutional mechanisms for self-regulation are part of the over-all development of

---

[31]National Co-operative Union of India, Fifth Asia-Pacific Co-operative Ministers' Conference: A Backgrounder, *The Co-operator*, Vol. XXXVII, No. 4, October 1999, pp. 126–128.

co-operatives. At the higher levels, this could mean the enforcement of standards that will strengthen democratic governance and operational integrity. The overall record of external assistance received by co-operatives has weighed more on the side of failure, with disastrous consequences to the image and reputation of co-operatives. This is so because this external input, while well intentioned, tended to ignore the very nature of co-operatives as self-help and autonomous organisations.

### New Challenges And Inadequate Responses

With the coming of economic liberalisation, demands for globalisation and the obligations arising from the membership of the World Trade Organisation, co-operatives will have to reorient their structures, functioning and management to meet the demands of the market economy. The co-operative sector will now have to face competition not only from the domestic private sector but also from imports. This has already happened in a number of areas, in which co-operatives used to have a significant share, such as sugar, textiles, milk and milk products, agro products and so on.

To enable co-operatives to cope with these new responsibilities, it will be necessary to enact a new co-operative law. Freedom from the shackles of government is as important in the case of the co-operatives as it is for the private sector. The Ardhanareeswaran committee appointed by the central government, reached a significant and perhaps far-reaching conclusion way back in 1985 that co-operative laws had operated against the democratic functioning and autonomy of the co-operatives and that the government had acquired undue powers. The committee pointed to the lack of co-operative character in the co-operatives, a stultification of the co-operative movement, and a dependency syndrome by which co-operatives had become an instrument of the state. The committee lamented that since Independence, while the number of co-operatives grew, the co-operative movement declined, paradoxically enough perhaps on account of the growth itself.

The planning commission constituted the Brahma Prakash committee in 1990 to review the status of the co-operative movement and suggest future directions. The committee was also expected to finalise the model co-operative societies Bill drafted by the planning commission. This was even before the forces of economic liberalisation were set in motion. Since then, the subsidies have gone down and state funding of co-operatives is drying up. The findings of the committee have therefore acquired a new urgency. But, neither the government of India nor the state governments took any follow up action on the report which the committee submitted in May 1991.

The conference of co-operative ministers held in December 1998, *inter alia*, discussed the factors which had led to disillusionment with co-operatives and the failures of the co-operative movement itself. The conference took note of concerns such as bogus societies, vested interests, inefficient functioning, non-viable co-operatives, lack of professional management and so on. One important area of reform identified was to make the co-operatives autonomous, democratic and accountable to members. Towards this end, the enactment of a new co-operative law was once again recommended.

In this context it is interesting to read the preamble of the Maharashtra Co-operative Societies Act, 1960. It makes no mention of any economic principles for management of co-operatives and is as vague as can be imagined. It states, 'Whereas, with a view to providing for the orderly development of the co-operative movement in the State of Maharashtra in accordance with the relevant principles of State Policy enunciated in the Constitution of India, it is expedient to consolidate and amend the law relating to co-operative societies in that State; it is hereby enacted...'. Thus, the law provides no particular focus to the working of the co-operatives. The law in fact does not treat them as business entities.

The national symposium on the future of co-operative advocacy organised by the co-operative initiative panel in September 1997 had, *inter alia*, highlighted a few elements as basic to a good co-operative law: First, it should be fundamentally and inalienably consistent with co-operative principles; second, it should enable not prescribe; third, except where the public interest is at stake—and that is normally the concern of other laws—co-operative law should leave matters to the members and their by-laws. Fourth, co-operative law should not duplicate, much less replace, other law—too often, misdeeds are protected by co-operative laws. Fifth, co-operative law should enforce the fiduciary responsibility of elected leaders and senior managers, holding them accountable for managing the affairs of a co-operative with the same prudence and integrity as they would their own. It lamented that spheres where co-operatives had proven their advantage were 'encroached' upon by the state itself besides the private sector in total defiance of the principle of a mixed economy. This approach of reservation of certain areas for co-operatives is quite contrary to the compulsions of the new era, referred to earlier, and can hardly be endorsed.

This brings us to the Self-Reliant Co-operatives Act (SRCA) drafted by the Co-operative Development Foundation (CDF).[32] As the introduction to the write-up highlights, it is important to focus attention on the co-operative form of business and the unreasonable and oppressive laws that it is subjected to. It asserts that, in India, we have managed to distort the definition, in practice, of a co-operative business, and have begun to believe it to be a government-controlled, government-promoted, monopolistic, public service institution. Today, co-operative laws in most states and at the union level are so appalling that:

- co-operative laws can prevent a group of people from conducting their business as a co-operative, by denying registration on irrelevant and unreasonable grounds;
- the voluntary nature of a co-operative is violated by law resulting in forced admission of persons as members, and in compulsory amalgamation/division/merger of co-operatives leading to involuntary change in membership;

[32] Co-operative Development Foundation, *Self Reliant Co-operatives Act, Referential Act: 1997*, Hyderabad.

- staff recruitment, pay, service conditions are as decided, not by the co-operative, but by the registrar of co-operatives (RCS) or the government;
- the conduct of elections, a responsibility of the co-operative, is by law, made the responsibility of the registrar, and between the registrar and the government, elections get postponed for reasons as obtuse as the Gulf War;
- co-operatives are denied elected boards for years on end, and even when elections are conducted, supersession of boards on the flimsiest of grounds is common enough, with government officers or nominees taking over the management of co-operatives;
- audit, the responsibility of owners of business, is the responsibility of the registrar, and the auditor reports, not to the general body, but to the registrar—and audit is in arrears in most co-operatives for years on end;
- the right to decide what activities a co-operative may undertake, and what it may give up, too, is interfered with by the registrar, through the standardisation and compulsory amendment of by-laws; and
- investment in the co-operative's own business requires the registrar's permission!

As all these restrictions have their origin in co-operative law, they apply equally to the small number of co-operatives which have government share capital, as to the large number which do not, being owned completely by their members. The CDF has proposed that the co-operative laws across the country need to be revised keeping in view the following principles:

- co-operative law should respect the definition, values and principles adopted across the world by co-operators, through the ICA—legal provisions should be supportive and not violative of these;
- unreasonable restrictions in existing co-operative law must go, and co-operative law should be one with fewer provisions but with such provisions as, with least external intervention, promote the effective practice of co-operative principles;

- co-operative law should facilitate and not obstruct the registration of new co-operatives, so that the right of groups of people seeking to engage in co-operative business is protected, and people's initiatives are allowed to bloom;
- the voluntary nature of membership in co-operatives should not be violated;
- co-operative law should ensure that co-operatives are managed democratically; and that the management is accountable to members;
- measures such as nominations to boards by government should not be permitted by law;
- both government policy and law should recognise a co-operative as an instrument of its members for their social and economic betterment, and should not perceive it as an instrument of the government for meeting various goals of the government, or as an instrument of any other external entity;
- the law should not permit government the right to give direction to co-operatives and government policy should require from co-operatives only such contribution to larger social objectives as are required of any form of business;
- the law should respect the freedom of co-operatives to run their own business, and may place on them only such restrictions as are applied to other forms of business—it should ensure that co-operatives have a level playing field in which to compete on equal terms with other forms of business; and
- co-operative law should recognise only genuine co-operatives, and parastatal or other forms of business should not be governed by co-operative law.

Special attention may be invited to the definition of term 'deficit' which means the excess of expenditure over income, arrived at, at the end of the financial year, *after the payment of interest, if any, on share capital.* (emphasis added). The use of the phrase 'interest on share capital' as opposed to 'dividend' seems to have been made to get out of the clutches of the Income Tax Act. Similarly, 'surplus' is defined to mean the excess of income over expenditure, arrived at, at the end of the financial year, after the payment of interest, if any, on share capital, and before the payment of surplus refund, and allocation of reserves and other funds. 'Surplus refund' means the refund from the surplus given/credited to the accounts of members, in proportion to their use of the services of the co-operative in accordance with the articles of association and resolutions of the general body.

Equally interesting is the definition of the term 'deficit charge' which means the amount collected from/debited to the accounts of members, in proportion to the use and/or non-use of the services of the co-operative, in accordance with the articles of association and resolutions of the general body, to meet deficit, if any, in whole or part.

It is interesting to note that equity capital, by definition, is to come from the owners of a business, i.e. from members in the case of a co-operative. It is for this reason that the SRCA does not permit a co-operative to raise equity capital from the government or from other non-members. It is often argued that but for government share capital, several co-operatives would never have come into existence. The CDF has rightly argued that all businesses, at all times, in all places, do not lend themselves to the co-operative design. If indeed potential members or members are not convinced about putting equity capital into a proposed co-operative venture, it appears illogical that an external party should bother to put that money in, and still try to run it as a co-operative with decision-making rights lying with the members. It is also argued that co-operatives should be permitted to raise capital from the market. Capital providers of other forms of business might be investor-owners, but are not expected to be user-owners. In the case of co-operatives, all owners are expected to be users, and therefore, the question of raising equity capital from the market does not arise. Attention may be invited to yet another important stand of the CDF. This pertains to the income tax liability of co-operatives. It is argued that a co-operative is essentially an agent of its members. It either pools member produce (including labour, skills, grain, etc.), adds value where possible and markets these, or it procures inputs (including credit, fertilser, consumer goods, etc.), based on needs of members, and supplies these to them. In both instances, it needs to hold back for itself only such margins as are needed to meet the costs of operation, or for further improvement/ increase in services to members. The rest of the surplus is returned to members, since the produce was underpaid for, or the inputs overcharged. Tax laws, therefore, must distinguish between the transactions between a co-operative and its members, and between a co-operative and non-members. While the latter may be treated on par with similar transactions in other forms of business, the former must receive separate treatment, as the service is one of pooling or indenting, and not one of purchase or sale. This is a very ingenious argument but flies in the face of the earlier argument of the CDF that co-operatives should have a level playing field vis-a-vis other forms of business. This is particularly relevant when co-operative ventures are to compete with other ventures in the private or joint sector.

Some of the other provisions of the model SRCA may be briefly brought out as under: co-operative identity as defined by ICA is incorporated as a schedule to the Act. There is no provision for making rules, compulsory amendment of by-laws, amalgamation, merger, division, supersession etc. by the registrar of co-operative societies (RCS) and various other powers entrusted by existing state co-operative societies Acts to the registrar and the government are drastically curtailed. The usual term 'by-laws' is replaced by the term 'articles of association' which are to provide exhaustively for the actual framework of the working of the society concerned. Membership is restricted to members who need and are able to use the core services provided by the co-operative. Government participation in share capital is omitted. Government loan or guarantee could however be on mutually agreed terms only under a memorandum of understanding. Special resolution is defined as a resolution with at least 51 per cent of all members with the right to vote voting in favour in the general body. The RCS has no powers to reject any amendment outright but will have to do so with the prior concurrence of the civil court. The admission or refusal of membership vests finally in the general body. Member education and staff and board education is the sole responsibility of the co-operative concerned. If more than 25 per cent of the services of a co-operative are availed of by non-members for a period of three years in a continuous span of five years, then such a co-operative having been considered as pseudo co-operative could be dissolved by the RCS after obtaining court orders.

The model SRCA also lays down that minimum use of services as specified in the articles of association will be a precondition for exercise of their rights by members. Provision of more than one vote for a member co-operative in a federal co-operative depending on the business conducted by the member co-operative is allowed as provided in the articles of association. There is also a provision for representative general body, if required. The powers of the general body extend to removal of members, conduct of elections, filling up vacancies on board, appointing statutory auditors, entering into partnerships with other co-operatives, voluntarily dissolving the society and considering registrar's report of enquiry. Disqualification as Directors to continue if (i) the general body meeting is not held on time, (ii) annual report and audited annual financial statements with statutory auditor's report for previous year are not submitted before the annual general body, and (iii) if elections are not held before the term of office of existing directors is over. Only active members, patronising services of co-operatives are allowed on the board of directors. Bar on holding office-bearers' posts for more than two terms and in more than two co-operatives was removed. Borrowing of funds from non-members is allowed. Investment of funds outside the co-operative sector in a non-speculative manner is allowed.

Andhra Pradesh was the first state in the country to pass a law on these lines in 1995. New co-operatives not receiving any share capital from the state government could get themselves registered under this Act. Co-operatives already registered under the Andhra Pradesh Co-operative Societies Act 1964 which had no share capital from the government could also get themselves registered under the new Act. Bihar enacted the law as above in 1996. Similar legislation is under consideration in a few other states.

The high powered committee relating to co-operative law and co-operative finance (Dubhashi committee) appointed by the government of Maharashtra in 1992 took the view that all non-aided co-operative societies may be brought under a separate chapter in the co-operative law so as to give them wider operational freedom, while those societies in which the government has large financial involvement should continue to be governed by the present law.[33] The committee defined unaided co-operative as one in whose balance sheet, at the close of the previous year, there would not be any liability in terms of government share capital, government loan, government guarantees, and any other form of government financial assistance including subsidies. The committee was of the view that any financial assistance received either from a government corporation or any other financial institution should not make the society a government-aided society.

A reference may be made to another set of recommendations of the Dubhashi committee. Some of these are at variance with those of the CDF. These pertain to the public funding of co-operative processing units. The committee felt that with the rapid development of co-operative processing, it would not be possible to meet the financial requirements of co-operative processing units through the existing channels of financing. It, therefore, recommended a new approach under which co-operatives will enter the open market for mobilisation of

[33]Commissioner for Co-operation and Registrar, Co-operative Societies, Government of Maharashtra, *Report of the High Power (Dr. Dubhashi) Committee relating to Co-operative Law and Co-operative Finance*, March 1992, Pune.

resources. The committee recommended the issue of preference shares to the general public and hoped that it would be possible to mobilise some portion of the income that is now generated in the rural areas through this method. Economically viable co-operative projects would be able to attract public financial support by way of preference share capital. Another recommendation was that national level institutions may also contribute to the shares of the co-operative processing societies. The committee looked into non-member share capital and felt that there was no objection in co-operative law for raising non-member share capital, and co-operative societies can raise deposits from persons who are not regular members. However, the rates of return will have to be sufficiently attractive. Some selected co-operatives can also raise debentures. A subsidiary organisation of the Maharashtra State Co-operative Bank (MSCB) could be established to raise debentures and mobilise resources. The committee also recommended the establishment of mutual funds in the co-operative sector by MSCB. The committee also recommended that the state government may move the RBI to permit the banking sector to invest a large proportion of funds collected from the rural areas for co-operative processing units.

Though the Dubhashi committee was not explicit, its recommendations would imply bringing in greater transparency and accountability in the functioning of co-operatives. It would also imply introducing the system of credit rating of co-operatives for the guidance of potential investors in this sector. Apart from anything else, it would mean running the co-operatives on a profit basis.

It can be seen that the Dubhashi committee differed with the recommendations of the CDF on some significant issues. As the discussion in the following section shows, the expert committee on co-operative sugar factories (CSFs) in Maharashtra has also taken a different view from the CDF on several important issues pertaining to the structure and functioning of co-operative business enterprises, in the larger interest of ensuring their viability. It is necessary that these issues are debated nationally to arrive at a consensus to meet the compulsions of the market place.

## A Case Study of Maharashtra[34]

More than a third of the co-operative sugar factories in Maharashtra are sick. The Government of Maharashtra (GOM) had appointed an expert committee to look into the reasons for this, to suggest remedial measures for dealing with it and to strengthen the CSFs. In view of the importance of the subject and its relevance for CSFs in a number of other states, the recommendations need to be discussed widely to arrive at a consensus on the critical issues in this sector. Some salient features of the report are given below.

India has made spectacular progress in the production of cane sugar. It has moved from being the third largest producer in 1976, following Brazil and Cuba, to being the largest in 1996, when it produced 19.47 per cent of the world's cane sugar. Maharashtra is the leading producer accounting for about a third of the annual sugar production in the country. But it is no means the most efficient producer of sugar in the world.

The sugar industry is the second largest agro-based industry in the country next to cotton textiles. But, unlike the cotton textile industry, it is located in rural areas, where it is the single largest employer with 3.5 lakh workers.

As on 28 February 1998, there were 460 installed sugar factories in the country. Of these, 254 were in the co-operative sector and accounted for more than 60 per cent of the total sugar production in India, with Maharashtra accounting for 116 CSFs. The CSFs had 16,02,677 shareholders of which, 14,53,328 were sugarcane growers.

The area under sugarcane, which is considered a lazy man's

---

[34]This section is partly based on this author's article entitled Co-operative Sugar Factories in Maharashtra: Case for a Fresh Look, published in the *Economic and Political Weekly*, February 5–11, 2000.

crop, increased steeply from 1.91 lakh hectares (ha) (1966–67 to 1970–71) to 4.60 lakh ha (1991–92 to 1995–96), though it varied a great deal from year to year.

The declining productivity of sugarcane has been a major cause for worry. The increase in sugarcane production since 1991–92 has been due mainly to the increase in the area under sugarcane in the state. The average productivity of cane during the last ten years has been only 83 M.T./ha. The sugarcane production per hectare in Maharashtra has steadily declined, except in a few years, from 97 M.T. in 1981–82 to 86 M.T. in 1991–92 and down to 75 M.T. in 1996–97. In the tropical belt, Tamil Nadu recorded the highest mean sugarcane productivity (107 M.T./ha), followed by Karnataka (86 M.T./ha). Maharashtra ranked third with mean productivity of 82.8 M.T./ha. While the productivity has increased in most northern states, it has declined in Gujarat and Maharashtra. Studies show that sugarcane productivity of 110 M.T./ha. should be achievable in Maharashtra. It is significant to note that in national crop competitions, farmers in Maharashtra obtained cane yield of as much as 338 M.T./ha.

Internationally, CSFs have to contend with a number of factors which lower their competitiveness. Typically, irrigated regions such as Burdekin in Australia have yields averaging 125 tonnes per ha and irrigated crops in Southern Africa (in Zimbabwe, Swaziland and Malawi) typically achieve yields over 100 tonnes per ha as against 80–85 tonnes in Maharashtra. The sucrose yield in India is lower than in Australia, Mexico and the US, though Maharashtra's yield compares favourably with that in other countries. There has been no increase in the sucrose content of cane in India during the last four decades. Unlike in many countries, payment for cane in India is made on the basis of weight and is not related to sucrose content. The Indian sugar industry has smaller factories as compared with the rest of the world where sugar units have much larger crushing capacities, many times higher than the average capacity of a unit in India.

It is interesting to note that the government of Maharashtra had appointed three committees since 1980 to look into sick CSFs. All these committees had recommended across-the-board relief to all CSFs classified as sick without going into the question of severity of sickness in each case. They did not recommend any institutional arrangement for examining sick CSFs on a case to case basis to recommend the kind of relief needed. Neither the central government nor the all India financial institutions were to be involved in deciding the relief, though the latter were expected to provide large assistance. The estimated overall burden of rehabilitation of sick CSFs on the state government was so staggering that all these reports remained without any action except for some *ad hoc* decisions.

The high powered committee on sugar industry (Mahajan committee) appointed by the central government which submitted its report in April 1998 practically glossed over the question of sickness in this vital industry.[35] Out of its 429-page report only three pages (pp. 348–350) were devoted to the subject of 'sick mills'. The seriousness of the problem, on an all India basis, can be gauged from the data given by the Mahajan committee in its report. As on 31 March 1997, of the 237 CSFs in the country, 157 were in losses, 74 had negative net worth, and 81 had negative/inadequate net disposable resources. In the case of Maharashtra, according to the committee, of the 113 CSFs, 60 were in losses, 20 had negative net worth, and 23 had negative/inadequate net disposable resources. Similar information about private mills was not available. However, according to the information supplied by the Industrial Finance Corporation of India (IFCI) to the Mahajan committee, out of 157 private sugar factories assisted by the IFCI, 61 were chronic defaulters, of which 39 were considered by IFCI to be sick, that is, their accumulated loss exceeded the net worth. Nine of these

[35] Government of India, Ministry of Food and Consumer Affairs (Department of Sugar and Edible Oils), *Report of the High Powered Committee on Sugar Industry*, Vol. I, April 1998.

companies are BIFR (Board of Industrial Finance and Reconstruction) cases and the remaining 30 are non-BIFR cases. The Mahajan committee has observed that, 'The financial position of the industry is not sound both in private and co-operative sectors. In the government sector, UP Sugar Corporation Ltd. and Bihar State Sugar Corporation Ltd. are two major government companies running several sugar factories. Most of the sugar mills under both the corporations have large accumulated losses'.

It is against this background that the recommendations of the expert committee on CSFs in Maharashtra deserve to be widely discussed and carefully considered. For its analysis of sickness in CSFs, the committee adopted the criteria enunciated by the Reserve Bank of India (RBI) for classification of sick industrial units comprising net worth in relation to paid-up capital and current ratio. In addition, the committee also took into account, for qualitative assessment, certain factors such as: (i) factories whose financial position does not permit payment of even the statutory minimum price and such payment is at the cost of depletion of all surplus in the previous three years; (ii) factories which have been incurring losses continuously for three years; (iii) factories which have continuously run below 75 per cent capacity for over three years, and (iv) factories which have been continuously in default of government dues for more than a year. Based on the RBI criterion, of the 116 CSFs, 10 fell into group C (below average) and 23 into group D (poor). In addition, according to early warning signals as above, 15 more CSFs were on the way to becoming sick.

As on 31 March 1998, the outstanding from CSFs totalled Rs 254.91 crore comprising equity yet to be redeemed (Rs 33.87 crore), purchase tax loan (Rs 185.00 crore) and other loans (Rs 36.04 crore). In addition were the guarantees recalled and paid for by the state government (Rs 63.41 crore). This was apart from guarantees invoked but not paid for (Rs 161.53 crore). Outstanding guarantees to CSFs were to the tune of Rs 1,604.29 crore.

The committee has proposed that the sick SCFs in group C, which have a reasonable chance of turning the corner, should be rehabilitated by the joint efforts of labour and employees, state government, central government (sugar development fund) and the concerned banks and financial institutions. For this purpose, a detailed programme has to be drawn up in consultation with all concerned including the shareholders of the CSF and strict conditionalities are to be laid down. A high level committee presided over by the chief secretary and comprising the representatives of the CSF, financial institutions and banks, and state and central governments is to prepare the rehabilitation packages for each CSF to suit its individual requirements. The rehabilitation package has to be approved by the shareholders in a special meeting so as to involve them fully in these efforts. The CSFs on the early warning list are also to be similarly treated before they become sick. The CSFs in group D which cannot be rehabilitated and/or turned around are to be put into liquidation or disposed off by sale or long term lease of property, and the resultant loss is to be shared by all the parties concerned including banks and financial institutions.

The committee has recommended a number of changes in the legislative framework governing the co-operatives. These include: enactment of a new law of self-reliant co-operative societies along the lines of the Andhra Pradesh Act and the points urged by the CDF. For this purpose, a self-reliant society is defined as one which does not, any longer, have any government share capital, any loan from the state government, and any subsisting state government guarantee for any financial accommodation availed of by it from any other financial institution. It is further recommended that, pending enactment of such a legislation, the CSFs which satisfy the above criteria should be freed from government control and not be made to ask for a number of permissions and approvals from the commissioner of sugar and the state government. The CSFs which have very small (less than Rs 10 lakh) involvement of the state government are also proposed to be freed from government control substantially.

Simultaneously, the committee has proposed over 40 amendments in the existing Maharashtra Co-operative Societies (MCS) Act for more effective monitoring and control of such other societies, particularly in the processing sector, in which the government's financial involvement will continue to be substantial for quite some time to come. The committee has underlined that if co-operatives are to work as industry and compete with the private sector, the provisions of the co-operative law, as compared with those of the Companies Act, 1956, will have to be examined carefully. Like, the private sector, the joint sector and the public sector, the co-operative is only a form of organisation of a business or industrial entity, and it must be governed by the same principles as are applicable to the other forms of organisation. In this light, the present provisions of the MCS Act need to be reviewed in their entirety.

With the aim of fixing the responsibility for the sickness of a CSF, the committee has recommended that not only should the management of the sick CSF be changed, but the out-going members of the board of directors should be debarred from holding any post in the same or any other co-operative society registered under the MCS Act for a period of five years from the date of termination of their term of office. To make management more accountable, it is recommended that personal guarantees/mortgage of property of the board members should be made compulsory before sanction of loans. Certain provisions of the Andhra Pradesh Act in this regard are also proposed for inclusion in the MCS Act.

A special reference may be made to the concept of 'interest on share capital' which is contained in the Andhra Pradesh Act. Apparently, this is to overcome difficulty regarding the income tax liability of the CSFs. The committee has highlighted that this play on words cannot be permitted to blur the important distinction between risk capital i.e. equity and loan funds. The return on the former is a dividend while that on the latter is interest. The committee has stated that the advocacy for income tax exemption is difficult to understand in view of the CDF's plea for a level playing field for co-operatives as compared with the private sector.

Since all shareholders hold one share each, there is no worthwhile financial stake of those who become the promoters of a CSF and later become its directors and office-bearers. The financial institutions therefore treat the state government as the promoter group of a CSF. This is clearly against the philosophy of a co-operative and its basic principles. The state government equity ranges from 1 (member's share):3 (government contribution) to 1:5 (in Vidarbha and Marathwada areas). Over 60 per cent of equity in most CSFs is held by the state government. The state government gives an unduly long period of 15 years for the redemption of equity. Elaborate procedures have been laid down for the creation of an equity redemption fund by each CSF but the instructions have been disregarded and, as a result, most of the government equity has not been redeemed. All this must change if the co-operatives are not to continue as government entities, floated and operated primarily with government funds or government guaranteed funds. The committee has, therefore, suggested that, wherever necessary in the interest of raising adequate equity capital or fulfilling the requirements (in respect of promoters) of the financial institutions, the concept of one member one vote may be given up. The upper limit for holding shares by any grower member may be 26 per cent of the total equity. However, a CSF may also have the liberty to choose the other alternative of one member one vote if it is in a position to raise adequate equity in this manner. In such an event, the CSF will have to enter into appropriate agreements with the financial institutions so as to be in a position to raise the required funds without the involvement of the state government.

As regards future financial involvement of the state government in CSFs, the committee has emphasised that the financial institutions should not treat the state government as a promoter group of all CSFs in the state. The state government also cannot be expected to take over the responsibility to make good any shortfall in funding requirements of CSFs. The state government is not a bank or a financial institution and should not be treated as such. The committee has recommended that, in future, the state government should not take any equity in the CSFs. The state government should also not give any government guarantee to loans raised by CSFs. The NCDC may also be requested to give its assistance to the CSFs directly, without going through the government. The state government should also not give any direct financial assistance by way of loans to CSFs from the state exchequer. However, as in the case of other private sector units assisted through the State Industrial and Investment Corporation of Maharashtra (SICOM), a suitable package of incentives may be evolved to assist the CSFs.

The committee has cautioned that a second look is necessary about funding any more CSFs by giving any assistance from the state government. If the promoters want to go ahead on their own they may be free to do so but the state government should keep itself scrupulously away from funding these proposals. The emphasis in the future should be on the expansion of capacity of existing units, wherever warranted, rather than on horizontal expansion by setting up new units.

The announcement of an unduly high cane price, year after year, by a committee presided over by the chief minister has been one of the main reasons for the sickness of CSFs. This has also led to competition among CSFs to pay higher cane prices though they are often not in a financial position to do so. An important recommendation of the committee, therefore, pertained to the setting up of a statutory five-member committee comprising a retired high court judge as chairman and two expert members with a background in agricultural economics and sugar technology. The fourth member should be a chartered accountant, and the fifth a representative of the all India financial institutions, and co-operative, commercial and urban banks which have extended assistance to the CSFs.

Yet another significant recommendation of the committee is that the present system of paying a uniform price for all varieties of cane, irrespective of their sucrose content be given up. A firm policy should be laid down that all CSFs will have to change over to the pricing based on sucrose content within three years at the latest. The committee has suggested that a beginning be made along the following lines:

(a) The factory, at the beginning of the planting season itself, should announce the varieties of cane with very low sucrose content which would not be accepted by the factory for crushing.
(b) Since sucrose content depends on a number of factors, to begin with, and before more sophisticated pricing techniques are evolved and used, payment for sugarcane should be differentiated at least on the basis of varieties according to their sucrose content. For this purpose, sugar factories may conduct tests of different varieties of cane.
(c) In the ultimate analysis, more scientific techniques may be adopted to relate the prices to sucrose content. For this purpose, pilot trials be carried out in a few factories with imported equipment to examine its suitability and consider the modifications needed therein to suit local conditions.

A series of recommendations relate to improving the financial management of CSFs. The committee has also suggested ways in which performance of machinery and equipment can be improved. The office of commissioner of sugar which supervises the work of CSFs has been looked at closely and a series of organisational, institutional and other changes have been suggested to make its working more accountable, transparent and effective. Audit is yet another neglected area of the work of CSFs. A number of measures are recommended for strengthening the audit department and also increasingly getting the audit done through a panel of chartered accountants.

An important part of the report pertains to the policy of water use. It is recognised that, particularly in the context of Maharashtra, evolving of policies for equitable use of water, keeping in view competitive demands, will pose formidable challenges. This aspect of public policy has received the least attention so far. It is therefore emphasised that every effort be made to conserve water and promote policies for conjunctive use of water to the maximum extent. The present practice of giving certificates of availability of water and consequent estimates of the possibilities of growing sugarcane in the command area of a proposed CSF was found to be grossly defective and a number of improvements are proposed.

The sickness of CSFs can be largely traced to the neglect of cane development. A series of steps are proposed to remedy this. One of the measures proposed is to set up seed farms to cater to the requirements of sugar factories by exempting the factories from the agricultural land ceiling law. This simple matter has remained unresolved so far. Certain changes in the policies of the central government, in so far as they relate to sugar development fund, are also proposed.

Considerable emphasis has been placed on cost control and continuous monitoring of all important elements of costs. Another area of serious concern relates to labor matters since there are large arrears of wages, gratuity and other labour dues amounting to over Rs 125 crore. A series of steps are proposed to deal with the complex issues in this field. One of the urgent steps proposed is to declare the sugar industry a seasonal industry. Once this is done, it is proposed that the Industrial Disputes Act may be amended so as to extend the provisions for permissible lay-off from 45 days as at present to one sugar year.

The committee has recommended that, to ensure the financial health of CSFs, the minimum distance between two sugar factories needs to be increased to 40 km, by making a representation to the government of India. This should hold good for a period of ten years. The matter could be re-examined thereafter in the light of experience. The committee has further proposed that every sugarcane grower should automatically become eligible for membership of the CSF in the area, if he so desires instead of at the discretion of the management of the CSF.

The committee has recommended that, looking at the conditions in Maharashtra, it would be best to lay down the minimum crushing capacity of 1,250 tonnes per day (tpd). As additional sugarcane becomes available, the capacity can be increased in a modular fashion.

The committee has suggested reintroduction of zoning as heretofore in the interest of ensuring the financial viability of CSFs and proper attention to the cane development programme.

The committee believes that the step of delicensing this industry was long overdue and needs to be welcomed by the CSFs. But mere delicensing is not enough. The policy should be carried to its logical conclusion by decontrolling sugar. The committee is also of the view that, as opposed to the recommendations of the Mahajan Committee, there need be no controls on monthly releases of sugar. The central government may continue the policy of supplying sugar through the public distribution system (PDS) only to those below the poverty line. For this purpose, it may introduce the policy of procurement of sugar from the market as is the case with foodgrains supplied through the PDS. (The central government has announced its decisions in this regard since the submission of the report of the committee.)

Delicensing the sugar industry is a major challenge and will call for structural adjustments in the way CSFs have been functioning so far. For the first time, they will have to face competition from newly established private sector factories, the first of which commenced production in January 2000 in the Usmanabad district. Scores of new private sector units have registered their applications in Maharashtra—the largest such number as compared to any other state in the country. As if this were not enough, there is the threat of imported sugar flooding domestic markets in the coming years. It is time the CSFs pay attention to this wake-up call, shed their complacency and do some serious introspection to meet these new challenges. Equally and perhaps more important will be the review, reorientation and redesign of the policies of the state government. Unfortunately, the report of the expert committee has been lying with the state government without any action since March 1999. Thus, there are no indications of any action on either of the two fronts. The drums are deafeningly silent.

The idea that co-operatives should not look to the government for financial support is still anathema to the leading co-operators and the ruling political elite in a number of states, particularly in Maharashtra. It cannot be forgotten that political parties like the Congress have been able to establish their grass-roots structure and support base on the financial assistance doled out by the state. Other political parties are now trying to catch up and establish parallel co-operative organisations of their own from the village level upwards. Thus, co-operatives have become an integral part of the powerful political structure in the state and have, by and large, not much to do with the ideology of the co-operative movement. Co-operatives have essentially become an instrument for capturing power. It is therefore not, surprising that the democratic front government has established the Maharashtra co-operative development corporation with an initial capital of Rs 1,000 crore to give financial assistance to co-operatives in the state through funds to be raised by the corporation from the market on government guarantee. In spite of the severe financial situation facing the state, the government has announced in June 2002 that it will give financial assistance of Rs 142 crore to 19 sick CSFs by way of equity and loan. Such moves will ensure that the ideal of promoting self-reliant and autonomous co-operatives will remain a distant dream.

The C&AG, in his report submitted in 2002, has brought out a number of irregularities in the setting up and financing of co-operative spinning mills in the state. From 1961 to 2001, Rs 752 crore were disbursed to 116 co-operative spinning mills. Of these, as many as 46 never came into existence, 12 have closed down and 15 are under liquidation. 39 spinning mills incurred a loss of Rs 381 crore. Nine mills were given more share capital contribution than what they were entitled to. (*Maharashtra Times*, 6 May 2002). These and many other irregularities show the shocking state of affairs in the co-operative spinning mills. In spite of the perilous state of the finances of co-operative spinning mills, such is their political clout that the state government has announced that it will give a government guarantee for raising Rs 1,000 crore from the market to give further financial assistance to the co-operative spinning mills.

## Assessment

It will be useful to take a look at the experience of a few other states. Co-operative institutions in Punjab depend heavily on the state government. This dependence is to the extent of nearly 50 per cent of their share capital. The state government also gives a liberal contribution to working capital as well as margin money requirements for raising loans. Chabbilendra Roul has underlined that, 'instead of being member-created, member-owned and member-controlled voluntary associations engaged in business, co-operatives have virtually become an appendage of government. Co-operative legislation has been rewritten and amended so as to vest with government virtually complete management authority and operational responsibility. Government can on its own amend the bye-laws of a co-operative, amalgamate and divide co-operatives, hold or withhold elections, veto, annul or suspend co-operative's decisions, appoint its own officers to manage co-operatives and nominate, suspend and remove committee members without cause. Such laws are inimical to the essential nature of the co-operative and professional management'.[36]

Co-operative policy in Himachal Pradesh has, in the last four decades, followed much the same course as in most other parts of India. 'State legislation has favoured overarching state control and direction. The perception that efforts at development have to be largely state-directed has seen the growth of state organised co-operatives and large doses of financial support to co-operatives by the state.'[37] Most co-operatives have been set

[36] Chhabilendra Roul, A Handshake of Sorts: The Punjab Experience in Sanjeev Chopra (ed.), *Creating the Space: Financial Disengagement of Government from Co-operatives*, Book World, Dehra Dun, 1998, pp. 30–31.

[37] Deepak Sanan, Himachal Pradesh: Co-operative Movement and Trends in Co-operative Policy in Sanjay Chopra (ed.), *Ibid*.

up either at the behest of state functionaries chasing plan targets to organise different kinds of co-operatives and disburse financial assistance to them or they have been promoted by groups of individuals or families because the state has extended special concessions or even reserved certain activities in different sectors for co-operatives.

There is a saying that one should not look a gift-horse in the mouth, but the injunction does not extend to white elephants! This is relevant in the case of lending by the National Co-operative Development Corporation (NCDC) to co-operatives in the states. Typically, the NCDC lends to co-operative institutions mostly through state governments; there is little, if any, direct lending. The state governments are responsible for the payment of the loan on due dates. The NCDC really 'piggy backs' on the states and resorts to 'risk free' lending. Its only risk is if the states default on their loan repayment liability which is rare. In such a situation, there is little motivation for the NCDC to evaluate and appraise proposals sent to it. As long as a proposal falls within its broad framework of schemes or projects, the NCDC lets it pass muster, funds permitting; after all, it has little or nothing to lose. The state government does not scrutinise the proposals with due care and diligence either. The general attitude is that when money is coming from NCDC why should the state not take advantage of it; and not infrequently, there are pressures at the field level and in the state secretariat to approve the proposal. It is not realised that the money is merely advanced by the NCDC and has to be finally paid for by the government if there is a loan default. The co-operative society has little stake in the venture; often its involvement in the share capital is just 10 per cent or even less. In quite a few cases, the co-operative society fails to come up with its prescribed share capital contribution, small though it is. But, that does not prevent it from demanding that the NCDC and state government disburse their assistance well ahead of their proportionate share capital contribution. The argument usually advanced is that if the moneys are not disbursed, the project or scheme will run into cost and time over-runs. This sometimes results in a situation where the NCDC and state government assistance is fully disbursed but the society's own modest share capital contribution is considerably in arrears. The irony is that with little investment of its own, the co-operative society is in command of large amounts of NCDC and state government money that stands disbursed. In a sense, this is the story of funding in all co-operatives, whether from the NCDC or through other institutions as most such lending is based on state government guarantees.

The series of scams and frauds which have come to notice in the co-operative banks in Maharashtra, Gujarat and several other states have once again brought into focus the rot which has set in the co-operative field. A number of major irregularities and deficiencies have come to notice in one of the biggest such banks, namely, the Maharashtra State Co-operative Bank. Co-operative banks have deposits of over Rs 70,000 crore. The government of Maharashtra took a decision in November 2002 to wind up 15 district land development banks. The state government has refused to hand over the investigation in the cases of co-operative bank scams to the CBI in spite of repeated suggestions by the central government. Action of forfeiture of property of the accused co-operators involved in the scams was taken only when a PIL was filed in the high court. Such is the political influence of leading co-operators that the state government has decided to amend the co-operative law to permit the office-bearers of co-operatives to continue to hold their offices even beyond 10 years.

Co-operative banks report to a multiplicity of regulators: RBI and RCS in the case of urban co-operative banks (UCB), and RCS and the national bank for agriculture and rural development (NABARD) in the case of district and state co-operative banks. This dual control is harming the co-operative banks. Unfortunately, the question of bringing all co-operative banks under the control of the RBI has been pending for an unduly long time due to political pressure and opposition by some states. Professional management is mostly at a discount in these banks. Corporate governance is totally missing at the board level. Most board members are not technically qualified and derive their strength from their political backing and background. In most cases, these banks are the preserves of one political party or faction. Basic requirements such as capital adequacy norms, diversification of investments, level of NPAs, and adherence to the guidelines of NABARD and RBI on investments are flouted with impunity. The audit leaves a great deal to be desired and not just the window-dressing but creative accounting is the order of the day. It is a matter of serious concern that even though the fraud in the Madhavpura Mercantile Co-operative Bank had come to light in March 2001, the surveillance over the co-operative banks has not been tightened by the regulatory agencies. As Mythili Bhusnurmath has brought out, less than 50 per cent of a total of 1866 UCBs were inspected during the period July 2000–June 2001. The position was no better in respect of the district and state co-operative banks. NABARD inspected only 175 of a total of close to 400 banks in 2000–01. As many as 22 per cent of these had negative capital adequacy ratios while another 15 per cent had ratios below the statutory minimum of 8 per cent.[38]

A reference must be made to a recent decision of the Supreme Court which has given a body-blow to the efforts to cleanse the co-operative movement of corruption. The court has held that the chairman and board of directors of co-operatives are not public servants. It is imperative that the implications of the judgement are examined so as to make the necessary amendments to the relevant enactments expeditiously.

The co-operative movement in India will complete a hundred years of its existence in 2004. This is therefore the proper time to do some serious introspection on the issues facing the movement. Even though co-operatives draw their strength from being part of the people's movement, public accountability and

---

[38] Mythili Bhusnurmath, End This Regulatory Apathy, *Economic Times*, 20/5/2002.

transparency have been eroded over the years. Governmentalisation has sapped the very roots of the movement. Co-operatives clearly do not seem to be equipped to handle the challenges facing the sector. It is high time serious note is taken by the co-operators of the formidable tasks ahead. For what is at stake is the very survival of the co-operative movement, particularly in the new era of economic liberalisation and globalisation.

# 6

# The Judiciary, the Media and Civil Society

Any discussion on public accountability and transparency must take note of three vital institutions which are crucial in any democracy. These are the judiciary, the media and civil society. They are responsible for overseeing those in authority, they are the watchdogs of freedom. Needless to say, they themselves have to be transparent and accountable in their dealings. The discussion in this chapter focuses on promoting public accountability and transparency in the working of these institutions.

### Judiciary: The Fulcrum of the System

Fortunately, India has a strong and independent judiciary. However, there are a number of institutional weaknesses in the judicial system which have become matters for serious concern. The first is the large number of cases that have been pending for inordinately long periods of time. While in the case of the Supreme Court, the number of pending cases has declined from 105,000 in 1990 to 21,600 in July 2000, the number of pending cases in the High Courts has increased from 19,00,000 to 34,00,000 during the same period. In the case of subordinate courts, there are nearly 20 million pending cases.[1] This is particularly relevant in criminal cases as undertrials have to languish in jails, often well beyond the maximum punishment prescribed for the offences for which they are charged. The severity of this has once again increased as the Constitution Bench of seven judges of the Supreme Court has, in April 2002, set aside that court's earlier decision to set free certain categories of undertrials if cases against them do not come up for hearing within a period of two years. (*Maharashtra Times*, 17 Apr 2002). Against this background, the NCRWC has recommended that a new article 30A, should be added in the Constitution to spell out a new fundamental right regarding access to courts and tribunals so as to provide 'reasonably speedy and effective justice'.

There are only 10–12 judges per million persons in India compared with 107 in the US, 75.2 in Canada, 50.9 in the UK and 41.6 in Australia. Moreover, in these countries only about 7 to 10 per cent of cases go up for trial, the rest are settled out of court. According to one estimate, if no new cases are admitted in the courts in India, it will take 320 years just to clear the present backlog of cases. The Law Commission of India had recommended in 1988 that the ratio of judges be increased from 10.5 per million population to at least 50 per million. This was to be done within a period of 10 years so that the ultimate target of 107 judges per million could be achieved. The problem of shortage of judges is further aggravated by the long delays in filling the vacancies of judges at various levels. Thus, in the case of the high courts, there were nearly 170 vacancies in November 2001.

This has inevitably meant long delays in deciding cases. In a recent case in Delhi, the accused was discharged after 33 years of trial. In a landmark judgement relating to human rights, a Calcutta trial court sentenced two former city policemen to one year imprisonment for torturing and physically abusing three innocent and respectable women in police headquarters 22 years ago. One of the victims was crippled as a result of the abuse, the

---

[1]Government of India, Planning Commission, *National Human Development Report 2001*, March 2002, p. 120.

lower part of her body having been paralysed. The case came to international attention when Amnesty International took it up. This is only the first round of what is seen as one of the longest criminal trials in India's judicial history since Independence. (*Hindu*, Chennai, 17 Jun 1996). Three liquidation cases in the Calcutta high court remained pending for more than 50 years. And India can claim the longest legal dispute in history—a land dispute in Maharashtra which lasted 650 years.[2] The land dispute even in a matter as explosive as the Babri Masjid, has remained pending in the courts for over 60 years. The appeal over the decision of the sessions judge in the case of rioting in the Godrej factory in Mumbai was decided by the Bombay High Court after 22 years. The final decision (after exhausting all appellate avenues) in the 1993 Mumbai bomb blast cases is not expected until we are well into the twenty-first century. The cases pertaining to the securities scam which rocked the country in 1991 are still at various stages in the court and, only in one case, that of Harshad Mehta, has the prime accused, been convicted. Had it not been for Mehta's death in 2002, the cases may have got indefinitely prolonged. This is in contrast to the case of Nicholas Leeson who was involved in a bank scam in Singapore. That case was decided by the Singapore courts in less than three years.

A recent and most welcome development in this regard is the decision taken in 2001 to set up fast track courts in pursuance of the recommendation of the eleventh finance commission. According to the reply given to a parliament question, out of 862 such courts approved for being set up in the country, 542 have started functioning. The distribution of these courts, across the states, is uneven—West Bengal has hardly 6 such courts, while Maharashtra has 94, Mahdya Pradesh 64, and Jammu and Kashmir and Rajasthan have 40 courts each. The impact of this step is seen in the fact that in the Kolhapur district of Maharashtra, for example, a criminal case is now decided within ten months of its being filed. There is no reason why this cannot

[2]Swaminathan A. Aiyer, Crowding out Justice, *Times of India*, quoted in *Common Cause*, Vol. XIX, No. 1, January–March 2000, p. 6.

be replicated in all states by setting apart adequate funds for the purpose. This clearly underlines the point made earlier (chapter 3) that the state and central governments must concentrate their attention and spending on the primary responsibilities of the government.

Appeals filed by the government against decisions of the courts in civil and criminal cases account for a large proportion of the workload of the courts. Often, appeals are filed in a routine manner without any regard for the time and money which will have to be spent on pursuing the action in the court. It is further noticed that the success rate of government appeals is extremely low. It is time ways were found to reduce the number of appeals by the government. In fact, efforts need to be made to review all appeals filed so far so as to withdraw those where it would be counter-productive costwise, or where no major question of interpretation of law is involved.

It is important to note that authentic data on such a vital subject as pendency of court cases are not readily available. There is an imperative need to have institutionalised arrangements for compilation, analysis, collation and publication of the relevant data by all high courts and the Supreme Court at regular intervals. This will enable trend analysis and help in understanding the problem areas for the future. This purpose can be served by all courts at the district, state and apex level bringing out annual administration reports of the working of the courts. Courts are no doubt independent and autonomous in their working but, surely, the people have a right to such vital information on a regular basis. This can be remedied to some extent when the central legislation on freedom of information is made applicable to the judiciary but, as brought out earlier, such a move was resisted by the Bombay high court when the government of Maharashtra sought its concurrence to extend the proposed new law on the subject to the judiciary in the state.

The other equally disconcerting feature of the judicial scene in recent times is the increasing number of judges who are found not to believe in the rule of law or whose conduct is highly unbecoming to the office they hold. The most celebrated case of its kind, at the highest level, was that of V. Ramaswamy, a judge of the Supreme Court, which was discussed earlier. Time and time again, cases of misconduct and misdemeanour of judges are reported in the newspapers. This shakes the confidence of the people not only in the subordinate judiciary but also in the higher judiciary. The list and range of such cases is mind boggling. In March 2000, an Allahabad high court judge created an unseemly spectacle and brought the judiciary to ridicule by holding open court at the New Delhi railway platform as he was not allotted a berth on an Orissa-bound train. A session judge who was dismissed from service by the Governor of Karnataka was reportedly a 'B-grade *goonda*' on the records of the Bhatkal police station in Uttar Kannada district. (*Times of India*, 5 Apr 2000). A sub-judge in Anakapally in Andhra Pradesh was caught in a scam involving grant of enhanced land acquisition compensation. (*Sunday*, 2–8 February 1997). The Gujarat high court has sacked a judge in Surat for dereliction of duties. (*Times of India*, 18 May 1997). A judge of the Calcutta high court created a stir by presenting a bill for reimbursement of Rs 39,000 for three pairs of spectacles. Sessions judge, J.W. Singh, in Mumbai who was alleged to have links with the underworld was absconding and had to be declared a proclaimed offender before he finally surrendered to the police. He was acquitted by the court in August 2002 for lack of evidence. A visit by a judge of the Madras high court to Malaysia raised a controversy. The judge not only travelled to Malaysia in the company of a real estate dealer, against whom several cases of cheating, wrongful confinement and rioting were pending but accepted the hospitality of an undesirable person. (*Frontline*, 3 Mar 2000). A high court judge of the Calcutta high court was arrested under the provisions of FERA. The Chief Justice of the Bombay high court, justice A.M. Bhattacharjee, was embroiled in a controversy over receiving $80,000 from an overseas publisher, Roebuck Publishing, UK, for his book *Muslim Law and the Constitution*. The bar council of Maharashtra and Goa demanded the resignation of the Chief Justice, alleging that the publisher concerned was not a bonafide publishing house. The

Chief Justice tendered his resignation with effect from 1 April 1995. Three high court judges of the Bombay high court had to resign due to pressure from the bar after allegations of large-scale corruption. In the year 2002 itself in-house mechanism was set in motion against seven high court judges of three states. It is, however, reported that the 'in-house mechanism' proved to be a failure as the indicted judges declined to step down. The list of judges who come to adverse notice on serious charges seems to be growing longer by the day, giving a clear indication that there is something intrinsically wrong about the state of the judiciary.

This brings us to the question of judicial accountability. Former Chief Justice of India (CJI), Justice J.S. Verma, while assuming office, had observed, 'These days we are telling every one what they should do. But who is to tell us?' This is the question which has evaded an answer for too long a time. As Justice V.R. Krishna Iyer has observed, 'The cult of the robe, on democratic probe, proves counterfeit, contempt power notwithstanding. A new Indian judicial order needs to be midwifed by a daring departure and a radical process.'[3] It is interesting in this context to refer to the statement of Justice J.S. Verma that judges of the Supreme Court and high courts should be brought under the ambit of a new law along the lines of the Prevention of Corruption Act to make them more accountable for their misconduct. 'Today, judges of the superior judiciary in India are not answerable to anyone for their misconduct as neither the impeachment procedure nor the internal judicial machinery is workable...Despite a majority judgement in the Veeraswami case, where it has been held that investigation into instances of misconduct by a judge could be ordered with the sanction of the Chief Justice of India, there is not a single instance of executive sanction of the CJI for making an investigation in any of the numerous cases where people had openly voiced allegations which many sections of society thought

---

[3] Justice V.R. Krishna Iyer, in *Quae Curia* (What a Court), *Frontline*, 19 June 1998.

required consideration...There were only two ways of ensuring accountability—either through an internal machinery that involved following conventions coupled with social sanction by the judicial community itself, or a new law', Verma added. He further said that while in earlier days, the internal machinery, evolved on the basis of healthy conventions, had been working for quite some time, it was obvious that every judge was on his own and there was no internal machinery to enforce accountability as it depended entirely on the judge against whom allegations were levelled to give his consent. If a judge does not agree, you cannot say anything to him, much less the chief justice. Neither can anyone else. The only other alternative is to provide legal sanction and for that you need to enact a new law. The former CJI said that he did not think the law could be deferred any longer because the longer it was deferred, the greater was the risk of erosion of credibility of the higher judiciary. (*Times of India*, 29 Aug 1998). Former union law minister Ram Jethamalani had asserted that the national democratic alliance government would enact a legislation to give effect to the code of conduct evolved by the Supreme Court. However, there is no unanimity on the subject and there is a cross-section of the judicial community which is opposed to passing of any such law or for that matter any stringent provisions for open public enquiries into the misconduct of the judges. For example, another retired CJI, A.M. Ahmadi, just prior to his retirement in 1997, had expressed views asking for much more protection for judges against such enquiries. (*Maharashtra Times*, 25 Mar 1997). In the judgement in the case of the controversial former Bombay high court chief justice, A.M. Bhattacharjee, the division bench of the Supreme Court held that only the CJI, considered to be the first among judges, can be the prime mover for taking action against an erring high court judge or chief justice whose bad conduct falls short of attracting impeachment. The court also, for the first time, gave legal sanction to an in-house proceeding to be adopted by the CJI for taking action against a high court judge or the chief justice.

As justice Rajindar Sachar has observed, 'The lament

"something is rotten in the state of Denmark" is echoed in the words of former Chief Justice S.P. Bharucha, who felt that the integrity of about twenty per cent of the higher judiciary was in doubt.'[4] Successive chief justices of the Supreme Court have bemoaned that the image of the judiciary is being tarnished due to corruption. Justice Bharucha deplored the fact that 'impeachment is a cumbersome process and which, as a recent instance showed (probably hinting at the developments concerning Justice V. Ramaswami in 1993) may not achieve the desired result for reasons that are political.' Alternatively, he claimed that the Supreme Court and the high courts had attempted to evolve an informal procedure to meet the situation but it was yet to be tested. In his Law Day address, he clearly suggested that the only alternative was internal, namely the in-house procedure, and that he would like it enforced wherever the conditions to do so existed. He did not elaborate what those conditions were.[5] A question which arises for consideration is whether there ought not to be more transparency in dealing with these matters. The NCRWC has recommended that a committee of the proposed national judicial commission (NJC) be constituted to examine complaints of deviant behaviour of judges and after the report of such a committee, recourse be taken to the provisions of the Judges (Inquiry) Act, 1968. However, we are still a long way from any consensus on the subject. After all, the judiciary cannot be a law unto itself and must be accountable to society at large. Former union law minister Shanti Bhushan has rightly emphasised that, 'the apex court owes not only to itself but also to the judiciary as a whole and even more so to the people of India to identify these corrupt judges and institute *suo motu* proceedings for criminal contempt against them'.[6] While one may not agree that such cases be dealt with under the Contempt of Courts Act, 1991, his sentiments

[4]Rajindar Sachar, Whither the Judiciary, *Hindu*, 15 May 2002, p. 10.
[5]V. Venkatesan, A New Chief Justice of India, *Frontline*, 24 May 2002, p. 31–32.
[6]Op. cit.

deserve wide and unstinted support. So far as the higher judiciary is concerned, the emphasis of the Supreme Court seems to be on making the tainted judges leave on their own rather than prosecuting them. There have also been instances where tainted high court judges have merely been transferred to other states leading to protests and sharp reactions in those states. It is time to consider whether this is the best policy and whether this will be able to retain the respect for the judiciary among the people at large. It is interesting to note in this context that a Vietnamese Supreme Court judge found guilty of taking bribes was sentenced by his peers to two years in prison. (*Times of India*, 26 Feb 1997). The union law minister has now announced that NJC would be established in 2003 to, *inter alia*, deal with allegations levelled against judges. (*Times of India*, 1 Dec 2002).

L.M. Singhvi has rightly underlined that the concept of independence of judiciary does not mean absolutely rigid separation and the concept of accountability is not a euphemism for judicial subordination. Accountability implies a control system, a system of dos and don'ts of ethics and a system of checks and balances. In that perspective, the two concepts are not only consistent and compatible but also complement, supplement and sustain each other.[7]

The parliamentary standing committee on home affairs has expressed its concern at the Allahabad high court judge holding open court on the platform (referred to earlier) and has asked the centre to formulate a code of ethics for judicial officers. It has suggested that early steps may be taken to ensure an 'institutionalised and transparent arrangement' in this regard. (*Times of India*, 21 Apr 2000).

It will be useful to refer to the observations of the superior courts themselves in certain matters decided by the lower courts. These, while enhancing respect for the higher courts, create misgivings in the minds of the public about the functioning of the courts in general. Just two instances should suffice to bring

[7]L.M. Singhvi, *Freedom on Trial*, Vikas Publishing House Private Ltd., New Delhi, 1991, p. 185.

home this point. Passing orders on a *suo motu* action as well as a petition from Delhi police to set aside the Madras [now Chennai] sessions court order, a division bench of the Madras high court severely castigated the principal sessions judge who had granted interim anticipatory bail to Sushil Sharma [accused in the notorious tandoor murder case]. The court expressed grave suspicion that there was 'something more than what meets the eye' in the circumstances in which the order was passed. (*Hindustan Times*, 13 Jul 1995). The other case is that of *R.C. Sood* v. *High Court of judicature at Rajasthan and others* (1998), 5 Supreme Court case 493, decided on 13 May 1998. Essentially, it is a judgement by which the Supreme Court quashed the proposed disciplinary proceedings as well as the placing under suspension of a member of the Rajasthan state judiciary. The Supreme Court was highly critical of the manner in which the Rajasthan high court dealt with the whole matter. The Supreme Court's remarks and observations though couched in sober and restrained language are still trenchant and make poignant and disturbing reading. The Supreme Court has stated in this judgement that a three judge committee was *looking for* a person who was ready to depose against the petitioner *even if he was an impostor,* that the person examined by the committee *was in all probability an impostor,* that the Supreme Court had no manner of doubt that *there was a complete lack of bonafides* on the part of the high court and finally that the high court *apparently stung* by an earlier judgement of the Supreme Court *retaliated* by launching a fresh set of charges.[8] (Emphasis added).

A point on which it is necessary to have some clarity pertains to the statements which the judges made while sitting on the bench. This has a direct bearing on the image of the judiciary in society. One would normally assume that any queries made from the bench would only be to seek clarifications rather than give vent to somewhat ill-tempered views and peremptory comments. The judges are also not expected to pass off-hand

[8]B.R. Ranade, Stranger Than Fiction, *Symbiosis Law Times,* July–August 1999, p. 11.

comments on any matters which are not directly related to the issues at hand. However, the recent trend is quite the opposite. During the hearing before the Bombay high court on a PIL on the Maharashtra state electricity board's award of a contract for retrofitting of generators, the presiding judge made a comment that the Maharashtra government administration was the worst in the country. The next day, this was widely reported in the Press. When, at the next hearing, the advocate general raised the matter to correct the record, the judge objected to the Press reporting his comments and cautioned the reporters in the court and directed that what was expected to be reported was only the orders of the court. This is difficult to understand. After all, the hearings in the court are public and the people have a right to know what transpires in the court. Ideally, a judge has to be careful in passing sweeping comments on matters which do not form part of the proceedings before the court. And, even if the judge believed that the state administration was the worst in the country, he should have brought it out in his judgement by arguing it cogently. It is reported that the Allahabad high court has prohibited the publication of any news pertaining to submissions made before it in the Ram Janmabhoomi–Babri Masjid case, till the case is decided. No articles are also to be published on the issues before the court. (*Sakal*, 22 Aug 2002).

In another instance, expressing deep concern over the alleged covert attempts being made to stall the investigation into corruption cases, the division bench of the Patna high court monitoring the animal husbandry scam probe observed that if things continued in this fashion there was every likelihood of India soon emerging as the number one country as far as corruption was concerned. The division bench made this observation while listening to the submissions of the CBI. (*Times of India*, 24 May 1997).

In yet another instance, the Patna high court said on 12 August 1997 that the 'State is a fit case for President's rule'. During a hearing on a PIL against the alleged misuse of funds meant for the national rural employment programme, a division bench ruled that it was not the Governor alone who was entitled to recommend imposition of President's rule, and that the court too could direct the use of Article 356 in appropriate cases! The merits of these observations are open to serious questions. The court's observation rocked parliament. The Lok Sabha was adjourned for 30 minutes on 13 August 1997 following a scuffle between members of the Rashtriya Janata Dal (RJD) and the Samata Party. The ruling RJD in the state and former chief minister Laloo Prasad Yadav considered the ruling a case of intrusion by the judiciary into the affairs of an elected government. (*Frontline*, 5 Sep 1997, p. 29).

Commenting on the issue of notice by the Allahabad high court to then prime minister Deve Gowda in a petition challenging his appointment as the prime minister, the *Hindustan Times* editorial commented, 'Judicial activism, whether it has achieved speedier dispensing of justice or not, seems to have made the judges of higher courts feel as if they are supra-Constitutional authorities... [But] when Supreme Court judges pass *obiter dicta*—"The nation should hang its head in shame" —on cases which are still being heard, they shroud the ends of justice...It is time the Chief Justice of the Supreme Court issues guidelines on what judges should say in the protected precincts of a judicial chamber. Nothing should be said by a judge which, if said or written outside the courts and parliament, can be legally actionable.'[9]

It is said that the judges should let their judgements speak for themselves. But, the need to maintain judicial restraint and decorum in writing judgements cannot be over-emphasised. As the Delhi high court observed in one of its judgements, 'the greater the power, the greater is the need for restraint'. Seen in this light, the observation of a Delhi TADA judge that parliament was like a fish market was most unfortunate. The judge had no business to comment that members of parliament were wasting the nation's time as well as public money. He took the liberty to pass free-wheeling judgements on MPs and ministers, all pining for 'a chance to sit at the feet of underworld dons and

[9]Editorial, Wanted Restraint, *Hindustan Times*, New Delhi, 27 July 1996.

base businessmen'. Predictably, these remarks led to protests in parliament and had to be struck off by the Delhi high court. The high court rightly observed, 'Judges these days do not speak through their judgements but use their special authority as a long sword taking broadsides at all other segements of society'.

While deciding a PIL in respect of Bengal bandh in June 2002, the Calcutta high court observed that 'protests without purpose' and a 'philosophy of no-work' were the twin contributions of Bengal and, as Bengalis, they hung their heads in shame. (Editorial, *Times of India*, 8 Jun 2002).

In the case pertaining to the conviction of former union minister, Kalpanath Rai, the *Hindustan Times* rightly argued editorially that the statements of the TADA judge that, 'a judge had to be sensitive to the social environment and the cry of society for justice' was dangerous logic because a judge's primary duty was to evaluate the evidence and give verdict on the merits of the case. Sensitivity to social environment can be part of the judicial *obiter dicta* but cannot be the basis of judicial punishment under the law. (*Sunday*, 30 March–5 April 1997, p. 51).

Obviously, judges who administer the law must be completely above any reproach and set an example of political neutrality and independence. In this light, a certain type of conduct by judges is simply not forgivable. A judge can have political ambitions but he must not be seen to be furthering his political prospects while sitting as a high court judge. Thus, a high court judge filing his nomination paper for election to the state legislature or parliament without first resigning from the high court, as happened in Assam, for example, some years ago is just not acceptable. A judge of the Bombay high court held a Press conference to declare his intention to contest the election to the state legislature on behalf of a political party. When he was denied the ticket, he merrily continued to function as the high court judge. To uphold the prestige and the image of the judiciary, such offenders must be brought to book.

Long delays in delivering judgements is yet another area of serious concern from the litigant's point of view of. The most recent such case was the Cogentrix power project case in

Karnataka in which the Supreme Court judgement was delayed considerably. There must be a reasonable time limit, of say three months from the conclusion of the arguments, laid down for giving the judgement and this must be adhered to scrupulously by all judges. Apart from the inconvenience caused to the litigants, justice itself may be a casualty of such delayed judgements as a judge is unlikely to remember all the nuances of the arguments pleaded before him by the parties after a lapse of several months. In the case of inordinate delays in delivering judgements, there have been cases where such judgements have been set aside. But, clearly, this is not an answer to the problem, particularly in a country in which the average time for disposal of a case is twenty years.

In a large number of cases, judges have applied for out of turn allotment of flats or land for construction of a house from the discretionary quota of the chief ministers or central ministers. As was observed by the Punjab and Haryana high court in one of its judgements, 'the record showed that a large number of judicial officers had applied for allotment of discretionary quota plots to the chief minister and some of the applications contained language which bordered on servility.' (*Times of India*, 23 Mar 1997).

As justice Hosbet Suresh has noted, 'The conferences of chief justices have always resisted framing of any formal code of conduct for obvious reasons'.[10] It is, therefore, a matter of some satisfaction that, after several years of procrastination, at last the higher judiciary has agreed to adopt a code of ethics, called 'restatement of values of judicial life'. As Krishan Mahajan has brought out, apparently, the apex court judges already had a code of conduct. But the code and its operation was a secret.[11] This is amazing, to put it mildly. There is no reason why a code of ethics needs to be kept secret. Not only the code but the manner in which it is applied and enforced must be clear for everyone to see. This is the public accountability and transparency that we are talking about.

[10] Justice Hosbet Suresh (Retd.), Who will judge the judges, *One India One People*, 16 January 1998.

[11] Krishan Mahajan, Let There Be Transparency, *Indian Express*, 8 December 1999.

As brought out by *Outlook* magazine, the 15-point code of ethics adopted by the higher judiciary is as under:[12]

— A judge shall not contest election to clubs, societies or other associations.
— A judge shall not hold elective office except in a society connected with the law.
— A judge must avoid associating with individual members of the bar, especially those who practise in the same court.
— A judge shall not permit any member of his family to appear before him or even be associated in any manner with a case to be dealt by him.
— He shall not allow a family member who practices to stay in the same residence.
— He shall strive for a degree of aloofness in keeping with the dignity of the office.
— He shall not enter into public debate or express views on political issues or air views on matters which are pending before the judiciary.
— He shall not speak to the media. The judgements speak for themselves.
— He shall not accept gifts or cordiality except from family members and close friends.
— He shall not play or speculate in the stockmarkets.
— He shall not seek or accept contributions or be associated with fund-raising.
— He shall always be under public gaze, and hence there should be no act of omission.
— He shall not hear or decide matters where he has financial interests, unless disclosed before hand.
— He shall not engage directly or indirectly in trade or business either individually or along with other persons.
— He shall declare his assets as well as those of other family members.

---

[12]Murali Krishnan, Milord, Judge Yourself, *Outlook*, 20 December 1999, p. 22.

This is a good beginning and it has not come a day too soon. The then Chief Justice of the Supreme Court, Justice A.S. Anand, hit the nail on the head when he pointed out at the chief justices' conference that 'every holder of a public office must be accountable to the people'. It is widely believed that bringing out the code was a pre-emptive move on the part of the judiciary against the possibility of the government taking the initiative to bring forth a suitable legislation on the subject or lay down such a code through the proposed NJC. Whatever the provocation, it is good sign that a code of ethics has finally been adopted by the judiciary. It is hoped that the implementation of the code will be transparent enough to instil a sense of confidence among the people that the judiciary is keen to set its house in order.

Any discussion on public accountability and transparency of the judiciary will have to take note of the Contempt of Court Act, 1971. The contemporary law of contempt, which seeks to prohibit any criticism of the judge, his judgement or the institution of the judiciary has become a matter of public debate. On 5 December 2002, the Karnataka high court initiated contempt of court proceedings against 56 persons from 14 newspapers and magazines for reportage that scandalised the image of the judiciary. (*Frontline*, 3 Jan 2003) This issue came up again prominently with the Supreme Court of India's ire being directed at Arundhati Roy, the Booker Prize winning author of *The God of Small Things*. The decision of the Supreme Court in March 2002 to 'symbolically' punish Roy by sentencing her to a day's imprisonment in Tihar Jail and a fine of Rs 2,000 on the ground that she had 'scandalised and lowered the dignity' of the apex court raised important issues relating to the scope of the freedom of speech and expression as a fundamental right, even though such right is, *inter alia*, subject to matters concerning contempt of court. The courts, in a number of other countries, seem to take a much more lenient view of criticism of the courts. As A.G. Noorani has brought out, the Australian high court has gone so far as to rule in 1992 that, 'so long as the defendant is genuinely exercising a right of criticism and not acting in malice or attempting to impair the administration of justice he or she is immune.' In a classic case decided in 1911 which Lord Justice Salmon approved in 1969 in his Report on the Law of Contempt in Britain, if there is a 'just cause for challenging the integrity of a judge...it could not be contempt of court to do so. Indeed it would be a public duty to bring the relevant facts to light'. (*Frontline*, 29 Mar 2002). S.P. Sathe has rightly underlined that the courts must give maximum freedom to the people to criticise their judgements and also their role in democracy...as long as it does not damage people's faith that the courts will do justice.[13]

As Fali S. Nariman has brought out, uncertainty shrouds the entire law on this subject. 'Scandalising' the court or the administration of justice 'in any manner' is punishable as contempt of court. To this marvellously evasive language there is another uncertain dimension: the inherent jurisdiction of high courts and of the Supreme Court. The Constitution expressly empowers the higher judiciary to punish for contempt of itself and leaves it to the judges to define contempt. In the end then, you can never win, simply because contempt of court is what the court says it is.[14]

Even more disturbing is the observation of the courts that truth cannot be the defence in a contempt of court matter. This puts severe limitations on any one raising matters pertaining to the judiciary in the public debate. As Soli J. Sorabjee has urged, 'This highly anomalous position needs to be judicially overturned or remedied by a legislative amendment whereby truth coupled with public interest can be a valid defence in a contempt action.'[15]

The US Supreme Court's views, in this behalf, are eloquently expressed in the words of Justice Black who wrote for the majority in 1941: 'The assumption that respect for the judiciary

[13]S.P. Sathe, NBA Contempt of Court Case, *Economic and Political Weekly*, 24 November 2001, p. 4342.
[14]Fali S. Nariman, No rescue for improper motives, *Economic Times*, Mumbai, 31 August 1999.
[15]Soli J. Sorabjee, Judge bashing, frivolity and sleeping on the bench, *Times of India*, 9 October 1997.

can be won by shielding judges from published criticism wrongly appraises the character of the American public opinion. For it is the prized American privilege to speak one's mind, although not always with perfect good taste, on all public institutions. And an enforced silence, however limited solely in the name of preserving the dignity of the bench, would probably engender resentment, suspicion and contempt much more than it would enhance respect.' History has proved Justice Black right. Also, the way forward may well lie in the words of Justice Amua Sekyi who reasoned that, 'The courts must have regard to the rights of every person to express himself freely and openly on all matters of public concern whether pertaining to the actions of the executive, the legislature or the judiciary.'[16]

The longest imprisonment awarded for contempt of court in independent India's history has been for three months. A secretary to the government of Karnataka was sentenced to one month's imprisonment for contempt of court for disobeying the orders of the court though the final decision in the matter did not lie with him. In contrast, a division bench of the Supreme Court gave only a nominal punishment to the former UP chief minister Kalyan Singh for contempt of court for violating its orders prohibiting the erection of a permanent structure in the Babri Masjid complex in Ayodhya in July 1992. The court awarded him a one-day, 'symbolic imprisonment' and a fine of Rs 2,000 though the state government had wilfully disobeyed the orders of the Supreme Court. The case pertaining to the contempt of court involving wanton demolition of the Babri Masjid, in spite of the solemn assurances given by the Kalyan Singh government to the Supreme Court to protect the structure, is still to come up for hearing before the Supreme Court though over 9 years have elapsed since the event! There is thus no consistency in the stand taken by the courts in contempt matters and it is best that the law is amended suitably to restrict the scope of the Act and to put reasonable restrictions

[16]Quoted in Zahid F. Ebrahim, Questions of Contempt, *Frontline*, 8 October 1999, p. 97.

on the powers of the courts. As brought out earlier (chapter 1, section III), parliamentarians are averse to codifying or restricting their own privileges because the courts enjoy such unlimited powers to punish for contempt of court.

Against this background, it is disappointing to see that the NCRWC has not recommended the review and amendment of the Contempt of Court Act. This is particularly striking in view of the fact that the commission has recommended that the privileges of the legislatures and parliament be defined and delimited! The only two recommendations of the commission on this subject are to restrict the power of the court to punish for contempt to the Supreme Court and the high courts and not to extend it to other courts, tribunals or authority by inserting a proviso in Article 129; and to add a proviso to Article 19(2) to the effect that, 'in matters of contempt, it shall be open to the court to permit a defence of justification by truth on satisfaction as to the bonafides of the plea and it being in public interest'. The union law minister has now called for a public debate on the efficacy and necessity of having the Act in its proper form. The central government has also decided to seek a consensus among all political parties on making truth as a defence in contempt cases. (*Times of India*, 15 Dec 2002)

Another area which requires careful attention pertains to matters relating to the setting up of commissions of enquiry and sparing judges for the purpose. It would be wrong to take the position that sitting judges should not be spared for such inquiries at all as often there is persistent demand that a commission of inquiry must be headed by a sitting judge. It is as much a duty of the judges to preside over such commissions of inquiry as it is to decide court cases coming up before them. But, the time has come to lay down a clear policy on certain matters.

Often, the appointment of a commission of inquiry is a convenient ploy adopted by the government to defuse the situation and to delay, and in most cases to defer indefinitely, taking any action on the issues at hand. There have also been instances of inquiries having been ordered outside the Commission of Inquiry Act. Such inquiries face a number of problems. Their public acceptability is quite low. Judicial officers associating themselves with such inquiries often come into controversy. This was the case, for example, when S.V. Puranik, a former judge of the Bombay high court, was appointed to look into allegations of corruption against two ministers of the government of Maharashtra. This inquiry was not ordered under the Commission of Inquiry Act. As a result, the report could never get public acceptability. Finally, the government had to set up another commission of inquiry under the Commission of Inquiry Act under the chairmanship of another retired judge of the high court. It is best that the high court does not nominate a retired or a sitting judge when a commission is not to be set up under the Commission of Inquiry Act. This will ensure that public respect for and the position of the judiciary are not compromised.

The second question is that the Contempt of Court Act does not apply to commissions of inquiry. This is a major lacuna and needs to be rectified. The reports of a commission could certainly be criticised but it is wrong to level personal attacks, criticism and innuendoes against the judge presiding over it, as happened in the recent case of the Srikrishna Commission inquiring into the riots and bomb blasts in Mumbai following the wanton demolition of the Babri Masjid. Denigrating the judiciary in this manner is not in the larger interest of the country.

The other troubling matter is the long delay in the publication of the reports of commissions. Reports of some commissions have not been published at all. One may as well ask why have a commission of inquiry at all if its report is not to be published. It is often seen that the government chooses its own politically convenient time to release the report of a commission. As happened in the case of the Srikrishna Commission, the government took several months to place the report of the commission before the state legislature but thereafter it gave hardly two days time, before the conclusion of the Assembly session, for the House to debate the report. It is necessary that the responsibility to publish the report is cast on each commission itself. Each commission should have the power to release its report to the public soon after it is submitted to the government.

The last and most crucial aspect pertains to the follow-up actions on the recommendations of a commission. The past record in this regard is scandalous. In most cases, the reports of commissions are lying unattended. According to an editorial in the *Times of India*, the Supreme Court faulted the UP government in September 1999 for the delay in implementing the report of the inquiry commission set up by it to study the unrest in Meerut in 1982...The late Justice G.D. Khosla headed several commissions of inquiry in the late 1960s and 1970s. But, in his autobiography *Memory's Gay Chariot*, he lamented that 'in the course of over a dozen inquiries and investigations, I often thought mine was an exercise in futility, for in no case were my recommendations fully and essentially acted upon'.[17] There are no simple and straightforward answers to this problem. It is only vigilance by the media, the legislature and public opinion which can force the government to act on the recommendations of the commission within a reasonable period of time.

There have been cases where judges presiding over commissions of inquiry which have given reports favourable to the government have been rewarded by the government by suitable and coveted postings, transfers, post-retirement assignments and so on. Justice K. Venkataswami who was heading the Tehelka inquiry commission was inadvisedly appointed as the chairman of a statutory body even before he had submitted the inquiry report. There must be a policy that any judge presiding over a commission of inquiry will not be considered for any assignment for a period of three years after the submission of the report of the commission.

A reference must be made in this context to the selection of the retired judges appointed on a number of oil selection boards (which fortunately have been abolished in early 2002) and similar other organisations. According to a news item in *India Today International*, at least six retired high court judges/chief

---

[17] Editorial, Errors of Commission, *Times of India*, 19 October 1999.

justices appointed on the oil selection boards were fired by the then minister for petroleum for defying the orders of the minister.[18] Thirteen more judges were similarly sacked during the tenure of the Atal Behari Vajpayee government. Obviously, the minister wanted them to do things which were irregular and not according to the rules on the subject. This is not the first time that the judges appointed on the oil selection boards have found it difficult to function. It is imperative that the Supreme Court lays down that retired judges will not be appointed in such posts unless they are given a fixed term and are protected against such arbitrary actions. For such actions bring down the image of the judiciary. It also creates an impression in the public mind that even high court judges are subservient to the executive.

Any discussion on the judiciary would be incomplete without a reference to judicial activism. There are a lot of misgivings on this subject. It was not therefore surprising that A.M. Ahmadi, the then Chief Justice of India, in his Zakir Hussain Memorial Lecture delivered in Delhi in February 1996 had to reassure the country that judicial activism in its current 'aggressive role' is a temporary phenomenon and at the root of the problem was the failure of the executive and the legislature to perform their constitutionally assigned roles. If all wings of Indian democracy perform their duties and obligations, there will be no need for the judiciary to advise them. He said fears of judicial tyranny are really quite unfounded because judges themselves are aware of the fact that the non-elected judiciary is neither meant nor equipped to act as a policy-making body.

As the *Hindustan Times* commented editorially, 'it will be unfortunate if the judiciary over-steps the constitutional role and is seen to pander to populism.'[19] At the same time, note must also be taken of the growing tendency on the part of the government at the centre and in the states to pass the buck to

[18] Greasier Than a Slick, *India Today International*, 3 May 1999, p. 23–24.
[19] Editorial, A Third Chamber?, *Hindustan Times*, New Delhi, 28 December 1995.

the judiciary wherever it lacks the political will to take a decision. The two major recent instances of this type were the recommendations of the Mandal commission report, and the Babri Masjid controversy.

While it is true that activism has been thrust on the judiciary due to ineffective, unresponsive and impervious legislative and executive processes, it is time to consider whether the perpetuation of this phase would not lead to further paralysis in important organs of the polity. The judiciary can and should direct these two institutions to take suitable action, but to take on itself the responsibilities which clearly fall in others' spheres is bound to harm the very foundations of democratic polity. Another real danger of judicial activism is that of direct confrontation between the vocal, organised and powerful vested interests in society and the judiciary...The grass certainly looks greener on the other side of the fence, but it is time each one tended the grass in his own backyard before casting longing glances at the neighbour's.[20]

Jeffrey Jowell, Professor of Public Law, University of London, while delivering a talk on 'the judges vs. the executive in England today' in New Delhi had this to say: The judiciary should not interfere in matters relating to policy, allocation of funds and welfare measures taken by the state. Judiciary should not, by expansion of its judicial powers, effect the transfer of decision-making right from the legislature and the executive to the courts in respect of matters of policy and allocation of funds. Referring to the limitations on the powers of courts to review administrative actions of the government, Jowell said that there were three principles—illegality, procedural unfairness and unreasonableness—which governed the powers of the courts in the area of judicial review. (*Hindustan Times*, N.D., 6 Jan 1996).

Based on these criteria, it can be seen that several decisions of the courts in public interest litigations have far exceeded the

---

[20]Madhav Godbole, Minding everyone else's business, *Indian Express*, 11 March 1997, *The Changing Times—A Commentary on Current Affairs*, Orient Longman, 2000, p. 47.

limits of judicial review. In fact, in recent years, a number of policy decisions have been taken by the government at the behest of the higher judiciary. These include: unauthorised constructions in Delhi, pollution of the Yamuna, preservation of historical monuments, cleaning Delhi, use of CNG for public transport vehicles, and so on. The Bombay high court directed the Bruhanmumbai municipal corporation to rapidly restore dug-up pavements in the city. In another PIL, the Delhi high court issued notices in October 1998 to the government of India and the Delhi government to let the court know the steps which were proposed to be taken to bring down the prices of onions and other vegetables and essential commodities. The Mumbai *Grahak Panchayat* filed a PIL urging the Bombay high court to direct the state government to stablilise the wholesale and retail prices of vegetables and edible oils. The division bench rejected the same. In yet another case, the Delhi government was directed by the court to take effective steps to check the spread of dengue fever.

In due course it was evident that the PIL was being used as much by vested interests, political opponents, lawyer politicians and publicity seekers as by bonafide public spirited men and women. In *Sachidananda Pandey* v. *state of West Bengal*, Justice Khalid was constrained to caution: 'PIL has now come to stay. But one is led to think that it poses a threat to the courts and the public alike. Such cases are now filed without any rhyme or reason. It is, therefore, necessary to lay down clear guidelines and to outline the correct parameters for entertainment of such petitions.'

The proliferation of PILs and the wide-ranging subjects on which orders came to be passed by the courts on PILs led the government to think of putting some curbs on PILs by imposing a large court fee for filing of a PIL. This was strongly opposed by a large cross section of people. But, even the courts have in recent times expressed reservations about the advisability of excessive resort to PIL.

It has to be admitted that while PILs have been effective in certain matters, in certain others they have proved to be unsuccessful as an instrument for safeguarding public interest. The three most prominent examples of the latter are the Enron,

Cogentrix and the telecom licencing scandals. In all these three matters, substantial public interest was involved but the courts failed to see the merits of the arguments made against the policies adopted and sanctions given by the government. In any future debate on PILs, it will be imperative to analyse the reasons for the failure of the PILs in these major cases.

This brings us to the question of long overdue judicial reforms. This is indeed a sad and disturbing chapter in the history of judicial administration in the country. Pious resolutions passed in seminars and conferences underlining the importance and urgency of the subject have remained on paper.

Law commissions appointed by the centre and the states as also reports such as the Malimath committee report in 1990 have made a series of recommendations in this regard. Unfortunately, most of the legislative changes proposed have not been made, even in basic laws such as the Indian Penal Code, the Indian Evidence Act, the Criminal Procedure Code and other laws. Either the government did not have the time to frame the necessary legislative proposals or Parliament did not have the time to consider them.

The legal profession has come to be looked upon as a business and as a result, any move to simplify the procedures, laws and rules is resisted by advocates who resort to agitation, strikes and so on. One such example was the agitation launched by advocates all over the country in February 2000 against certain amendments made in the Civil Procedure Code. This was again repeated in 2002. The Supreme Court has held that legal professionals have no right to strike and that if they do so, they would have to compensate their aggrieved clients. In spite of this injunction, lawyers resorted to strike in December 2002 to protest against the Legal Services Authorities (Amendment) Act, 2002 providing for *lok adalats* in every public utility department of government. Lawyers in West Bengal were on a 44-day long strike in November–December 2002 against the court fee increase. Lawyers in Maharashtra boycotted the courts in December 2002 to protest against the increase in the sitting time of the courts by 45 minutes! The experiment of setting up of administrative tribunals was undertaken with the intention of reducing judicial delays but it has failed for more than one reason.

The reasons for the large number of cases pending are well known but there is scarcely any political or administrative will to take necessary remedial measures. Some suggestions mooted in this behalf include reducing the number of holidays and vacations for the courts, increasing the number of courts, holding court hearings in two shifts to use the available infrastructure more intensively, more rigorous training of judges and so on.

The question of setting up of the NJC has been under discussion for many years but no consensus has yet emerged on the subject. It will be relevant in this context to refer to the observation made by then CJI, Justice A.S. Anand, at the golden jubilee celebrations of the Supreme Court of India on 26 November 1999. Justice Anand said, 'The suggestion for setting up a national judicial commission for the appointment and transfer of judges was prompted by a desire to have wider consultation and not to leave it to any one individual to make the choice. The answer of the 9 judge bench to the Presidential Reference, which provides for wider consultation by a collegium, meets that requirement. It must be given a fair chance to prove its worth.'[21] The NCRWC has recommended the setting up of a NJC but its composition— CJI as chairman, two seniormost judges of the Supreme Court, union law minister and one eminent person to be nominated by the President in consultation with the CJI—is too heavily weighted in favour of those occupying high judicial positions. It is unlikely that such a commission will find wide public acceptance or serve the purpose underlying the setting up of such a commission.

The rule of seniority for appointment to the post of chief justice of India has led to several incumbents having very short tenures. In 2002 itself, the country has seen four chief justices of India. It is time to lay down statutorily that any person eligible for consideration will have to have at least one year of

[21] *Symbiosis Law Times*, February 2000, p. 7.

service left and when appointed will hold office for at least two years.

The question of establishing an All India Judicial Service is similarly pending resolution. As referred to earlier, there should be a special law for taking disciplinary action against and prosecution of high court and Supreme Court judges if the need arises. Issues which came up in the impeachment proceedings of Justice V. Ramaswamy should be analysed so as to take corrective action, wherever necessary. This will avoid unnecessary controversy in similar proceedings in future.

Simple procedural changes which have been adopted in a number of other countries are resisted in India. The first of these relates to the procedure for giving adjournments. There must be an upper limit on the maximum number of adjournments which can be permitted in any one case. Second, the maximum time for which an adjournment is to be permitted must be specified in the rules. Third, any stay given in a case should not be for a period of more than three months and if the stay is not vacated earlier, it should stand automatically vacated at the end of three months from the date of the stay. Fourth, the normal rule must be to make all submissions to the court in writing. Oral hearing may be permitted only in cases where clarifications are considered necessary. Fifth, there must be a maximum time limit of 30–45 minutes for making oral arguments by each side. Sixth, the judgements must be precise and to the point and not compete in length with Ph.D. dissertations.

The 'court clerk' system prevailing in the US Supreme Court and high courts needs to be given a serious trial in India. Under this system, eminent law academics assist the judges by following the arguments, summarising details, identifying and retrieving the relevant case law, and even writing draft judgements which may be finally approved by the judges with such changes and modifications as they may consider appropriate. This would relieve the judges of a great deal of work and help in the speedy disposal of cases.

The Law Commission's proposal to bifurcate the Supreme Court bench into a constitutional and an appellate division also merits serious consideration. As J.K. Jain has brought out, 'Perhaps if the Supreme Court were to have a constitutional court that sat *en banc*, the jurisprudence of the court would grow more coherently. And if the jurisprudence of the court became more coherent, the flood of litigation would certainly recede.'[22]

Finally, the granting of financial and administrative autonomy to the judiciary will go a long way in curing the ills of the system. There is substantial scope for incurring further additional expenditure on the judiciary. After all, administration of justice is one of the primary responsibilities of the government. The expenditure on the judiciary in this country is only 0.2 per cent of gross national product (GNP) as compared to 4.3 per cent in the UK. More than half the expenditure on the judiciary is from the revenue generated by the judiciary itself through court fees, fines etc.

One would have expected a high-level commission such as the NCRWC to delve into the complex issues in the field of judicial administration in the country, particularly since a majority of its members were judges of the superior courts or jurists. The report of the commission is, however, very disappointing on this as also on various other scores. As stated earlier, the discussion herein is confined only to certain facets which have a bearing on the theme of this book. But, clearly the time has come to appoint a Judicial Reforms Commission which, hopefully, will have a greater representation of the various stakeholders and not just the members of the judicial fraternity.

### Media: Who Will Watch the Watchman?

The print and electronic media have been fast expanding their hold and reach in India. The national readership council study 2002, released in June 2002, shows that the reader base of the daily newspapers has gone up by 20 per cent over the last two years from 131 million in 1999 to 156 million at the beginning of 2002. Despite this growth, as many as 248 million literate

---

[22]C.K. Jain (ed.), *Constitution of India—In Precept and Practice, op. cit*, p. 136.

adults still do not read any publication. This shows the growth potential for the future. Of the estimated 180 million readers of the print media, the share of rural readers has been growing steadily and now contributes 48 per cent of the total readership. The two top dailies, *Dainik Bhaskar* and *Dainik Jagran* have a large rural readership of 5.2 million and 5.9 million respectively. Television comprises the major share of media consumption though it does not seem to have affected reading time. The average reader in urban India still spends 16 per cent of total media time, or 18 minutes a day reading a daily or a magazine. Predictably, cable and satellite television are extremely popular, covering 40 million homes in 2002 as compared to 29 million in 1999, recording a 31 per cent growth. In view of the rapid spread of the electronic media, it is better to talk now of the freedom of the media rather than mere print media.

In 1959, the Supreme Court echoed the view of Lord Shaw and argued that since the freedom of the press was 'only a right flowing from the freedom of speech and expression', the liberty of the press in India stands on no higher a footing than the freedom of speech and expression of a citizen and that no privilege attaches to the press as such, that is to say, as distinct from the freedom of the citizen. (*M.S.N. Sharma* v. *Srikrishna Sharma*, 1959). So it is a good sign that the NCRWC has recommended that the freedom of the press and other media should be explicitly recognised as a fundamental right by amending Article 19(1) of the Constitution.

As Nani Palkhivala has asserted, to talk about democracy without the freedom of the press is a contradiction in terms. A free press is not an optional extra in a democracy. If the press does not function as the watchdog of democracy, it has no reason for existence.[23] Jawaharlal Nehru, strongly advocated the freedom of the press. He said, 'To my mind, the freedom of press is not just a slogan...but it is an essential attribute of the democratic process...I would rather have a completely free press with all the

---

[23] Nani Palkhivala, Press Must Not Be A Poodle, *Indian Express*, New Delhi, 6 August 1995.

dangers involved in the wrong use of that freedom than a suppressed and regulated press.' The same sentiment was expressed by Thomas Jefferson who said, 'If it is left for me to decide whether we should have a government without newspapers or newspapers without a government, I should not hesitate to prefer the latter'.

Let us look at the various prerequisites needed for making such an independent, vibrant media a reality. The Press Council of India (PCI), in a recent ruling, has rightly pointed out that 'the media has an adversarial role to the extent that it questions authority, all authority, to look at the other side. This must be understood as a relationship of creative tension and accepted as a democratic necessity.'[24] As A.H. Sulzberger, President of the *New York Times*, said, press freedom is not the publisher's freedom to print; it is rather the citizen's right to know. The survey made by Freedom House, a US human rights group, mentioned four principal criteria to evaluate press freedom, namely, country laws and administrative rules; economic influence; political pressure; and overt restrictive action against reporters. It considered the Indian press only 'partly free'. The English language press in India was reported to be freer than the Indian language press according to the US based Committee to Protect Journalists.[25] It is equally important to make the media transparent in its working and accountable to the people.

Looked at from this point of view, one can see that the freedom of the media in India is rather fragile. Mulayam Singh Yadav, then chief minister of UP, adopted a multi-pronged strategy to get the media to report in his favour which included, among others, the following:

- Humouring the owners of the newspapers of Lucknow and Delhi as well as divisional publication centres of UP with plots of land, sugar mills, excessive advertisements and government

[24] Press Council Rejects Army Complaint Against Outlook, *Outlook*, 27 December 1999, p. 18.

[25] Press Council of India, *16th Annual Report (April 1, 1994—March 31, 1995)*, p. 16.

patronage to the sister-industries of the newspaper owners. The two newspaper owners, who could not be 'managed', had to face the *halla bol* (declare a war programme) of Mulayam's party. The house of an editor was attacked. Newspaper vans were set on fire. At many places, newsmen were beaten up. This continued for several months. Even the Editors' Guild of India had to send reputed editors to inquire into the matter.

- Bribing journalists on an unprecedented scale. About 100 scribes and their organisations were paid Rs 4.5 crore from CM's discretionary fund. He distributed out-of-turn plots in Lucknow, NOIDA and elsewhere. The general secretary of the Samajwadi Party, Raghu Thakur, brazenly asked, 'What is wrong in it?'[26]

Mulayam Singh spent over Rs 1 crore wining and dining scribes. (*Newstime*, Hyderabad, 19 Jul 1995). The fund was even used for lavish parties given by journalists to celebrate the birthdays of their wards or their own marriage anniversaries. Their airfares and stays at five-star hotels in other cities was also paid for from the fund.

A *halla bol* agitation was launched in UP on 12 October 1994. An appeal was issued to people to boycott reading *Dainik Jagran* and *Amar Ujala*, the two Hindi dailies which had refused to succumb to pressure. As many as 111 journalists demanding the withdrawal of the *halla bol* call were arrested in Muzaffarnagar on 27 October 1994. The BSP kept away from the *halla bol* but viciously described the press as *manuwadi* (subscribing to the ideology of Manu).

UP was not alone in terrorising the press in this manner. In Maharashtra Shiv Sena activists attacked Nikhil Wagle, editor, *Mahanagar* and attacked the offices of the newspaper in 1993. Shiv Sena workers beat up 9 journalists in Aurangabad on the premises of a hotel when Bal Thackeray was addressing a press conference. (*Tribune*, Chandigarh, 20 Feb 1994).

[26]Dina Nath Mishra, Scribes who Take Bribes, *Observer*, New Delhi, 4 August 1995.

In the wake of the demolition of the disputed structure at Ayodhya on 6 December 1992, came the reports of numerous attacks on members of the media photographers/cameramen who were covering the happenings at Ayodhya. A special inquiry committee headed by the chairman of the PCI was set up to inquire into the matter. The chairman also appealed to the authorities to ensure that the press was allowed to function freely and fearlessly to disseminate information on matters of public importance.

It is necessary to note that the media is as much at risk from within its ranks as from outside. Ravindra Kumar, in his article in the *Statesman* says, 'I was in Bombay [now Mumbai] last February [1994] to interview candidates for a financial correspondent's position with the *Statesman*. The response, as might have been expected, was good. At least one of the candidates was uninterested in what the *Statesman* could offer; on the contrary, he was prepared to pay us a monthly sum for the privilege of being our financial correspondent. Now that was a surprise and led to obvious questions. The answers were distressing. A business journalist stands to take home a sum close to Rs 70,000 a month. When I first drew attention to the fact of corruption in business journalism, I received calls from some journalists asking whether I knew that sports and film journalists were no better and were both heavily subsidised by interested parties. I was asked whether I had ever cared to inquire into the lifestyles of film journalists in particular. Honestly, it never occurred to me.'

Kuldip Nayar, a veteran and highly respected journalist, laments that the credibility of the press has taken a nose-dive. Newspapermen change their views and sides—like chameleons. And they seem to convey the impression that they have a price which is in proportion to the position they occupy or the beat they cover. Most newspapers are a product of business—what can sell and how...Journalism is a profession only in name; in reality it is an industry...The best journalists are available to the higher bidder, whatever his source of income. In the circumstances business interests and political pressures have the better of the press. The truth about the Indian press is that it is already too nice, altogether too refined, too ready to leave out.[27]

In yet another blunt assessment, Bharat Bhushan lashes out at the corruption in journalism. He says, it is not uncommon in newspaper offices to come across the naive villager with his petition against some local official asking, 'How much will you charge for publishing this news item?' But in that naiveté is the essential truth of Indian journalism today. In the public mind, journalism is a corrupt profession. According to Bharat Bhushan, the first signs of the changing nature of corruption in Indian journalism came barely 10–15 years ago with the rise of new industrial houses trying to make it to the top in the *licence-permit raj*. They needed to control both the politicians and the media...Journalism must be the only profession in India where professional bodies take no notice of the unethical practices of their members...It is in journalism alone that the more corrupt one is, the more powerful one becomes in the profession—colleagues are in awe of you, the state machinery salutes you and the newspaper owners are afraid of reprimanding you. 'Throw a bone or two at the watchdogs of democracy and they will stop barking', avers Bharat Bhushan.[28]

Against this background, it was not surprising that the Malegam committee on disclosure requirements in offer documents made a recommendation that 'SEBI should, in consultation with the Press Council of India, evolve a code of conduct for financial journalists'. It is important to note that the Malegam committee had not singled out financial journalists in this regard. The committee had also recommended that SEBI should, in consultation with the stock exchanges and the Association of Merchant Bankers, evolve a code of conduct for brokers, lead managers, etc. in respect of communications to

[27]Kuldip Nayar, Niminy-Piminy Press—Fourth Estate Has Deviated From Principles, *Indian Express*, New Delhi, 11 July 1994.
[28]Bharat Bhushan, Bribes and Journalists—Second Thoughts, *Indian Express*, 13 August 1995.

clients on new issues and rights issues.[29] However, the same media which teaches everyone the virtues of laying down codes of conduct is reluctant to have any such code prescribed for itself. R. Vijayaraghavan, for example, believes that 'the [Malegam] committee enters the realm of the fatuous when it suggests that SEBI evolve a code of conduct for financial journalists...It can approach the PCI and evolve any number of codes of conduct. Journalists will accept these only if they feel that it will help them in their duty of providing information to the public'. (*Economic Times*, 24 Jul 1995). This is a strange logic indeed. Why should the same logic not be acceptable in the case of all other sections of society including the judiciary? Further, the limitations of self-regulatory bodies of professionals must be kept in view. There is not much that such bodies can do to discipline the professions. It is also necessary that society at large is able to judge the conduct of any given profession by referring to its code of conduct. Public accountability of journalists is as important, and in a sense more important than that of all other sections except the judiciary.

From this point of view, it is important to note that the journalists of the *Times of India* (TOI) group have, in the interest of transparency, felt the need to lay out some specific guidelines as under:

- Journalists of the TOI group should desist from accepting gifts, favours, concessional benefits such as loans, discounts, preferential shares and the sort from corporate bodies or other entities that they deal with in their professional capacity. Though nothing of value should be accepted, a commonsensical approach can be adopted towards accepting, say, a modest box of sweets, inexpensive pens, diaries, calendars and such other tokens of courtesy.
- All invitations for sponsored trips should come to the editor for nominating a representative of the newspaper. Under no

[29]Sanjiv Agarwal, *Bharat's Manual of Indian Capital Market*, 2nd edition, Bharat Law House, New Delhi, 1997, pp. 621–628.

circumstances should the individual journalist accept such an invitation on his own. The name of the host inviting agency and the fact that the trip was sponsored by it should be mentioned at the conclusion of subsequent articles. Given the sensitive nature of political journalism, no hospitality from an individual politician or party should be accepted. In order to preserve its independence, the TOI group would not like its journalists to accept the hospitality of governmental or non-governmental institutions in India. In cases where, for convenience in covering a story, the transportation is provided by the government, or a private company or other institution needs to be used, the company will pay an amount equal to the ordinary commercial costs of similar facilities.

- Every journalist should ensure that professional objectivity is not influenced by personal likes, dislikes, friendships and ideologies. Journalists should refrain from being members of political organisations. Involvement in political activities, community affairs, demonstrations and social causes that could cause a conflict of interest with the discharge of professional duties should be avoided. Any situation of potential conflict of interest (such as covering the activities of a club, organisation of which one is a member) should be brought to the attention of the editor by the journalist concerned.
- Reports which might be damning to an individual or organisation should not be carried without every effort being made to contact the affected party and obtain his or its views. In case no comment is available, the effort made to speak to the affected party should be reflected in the report.
- A journalist should not use the normal requirement of protecting the confidentiality of his sources as a cover to write unsubstantiated or sensational reports. The journalist concerned must be armed with enough information and argument to satisfy the editor about the authenticity of his report, should the occasion for any doubt or question arise. While a journalist should make every effort to ensure objectivity and accuracy, the newspaper should publish corrections and acknowledge errors.

- A journalist who holds shares in a particular company must inform his head of department/editor before writing a story related to the company. Insider trading by a journalist on the basis of privileged information is a gross violation of professional ethics.
- Journalists of the *Times of India* group should not acquire flats/houses/land at concessional rates courtesy any government quota. In case there are any who have already acquired such property out of such quota, they should declare to the company the acquisition along with the price paid. Accredited journalists occupying government accommodation on rent should conform to the newly announced guidelines of the PCI in this regard: payment of a monthly licence fee to the government plus the house rent allowance given by the employer, declaration to the government on March 31 every year of details regarding salary, property acquired etc.; vacation of accommodation on expiry of allotment, etc. Information on all these aspects should be declared to the editor.
- An advisory committee of staff journalists selected by the editor will be set up to inquire into complaints of misdemeanour or bias against any journalist. The committee may call upon the journalist in question to submit a list of his assets or a record of his investments or any relevant document should the need arise. The committee's recommendations will be carefully considered by the editor before taking action.

The allotment of central government residential accommodation to journalists has been frowned upon by a number of responsible persons as a way of bringing to bear undue influence on the journalists. B.G. Verghese, a well-known journalist, is of the view that there is no reason why this policy need be continued. Justice R.S. Sarkaria, the then chairman of PCI had felt that there was no objective criteria for deciding who should get government accommodation and who should not. Such a decision should ideally be taken by the PCI, in conjunction with a government committee. He had regretted that the PCI had no such powers. (*Times of India*, New Delhi, 21 Jul 1995).

The All India Newspaper Employees Federation, Federation of the Press Trust of India (PTI) Employees Unions, and the United News of India (UNI) Employees Federation, in a joint memorandum to the prime minister, had, *inter alia*, demanded that:

- An inquiry be held by an intelligence agency into the use of state funds during the last 15 years by the central and state governments to influence journalists and newspaper proprietors through various means.
- The probe should cover similar practices indulged in by the industrial and corporate sectors.
- Gift coupons to journalists or others in management of newspapers and news agencies be legally banned.
- Strict control be exercised on discretionary funds of the central and state governments, and
- All privileges to journalists such as subsidised housing, travel, grant of land and flats etc. should be discontinued. (*National Herald*, New Delhi, 10 Oct 1995).

'Chequebook journalism' has become a matter of serious concern. M.V. Kamat, a veteran journalist, has observed that, the corporate world took over where the government left. In order to get favourable publicity, business houses began to 'buy' journalists, at first with ordinary gift items...and then, with greater daring, with offers of all-paid holidays for journalists and their wives to distant places (Srinagar, Mauritius, Colombo and even Paris). Obviously, this has been a paying proposition. There are three parties to this form of corruption: corporate houses themselves, journalists and newspaper managements. It is clear that newspaper managements themselves have been lax in controlling their reporters.[30]

Section 13(2)(b) of the Press Council Act, 1978, requires the council 'to build up a code of conduct for newspapers, news agencies and journalists, in accordance with professional standards'.

[30] M.V. Kamat, Code of Ethics for Financial Journalists, in Mediawatch, *Tribune*, Chandigarh, 24 December 1995.

But the Council has consistently adhered to the view that it is neither desirable nor necessary to formulate an exhaustive code in abstract, and that the Council is, in consonance with the letter and spirit of Section 13(2)(b) of the Act, building up a set of principles and guidelines through its adjudications on a case-to-case basis. During 1993, 'A Guide to Journalistic Ethics' was prepared and released by the PCI. It is a compilation of the principles of journalistic ethics sorted out from the adjudications of the PCI and the guidelines issued by it in their wake. According to PCI, in substance, many of the basic principles set out in the guide are universally recognised. These are not cast-iron statutory rules but broad general principles, which, applied with due discernment and adaptation to the varying circumstances of each case, will help the journalist to self-regulate his or her conduct along the path of professional ethics.[31]

Questions do, however arise when, in spite of the code of ethics, the management of a newspaper decides to use its newspaper to launch a campaign against government agencies doing their duty to interrogate and prosecute the management for the breach of law. This happened when Ashok Jain of the *Times of India* group was being interrogated by the Enforcement Directorate (ED) for violations of certain provisions of FERA. The newspaper was used in an unabashed manner to create an impression that the government agencies were at fault in pursuing the investigation. Time and again, it was propagated that the authorities were misusing their position and violating the human rights of the accused. The matters went to a stage where the PCI, on complaints filed by two organisations and a reader of the newspaper, censured the TOI. Briefing the reporters after the meeting of the Council, the then chairman, P.B. Sawant, said the Council found the newspaper guilty of three lapses—communalising the issue, distorting statements and trying to pressurise the Enforcement Directorate. The Council took the view that the daily violated ethics. (*Hindustan Times*, 6 Aug

[31]Press Council of India, *Annual Report (April 1, 1995–March 31, 1993)*, New Delhi, p. 20.

1998). This case has important lessons about the manner in which the managements of newspapers have to conduct themselves.

In chapter 1 we had referred to the question of non-codification of privileges of the legislature and the manner in which this has led to circumscribing the rights of various persons from time to time and adversely affected the freedom of press. Unfortunately, the Privileges Committee of the Lok Sabha, in its fourth report presented in December 1994, has recommended against any legislation to codify parliamentary privileges. The recommendation is said to be based on the committee's finding that there was no evidence to show any misuse of the privileges.

Newspapers have, however, faced the wrath of the legislatures again and again on this score. There have been ever increasing incidents of privilege motions against the press. Nikhil Wagle, editor of *Aple Mahanagar* was, for example, sentenced to four days civil imprisonment by the Maharashtra Legislative Assembly for publishing an article entitled 'Why this Hypocracy' on 26 March 1992. The resolution was moved by then chief minister Sharad Pawar and adopted unanimously. There have been several such cases all over the country. The Tamil Nadu government had to pay a notional compensation of Rs 1000 on orders from the Madras high court to S. Balasubramaniam, editor of the Tamil weekly *Ananda Vikatan*, who was sentenced to three months' rigorous imprisonment by the Tamil Nadu Assembly in April 1987 for publishing a cartoon allegedly denigrating MLAs and ministers. The most significant aspect of the divisional bench judgement is not so much the award of damages to Balasubramaniam, but the assertion that the powers, privileges and immunities claimed under Article 194(3) cannot be the exclusive domain of the legislature. It is also open to the judiciary to decide whether legislative authority has been exceeded or the fundamental right of a citizen has been contravened. In effect, the court said that a legislature cannot claim judicial immunity when it arbitrarily deprives a citizen of his liberty.[32]

[32]Press Council of India, *16th Annual Report (April 1, 1994–March 31, 1995)*, New Delhi, pp. 19–20.

Alarmed over increasing instances of privilege motions, the PCI recalled the recommendations made by it in the study conducted in collaboration with the Indian Law Institute way back in 1982 and released the recommendations to the press, once again, on 2 May 1992 for the benefit of the general public.[33]

In a historic *diktat*, the chairman of the Maharashtra Legislative Council directed that the proceedings of the House in its Nagpur session in December 1996 should not be reported by the press on the ground that it would adversely affect the law and order situation in the state. When a number of persons questioned this ruling, the chairman clarified in defence that it was during World War II that a similar order had been issued! Presiding officers often order the concealment of certain parts of the proceedings in the House or the expunging of certain others. This is clearly a dubious practice as the people have a right to know what transpires in the legislatures. Often, during the periods of pandemonium in the House, even the live telecast is switched off. It is in everyones interest that the privileges of the legislature should be codified. This will remove the present ambiguity and help people and the media understand where they stand vis-a-vis the privileges of the legislature. It will also make the privileges justiciable. Perhaps for the same reason, the legislatures are reluctant to codify the privileges.

Any discussion on the freedom of the press will not be complete without a reference to the right to privacy. Many years ago, a noted American jurist, US Supreme Court Justice Louis D. Brandeis (1856–1941), defined the right to privacy in the simplest of terms. He called it, 'the right of the individual to be left alone'. In India the Supreme Court has held that the right to privacy is implicit in the right to life and liberty guaranteed to a citizen of the country by Article 21. A citizen has a right to safeguard the privacy of himself, his family, marriage, procreation, motherhood, child-bearing and education, among other matters. No one can publish anything concerning the above matters

[33]Press Council of India, *Parliamentary Privileges and the Press*, 1984.

without his consent whether truthful or otherwise and whether laudatory or critical. If he does so, he would be violating the right to privacy of the person concerned and would be liable in an action for damages. The position may, however, be different, if a person voluntarily thrusts himself into controversy or voluntarily invites or raises a controversy. (*R. Rajagopal* v. *State of Tamil Nadu*, AIR, 1995, SC 264). However, the publication of material concerning privacy is unobjectionable if it is based upon reports including court records.

A reference must be made in this context to the investigation of issues of private grief by the Indian press. On a complaint received in the matter, the PCI went into this question but came to the conclusion that a case-by-case consideration in such matters with due regard to the circumstances and facts of each case is necessary and no absolute rule can be laid down. The PCI held that a newspaper photographing the havoc wrought by a tragedy may not be wrong but if the near relations of the deceased object to the taking of the photograph or its publication in the press, in deference to their wishes, it should refrain from doing so. Photo journalism is an important part of the print media today and, while intrusion through photography into personal grief likely to hurt sentiment or arouse communal passions should be avoided, publication of photographs serving the larger public interest cannot be termed as unethical or in bad taste.[34] This view certainly requires to be reconsidered. The dignity of a human being should not be allowed to be compromised or demeaned even in death. The relatives of the deceased who are overcome by grief cannot be expected to object at the time of the tragedy to the intrusion of the press. Further, a large number of illiterate and poor people in this country do not even know that they have a right to so object to the intrusion by the press. The guidelines themselves ought to be stricter.

As L.M. Singhvi has explained, on the question of privacy, Indian law lags behind laws in other countries. The Second Press

[34]Press Council of India, *Annual Report (April 1, 1990–March 31, 1991)*, New Delhi, p. 23.

Commission did not consider it necessary to recommend legislation on privacy except to endorse the recommendation of the Law Commission to amend the Indian Penal Code to include the offences against privacy with regard to eavesdropping and unauthorised publication of photographs, not only because the concept of privacy is vague and nebulous, but also because privacy is greatly limited in Indian society and this is a known sociological fact. That is why the common law of privacy or any attempt to encapsulate it in a statutory form would be slow and late in the Indian context. It is, however, interesting to note that an amendment of the Press Council Act of 1978 was suggested by the Second Press Commission and it was recommended that the words 'including respect for privacy' be added after the words 'the maintenance of high standards of public taste'.[35]

The PCI has, in one of its annual reports, dealt with the concept of right to privacy and the guidelines therefor. One of the important points made in this report is that 'of interest to the public' is not synonymous with 'in the public interest'. The PCI has warned that there may be cases where a report is legitimate and proper, but the means by which the information was gained entails an unwarranted intrusion into the privacy of an individual. The guidelines rightly suggest that it would be an invasion of privacy to name the family or associates of a wrong-doer when they are totally innocent of the crime and no public interest is involved. Suggestive guilt by association would be unfair to the privacy of others.[36]

Against this background, it is important to note that the NCRWC has recommended that the right to privacy be recognised as a fundamental right by inserting a new Article 21 B to the effect that, 'Every person has a right to respect for his private and family life, his home and his correspondence'. This is to be subject to reasonable restrictions by the state in the

[35]L.M. Singhvi, *Freedom On Trial*, Vikas Publishing House Private Ltd., New Delhi, 1991, p. 69.
[36]Press Council of India, *Annual Report (April 1, 1991–March 31, 1992)*, New Delhi, p. 383–384.

interest of security of the state, public safety or for prevention of disorder or crime etc.

A reference must also be made to the right of an individual to reply vis-a-vis the press. Efforts have been made four times since 1988 to give legal shape to this right but this has been strongly resisted by the press. The latest such attempt was the late V.N. Gadgil's private member's Bill in 1994 on the right to reply in the press. The Bill sought to give members of the public the right to reply to allegations made against them, misreporting or misrepresentation of facts concerning them and matters connected therewith. It asserted the right to reply to a 'factually incorrect or distorted report' and made it obligatory on the newspaper or the journal that the reply shall be printed on the same page at the same position and in the same type as the report replied to. The disputes were to be referred to a three-member panel of the PCI. It provided for a fine for failure to publish the reply and also a fine for initiating proceedings without sufficient grounds.

The Bill on the right to reply derived its inspiration from a similar Bill pending before the British Parliament. Though the Bill was reportedly dropped at the report stage, it had rapidly received two readings with the support of all sections of the House. While dropping the Bill, the Minister declared it should be a last warning to the press that they should restrain themselves from publishing objectionable, unethical writing. Otherwise, statutory regulations will become inevitable. Reportedly, there are similar laws on the statute books of France, Germany, Canada and Denmark.

The Bill was stoutly opposed by the Editors' Guild of India. Mrinal Pande, general secretary of the guild called it 'regressive'. Veteran journalist Nikhil Chakravarty called it 'Gadgil's gag'. R.S. Sarkaria, then chairman of the PCI, questioned the Bill on grounds of its 'necessity, propriety, viability, workability and above all its constitutionality'. The PCI felt that the Bill had a potential of doing more harm to public interest than the stray lapses on the part of the newspapers to publish the reply of an individual affected by the report. The Council expressed its concern over the deteriorating standards of a section of the press, but it noted that, by and large, newspapers had always honoured the principle of the right to reply. The PCI itself urged the press to accept this as an ethical responsibility and has laid down a norm—Norm 9 in its publication 'A Guide to Journalistic Ethics'. It reiterated its resolve to put on fast track the complaints relating to the right to reply. The PCI felt that there was no necessity or justification for making the right to reply statutory.

The PCI has laid down guidelines, through its various adjudications, in regard to the principle of the right of reply. These include the following: The newspaper should promptly publish at the instance of the person feeling aggrieved/or concerned by the impugned publication, a contradiction/reply/rejoinder sent to the editor in the form of a letter or a note. The editor has the discretion either to publish it in full or publish its abridged and edited version, particularly when it is inordinately long. But the remainder should be an effective reply to the allegations. However, the editor is not entitled to alter, omit or refuse to publish important portions of the reply/rejoinder which effectively deal with the material allegations in the news item. If the editor doubts the truth or factual accuracy of the contradiction, it is still his/her duty to publish it with an editorial comment doubting its veracity, but only when the doubt is reasonably founded on unimpeachable documentary or other evidential material in his/her possession. The editor should not, in a cavalier fashion, without due application of mind, append such a note, as: 'we stand by our story'. It must be remembered that the liberty to append an editorial comment to a rejoinder or a reply is not an absolute right. It is a concession which has to be availed of sparingly with due discretion and caution in appropriate cases.

But, like the opposition to the code of conduct for journalists, it is difficult to understand this one-sided stand of the fourth estate and the PCI. In a sense, the right to reply can also be read into the same source, namely, Article 19(1)(a) of the Constitution and is further strengthened by the right to privacy referred to earlier. The to reply is, in a sense, a reader's right to know. How can it be denied to him? Unfortunately, the Bill was later withdrawn by V.N. Gadgil.

While the PCI has consistently argued against arming itself with punitive powers, in June 1993, it decided that in the event of a paper being censured twice in a span of three years, the adjudication in such cases shall be sent to the Cabinet Secretary to Government of India and the state Chief Secretary for such action as they may, in their discretion, deem necessary in the circumstances of the case.

The Constitution of India, under Article 19(1) and 19(2) guarantees the freedom of speech and expression subject to reasonable restrictions in the interests of the sovereignty and integrity of India, the security of the state, friendly relations with foreign states, public order, decency and morality or in relation to the contempt of court, defamation or incitement to an offence. These reasonable restrictions are particularly relevant to reporting on matters relating to communal riots. The Madon Commission found that the communal riots in Jalgaon and Mahad were fanned by the news of the Bhiwandi disturbances and recommended that it was necessary that there should be pre-censorship of news relating to communal disturbances before it is published in the newspapers.

The second press commission (1982) observed that the newspaper coverage of four communal riots viz. in West Bengal in 1964, in Gujarat in 1969, in Aligarh in 1978 and in Jamshedpur in 1979 left a great deal to be desired. The first day's sensationalism and communal reporting of incidents in many Indian language papers was followed by an intensification of communal conflict over a wider area. The PCI, in its report in January 1991, had, in respect of the Ayodhya communal riots in October-November 1990, censured four Hindi dailies for their gross irresponsibility and impropriety in offending the canons of journalistic ethics to promote mass hysteria on the basis of rumours and speculation.

In January 1990, R.S. Sarkaria, then chairman of the PCI, opined that while reporting communal disputes or riots, the press should not cite communitywise figures of the victims as this was likely to aggravate the situation. He used the example in the *Rigveda*: the truth is one but wise men tell it in many ways.

The PCI has laid down certain salutary principles in regard to communal and casteist writing. In 1993–94, the PCI underlined in the adjudication principles that India is a secular, democratic republic and people belonging to different religions, castes, creeds, etc. are all equal in the eyes of law. Newspapers should promote a sense of unity and integrity of the country by encouraging the secular way of life. The PCI also urged that news, views and comments relating to communal disputes, clashes and tensions should be disseminated in a manner that is conducive to the alleviation of strain in inter-communal relationships and the restoration of communal harmony, amity and peace.

All these issues have come into prominence once again in relation to the role of the media in reporting the communal violence in Gujarat in 2002. The palpably wrong and misleading email sent in the name of some journalists in Gujarat to justify the burning of train coaches at Godhra and inflame communal feelings was widely used by a section of the media without verifying its accuracy. The complicity of the state government in turning a blind eye to the communal riots, the connivance of the police as also the dereliction of the Constitutional responsibilities by the central government were matters of grave national concern and certainly needed to be raised and addressed. But, perhaps, till the situation was brought under control, the most important thing was to create a climate for communal harmony and peace. The exaggerated reporting by a section of the media, particularly the Gujarati language press, was responsible in no small measure in creating more communal tension and increasing the divide between the two communities in the state. This brings out once again the need for more responsible reporting and coverage of news by the media in the larger interest of controlling communal violence as quickly as possible.

The ownership of the media and editorial independence is another vital aspect of the freedom of the press. The two press commissions had suggested diffusion of ownership or delinking the proprietors from the editorial department. It was suggested that a board of trustees or a directorate should be interposed through legislation to act as an umpire between the managing company and the editorial department. But, there was no unanimity on the subject. If real accountability and transparency are to be brought about in the media, ways will have to be found to curb the influence of large houses, industrialists and business establishments in a perceptible manner.

Mannika Chopra has lamented that aggressive newspaper managements had attenuated autonomy in the country's three leading dailies, the *Times of India*, the *Indian Express* and the *Hindustan Times*, with a combined circulation of well over 16 lakh, resulting in an unseemly spate of resignations. At the core of these changes is the old question of editorial independence versus interference by the management. The debate in 1994 had merged with the larger question of whether newspapers should be considered a business venture like any other industry.[37]

This brings us to the question of the policy on advertisements. The PCI has urged, from time to time, that government authorities cannot single out newspapers critical of the government for discriminatory treatment in providing facilities or releasing advertisements. In its meeting in March 1994, for example, the PCI held the note by the chief secretary of Tamil Nadu threatening to launch criminal proceedings against certain newspapers as being contrary to the fundamental right of freedom of speech and expression guaranteed by the Constitution. The PCI also said that the release of advertisements should be done on the basis of a notified policy formulated on some rational criteria and political considerations should not weigh on the issue. Distribution should be equitable and the basic criteria should be the circulation and reach of a

[37] Mannika Chopra, The Latest Endangered Species: Editors, *Telegraph*, Calcutta, 18 March 1994.

paper. It further advised that special consideration should be given to small newspapers. These principles have been reiterated by the PCI in its annual reports year after year but all the exhortations of the PCI have failed to make any discernible impact on the authorities.

For the purpose of the release of advertisements and other favours, newspapers are often judged by the government on the basis of 'positive reporting' as opposed to 'negative reporting'. As K.K. Katyal has pointed out, it was during the Emergency that the expression 'positive reporting' gained currency, thanks to the over-zealousness of officials of the Press Information Bureau in enforcing the rigid 'does' and 'don'ts' under the censorship regulation. A variation of this doctrine was sought to be applied in Tamil Nadu. Else, what is the meaning of a reference in the statement of then chief minister, Ms Jayalalithaa, to 'negative reporting' as a part of the three-page indictment of the *Hindu?*, asks Katyal.[38]

The PCI has formulated a model advertisement policy. A welcome feature of this policy is that the list of newspapers eligible for empanelment should be made a public document available on request. The list is to be periodically sent to the PCI, the RNI and also to recognised newspaper associations. All disputes regarding inclusion/non-inclusion/removal from the approved list for release of advertisements should be referred to an independent body. This will help make the exercise transparent.

Advertising being the lifeblood of commercial publishing, major advertisers wield considerable potential power. This is as true of business advertisements as of government advertisements. In the era of public accountability and transparency, the misuse of this power for wrong ends needs to be deprecated and set right as much for private sector advertisers as for the government.

Two other issues vital for the freedom of press are the right to information and the need for drastic amendments in the

[38] K.K. Katyal, The Doctrine of Positive Reporting, *Hindu*, Chennai, 15 May 1995.

Official Secrets Act. These have been discussed at some length earlier in chapter 3.

The question of contempt of court is equally important. A number of newspersons have been hauled up under this Act. As L.M. Singhvi has underlined, there are circumstances when contempt of court and freedom of expression are implacable adversaries. There is a feeling in the press that there is something awesome in the powers of the courts to punish for contempt. In the case of contempt of court proceedings, there is a feeling among journalists and articulate citizens with a radical republican approach that more often than not they must yield by way of contrition and apology. There are some cases in the interpretation and application of contempt powers which lend some justification to these reservations and call for a new and different approach.[39] In the discussion in the earlier section on the judiciary, we have suggested that the Act be revised suitably to reduce its severity and unpredictability.

One question which has repeatedly come up for discussion is whether the PCI should be given penal powers over the press. Although the PCI has no legally enforceable punitive sanction, it wields a great deal of moral authority. Its essence is that journalists can be kept on the path of professional rectitude through moral castigation by their peers and not by punitive sanctions imposed through a plethora of restrictive laws. As Mahatma Gandhi put it, 'If the control is from without, it proves more poisonous than want of control; it can be profitable only when exercised from within'. The PCI believes that, by and large, the powers of admonition, warning or censure exercised by it under the statute have proved to be sufficient for the preservation of the freedom of the press and for maintaining the standards of newspapers and news agencies. For punitive sanctions, there are courts of law and there is already, in the armoury of the state, a battery of draconian laws to punish flagrant abuses. Besides, the PCI considers and decides complaints not only against the press but also by the press. Most

[39] L.M. Singhvi, *op cit.*, p. 74.

of the complaints by the press are against the authorities. In such cases also, the Council only has moral authority, not punitive power. Under section 15 of the Press Council Act, 1978, the Council is empowered to make such observations as it may think fit in any of its decisions or reports respecting the conduct of any authority including government.[40]

It is pertinent to note that there is already opposition to the amendment of the Press Council Act so as to increase the representation of working journalists in the proposed council and to increase the powers of the PCI to levy higher fines on erring newspapers. There are periodical outbursts from various sections of the newspaper world against the PCI. In one such recent case, the Indian Newspaper Society (INS) criticised the then chairman of the PCI for his hostile attitude towards the newspaper industry. Somehow, all this only serves to give the impression that the PCI is on the right track and deserves the support of all right-thinking people!

Several newspapers in the US have appointed an 'ombudsman' to review the performance of the paper, check the fairness and adequacy of its coverage and comments, monitor the performance of the paper on a daily basis and deal with complaints from readers. The *Times of India* group has set up an ombudsman for its newspapers. This is a welcome step and needs to be emulated by others.

In India, the press has come under pressure in Punjab, Jammu and Kashmir, Assam, Tamil Nadu (in relation to LTTE-related activities), the Naxalite belt in northern Andhra Pradesh, and in parts of Bihar. But nowhere has the pressure been more evident than in Punjab and Jammu and Kashmir.

The insurgency and terrorism in Punjab in the late eighties and early nineties brought the media face to face with a new problem. In December 1990 the PCI set up a sub-committee consisting of B.G. Verghese (convenor), Jamna Das Akhtar and K. Vikram Rao to examine the pressures and problems

---

[40] Press Council of India, *Annual Report (April 1, 1990–March 31, 1991)*, New Delhi, pp. 28–29.

confronting the press and its personnel in the state of Punjab. The sub-committee brought out a report entitled 'Overcoming Fear' which contained a number of important recommendations. These included the following: While exercising due caution in disseminating 'press notes' issued by terrorist groups, the press must also be vigilant against being used for official plants. The media cannot be anybody's handmaiden or cat's-paw. Credibility is vital. Apart from spot news, far more investigative and analytical reporting and writing is required to portray the human tragedy being enacted in Punjab and acts of courage and camaraderie by ordinary citizens and communities who have resisted threats and murderous assaults and refused to yield ground or give up their convictions. The social, economic, political and religious aspects of the struggle in Punjab must be understood and highlighted. The media will have far less to fear if its coverage is balanced and honest. True professionalism is respected by all, even one's opponents. There is no other code the committee would prescribe. Anything less would be incomplete, anything more unnecessary.

The PCI brought out a further report entitled 'Postscript on Punjab' on matters arising from terrorism in Punjab and its impact on the press. This report dealt with the censorship imposed by terrorist groups as also objectionable advertisements and subversive writing by terrorist groups.

A similar report was brought out by the PCI on threats to the media in Jammu and Kashmir from militant organisations in 1994. The committee noted that both the press and the electronic media were under constant threat of ban, violence, arson and bomb attacks and abduction of employees and their families and physical liquidation. The committee made a number of important recommendations on dealing with the complex problems on hand.

Yet another noteworthy report of the PCI was entitled 'Pen and Sword: Towards More Openness in Defence Coverage'. The committee which went into the matter was categorically of the view that greater transparency was needed regarding defence-related matters. This was not merely desirable but possible without detriment to national security. The concept of national security is both too narrowly and too broadly defined. The security of the state is sometimes confused with the security of the government, and the latter with the interest of the military-bureaucratic-political complex that makes up the defence establishment. The committee has made a number of major recommendations to deal with shortcomings in the present policies in this field.

There is as yet no legal, institutional or policy framework for exercising supervision over the electronic media in the country though it has expanded its reach and coverage considerably over the years. This delay is reported to be due to the delay in the passage of the Convergence Bill by parliament. The jurisdiction of the PCI is confined only to the print media. It is imperative that a similar autonomous organisation be created for the electronic media as soon as possible.

There is also as yet no national media policy in the country. It is necessary that such a policy is formulated with as wide ranging consultations as possible. Such a policy will clarify the limitations on the powers of the government. It could simultaneously address itself to a number of the issues brought out in the foregoing discussion. It will also bring into sharp focus the issues of public accountability and transparency of the media.

This brief survey brings out the various issues in making the media an effective watchdog of democracy. Just as the media has to keep a watch on others, it also has to watch itself carefully. This is particularly important from the point of view of the aversion of the media for control and supervision over it by any outside agency such as even the PCI. Clearly, there are a number of areas in the working of the print and electronic media which are of serious concern from the perspective of public accountability and transparency. It is time these issues are addressed by the media with some urgency and sensitivity.

## Civil Society

As one looks around, it is a matter of pride that Indians are doing so well in so many parts of the world in the most competitive environments. For example, in the US, 38 per cent of doctors, 12 per cent of scientists, 36 per cent NASA employees, 34 per cent Microsoft employees, 28 per cent IBM employees, and 17 per cent INTEL employees are Indians.[41] With this kind of reservoir of talent and manpower, the question often asked is why is India at the bottom of the pile based on several criteria for judging a country's progress. A part of the answer lies in the lack of public accountability and transparency in the country.

As Edmund Burke said long ago, 'The only thing necessary for the triumph of evil is for good men to do nothing'. And, it is necessary to remember that, in these endeavours, even the power of one can make a difference. The struggle for public accountability and transparency will have to be raised by civil society, its multifarious organisations of professionals, non-governmental bodies, and socially conscious individuals. Clearly, you cannot win a war if you are not going to wage it.

The test of real democracy is not the holding of elections at regular intervals, but what happens between them and the extent to which we exercise our rights as citizens between the elections. The pressure for change will have to be built up from within civil society and that is where we find the most weaknesses today. Unless the battle for public accountability and transparency is fought by civil society, it is not likely to make much headway.

A refrence was made earlier to the report of the Committee on Standards in Public Life (Nolan Committee), in Britain, which has recommended that all public bodies should draw up codes of conduct incorporating seven principles. (See chapter 1). Internal systems for maintaining standards should be supported by independent scrutiny. The committee has also suggested that

[41] *Common Cause*, Vol. XIX, No. 2, p. 20.

more needs to be done to promote and reinforce standards of conduct in public bodies, in particular through guidance and training, including induction training.

Looked at from this perspective, it is disappointing to see the performance of self-regulatory bodies of professionals such as doctors, advocates, chartered accountants, architects, engineers and others. Concerted efforts made by this author to get even rudimentary information from these bodies regarding steps taken by them to regulate, oversee and supervise their own professions met with silence. Most of these bodies do not seem to believe that they owe a duty to society to let the people know about the work done by them. In most cases, annual reports are not produced at all and if they are published, they do not contain the kind of information one would like to see. Thus, for example, in most cases, no details are available of the complaints received against their members from the public, the inquiries which were made and the action, if any, taken against the members. Hardly any organisation has laid down a code of conduct for its members. And, since there is no code of conduct, there are no arrangements for monitoring adherence to it. It is thus a travesty that the creation of these statutory and other bodies has not yielded any results. Neither have the central and state governments bothered to rectify matters. The recommendations made by these bodies for the amendment of the relevant statutes are reported to be pending with the government for years together. The Institute of Chartered Accountants of India (ICAI), is reportedly seeking more powers to regulate auditors. However, it is doubtful whether this will serve any purpose in the light of the performance of ICAI so far. This is amply borne out by just two recent decisions of the ICAI. It was in September 2002 that the ICAI decided to suspend the membership of one of Ferguson's senior partners in a ten-year old case. In the same month, in another case pertaining to 1991–92, it decided to suspend a partner of C.C. Choksi & Company Thus, while the government has left the regulation of these professions to their own bodies, these bodies have been totally ineffective except where the promoting and safeguarding of the interests of their own professions are concerned. Both transparency and accountability seem to be anathema to these bodies of professionals. It is interesting to see that these articulate sections of society wax eloquent on these matters when they relate to other sections of society. Serious thought needs to be given to the whole question of restructuring these bodies and amending of the relevant laws and/or passing new laws so as to make them effective.

Take for example, the case of just one profession, namely the medical profession. The affairs of the Maharashtra Medical Council (MMC) have become highly controversial over the years. The electoral malpractices alleged in the elections of the council are reportedly even worse than those in the legislative assembly and parliament elections. One is forced to consider why it is so lucrative to be an office-bearer of the Council (*Maharashtra Times*, 8 Oct 1999). Matters came to such a pass that the Bombay high court stayed the elections held in July 1999 and extended the term of the existing committee. Dr Arun Bal has shown how the MMC has lost all credibility. It neither helps patients nor protects doctors. It has failed to enforce ethical standards. The MMC functions more as a body of vested interests than as an agency for ensuring discipline. Powers conferred on the council by the Act are either misused or not used at all. A strong indictment indeed but particularly valuable as it comes from a person within the medical fraternity.[42]

Orders of Bombay high court to give copies of case papers to patients have not been implemented and a contempt petition had to be filed in April 1998 for their implementation. As the *Times of India* (2 Apr 2000) reported, the Maharashtra Medical Council's faded booklet of ethical guidelines could be a reflection of the medical profession today. According to many doctors, ethics in medical practice is almost as *passé* as the council's 30-year-old publication is outdated. It is, therefore, a welcome development that a new code of medical ethics, the

---

[42] Arun Bal, Maharashtra Medical Council Act (1965): Suggested Amendments, *Medical Ethics*, Vol. 3, No. 1, January- March 1995, p. 8.

'Indial Medical Council' (Professional Conduct, Etiquette and Ethics) Regulations, 2002 has been released. This is the first major change since 1956 when the Medical Council Act was first revised in independent India. In a further move, the MCI has now made it mandatory for doctors to log 30 hours of continued medical education every five years to retain their registration.

As the *Economic and Political Weekly* has underlined, 'State MCIs have become fiefdoms controlled by a few individuals who distribute largesse, protecting wrong-doers and violating norms and regulations on admission to medical colleges, setting up of new colleges and other aspects of medical training and practice. The recent case of Ketan Desai who headed the MCI as well as the Indian Medical Association (IMA) and was found guilty of corruption and abuse of power by the Delhi high court and summarily ordered to be removed from his post in the MCI is not so much an exception even if it may not be quite the rule.'[43] These and other issues were once again brought into focus by the 148-page judgment of the Chief Judicial Magistrate in Kolkata in 2002 indicting two well known medical practitioners and ordering three years' rigorous imprisonment and also imposing a fine of Rs 3,000 to be paid to the complainant. The West Bengal unit of the IMA has severely criticised the court judgment and threatened a strike![44]

What is true of these bodies of professionals is also largely true of non-governmental organisations (NGOs). Their clout, visibility and impact has increased over the years, both nationally and internationally. It cannot be denied that NGOs have become a force to reckon with because they are working towards the strengthening of civil society based on collective self-reliance. Internationally, NGOs have started asserting themselves on environment and trade issues, World Bank and IMF matters, WTO and so on. Nationally too they have become an important voice in various causes. In a sense, NGOs reflect the voice of civil society.

[43] A Paper Code, *Economic and Political Weekly*, 18 May 2002, p. 1856.
[44] Medical Practice: Shirking Responsibility, *Economic and Political Weekly*, 8 June 2002, p. 2190.

A more common purpose of NGOs is the empowerment of the poor and the oppressed. They also strive to build and strengthen people's organisations. The third stream of NGOs' activity is strengthening, re-energising and rejuvenating social movements. The fourth is the trend towards anti-authoritarianism.[45]

Three specific areas in which there is considerable scope for strengthening the NGO network in the country pertain to their role as think tanks, as catalysts in the public policy area and as specialists in specific sector issues. Though India has a large number of NGOs, they are acutely in short supply in these three areas which have emerged as important gaps in the work and presence of NGOs.

Influencing public policy, as a deliberate step by NGOs, is a recent phenomenon. In this regard, three different routes have been taken. The first is to influence the key decision-makers at the state and central level by introducing them to innovative ideas. The second is to influence policy through organised interest groups. In recent years, NGOs have found yet another way to influence public policy. This is through the institution of PIL.

The coming years will see the setting up by the government of a large number of independent statutory regulatory authorities in various sectors. One such example is that of the electricity regulatory commissions set up in a number of major states in the country. As the experience in Maharashtra has shown, advocacy by active, vociferous and knowledgeable NGOs, enabled the consumers' point of view to be ably represented before the Maharashtra electricity regulatory commission and as a result, the electricity board's demand for revision of tariffs was substantially pared. The experience of consumer fora in a number of states in the country has been similar. The credit for exposing the wrong-doings in major power projects such as Enron and Cogentrix will have to be largely given to the NGOs. This brings into focus what can be achieved through alert and organised NGO action.

[45]Voluntary Action in Adult Education, *NGO Government Relations—A Source of Life or A Kiss of Death?*

As Neeraj Kaushal has explained, interestingly, the World Bank has been lending straight to some of its former critics, the NGOs. During 1973–88, NGOs were involved in only six per cent of all World Bank-financed projects. By 1990, NGO involvement increased to 22 per cent of the projects, and by 1998–99, it rose to as much as 54 per cent. Even among the NGOs, the bank is reaching out to more local NGOs now than before. During 1973–91, 40 per cent of all NGOs the Bank worked with, were international. Today, this ratio has fallen to a quarter of all NGOs. These are encouraging trends.[46]

If the government is to be divested of a large number of responsibilities and if some of these are to be entrusted to NGOs in suitable cases, the NGOs themselves will have to be made answerable to society at large. The experience in this regard is somewhat mixed. While some NGOs have been scrupulous about maintenance of accounts, audit of revenues and expenditures, and placing before the people annual account of the work done during the year, some others have been equally lax. The parliamentary standing committee has therefore rightly recommended that steps should be taken by the Council for Advancement of People's Action and Rural Technology (CAPART) to verify the use of funds carefully. The committee has noted that, 'there is no auditing of accounts of the different CAPART assisted voluntary organisations by CAPART…certain percentage of funds for CAPART should be earmarked for monitoring and evaluation of activities of voluntary organisations. The government should think of some foolproof mechanism for the monitoring of voluntary organisations so as to avoid misappropriation of funds by them. They would also like that the government should evolve some foolproof mechanism to check the entry of bogus NGOs'.[47] To deal with the problem,

---

[46]Neeraj Kaushal, Banking on HRD, Ecoscope, *Economic Times*, 28 December 1999.

[47]Lok Sabha Secretariat, *Standing Committee on Urban and Rural Development (1998–99), Twelfth Lok Sabha, Ministry of Rural Areas and Employment (Department of Rural Development), Demands for Grants (1998–99), Fourth Report,* New Delhi, July 1998.

CAPART has constituted a national standing committee on monitoring and evaluation. To check entry of bogus NGOs, revised guidelines on the functioning of CAPART have been formulated in consultation with reputed NGOs.

A reference may be made in this context to a study of 140 NGOs in the Solapur district of Maharashtra. It was found that only 57 per cent of the organisations had their accounts audited. It was also found that the non-maintenance of accounts was because of three reasons: (a) accounts had not been maintained (53 per cent); (b) had no knowledge of accounts (33 per cent); and (c) were not considered necessary (13 per cent).[48]

The deputy chief minister of Madhya Pradesh, Subhash Yadav, has claimed that according to his information, all NGOs working in the country receive annual financial assistance of Rs 2,000 crore from abroad. Of this amount, Rs 200 crore was received by NGOs operating in Madhya Pradesh alone. He has urged that the centre should institute appropriate inquiries into the use of these funds (*Times of India*, 9 Sep 1997). The point to be noted is the large scope for public accountability and transparency in the working of the NGOs in the country.

The common perception is that NGOs are 'by their very nature' flexible, participatory, gender sensitive and transparent and it is only the government which carries the baggage of red-tapism and rigidity. However, experience has shown that there is tremendous variation in both sectors. As Vimala Ramachandran contends, some government programmes and departments have functioned with remarkable sensitivity and transparency under a dynamic head but there have also been instances when NGOs have been rigid, rule bound, corrupt and insensitive. Be it NGOs or government institutions, both are rooted in society, and changing values are manifested in all institutions. Corruption, manipulation, power and control are

---

[48] B.T. Lalwani, *NGOs in Development—A Case Study of Solapur District*, Rawat Publications, Jaipur, 1999.

not the exclusive preserve of government institutions, and NGOs certainly are not free from it.[49]

More enlightened international public opinion is likely to help in these endeavours. The World Bank has warned that it will not tolerate corruption in borrower countries and would provide 'advice, encouragement and support' to governments that wish to fight the malaise. The president of the Bank said that corruption is a major barrier to sound and equitable development and the Bank would help member countries to implement national programmes that discourage corrupt practices. The statement of G-7 finance ministers and Central Bank Governors, issued after their meeting in Washington DC on 15 April 1998 called for multinational development banks to establish uniform procurement rules and documents of the highest standards to fight corruption and bribery. Similar requests had been issued after the previous meeting and in the communique issued by the Development Committee during its meeting on 22 September 1997 in Hong Kong.

The OECD's convention on corruption is a worthy effort to stop grand corruption at its source—the multinational companies that bribe their way to contracts, mainly in poor countries. Every other trading country should likewise make bribery a criminal offence.[50] 'A global war against bribery has at last been declared. Victory, alas, is by no means certain', *The Economist* has prophesied.[51] Cajoling by outfits like the World Bank will not achieve much, *The Economist* rightly emphasised, unless the ordinary people most affected by corruption take up the fight themselves. Where this is happening, results are heartening. For example, *jana sunwais* (public hearings) in Rajasthan, UP and some other states on how money is spent by

[49]Vimala Ramachandran, Equality Among Unequal Parties: Relationship Between NGOs and Government, *The Administrator*, Vol. XL, July–September 1995, p. 121.

[50]Stop the Rot, *The Economist*, 16 January 1999, p. 19.

[51]A Global War Against Bribery, *The Economist*, 16 January 1999, pp. 22–24.

village panchayats by comparing official documents with work actually done has led to corrupt functionaries refunding the money made illegally. Thus, there is no substitute for the involvement of the common person and civil society in these endeavours.

We had commenced the discussion in this book with a poem by Rabindranath Tagore. There can be no better way to conclude than with the passage written by the German intellectual, Pastor Neimollar, on the Nazi ascendancy:

> First they came for the Jews
> and I did not speak out
> because I was not a Jew.
> When they came for the communists
> then I did not speak out
> because I was not a communist.
> Then they came for the Catholics
> and I did not speak out
> because I was not a Catholic.
> Then they came for me
> and there was no one left
> to speak for me.

# Abbreviations

| | |
|---|---|
| AERB | Atomic Energy Regulatory Board |
| AI | Air India |
| APS | Atomic Power Station |
| ANTR | Action Not Taken Report |
| ASSOCHAM | Association of Chambers of Commerce |
| ATR | Action Taken Report |
| BEST | Brihanmumbai Electric Supply and Transport |
| BIFR | Board for Industrial and Financial Reconstruction |
| BJP | Bharatiya Janata Party |
| BPCL | Bharat Petroleum Corporation Limited |
| BS | Business Standard |
| BSP | Bahujan Samaj Party |
| C&AG | Comptroller and Auditor General of India |
| C&AG (DPC) Act | Comptroller and Auditor General of India (Duties, Powers and Conditions of Service) Act |
| CALPERS | California Public Employees Retirement System |
| CAPART | Council for Advancement of People's Action and Rural Technology |
| CBDT | Central Board of Direct Taxes |

# Abbreviations

| | |
|---|---|
| CBI | Central Bureau of Investigation |
| CC | Citizen's Charter |
| CDF | Co-operative Development Foundation |
| CDFA | Co-operative Development Finance Agency |
| CEC | Chief Election Commissioner |
| CEO | Chief Executive Officer |
| CFC | Central Finance Commission |
| CII | Confederation of Indian Industry |
| CLM | Commissioner for Linguistic Minorities |
| CM | Chief Minister |
| COROAL | Commission on Review of Administrative Laws |
| CREF | College Retirement Equities Fund |
| CSF | Co-operative Sugar Factory |
| DMK | Dravida Munnetra Kazagam |
| DAE | Department of Atomic Energy |
| DM | Defence Minister |
| DPC | District Planning Committee |
| DOT | Department of Telecommunication |
| EC | Election Commission |
| ED | Enforcement Directorate |
| ERC | Electricity Regulatory Commission |
| FCA | Federal Court of Audit |
| FCRA | Foreign Contribution Regulation Act |
| FERA | Foreign Exchange Regulation Act |
| FI | Financial Institution |
| FICCI | Federation of Indian Chamber of Commerce and Industry |
| FIR | First Information Report |
| FM | Finance Minister |
| GAIL | Gas Authority of India Limited |
| GAAP | General Audit and Accounting Practices |
| GDP | Gross Domestic Product |

| | |
|---|---|
| GOG | Government of Gujarat |
| GSDP | Gross State Domestic Product |
| HM | Home Minister |
| HPCL | Hindustan Petroleum Corporation Limited |
| IAF | Indian Air Force |
| IAS | Indian Administrative Service |
| IB | Intelligence Bureau |
| IBP | Indo-Burma Petroleum |
| ICA | International Co-operative Alliance |
| ICICI | Industrial Credit and Investment Corporation of India |
| IDBI | Industrial Development Bank of India |
| IFCI | Industrial Finance Corporation of India |
| IFFCO | Indian Farmers' Fertilisers Co-operative Limited |
| IGNCA | Indira Gandhi National Centre for the Arts |
| IMF | International Monetary Fund |
| INS | Indian Newspaper Society |
| IPC | Indian Penal Code |
| IPCL | Indian Petrochemicals Limited |
| IPS | Indian Police Service |
| IRS | Internal Revenue Service |
| ITC | India Tobacco Company |
| J&K | Jammu and Kashmir |
| JMM | Jharkhand Mukti Morcha |
| JPC | Joint Parliamentary Committee |
| LTTE | Liberation Tigers of Tamil Elam |
| MCC | Model Code of Conduct |
| MLA | Member of Legislative Assembly |
| MHA | Ministry of Home Affairs |
| MIC | Mayor-in-Council |
| MMC | Mumbai Municipal Council |
| MMC | Maharashtra Medical Council |
| MOD | Ministry of Defence |

| | |
|---|---|
| MOF | Ministry of Finance |
| MP | Madhya Pradesh |
| MP | Member of Parliament |
| MPLADS | Member of Parliament Local Area Development Scheme |
| MSC Act | Maharashtra State Co-operative Act |
| MSCB | Maharashtra State Co-operative Bank |
| MTNL | Mahanagar Telephone Nigam Limited |
| MW | mega watt |
| NAA | National Audit Act |
| NAO | National Audit Office |
| NAV | Net Asset Value |
| NCC | National Cadet Corps |
| NCDC | National Co-operative Development Corporation |
| NCRWC | National Commission to Review the Working of the Constitution |
| NDMC | New Delhi Municipal Committee |
| NGO | Non-Government Organisation |
| NIPFP | National Institute of Public Finance and Policy |
| NHRC | National Human Rights Commission |
| NPA | Non-Performing Asset |
| NPC | National Partnership Council |
| NPC | National Police Commission |
| NRI | Non-Resident Indian |
| NPR | National Performance Review |
| OECD | Organisation for Economic Co-operation and Development |
| OIDB | Oil Industry Development Board |
| ONGC | Oil and Natural Gas Corporation |
| OSRC | Other Services Regulatory Commission |
| PAC | Public Accounts Committee |
| PB | Performance Budget |

| | |
|---|---|
| PBS | Public Broadcasting System |
| PCA | Prevention of Corruption Act |
| PCI | Press Council of India |
| PDS | Public Distribution System |
| PIL | Public Interest Litigation |
| PM | Prime Minister |
| PSU | Public Sector Undertaking |
| PUC | Public Undertakings Committee |
| QPM | Questions of Procedures for Ministers |
| RAW | Research and Analysis Wing |
| RBI | Reserve Bank of India |
| RCS | Registrar of Co-operative Societies |
| RJD | Rashtriya Janata Dal |
| RPA | Representation of People Act |
| SAIL | Steel Authority of India Limited |
| SC | Scheduled Caste |
| SEBI | Securities and Exchange Board of India |
| SEC | Securities and Exchange Commission |
| SFC | State Finance Commission |
| SHRC | State Human Rights Commission |
| SICOM | State Industrial and Investment Corporation of Maharashtra |
| SPG | Special Protection Group |
| SRCA | Self-Reliant Co-operatives Act |
| SSSC | Statutory State Security Commission |
| ST | Scheduled Tribe |
| TADA | Terrorist and Disruptive Activities Act |
| TI | Transparency International |
| TIAA | Teachers' Insurance and Annuity Association |
| TRC | Transport Regulatory Commission |
| UK | United Kingdom |
| UNICEF | United Nations International Children's Emergency Fund |

| | |
|---|---|
| UNDP | United Nations Development Programme |
| UP | Uttar Pradesh |
| UTI | Unit Trust of India |
| USA | United States of America |
| VFM | Value for Money |
| VIP | Very Important Person |
| WRC | Water Regulatory Commission |
| WTO | World Trade Organisation |
| ZBB | Zero Base Budgeting |

# Index

Abdullah, Farooq, 152
Abdullah, Sheikh, 153
Advani, L.K., 66, 75, 99, 177
Agarwal, Sanjiv, 356
agriculture, committee on, 12
Ahmadi, Justice A.M., 329, 344
Aiyer, Swaminathan A., 89, 325
Akhtar, Jamna Das, 372
Alexander, P.C., 72
Ambedkar, Dr. B.R., 245
Ambani, Dhirubhai, 291, 278
Ambani, Mukesh, 291, 292
Anand, Justice A.S., 338, 348
Andhra Pradesh, 62, 153, 173, 178;
   co-operatives legislation, 304;
   judiciary, 327;
   Lok Ayukta system, 194–95, 255, 261–63;
   panchayats in, 123, 128;
   pressure on Press, 372;
   regulation of government appointments, 204
   *see also* state budgets
Anti-Defection Act, 67–70
anticipatory bail, 214
Argentina, 45, 201, 205
Ashoka Mehta Committee on Community Development (1978), 120
Assam, 55, 223;
   Lok Ayuktas in, 255;
   panchayats in, 124
ASSOCHAM (Associated Chambers of Commerce and Industry), 287
Athreya, Mrityunjay, 281
Atomic Energy Regulatory Board, 10–11
audit of public expenditure in Germany, 242–45;
   in India, 245, 246–51;
   in UK, 239–42, 249
Australia, 45, 225, 307, 325;
   contempt laws in, 338;
   ombudsman in, 252–53;
   parliamentary privilege, 28–29;
   police, 211;
   public hearings of parliamentary committees, 57
Ayodhya controversy, 3, 354;
   press coverage of communal riots, 367; *see* Babri Masjid

Baba Amte, 74

Babri Masjid, demolition of, 65–66, 145, 155, 325, 340, 342
Bahujan Samaj Party (BSP), 39, 69, 94
Baker, James, 15
Bal, Arun, 377
Balachandran, V., 151, 152
Balasubramaniam, S., 361
Bali Declaration (1988) in role of audit, 245
Balwantrai Committee on Community Development (1957), 120
Balayogi, G.M.C., 7, 52
bank scam, 3, 59
Basu, Chitta, 83
Basu, Debashis, 36, 284
Basu, Jyoti, 71
Bhandare, Murlidhar C., 54
Bhagwat, Admiral Vishnu, 151
Bhardwaj, R.C., 1
Bharucha, Justice S.P., 330
Bhatnagar, Rakesh, 88, 138
Bhatnagar, S.K., 34
Bhatt, Chandi Prasad, 74
Bhattacharjee, A.M., 327, 329
Bhushan, Bharat, 355
Bhushan, Shanti, 330
Bhusnurmath, Mythili, 271, 321
Biffen, John, 42
Bihar, 55, 62, 65, 94, 113, 207, 215, 250;
civil servants agitation, 27–28;
communal riots, press coverage, 367;
co-operatives legislation, 304;
electoral malpractice, 77;
Lok Ayukta in, 255, 264–65;
panchayats in, 124

BIMARU states (Bihar, Madhya Pradesh, Rajasthan and UP), population growth in, 106, 111
BJP (Bharatiya Janata Party), 27, 53, 62, 94, 113, 125, 145, 167
Black, Justice, 339, 340
Bofors contract, 22–24, 59, 159, 211
Bosu, Jyotirmoy, 85
Brahma Prakash Committee on Co-operative Movement, 297
Brandeis, Justice L.D., 362
bribery, global war against, 382
Britain, *see* UK
Budget Management and Fiscal Responsibility Bill, 18
budget reforms, 239–45
Burke, Edmund, 375
Butler, David, 75
Byrd, Senator R., 21

C&AG (Comptroller and Auditor General) India, duties and powers, 246–49;
recommendations by NCRWC,
setting up audit board, 250;
external audit system, 250–51
Cadbury Committee Report, UK, 268–69, 288, 293
Callaghan, James, 147
Camdessus, Michel, 267
Canada, 197, 225, 324, 365;
Auditor General's role, 249–50;

# Index

legislature, supervisory role of, 9;
ombudsman system, 252, 254;
parliamentary privilege, 30;
police, 211
CAPART (Council for Advancement of People's Actions and Rural Technology), 380–81
capital flight, 15–17
caretaker government, 102
Carter, President J., 44
CBI (Central Bureau of Investigation), 159
   need for central law on, 217–18
Central Viligance Commission, 18
Chagla, M.C., 82
Chakravarthy, S., 290
Chakravarty, Nikhil, 365
Chandrashekhar, 63, 68
Chatterjee, Somnath, 75
Chautala, Om Prakash, 77
Chavan, Y.B., 82, 83
Chelliah, Raja, 120
Chattisgarh, panchayats in, 123
Chief Justice of India, appointment of, 348–49;
   see also Judicial, judiciary
Chopra, Mannika, 369
Chopra, Sanjeev (ed.), 294
CII (Confederation of Indian Industry) task force on corporate governance, 269, 284, 287, 290
citizen-friendly government, 181;
   citizen's charter, 194;
   criteria for beneficiaries, 192–93;
   delegation of power, 183–84;
   discretionary powers, codification of, 191–92;
   exit polls in government offices, 188;
   increasing validity period of licences, 189–90;
   Lok Ayukta system, 194–95;
   office discipline, 181–82;
   payment of dues through post-offices/banks, 188–89;
   prolification of useless information, 183;
   public grievances, redressal of, 193;
   publication of standing orders, guidelines for, 186;
   quarterly meetings, 195;
   reduction of paperwork, 186–88;
   sale of stamp paper at banks/post-offices, 189;
   self-contained orders, 192;
   single-window approach, 190;
   suo-motu publication of information, 185–86
   telephone use, more purposeful, 190–91;
   time-limit on stays, 192;
   unproductive meetings, 182–83;
   upkeep of government offices, 181;
civil service reforms, 176–80,
   amendment of rules, 180;
   back to basics, 176–77;
   extension and re-employment, 180;
   publication of annual property returns, 180;

statutory Boards, 177–78;
transfer policy, 178–79
code of conduct for MPs/MLAs
and Ministers, 48–49
Cogentrix, 347, 379
Colvin, Geoffrey, 275
Commission of Inquiry Act,
India, 341–42
'Common Cause' (NGO,
India), 87, 255
communal riots, and press
coverage, 367–68
Communist Party of India
(Marxist) (CPI(M)), 71, 89
communist parties, 39, 129
community development, 120–22
Congress Party, 7, 66, 82, 85,
89, 118, 127, 152, 153, 167,
220, 285
Constitution of India,
see NWRWC
Constitutional Offices, one term
for, 71–72
Contempt of Court Act, 1971
(India), 338, 340–42, 371;
need for amendent, 341
co-operative Banks, 320–21
co-operative sugar factories, case
study of, 306–18
co-operatives,
major issues, 295–96;
philosophy of, 294–95
co-operatives in India, 293–322
assets, 293;
contribution of sector,
293–94;
credit to, 319–20;
future of, 297, 321–22;
need for new laws, 296–97;
number, 293

COROAL (Commission on
Review of Administrative
Laws), 139–42
corporate governance, 267–69;
in India,
audit committee format,
need for, 287;
corporate wrong doing,
292;
credit-rating agencies, 291;
and economic liberalisation,
287;
excessive salaries, 291;
illegal activities, 279–80;
independent directors on
boards, 282;
nominee directors, 285–86;
non-performing assets,
283–84;
petrochemical sector,
289–91;
regulatory mechanisms,
need for, 288–92;
shareholder activism, need
for, 292;
social audit committee,
283;
three-step process for
transforming of, 281
international experience,
270–78
corporate sector and
Government, major
difference between, 267–68
corruption, zero tolerance for,
176
criminals, politicians and
bureaucrats, nexus between,
39–40

## Index

custody,
  crimes during, 214–15;
  draft bill on basic principles, 216–17

Dadiseth, K.B., 281, 282
decriminalisation of politics, 93–97
Defence expenditure of India, 11–12
Defence issues in India, secrecy about, 149–51
Delhi, 215, 217
democratic decentralisation, 119,
  constitutional amendments for, 120–22;
  implementation of, 121–23;
  hurdles, 134
    opposition from legislators, 134;
  recommendations of NCRWC, 135–36;
  see NCRWC;
  urban areas, 127;
  see also local bodies, panchayati raj, self-government
Denmark, 251, 365
Desai, Balasaheb, 154
Desai, Gurunath, 27
Desai, Ketan, 378
Desai, Justice P.D., 37
Deshmukh, Nanaji, 118
Deve Gowda, H.D., 64
disclosure of assets by
  legislators, 45
  ministers, 50;
  MLAs/MPs, 49
discretionary quotas for MPs, 52–53

downsizing Government, 196–98
  employees, 200–02;
  benefits for, 202;
  recruitment, 203–05;
  wage bill, 202–03;
  simplifying regulations, 198–99
Downs, Stephen J., 42
Drucker, Peter, 199

Ebrahim, Zahid F., 340
economic liberalisation, 13, 287, 292, 293, 296, 322
Election Commission of India (EC), 69–70, 75–76;
  code of conduct issued by, 75;
  need to supervise poll surveys, 114;
  powers of, 76–77
    need for widening of, 77–79;
election petitions, 107
elections, 109–10;
  candidates, 74, 97–99;
  expenditure, 73–74;
  model code of conduct, 75, 78–79;
  from more than one constituency, 99;
  see also electoral
electronic media, no supervision over, 374
electronic voting machine, 104–05
electoral,
  funding, 81
    and black money, 81–83;
    by business and industry, 89–90;
    foreign money, 83–86;

state funding, 90–93
committees on, 90
litigation, 74;
offences, punishment for, 100;
reforms, 73–76;
committees on, 79, 90;
Law Commission Report, 90–91;
neglect of, 75
Emergency, the, 101, 153, 370
Enron Corporation, 270, 272, 346, 379
Ethics in Democracy Act, need for, 66–67, 70
Ethics in Government Act, 1978 (US), 44
Evans, Harry, 29
executive, delegation of powers to, 19
exit polls; *see* opinion and exit polls

Fernandes, George, 250
FICCI (Federation of Indian Chambers of Commerce and Industry), 287
first-past-the-post system, 109–10; *see also* elections
financial control of Parliament over executive, 239–42
financial journalists, code of conduct for, 355–56, 359
Finland, 198, 251, 273
France, 196–97, 365

Gadgil, V.N., 365, 367
Gandhi, Indira, 9, 70, 82, 85, 99, 157, 278, 285
Gandhi, Mahatma, 371

Gandhi, Rajiv, 3, 9, 10, 77, 118, 151, 155, 158
Gandhi, Sonia, 99
Gavin and Klinefelter, 274
Gawli, Arun, 93
Germany, 45, 196, 365;
budget law reform, 242–45;
corporate governance, 270
globalisation, 13, 287, 292, 293, 296, 322
Gilani, 220
Gill, M.S., 69, 102, 113
Gill, S.S., 10, 151
Giri, V.V., 82
Goa, panchayats in, 124
good governance, concept of, 168–69
Gopal, S., 156
Gopalakrishnan, A., 149
Gopinath, Vrinda, 114
Gore, Al, 198, 199
Goswami Committee in Electoral Reform, 79, 90
Gowswami, Onkar, 282
government employees, 200;
*see also* Civil Services, citizen-friendly government
Greece, 198
Grover, A.N., 23
Gujarat, 66, 94, 104, 113, 117, 307;
communal violence, 2
press coverage of, 368;
judiciary in, 327;
Lok Ayukta in, 255, 263–64;
panchayats in, 120, 124, 127, 130
Gujral, I.K., 13, 85
Gundewar Commission, 155
Gupta, Kanwar Lal, 84

## Index

Gupta, Ramprakash, 62
Guyon, Janet, 273, 274

Habib, Irfan, 155
Haryana, 77,
 Lok Ayukta in, 255, 257;
 Lok Pal, 257–58;
 panchayats in, 123
Hazare, Anna, 93
Himachal Pradesh,
 cooperatives in, 318–19;
 Lok Ayukta in, 255, 259–60, 261;
 panchayats in, 123
Hinduja, S.P., 16, 86
Hindujas, 33, 211
Hong Kong, 197,
 ombudsman in, 253
human rights, 205–08, 324
 abuses, 209; *see also* custody
Hurriyat Conference, 220

IMF (International Monetary Fund), 267
Inder Jit, 41, 56, 63, 69
Indonesia, 279
Indrajit Gupta Committee on State Funding of Elections, 90
Institute of Chartered Accountants of India (ICAI), 376–77
insurgency, 218–19
intelligence agencies in India, 151–54
 misuse of, 153
internal security, 218–22
 political parties stance on, 221
International Co-operative Alliance (ICA), 294–95
Italy, 198

Iyer, Justice V.R. Krishna, 328

Jain, Ashok, 360
Jain, J.K., 350
Jamir, S.C., 250
Jammu and Kashmir, 81, 104, 113, 155;
 fast track courts in, 325;
 insurgency in, 220–22, 223;
 local bodies in, 128;
 pressure on press, 372
Janata Dal, 63
Japan, 45, 197, 198, 199
Jayalalitha, J., 55, 96, 370
Jefferson, T., 352
Jethmalani, Ram, 329
Jharkhand,
 panchayats in, 124
JKLF (Jammu and Kashmir Liberation Front), 220
JMM (Jharkhand Mukti Morcha) case, 7, 24, 26, 54, 279
Johnson, President Lyndon, 154
Joint Committee of Parliament, 59–60
Joshi, Manohar, 65
Jowell, Jeffrey, 211, 241, 345
JPC (Joint Parliamentary Committee) on
 bank scam, 34–36;
 Bofors contract, 32–34
judicial activism, 344–46;
 commissions, 155
 reforms, 347–50
judiciary in India, 245
 accountability, 328–32;
 backlog of cases, 323–24;
 code of ethics, 337;

Commissions of Inquiry,
  341–42;
  adjournment procedures,
    349;
  autonomy for, 350;
  delay in publishing
    reports, 342–43;
  expenditure on, 350;
  follow-up action on
    recommendations, 343;
  selection of retired judges,
    343–44
delay in judgements,
  324–25, 335–36;
fast track courts, 325;
judges,
  conduct of, 326–28, 332,
    334–35, 336;
  ratio of, to population,
    324–25;
  remarks by, 332;
  restraint, need for, 334–35

Kalani, Pappu, 94
Kamat, M.V., 359
Kania, H.M., 283
Kantharia, H.N., 258
Karnataka, 62, 97, 141, 200,
  307;
  judiciary in, 327, 338, 340;
  Lok Ayukta system in, 255,
    260, 266;
  panchayats in, 120, 123,
    124, 127–28
Karunakaran, K., 55
Kashmir; *see* Jammu and
  Kashmir
Kashyap, Subhash C., 1, 23
Kasmi, Azhar, 274, 275
Kasturi, T.S., 153

Katyal, K.K., 370
Kaul, M.N., 26
Kaushal, Neeraj, 380
Kerala, 55, 159, 205;
  Lok Ayukta in, 255;
  panchayats in, 123, 124,
    129–30
Kesari, Sitaram, 85, 86
Khalid, Justice, 346
Khan, Khurshid Alam, 71
Khosla, Justice G.D., 343
Krishna, Raj, 82
Krishnan, Murali, 337
Kumar, Ravindra, 354
Kurien, Verghese, 74

Lalwani, B.T., 382
Law Commission of India, 212,
  214;
  list system, 109–10;
  recommendations on:
    political parties, 80–81;
    size of constituencies, 106;
  report on electoral reforms,
    90–91, 95
  speedy justice, 215
laws in India,
  amnesty schemes, 144–45;
  anticipatory bail, 145–46;
  delay in notification of, 144;
  lack of respect for, 146–47;
  outdated, 137–38;
  penal, 143;
  repeals and amendments,
    139–42
Laxman, R.S., 1
legislatures,
  and executive, 9;
    *see* Parliament;
  size of, 105–07;

supervisory role of, 9;
see C&AG
legislators, 108–09; see MPs
Lieber, Ronald B., 273
Limaye, Madhu, 80
list system, 109–10
Lok Ayukta system, 72,
194–95, 251, 254;
All India Conference model
bill, 255–57;
functioning of, 257–66
Local Area Development
Scheme, 50–51, 91, 101, 133
local bodies,
devolution to, 232;
functioning of, 122, 130–34
Lok Pal Bill, 38–39; see Lok
Ayukta system above
Lok Sabha, 1, 4, 111–12; see
elections, MPs, Parliament,
Rajya Sabha

Macdonald and Dunleavy, 275
Mackintosh, J.P., 9
Madhya Pradesh, 207, 381;
fast track courts in, 325;
Lok Ayukta in, 255, 259, 260;
panchayats in, 123
Mahajan, Krishan, 336
Mahajan, Pramod, 66
Mahanta, Prafulla Kumar, 55
Maharashtra, 5, 22, 28, 53, 66,
67, 94, 154, 155, 167, 178,
200, 203, 207, 215, 326, 345;
budget,
demystification of, 224–25;
making process,
recommendations,
226–39;
zero base budgeting, 204–05;

co-operative societies Act,
1960, 297, 304–06;
spinning mills, 317–18;
sugar factories,
case study, 306–18;
cane development,
315;
concept of interest
on share capital,
311–12;
delicensing, 316;
expert committee
recommendations,
309–17;
improving financial
management, 314;
Mahajan Committee,
308–09;
number, 306;
productivity, 307;
water-use policy,
314–15
democratic decentralisation
in urban areas, 127;
fast track courts in, 325;
government, 24, 145;
Legislative Assembly, 5, 22;
conduct in, 3
Lok Ayukta System, 255,
257, 258, 260–01, 266
Medical Council, 377–78;
media in, 353;
privilege motions against,
361;
NGOs in, 379, 381;
panchayats in, 120, 123;
three-tier system, 124–27,
130;
Right to Information
Ordinance, 167, 168, 206

Malegam Committee on disclousure, 355–56
Malik, M. Yaseen, 220
Mangeshkar, Lata, 119
Manipur, 137
Mathew, Justice K.K., 147
Mathur, O.P., 123
Mayawati, 178
media in India,
advertisements in, 369–70;
electronic, 350;
ethics, 353–61;
and government, 175–76;
and human rights, 222–23;
ownership and editorial independence, 369;
print, 350–51;
reach, 350–51;
reporting of communal violence, 367–68;
see also freedom of the press
medical profession, self-regulation, 377–78
Mehta, D.R., 288
Mehta, Jaswant B., 68
Mexico, 217, 307
ministry, image of, 64–67;
upper limit on size, 62–64
Minorities Commission, 201–02
Mishra, Dina Nath, 353
Mishra, Jagannath, 55
Moynihan, Daniel P., 84
MPs (Member of Parliament), 4
code of conduct for, 48–49;
discretionary quotas for, 52–53;
local area development scheme, 50–51, 91, 101, 133;
pay and allowances, 50;
as public servants, 7–8;
see also elections, Parliament, Rajya Sabha
Mullick, B.N., 153, 154
municipal bodies,
powers and functions, 120–22;
study by National Institute of Public Finance and Policy, 122–23
Murthy, N.R. Narayana, 201, 291
Muslims,
representation in Lok Sabha, 111–12
Women's Act, 138

NABARD (National Bank for Agriculture and Rural Development), 320–21
Nagaland, 250
Narayanswamy, R., 288
Naresh Chandra Committee on Corporate Governance, 269, 287
Nariman, Fali S., 339
National Audit Act (NAA) UK, 239–42
significant features, 241–42
National Cooperative Development Corporation (NCDC) India, 319–20
national crime agency in India, need for, 218
National Democratic Alliance government, 39
National Human Rights Commission (NHRC), 137
national judicial council, need for, 348

national media policy, need for, 374
Nationalist Congress Party, 66, 67
Nayanar, E.K., 159
Nayar, Kuldip, 354, 355
Nehru, B.K., 142, 152
Nehru, Jawaharlal, 40, 41, 155, 158, 351
Neimollar, Pastor, 383
Netherlands, 198
New Zealand, 113, 200;
  Auditor General's role, 249–50;
  ombudsman in, 251
NGOs (Non-governmental Organisations), 162, 175, 180;
  in India, 378–79
    accountability of, 380–82;
    funding of, 380–82;
    and public policy, 379–83;
    role of, 379
NHRC (National Human Rights Commission) India, 205, 212, 213–15, 220
  cases registered, 205–06;
  and national security, 220, 221
Nolan Committee Report on Standards in Public Life, 46–47, 375–76
Noorani, A.G., 147, 338
Norton, Philip, 9
Norway, 251
NWRWC (National Commission to Review the Working of the Constitution), 5, 24, 31, 38, 63, 96, 98, 107, 117, 161, 206, 215, 330, 348, 350, 351, 364
nuclear energy, peaceful uses of, 149

Official Secrets Act, 1923, 147–48, 159–60, 166
  need for amendment, 370–71
ombudsman, 251–54
  in India, 254; *see* Lok Ayukta;
  key criteria, 251–52
Oomen, M.A., 129
opinion and exit polls, 112–15;
  merits of, 115;
  rating of agencies, 114;
  supervision of EC, need for, 114
opposition parties in India, 56, 80
Orissa, 8, 203
  Lok Ayukta in, 255, 258;
  panchayats in, 123, 124

Pakistan, 154
Palkhiwala, Nani, 351
Panchayati raj, 120–22
  three tier system, 124–27
Pande, Mrinal, 365
Pandey, T.N., 87
Paperwork Reduction Act, US, 186–87
Parliament,
  adjournments of, 3–4;
  budgetary allocation, 4–5;
  budgets, discussions on, 6;
  expenditure control, 20–22;
  information, dissemination of, 60;
  legislative business, time spent on, 5–6;
  questions in, 7;
  sessions, length of, 5
Parliamentary Committees, 9–14;
  calling ministers before, 59;
  financial control over, 61;

functioning of, 56–58;
Joint Committees, 59–60;
as mini-legislatures, 15;
relevance to policy-making, 14–15
parliamentary privilges, 22–31, 54, 361;
proceedings, telecast of, 1–2;
reforms, 40–45
Patel, H.M., 84
Patil, Shivraj V., 10, 25, 26, 48, 68
Paul, Justice John, 45
penal laws, 143
Pendse, D.R., 21
performance budgets, need for, 22
Phoolan Devi, 27
Pilot, Rajesh, 220
PILs (Public Interest Litigation), proliferation of, 346
Pinto, Marina, 127, 128
Poland, 225
police,
autonomy, concept of, 210–12;
communalisation of, 210;
custodial crimes, 214–15;
and human rights, 205–06, 207–09, 216–17;
lack of representation from all sections, 210;
public image of, 208–09;
Rebeiro Committee, 212–14;
reforms, 137;
women officers, 214
political parties in India,
audit of accounts of, 86–89;
functioning of, 79;

Law Commission recommendations, 80;
registration of, 79, 80;
structure of, 79
POTA (Prevention of Terrorism Act), 218, 220, 221
Pradhani, K., 84
Premchand, A., 22
Prasad, Rajendra, 158
President, powers of, 158, 59
President's rule, 102–03
press,
communal riots, reporting of, 367–68;
corruption of, 352–53, 355, 359;
credibility of, 352–55;
guidelines for transparency, 356–58;
privilege motions against, 361–62;
and right to privacy, 362–65;
and right to reply in the press, 365–67
Press Council of India (PCI), 352, 355, 358, 374;
Guide to Journalistic Ethics, 360–61, 366;
model advertisement policy, 369–70;
moral authority of, 371–72;
principles on casteist and communal writing, 367–68;
Report on Defence Coverage, 373–74;
and right to privacy, 363–64;
right to reply in the press, 365–67;

# Index

sub-committees on press problems, 372–73;
reports on Kashmir, 373;
Punjab, 372
Prevention of Corruption Act, 146
Prevention of Money Laundering Bill, 1988, 17
privilege motions against the press, 361–62
private sector, 161;
see corporate government
public office, age limit for, 70–71
public policy, 169,
autonomous regulatory commissions, 171–72;
citizens' interface with government, 172–73;
media and government, 175–76;
NGOs as development partners, 175;
primary responsibilities of government, 173;
segregation of IT and non-IT streams, 173–75;
social audit, 170–71;
'sunset' provision, need for, 169–70;
zero tolerance for corruption, 176;
public sector, streamlining of, 197–98
Punjab, 81, 104, 203, 223;
cooperatives in, 318;l
Lok Ayukta scheme in, 255;
Lok Pal in, 258;
panchayats in, 123;
pressure on press, 372–73
Puranik, S.V., 342

Rabri Devi, 62
Rai, Kalpanath, 335
Rajasthan, 104
Assembly, conduct in, 3;
fast track courts in, 325;
judiciary in, 332;
Lok Ayukta in, 255, 258–59, 265–66;
panchayats in, 122, 123, 124, 382
Rajya Sabha, 4,
composition of, 117–18;
elections, 115–17;
nominated members, 118–19
Rakesh Mohan Committee, 202
Ramachandran, Vimala, 381, 382
Ramamurthy, V., 52
Ramaswamy, Justice V., 37, 327, 330
Ramaswamy, Sushila, 111
Rao, Bhaskar, 113
Rao, J. Vengala, 153
Rao, K. Vikram, 372
Rao, P.V. Narasimha, 7, 25, 50, 63, 64, 76, 89, 104
Rao, S.L., 150
Rawle, Mohan, 27
Ray, Rabi, 68
Ray, Subir, 285
Records of Government, release of, 159–60
Reddy, Anji, 291
Reddy, Chenna, 55
Reddy, D. Chinappa, 37
Reddy, Sanjeeva, 153
Representation of the People Act, 1951 (RPA), 69, 75, 92, 95, 100
shortcomings of, 79, 96, 97

Reserve Bank of India, 156,
   advisory group report, 269
Right to Information, 160–68,
   370
Right to Privacy, 362–65;
   Indian law on, 363–64
Right to Reply in the Press,
   365–67
Robinson, Ann, 20
Roul, Chabbilendra, 318
Roy, Arundhati, 338
RSS (Rashtriya Swayamsevak
   Sangh), 3, 118, 177
rule of law, 137, 142–43;
   and legislators, 53–54;
   setback to, 145
rural development, 13;
   see Panchayat
Rye, Michael, 42

Sachar, Justice Rajinder, 329
Salmon, Lord, 54
Samajwadi Party (SP), 94, 353
Sanan, Deepak, 318
Sanction of Prosecution of
   PM/CM/Ministers, 54–55
Sangma, P.A., 2, 26, 52, 70
Sarkaria Commission on
   Centre-State Relations, 62–63
Sarkaria, Justic R.S., 265, 358,
   367
Sastry, Peri, 77
Sathe, S.P., 339
Sawant, P.B., 37, 360
SEBI (Securities and Exchange
   Board of India),
   powers, 288;
   report, 269, 355

SCs/STs (Scheduled Castes/
   Scheduled Tribes), 145, 208,
   reservations for, 121, 122
Scandinavia,
   women's representation in,
   110–11
secessionist movements,
   218–19, 220
secrecy, 147–50
   regarding, defence
   expenditure, 150–51;
   intelligence apparatus,
   151–53;
   judicial commissions, 155;
   railway accidents, 156–57;
   see also Official Secrets Act
securities scam, 325
Sehgal, Rattan, 153
Sekyi, Justice Amua, 340
self-government, 120–22;
   need to strengthen, 135–36
self-regulatory bodies of
   proffessionals, performance
   of, 376–78
Self-Reliant Co-operative Act
   (SRCA), 298–304
   provisions, 298–304
Seshan, T.N., 76, 104
Shad, S.R., 274
Shah Commission of Enquiry,
   153
Shakdar, S.L., 76, 81
Shamsul Haq, M., 198
Shankar Acharya, 203
Sharma, Justice M.B., 258–59
Sharma, Shankar Dayal, 116
Sharma, Gen. V.N., 149
Shastri, Lal Bahadur, 154
Shenoy, T.V.R., 85

Shiv Sena, 27, 53, 79, 93–94, 100, 125, 145, 146, 353
Shiv Shanker, P., 26
Shourie, Arun, 155
Shourie Committee, 163, 166
Shourie, H.D., 138
Sibal, Kapil, 38
Sikkim,
   panchayats in, 124
Singapore, 45, 197, 199–200
Singh, H. Borobabu, 137
Singh, Jaswant, 66
Singh, Justice Kuldeep, 93
Singh, Kalyan, 62, 65, 145, 178, 340
Singh, K.N., 67
Singh, Manmohan, 117
Singh, V.P., 68, 75–76, 77, 81
Singh, Giani Zail, 157
Singhvi, A.M., 85
Singhvi, L.M., 331, 363, 364, 371
Sinha, Yashwant, 63
Sivaramakrishnan, K.C., 122
Sorabjee, Soli J., 68, 339
South Africa, 9, 111
Southern Africa, 307
special legislation, need for, 218–22
Sri Lanka, 154
Srikrishna Commission on Mumbai riots, 146, 155, 210, 342–43
Srinivasan, Kannan, 16
standards in public life, 375–76
Stark, 274
State budgets, 223–39
   need for transparency, 223–25;
   demystification of, 224;

budget-making process, 225
   and presentation, 225–26;
need for pre-budget consultations, 226;
prior circulation of documents, 226–27;
budget-at-a-glance, 227;
budget in brief, 227–8;
finances, significant pointers, 228–33, 238, 239;
contingent liability, 229–30;
debt, classification, 229;
   profile, 229;
decisions with prospective effect, 23;
devolution to local bodies, 231;
multi-year budgeting, 230–31;
off-budget transactions, 233;
overdrafts, 233;
pension liability, 232–33;
performance budgets, 233–34;
quarterly financial information, 229;
reduction in number of grants, 228–29;
salaries and allowances, 232;
targets and estimates, 230;
tax expenditure, 233;
works in progress, 231
Accounts of Departmental Commercial undertakings, 235;
aided institutions, 238–39;
budget manual, 237;

centrally-sponsored concerns, 237;
committed expenditure, implications of, 236;
dissemination of budget documents, 239;
policies likely to impact budget, 236;
PSUS (Public Sector Undertakings),
accounting of debt liability, 234;
book adjustments vs. cash flow, 235;
credit rating, 237;
information on resources, 234–35;
release of share capital to, 234
Reserve Funds, 235–36;
Risk Analysis, 237–38;
Sinking Fund, 236
stock market scam, 59
Sturgess, G., 199
Subordinate Legislation Committee, 9, 18–20, 61
Subrahmanyam, K., 148, 150
Sukh Ram, 3
Sulzberger, A.H., 352
Supreme Court, 40, 87, 88, 137
bifurcation into appellate and constitutional divisions, 349–50;
*see also* Judiciary
judgement in JMM case, 7, 24;
removal of a Judge, proceedings for, 36–38;
Suresh, Hosbet, 336
Swami, Agnivesh, 23
Swami, Parveen, 153

Sweden, 198, 251
Switzerland, 197

TADA (Terrorist and Disruptive Activities Act), 143, 220
Tagore, Rabindranath, 383
Taiwan, 197
Tamil Nadu, 55, 97, 167, 178, 207, 307;
Assembly, conduct in, 2–3;
local bodies, 122;
panchayats, 123;
press in, 369, 370;
privilege motions against press, 361
Tata group, 89, 278
telecom licensing scandal, 3, 347
terrorism, 218–19, 222
Thackeray, Bal, 93, 94, 100, 145, 146, 197, 353
Thatcher, Margaret, 2, 42, 197
Tripathi, K.N., 68

UK (United Kingdom), 45, 145, 157, 196, 197, 324, 350, 375,
budgets in, 225;
corporate governance, 268–69, 288;
electoral law, 74;
law of contempt, 339;
ombudsman concept, 251;
in local government, 253–54;
parliamentary control over public spending, 20, 239–42;
privilege, 29–30;
reforms, 41–44, 46–47

public hearings of
  Parliamentary
  Committees, 57;
right to reply in the press,
  365;
Serious Fraud Office, 249
United Front government, 118,
  167
UP (Uttar Pradesh), 62, 65, 68,
  69, 94, 113, 145, 178, 207,
  215, 343;
  Legislative Assembly,
    conduct in, 2;
  Lok Ayukta in, 255;
  media, 352–53, 354;
    coverage of communal
      riots, 367; see also
      Ayodhya, Babri Masjid
  panchayats in, 123
Urban Land (Ceiling on
  Holding) Act, 1976, 19
US (United States), 145, 150,
  154, 186, 196, 198–99, 307;
  budget-making process, 225;
  corporate governance, 270–78;
  court clerk system, 349;
  law of contempt, 339–40;
  legislature, reforms, 4–45, 47;
    supervisory role of, 9;
  ombudsman for press, 372;
  police autonomy, 210–11;
  right to privacy, 362
Useem, Michael, 273
Uttaranchal, panchayats in, 123

Vajyapee, A.B., 63, 66, 75
  government of, 78, 100,
    112, 119, 177, 344
Vajpayi, S.C., 252
Venkatachaliah, M.N., 137

Venkataraman, R., 85
Venkataswami, Justice K., 343
Venkatesan, V., 330
Venkataramanan, S., 21
Verghese, B.G., 358, 372
Verma, A.K., 152
Verma Committee, 156
Verma, Justice J.S., 328, 329
Vietnam, 225
Vijayaraghavan, R., 356
village panchayats,
  functioning of, 123;
  powers and functions,
    120–22
violence,
  causes and containment of,
    218–22
Viswanathan, R., 291
Vohra Committee, 212
voter identity cards, 103–04

Wagle, Nikhil, 353, 361
West Bengal, 215, 251;
  communal riots, press
    coverage of, 367–68;
  fast track courts, 325;
  panchayats in, 123, 124,
    129, 382
White papers, importance of, 61
Williams, Sandra, 43
women legislators in Lok Sabha,
  110–11
  police officers, 214;
  reservations in self-government
    projects, 121, 122;
  rights of, 208
World Bank, 157, 201, 378,
  382
  and NGOs, 380

Yadav, Chaudhuri Harmohan Singh, 118
Yadav, Laloo Prasad, 55, 65, 96, 250
Yadav, Mulayam Singh, 52, 99, 178;
and media, 352–53
Yadav, Pappu, 94
Yadav, Subhash, 381

Zavelberg, H.G., 242
Zdanowicz, John S., 16
Zelnick, B., 198
zero-base budgeting (ZBB), 22, 204–05